Springer Series on ADULTHOOD and AGING

Series Editor: Bernard D. Starr, Ph.D.
Advisory Board: Paul D. Baltes, Ph.D., Carl Eisdorfer, Ph.D., M.D., Donald E. Gelfand, Ph.D., Lissy Jarvik, M.D., Ph.D., Robert Kastenbaum, Ph.D., K. Warner Schaie, Ph.D.

O.P. = Out of print

Donald E. Gelfand, Ph.D., is a Professor at the Institute of Gerontology and Department of Sociology at Wayne State University. His interests span both basic and applied areas of aging. He is co-editor with Charles Barresi of *Ethnic Dimensions of Aging* (Springer Publishing Company, 1987) and a contributor to many journals in the field of aging. He has conducted research on senior centers, board and care homes, and on the relationship of ethnicity to aging among many groups. In 1990, he was a Visiting Research Fellow at Australian National University and a Senior Fulbright Fellow in Darmstadt, Germany, in 1982. He has also served as Associate Director of the National Policy Center on Older Women and as a Senior Research Associate at the National Council on the Aging.

Fourth Edition

THE AGING NETWORK
Programs and Services

Donald E. Gelfand, Ph.D.

SPRINGER PUBLISHING COMPANY
New York

Copyright © 1993 by Springer Publishing Company, Inc.

Springer Publishing Company, Inc.
536 Broadway
New York, NY 10012-3955

First edition published, 1980
Second edition published, 1983
Third edition published, 1988

96 97 / 5 4

Library of Congress Cataloging-in-Publication Data

Gelfand, Donald E.
    The aging network: programs and services / Donald E. Gelfand. —
4th ed.
       p. cm. — (Springer series on adulthood and aging)
    Includes bibliographical references and index.
    ISBN 0-8261-3056-9
    1. Aged—Services for—United States. I. Title. II. Series.
HV1461G44. 1993
362.6'0973—dc20

93-19615
CIP

Printed in the United States of America

Contents

Appendixes

Preface to the Fourth Edition

With each edition of *The Aging Network* there is a temptation to provide increased detail about all programs and services in the field of aging. As federal programs and services gain in complexity, some additional detail is needed to keep the reader current. Although information is provided in this edition on regulations of such programs as Medicare and Medicaid, no effort has been made to cover every aspect of every program and service. My intent is to highlight the primary components of specific programs and services and to emphasize the most recent and important changes. Although positive or negative aspects of existing programs and services are mentioned, a comprehensive evaluation of all income maintenance, health, and aging network programs is beyond the scope of this volume.

As in earlier editions, the most recent authorization of the Older Americans Act forms the basis of most of the discussion; but there are many details in the Act that are not directly discussed. Readers are encouraged to peruse the 1992 amendments (Appendix B) and to consult other publications about particulars of the Act not covered in this volume. Many of these publications are available from the organizations listed in Appendix A. There are, of course, many programs and services initiated and funded by states and localities, and an effort has been made to highlight some of these important and innovative efforts.

Unlike the 1970s, or even much of the 1980s, the 1990s promise to be a period in which existing programs and services for older persons will need to be rejustified. In Chapter 16 I have tried to provide a brief look ahead to the remainder of this decade and the major issues that confront practitioners, researchers, and older Americans as we move towards a time when 20% of the American population can be termed "aged."

As in the past, I am grateful to the staff of Springer Publishing Company for their support in the development of this volume. I am particularly grateful to my wife, Katharine, for her patience during the cumbersome process of preparing this edition.

Introduction

The problems facing practitioners working the field of aging are numerous. First, they have to constantly confront their own attitudes about aging. Second, they have to acquire skills in a field that is by nature complex and interdisciplinary. Third, unlike practitioners and students in the 1950s or 1960s, they have to gain an understanding of a seeming myriad of programs and services. Many of these programs and services seem to crosscut each other. Similar efforts often appear to be available under different governmental or private auspices. This complexity is related to the primary organization of the American federal system along functional lines such as education, employment, housing, and transportation. Agencies dedicated to population groups such as children or the aged are both smaller and very recent in organization.

The experiences of the 1970s and 1980s reinforce the sociological axiom that there are unanticipated consequences to every policy initiative. In the field of aging, one of the consequences has been the development not of a seemingly clear-cut continuum of programs and services, but rather what can be drawn almost as a maze.

The last half of the 1980s appeared dedicated to simplifying the complexity of obtaining access to these programs for older persons. There still remain problems of fragmentation and lack of coordination, or even communication, among various service providers. Access to services may be stymied by problems of fragmentation and a lack of coordination or even communication among various service providers. The most important effort of the 1980s was probably the development of mechanisms that "channel" individuals into services that best meet their needs by having a central intake system at the local level or the development of a case management approach. With this emphasis, in part generated by a reduction in available funding, it is necessary for providers and students to have a clear understanding of existing programs and services and how they can intermesh and operate more efficiently. Throughout this volume the reader will find an effort to clarify the goals, target populations, and important components of specific programs and services. Each chapter also outlines the background, past and present funding, and variations in these programs and services as they are delivered to older populations across the country.

ORGANIZATION OF THE BOOK

Part I focuses on the present status of older Americans and the general thrust of programs and services in aging. After a brief glimpse at the characteristics of older adults in Chapter 1, Chapter 2 moves into an extensive examination of federal legislation authorizing programs and services for the aged. The major emphasis is on the provisions of the Older Americans Act.

In Part II, the complex but crucial topic of income maintenance programs is explored, including both the burgeoning private pension plans and the major public programs such as Social Security, Supplemental Security Income, Medicare, and Medicaid.

Part III provides readers with details on major programs in aging, ranging from information and referral efforts to crime prevention programs throughout the United States.

Part IV moves on to a discussion of the enlarging service delivery systems for the elderly, including senior centers, the growing in-home services, and adult daycare centers. This part concludes with an examination of the always controversial but important nursing homes.

Having discussed the myriad efforts that fall under each of these headings, Chapter 16 provides an opportunity to reflect on the factors that have allowed for such rapid development of these programs and services and their probable future.

Part I

The American Elderly and Programs

The end of the 1980s probably saw an end to any rapid expansion of programs and services for the American older population. Rather than being stereotyped as sick and unable to care for themselves, the older population was being portrayed as stereotyped "greedy geezers." Obviously neither stereotype is completely valid. By examining relevant statistical data, Chapter 1 reviews the current status of the aged in the United States in a perspective helpful to the planning and development of programs.

The groundwork having been laid, Chapter 2 plunges into an in-depth examination of the programs and services for the aged. The focus is on program authorizations and funds emanating from the Older Americans Act and on related programs stemming from a variety of federal and state legislation. The complexity of existing legislation will be quickly evident to the reader, but an understanding of the titles and acts discussed is imperative for the student and practitioner planning to work in the field of aging.

1

The Older American

THE ELDERLY POPULATION

Before we examine any programs, some attention must be paid to the number and characteristics of older Americans. This foundation should enable the reader to assess critically the specific programs and services discussed in the remaining chapters of this book. Rather than viewing characteristics statically, the focus will be on the changing status of the elderly during the twentieth century.

Size of the Population

Many Americans seem surprised when they first become acquainted with the significant increase in the number of older adults in the United States. This increase is occurring in every major industrialized country in the world. The ratio of older Americans to the general population will continue to increase during the next century. In 1900, individuals over 60 comprised only 6.4% of the population and individuals over 65, only 2.9%. These figures had more than tripled by 1977, with adults over 60 making up 15% and those over 65, 12% of the nation's citizens. By 2000, Soldo and Agree (1988) project a median age of 35.3 years for the United States with the population over the age of 65 comprising 13% of the total population. By 2030 they estimate that the elderly will comprise 21.2% of the American public (Soldo & Agree, 1988).

Children born in 1989 could expect to live 75.2 years. This is 28 years longer than a child born in 1900 (American Association of Retired Persons, n.d.). Unfortunately, these positive life expectancy figures hide some important inter-group differences. Minority elderly still have lower life expectancy rates than white elderly, the result being an excess mortality of 60,000 lives per year. The shortest life expectancy is found among American Indians: 65.6 years compared to 73.3 years for non-Indians (American Society on Aging, 1992).

Perhaps the most important figures concern the life expectancies for individuals who reach the age of 65 and 85. In 1990, men who reached the age of 65 had an average life expectancy of 15.1 more years, women 19.1 years. At age 85, the average life expectancy for men was 5.4 years and for women 6.8 years (Soldo & Agree, 1988). By the year 2020, the life expectancy for men at age 65 will be over 16 years and for women almost 21 years. The life expectancy at age 85 will be 6.3 and 8.5 years for men and women respectively. Based on these figures the growth of the population in their seventies and eighties is not surprising. Some scientists, however, argue that age 85 is the upper limit for life expectancy (Olshansky, Carnes, & Cassel, 1990).

There were 12 million persons over the age of 75 in the mid 1980s. By the year 2000, the population over the age of 75 will represent 45% of the elderly (Stone & Fletcher, 1988). The over-85 population will increase from approximately 3 million individuals in 1988 to over 6 million by 2015 (U.S. Bureau of the Census, 1989).

The proportion of black and Hispanic elderly in the American population will continue to grow in the next century. By 2050, black elderly will comprise 14% of the older population as opposed to 8% in 1990. Although Hispanic elderly were only 4% of the older population in 1990, their numbers will increase to 12% of this age segment by 2050 (Cantor, 1991).

HEALTH STATUS

The major problems of older persons are not acute illnesses but chronic conditions that affect their functioning. Problems in functioning are usually assessed on the basis of the relative inability of the individual to carry out basic Activities of Daily Living (ADL)—bathing, dressing, feeding oneself, reaching and using the toilet, and transferring between bed and chair. The Instrumental Activities of Daily Living (IADL) include the ability to perform household tasks such as meal preparation, housecleaning, money management, shopping, and getting around in the community. The National Medical Expenditures Survey (Leon & Lair, 1990) of 1987 indicates the current functional limitations of the noninstitutionalized American population.

Overall, 12.9% of the elderly had difficulty with walking or one of the

ADLs. Although 17.5% of the respondents reported difficulty with at least one IADL, the largest number of older persons had difficulty with bathing (8.9%) and walking (7.7%). Lesser percentages had difficulty with transferring from bed to chair (5.9%), dressing (5.1%), toileting (3.5%), and feeding (1.1%). Among the IADLs, more older people encountered difficulty with "getting around the community" (13.5%) than the other activities. Difficulties were also reported with shopping (11%), doing light housework (10.1%), preparing meals (7.5%), handling money (6.3%), and using the telephone (4.4%). As expected, the percentage of persons reporting difficulties with either set of indicators increased with age. Black elderly had more ADL/IADL difficulties (26.3%) than whites (19.1%) or Hispanics (14.1%).

A second large scale survey (U.S. Bureau of the Census, 1990) provides information on the older population's assessment of their need for help with basic activities. There were age differences among individuals who reported needing assistance with specific activities. Consistent across all of these differences is the greater need for assistance among the oldest age cohort (85 and older). As in the study of difficulties with ADL/IADLs a greater need for assistance was reported by black elderly than white or Hispanic elderly. Overall, 86% of the elderly have some chronic condition. These conditions limit the activity of 47% of older persons living in the community and approximately 18% are severely disabled.

A large proportion of problems in functioning among older persons stems from chronic conditions. The most common chronic conditions among older persons are shown in Table 1-1. The most remarkable of these statistics is that over half of all persons over age 75 are afflicted by arthritis. Beyond the pain associated with arthritis, the impact on the older person may include difficulty in feeding themselves, cooking, taking medicines, or even walking. The other conditions listed can also have a major impact on the daily lives and activities of older people. As the American population continues to age, the prevalence of other diseases may dramatically increase. One example of this change is the 17% increase in diabetes between 1980 and 1987, a change explained in large part by the increase in the number of older persons.

LIVING PATTERNS

There are now 1.5 million nursing home beds in the United States, but the over-65 population in nursing homes still represents less than 6% of

Table 1-1. Number of selected chronic conditions per 1,000 elderly persons by age and family income, 1986.

		Age	
Type of chronic condition	All elderly	65–74	75 and over
Arthritis	480	443	540
Cataracts	141	84	223
Hearing impairment	296	244	378
Deformity or orthopedic impairment	173	158	196
Hernia of abdominal cavity	61	47	85
Diabetes	98	82	109
Heart disease	277	250	319
High blood pressure	394	385	409
Emphysema	40	45	33

Source: U.S. House of Representatives, 1990

the total number of older American adults. The vast majority of older Americans want, and will continue to maintain, their residence in the community.

One of the most striking statistics of recent years is not the number of the older people living in the community, but the increasing proportion of older individuals who are maintaining their own households. In 1960, only one-sixth of the noninstitutionalized elderly lived alone. Among individuals over age 75, 38% in 1989 were living alone. This figure increases to 47% among individuals over age 85. Approximately one-third of all older blacks and whites live alone but a smaller percentage (22%) of older Hispanics lived alone in 1989 (U.S. Senate et al., 1991).

While longevity accounts for much of this increase, living alone requires reasonably stable financial resources. In part these resources can be provided by a combination of increased Social Security benefits, Supplemental Security Income (SSI), or private pensions. The increased number of elderly living alone also reflects the dispersal of families over a wide area. Poorer families consistently live closer to their elderly relatives. It has been shown that family income is positively related to the use of long-term care residences for elderly parents. Poorer families who cannot afford nursing home care are thus more likely to have an older family member living with them.

During the 1970s and 1980s, rural states such as Iowa, Arkansas, and Missouri had high proportions of elderly. In these states younger families have moved to more urbanized regions and have not been replaced by any significant numbers of new residents, although a proportion of the elderly have joined in the migration to the suburbs and many suburban residents have grown old in their neighborhoods. Thus, 40% of the white elderly in metropolitan areas were living in the suburbs in the 1980s as compared to one-third in 1960 (U.S. Senate, 1982). As research continues to show, older people tend to remain in communities where they have lived for a long period of time. Between 1982 and 1983, only 4.9% of older persons moved, compared with 16.6% of all age groups (U.S. Senate, 1986). This "aging in place" phenomenon has produced a new situation. As Logan and Spitze (1988) have noted in their analyses, there are now more older people living in suburban communities than in central cities.

Cultural Backgrounds

Although many senior advocacy groups speak out against stereotyping, there is a continued tendency to discuss the elderly as a homogeneous group whose values and beliefs are defined by their age. In reality the cultural backgrounds among the present generation of individuals over 60 are enormously varied. In 1960, 4.2 million of the American elderly had been born overseas. This group had declined to 3.7 million in 1970, comprising approximately one-seventh of the population over 60. In 1975, the Bureau of the Census reported that 5% of the over-65 population still primarily relied on a language other than English (Fowles, 1978). This diversity has been increased in recent years by the entry of substantial numbers of Hispanics from Central and South America and Asians from Korea, China, Cambodia, India, Laos, and Vietnam into the United States. Although Hispanics and Asians tend to have a relatively young median age, demographic data indicate an increase in the proportion of elderly among each of these groups. Differences in cultural attitudes toward aging and utilization of services, as well as a lack of fluency in English among foreign-born elderly, may create problems for providers attempting to implement aging programs.

Education

The minimal educational background of many present-day elderly also creates problems for service providers. The service provider must understand that many present-day older adults possess limited verbal, writing, and reading skills. Programs that involve extensive reading and discussion may thus not be practical for many elderly. At a more basic level,

many elderly will have difficulty understanding and following instructions on medication and may utilize their medication improperly. As the
differentials in educational background between the elderly and the general population become less distinct, these problems will abate. The improvement in educational background is already evident if data for the
years 1980–1989 is examined. During this period the median years of
school completed by whites over 65 increased from 8.7 to 12.0 (Soldo &
Agree, 1988). There are still substantial differences in the educational
backgrounds of white and minority elderly. In 1989 black elderly had a
median of 8.5 years of school completed and Hispanic elderly had a median of 8 years of school background. These statistics show that 58% of
whites over age 65 graduated from high school while only 25% of black
elderly and 28% of Hispanics had high school diplomas (U.S. Senate et
al., 1991).

Employment and Income

Recent changes in American work patterns have not been of major benefit to many American and foreign-born elderly. The inability of these
older adults to obtain higher education during the early 1900s relegated
them to careers as blue-collar workers. Men and women whose work has
centered around low-paying jobs have meager financial resources for
their old age. Low wages have meant low Social Security benefits and inadequate or nonexistent pensions. Part-time and intermittent work has
prevented many women from accumulating enough quarters to qualify
for Social Security.

Many of the elderly being served by present-day programs are individuals with limited ability to pay for costly programs. Income maintenance
programs such as Supplemental Security Income (SSI), Medicare, food
stamps, and housing subsidies have helped to raise the income floor of
the elderly.

In 1991, 14.2% of the population was living below the official government poverty line, while only 12.4% of individuals over age 65 fell into
this category of the poor. Unfortunately, this positive indicator of the income status of older Americans did not extend to older women, 15% living in poverty in 1990. The situation was even worse among the minority
elderly: In 1990 21% of Hispanic elderly and 34% of black elderly, compared to 12% of white elderly, were below the official poverty line
(American Association of Retired Persons, n.d.). Unfortunately, compensation for long-term employment in low-paying occupations can
never be totally achieved. Women and minority groups have had concen-

trated employments in low-paying industries. The slowest declines in poverty rates during the 1970s were thus among women, minorities, and individuals living alone. It is thus doubtful that efforts by the private sector to expand services available to the elderly will meet the needs of present-day older citizens unless these services are included under government reimbursables (Medicare, etc.).

Although their status has been improved on many fronts, the elderly still suffer from a variety of deficits which require the assistance of formal and informal services. After examining the existing programs, we will return in Chapter 16 to a discussion of the anticipated effects of economic, social, and health changes among the elderly on contemporary service delivery systems.

REFERENCES

American Association of Retired Persons. (n.d.). *A profile of older Americans, 1990*. Washington, DC: Author.

American Association of Retired Persons. (n.d.). *A profile of older Americans, 1991*. Washington, DC: Author.

American Society on Aging. (1991). *Serving elders of color: Challenges to providers and the aging network*. San Francisco: Author.

Cantor, M. (1991). Family and community: Changing roles in an aging society. *The Gerontologist, 31*, 337–346.

Fowles, D. (1978). *Some prospects for the future elderly population*. Washington, DC: Administration on Aging.

Leon, J., & Lair, T. (1990). *Functional status of the noninstitutionalized elderly: Estimates of the ADL and IADL difficulties*. Rockville, MD: Public Health Service, Agency for Health Care Policy and Research.

Logan, J., & Spitze, G. (1988). Suburbanization and public services for the aging. *The Gerontologist, 28*, 644–652.

Olshansky, S., Carnes, B., & Cassel, C. (1990). In search of Methusela: Estimating the upper limits to human longevity. *Science, 250*, 634–650.

Soldo, B., & Agree, E. (1988). America's elderly. *Population Bulletin, 43*(3), Washington, DC: Population Reference Bureau.

Stone, L., & Fletcher, S. (1988). Demographic variations in North America. In E. Rathbone-McCuan & B. Havens (Eds.), *North American elders*. Westport, CT: Greenwood Press.

U.S. Bureau of the Census. (1989). *Current Population Reports, Population Estimates and Projections*, Series P-25, No. 1018, January. Washington, DC: U.S. Government Printing Office.

U.S. Bureau of the Census, (1990). Current Population Reports, Series P-70, No. 19. *The need for personal assistance with everyday activities: Recipients and caregivers*. Washington, DC: U.S. Government Printing Office.

U.S. Senate, Special Committee on Aging (1982). *Developments in Aging, 1981: Part I*. Washington, DC: U.S. Government Printing Office.

U.S. Senate, Special Committee on Aging. (1986). *Developments in aging, 1985: Part III*. Washington, DC: U.S. Government Printing Office.

U.S. Senate, Special Committee on Aging, American Association of Retired Persons, Federal Council on the Aging, & U.S. Administration on Aging. (1991). *Aging America: Trends and projections, 1991 edition*. Washington, DC: Authors.

2
Legislative Bases for Programs and Services

The present generation of elderly benefit from the "categorical" programs designed to serve all individuals who fall into a specifically defined group (in this case older adults) and generic programs that benefit all age groups. In this chapter we will intensively review the legislation underlying existing aging programs. After highlighting the important legislation, we will examine other sources of programs and services for the aged and the major funding mechanisms underlying these services. Our attention will focus on the legislative initiatives and programs formulated at the federal level and implemented by state and local governmental units.

The major influence on programs for older adults has been the Older Americans Act (OAA) initially passed by Congress in 1965. Many of the features of the Act were influenced by the 1961 White House Conference on Aging. The Act has been amended 11 times; and the eleventh amending of the Older Americans Act was signed into law by President Bush and reauthorized the OAA through fiscal 1995.

The 1992 amendments added a large number of possible initiatives to the activities of the Administration on Aging. There is also an increased specificity throughout the amendments on the need of state and local providers to target their efforts towards the most "needy" older individuals, including needy minority elderly. It is important to note that a unique element of the Older Americans Act has been that all authorized programs and services are offered free of charge to the client. During the late 1980s there was sentiment on the part of many provider agencies for initiation of "cost-sharing" on the part of clients based on their income. The agencies assert that cost-sharing would increase their income and allow them to expand more programs and services. Other groups believe that cost-sharing would stigmatize OAA programs and reduce the participation of many elderly, particularly minority elderly (Gelfand & Bechill, 1991). This chapter will examine the basic thrust of each of the titles of the OAA and compare important changes in the 1992 amendments with previous versions of the Act. The complete text of the OAA can be found in Appendix B. The specifics of individual programs and services are provided in subsequent chapters.

THE OLDER AMERICANS ACT

Purpose of the Act

The basic purpose of the Older Americans Act is to "help older persons" by providing funds to the states for services, training, and research. All three of these activities are to be coordinated through the Administration on Aging (AoA). As part of a reorganization plan, the Office of Human Development Services was abolished in 1991. The Administration on Aging was a major component of this Office. As a result of the reorganization, the AoA became an independent agency that reports directly to the Secretary of the Department of Health and Human Services.

TITLE I: OBJECTIVES

In 1965, the goals of the OAA were couched in sweeping language which encompassed 10 difficult but laudable objectives:

1. An adequate income
2. The best possible physical and mental health
3. Suitable housing
4. Full restorative services
5. Opportunity for employment without age discrimination
6. Retirement in health, honor, and dignity
7. Pursuit of meaningful dignity
8. Efficient community services when needed
9. Immediate benefit from proven research knowledge
10. Freedom, independence, and the free exercise of individual initiative (Butler, 1975, p. 329)

In 1978, a new stress was placed on the provision of community services that enable the older person to make a choice among a variety of subsidized living arrangements. In 1987 objective 7 was altered to emphasize the participation of older persons in "meaningful activities" and objective 10 was expanded to guarantee "protection against abuse, neglect and exploitation." The 1992 amendments expanded objective 4 to not only include impaired elderly but also support services for the caregivers of impaired elderly. The target population of the OAA was originally individuals over the age of 65. In 1973, this was changed to 60 without extensive opposition in Congress. Part of the logic in the reduction of the eligible age was that the programs and services developed under the Act's provisions would assist older individuals in preretirement planning. A review of the history and titles reveals that the Administration on Aging has become responsible for the operation of an extensive service delivery program for older people (Gelfand & Bechill, 1991).

Title II: Administration on Aging

A direct outcome of the enactment of the OAA was the organization of the Administration on Aging. Directed by the Commissioner of Aging, AoA is charged with carrying out the provisions of the OAA. The Commissioner is appointed by the President and confirmed by the U.S. Senate.

As can be seen by even a quick perusal of the OAA, the responsibilities of the AoA are extensive. They range from providing information on problems of the aging to planning, gathering statistics, setting policies, and coordinating ongoing efforts in aging at federal and local levels with private and public organizations. The data-gathering responsibilities of the AoA were increased by the 1987 OAA amendments. These responsibilities include gathering information on services funded, individuals served, and the extensiveness of support by the Area Agencies on Aging for elderly with the greatest economic and social needs, particularly low-income minority elderly, low-income elderly in general, and frail older persons. This latter group would include individuals with mental as well as physical handicaps. The 1973 amendments to the OAA also authorized the Federal Council on the Aging, appointed by the President to provide advice to the President on concerns of the elderly.

The 1978 OAA amendments outlined a role for the AoA as an advocate of aging programs throughout the federal government (Sec. 202a). Sections 202 and 203 also stressed the importance of the Commissioner's intervention in a variety of planning, regulatory, and coordinating activities.

Recent reauthorizations of the OAA stress the role of the Commissioner and his/her responsibility to consult with other federal agencies concerned with programs that have an impact on the elderly. The 1992 amendments establish an Office of Long-Term Care Ombudsman Programs within the Administration on Aging. The mandate of this office is to recommend policies regarding ombudsman programs. One staff person is also to be designated by the Commissioner as a Nutrition Officer responsible for the administration of all nutrition programs funded through the OAA. In addition, the Act authorizes the establishment of a National Center on Elder Abuse and a National Aging Information Center.

Title III: Grants for State and Community Programs in Aging

Title III is the most important component of the Older Americans Act. This title outlines the types of services that should be provided at the local level in order to develop "comprehensive and coordinated services" enabling older adults to maintain "maximum independence" (Sec. 301). The basic foundation for providing these services is an agency designated by the governor of each state with responsibility for aging services. In many states this agency has been a newly formed office on aging. State offices on aging are not always provided with a mandate to oversee all aging programs, some remaining within already established departments. In 28 states, the office on aging is part of a human services department while in another 21 states the office on aging is independent. The state offices and Area Agencies on Aging are forbidden actually to provide rather than contract for services unless absolutely necessary "to assure an adequate supply of such services" [Sec. 307(a)(10)].

The agency designated by the governor is responsible for the development of a three-year statewide plan for serving the elderly. Geographic service areas must be designated by the agency, and local Area Agencies on Aging (AAAs) must be established. Within each of these areas the state agency has latitude in outlining geographic service areas. In many states these areas have coincided with health and mental health planning units.

The AAA develops its own three-year service plan, which must be submitted for approval by the state agency. An area agency can be a unit of county, city, or town government or even a private nonprofit agency. Preference must be given to an already established office on aging. In 1990 approximately 680 AAAs were already in existence across the country. In 13 states, the state agency is also the AAA.

Since its original passage, the categories of services that need to be addressed in an AAA service plan have grown. The 1987 amendments added disorders related to Alzheimer's disease and the 1992 amendments add case management as an appropriate service. The State and AAA plan must set "specific objectives" [Sec 306a(5)(A)(i)] to identify a variety of older individuals who need services; rural elderly; older individuals with greatest economic need; older individuals with greatest social need with a particular emphasis on low-income minority elderly; severely disabled elderly; elderly whose ability in English is limited; older persons suffering from Alzheimer's and related disorders. The area plan must demonstrate coordination of services provided through the AAA and services provided through other agencies, including community action agencies.

In the 1975 amendments, four priority areas were noted: transportation, in-home services, legal services, and home repair and renovation programs. In 1978, the three priority areas were access services (transportation, outreach, information, and referral), "in-home services" (homemakers, home health aides, visiting, and telephone reassurance efforts), and legal services. In 1987 the OAA required that the area plan demonstrate coordination of in-home, access, and legal services with ongoing activities of other community organizations working with Alzheimer's disease patients and their families. In 1992, case management was classified as an access service.

Supportive Services

Supportive services as defined in the Act include a wide range of programs ranging from health care efforts to transportation, housing assistance, residential repairs, and an ombudsman program designed to "receive, investigate and act on complaints by older individuals who are residents of long-term care facilities." The 1981 amendments also authorized a number of new initiatives, including efforts formerly undertaken by other federal agencies. These efforts include crime-prevention and victim-assistance programs, the installation of security devices, job-counseling programs, and the Senior Opportunities and Services Program (formerly operated by the Community Services Administration), which focused attention on the poor elderly.

The 1992 amendments add a number of supportive services to the already substantial list. These include translation services for non-English speaking elderly, representation in guardianship cases, counseling for older individuals who provide care to adult children, expanded types of therapies, expanded counseling in regard to various types of insurance, "lifestyle changes, relocation, legal matters, leisure time, and other appropriate matters," support services for family members caring for older individuals needing long-term care, services for individuals who are currently, or may become, guardians, and services that will "encourage and facilitate interaction between school-age children and older individuals. . ." [Sec. 313]. If the need for funds is less for supportive services than for nutrition, states can transfer 30% of supportive service funds to nutrition programs in FY 1993. This figure is reduced to 25% for FY 1994 and 1995 although the AoA Commissioner can approve additional transfers of 5%.

In 1981, the Senate introduced an amendment to the OAA requiring specific state programs for geographically concentrated groups of non-English-speaking elderly. A full-time AAA employee was to be assigned to provide counseling, as well as information and referral, to non-English-speaking older persons. This staff member would also have the responsibility of ensuring that local service providers are "aware of cultural sensitivities and . . . take into account effectively linguistic and cultural differences" [Sec. 307(a)(20)].

Nutrition Programs

Until 1978, nutrition programs comprised Title VII of the Older Americans Act. In 1978, Title VII was deleted and reclassified as Section C of Title III. While in 1978 the Act stressed the provision of congregate meals, the 1981 amendments asked for increased flexibility—only noting that primary consideration be given to congregate meals settings but allowing an AAA to award a grant to an organization that provided only home-delivered meals. Another major change was the restriction by Congress on the diversion of funds earmarked for nutrition to supportive services such as recreation, information and assistance or counseling. The ability to use funds for supportive services that was part of the 1978 amendments was important in allowing nutrition programs to expand their efforts. Congregate programs accept donations, and home-delivered meals programs are permitted to charge for their services based on income levels in the community, These funds obtained by these charges can be used for supportive services and to facilitate access of the older person to the meal sites.

The 1992 amendments include a new initiative to offer school-based meals for older persons who volunteer in schools, and fund intergenerational, social, and recreational programs for older volunteers [Sec. 316]. OAA funds can be used to pay 85% of the costs of these meals or intergenerational activities that involve older people and students. Under the 1992 OAA amendments, 30% of the nutrition funds can be transferred between congregate and home-delivered meals. Waivers for limited additional transfers can be approved by the Commissioner.

Senior Centers

In 1981, Title V (first included in the 1973 amendments) dealing with multipurpose senior centers also became part of Title III. The 1981 amendments again recognize that the multipurpose senior center is not a separate service entity but rather a "community facility" for organizing and providing the gamut of social and nutritional services authorized by the OAA. In 1978, the House-Senate conferees were unwilling to authorized separate funding for multipurpose senior centers. This unwillingness represents the viewpoint that centers are part of the social services delivery network of the state and its AAAs (U.S. House of Representatives, 1978). In fact, Title III stresses that "where feasible, a focal point for comprehensive service delivery" should be created with "special consideration" given to "designating multipurpose senior centers as such focal point" [Sec. 306(a)(3)]. The AoA is authorized to make grants to the states for construction, acquisition, and renovation of buildings usable as senior centers. Mortgages for these centers can be insured by HHS, and social services funds can be used for the centers' operating costs.

Although the exact amount of funds expended for each of these Title III activities will vary from state to state, the 1987 amendments required that the state plans specify a minimum percentage of funds that each AAA must spend on each service and program. In addition, documentation is now required from AAAs on how service providers will meet the needs of low-income minority aged. In this effort service providers must attempt to provide services to low-income minority elderly in proportion to their representation in the population of older adults in the area. Thus, if low-income minority elderly are 10% of the elderly population in an area, 10% of the services providers' funds should be targeted to their needs.

Additional Programs and Services

Besides the supportive and nutrition services already mentioned, a number of new elements were added in 1987 to Title III. These include in-home services for frail elderly and their families [Sec. 341], funds for services such as transportation designed to meet the "special needs" of older individuals [Sec. 351], and disease prevention and health promotion services [Sec. 361]. The 1992 amendments include an extensive list of 12 disease prevention and health promotion services that range from health assessments and screening through nutritional counseling, physical fitness and dance, and music and art therapy. Supportive activities for caregivers of frail elderly are a new component of the 1992 OAA amendments but reflect the increased focus on families as well as older individuals. These activities involve training, technical assistance and information.

Title IV: Training, Research, Discretionary Projects and Programs

Title IV has been a mainstay of training and research efforts in the field of aging. This includes efforts of state and local governments as well as a variety of public and private organizations. Under Title IVA, diverse training projects have been funded, including short-term training courses, in-service institutes, and seminars and conferences. Concern about a shortage of trained personnel to serve the aging is growing in Congress, and the 1978 amendments encouraged a coordinated approach to expanded training activities, especially training directed at serving minority elderly.

Since 1965, Title IVB research priorities have reflected changing concerns in the field of aging. In recent years the research priorities have reflected the government's interest in problems faced by family caregivers as well as in dissemination of information about programs for older persons. Increased emphasis has also been placed on the funding of projects conducted by AAAs and state units of aging.

As was true of previous enactments, the 1992 amendments authorize a substantial number of demonstration and research efforts. Among them are special programs in long-term care, demonstration projects of multigenerational programs, supportive services in federally assisted housing, transportation demonstrations that improve the mobility of older persons, demonstration programs for older persons who have developmental disabilities, ombudsman programs in publicly assisted housing, demonstrations that provide information and counseling about retirement and pension benefits, and demonstrations on how increased resources from non-federal funds can be obtained for aging programs. An interesting innovation is the "Neighborhood Senior Care Program," which aims to increase the number of professionals who volunteer their time to older local residents who are at risk of being placed in hospitals or nursing homes.

Title V: Community Service Employment

Title V of the 1981 OAA was formerly Title IX. Title IX had originally been added to the OAA in 1973. The stress in Title V is on coordination of projects underway in a variety of state, federal, and private agencies. The title also attempts to delineate the role of groups that contract to provide community service employment for older adults. As in the past, the priority recipients of community employment services are individuals over 55 who are unemployed or whose prospects for employment are limited. Individuals with an income equal to or less than the intermediate budget for retired couples developed by the Bureau of Labor Statistics are eligible for Title V programs. The OAA also stresses second career training in "growth industries and in jobs reflecting new technological skills" [Sec. 502(e)(2)].

Title VI: Grants for Native Americans

This title authorizes funds for Indian tribes to develop social and nutritional services for the aged if Title III programs are not already providing adequate services. The enactment of a separate title on Indian elderly represents an enlargement of the 1975 amendments to the OAA, which encourage states to directly fund Indian tribes interested in providing services to the elderly if these services are not already available. In 1987 OAA amendments explicitly recognized the needs of older Alaskan natives and Native Hawaiians as well as programs and services needed by older Native Americans. The amendments also strengthened the role of native tribal organizations in the provision of services and provide guidelines for application for and use of Title VI funds (Sec. 614). A similar section (Sec. 623) relates to funding for Native Hawaiians.

Title VII: Vulnerable Elder Rights Protection Activities

This new Title VII was adopted in 1992 but some of its components were formerly included in Title III. Title VII has four major components: The "State Long-Term Care Ombudsman Program" [Sec. 712]; "Programs for Prevention of Elder Abuse, Neglect and Exploitation" [Sec. 721]; "State Elder Rights and Legal Assistance Development" [Sec. 731]; "State Outreach, Counseling and Assistance Program for Insurance and Public Benefits" [Sec. 741]. The sections reflect concern that older people do not receive the benefits to which they are entitled, as is certainly the case with the Supplemental Security Income program. The title thus aims to "expand State responsibility for the development, coordination and management of statewide programs and services directed towards ensuring that older individuals have access to, and assistance in securing and maintaining, benefits and rights" (Congressional Record, 1992, p. 8989). In addition to the funds authorized for the different parts of this title, $5 million for fiscal 1992 and "such sums as necessary" are authorized for organizations involved in protecting the rights of vulnerable Native American elderly [Sec. 751].

In the effort to assist AAAs and other state agencies in understanding issues related to the rights of older people, the state has to appoint a focal point for state-level policy review, analysis, and advocacy on these issues. Personnel who will be involved with these issues must be designated, including a "State legal assistance developer." The State Outreach, Counseling and Assistance Program will help older individuals compare available Medicare supplemental policies and obtain those benefits to which they are entitled. The program will also help older people compare life insurance, other insurance, and pension plans. When needed, the program will help the individual obtain benefits and refer the older client to legal assistance when appropriate.

FUNDING OF AGING PROGRAMS

Prior to 1973, funding for aging programs and services was minimal. Gold (1974) has characterized the programs and services supported in the 1960s as community demonstrations. The passage of the Nutrition Services Act in 1972 was thus a major breakthrough in its focus on large-scale direct services for the elderly. Until 1981, Congressional appropriations for activities under the OAA had increased dramatically, enabling the implementation of a wide range of programs and services.

During the 1980s, federal funds appropriated for Title III-B programs increased by only 10%. In FY 1990, Congress appropriated only 74% of the funding authorized by Congress (Kutza, 1991). This funding gap has forced states and localities to increase their financial support for many programs and services authorized through the Older Americans Act. Approximately $800 million is estimated to be the share of funds contributed by state, local, and voluntary agencies to programs and services for the elderly (Gelfand & Bechill, 1991). Table 2-1 shows the authorizations for the OAA amendments passed in 1992. With one exception, these amendments only specify the authorizations for FY 1992. For FY 1993, 1994, and 1995, "such sums as necessary" are authorized for all pro-

Table 2-1. Older Americans Act Authorizations FY '92

Components	$ in millions
Federal Council on Aging	.3
White House Conference on Aging	SS*
Title III	
Supportive services	461
Congregate meals	505
Home-delivered meals	120
Surplus commodities	250
In-home services for frail elderly	45
School based meals	15
Caregiver support	15
Additional assistance/special needs	SS*
Disease prevention and health promotion	25
Title IV	
Training, research, and discretionary projects	72
Title V	
Senior Community Service Employment Program	471
Title VI	
Grants for Native Americans	30
Title VII	
Ombudsman program	40
Elder abuse prevention	15
Elder rights	10
Outreach activities	15

*SS, such sums as necessary

grams except surplus commodities. For this effort, $250 million was authorized in FY 1992. The amounts authorized increase to $310 million, $380 million, and $460 million in FY 1993, 1994, and 1995, respectively.

Geographic Funds

A crucial element in the development of aging programs and services is the formula used by individual states to distribute funds they receive from the federal government. The percentage of minority elderly, poor elderly, and individuals over age 75 have all been common elements in intrastate formulas. As a United States General Accounting Office study (1990) noted, the Administration on Aging did not officially approve or disapprove particular state formulas and there was a large diversity of formulas. The formulas came under scrutiny when a Florida court ruled that the State's formula was discriminatory. The 1992 OAA amendments require that state intrastate formulas be developed in consultation with Area Agencies on Aging and in accordance with guidelines set by the AoA Commissioner. AoA must also approve all intrastate formulas. The formulas must take into account the distribution of older people in the state as well as the geographic distribution of older persons with "the greatest economic need and older individuals with greatest social need, with particular attention to low-income minority old individuals" [Sec. 305(a)(2)]. Each state must specify how it will meet the needs of low-income minority elderly in each local area.

"Economic" and "social" need is more precisely defined in the 1992 amendments than it has been in earlier OAA authorizations. "Economic need" is defined as an income below the federal poverty line. "Social need" can be caused by a variety of factors that include "(A) physical and mental disabilities; (B) language barriers; and (C) cultural, social, or geographical isolation, including isolation caused by racial or ethnic status that (i) restricts the ability of an individual to perform normal daily tasks; or (ii) threatens the capacity of the individual to live independently" [Sec. 102]. Local Area Agencies on Aging must indicate the extent to which they have been able to serve older persons who fit these criteria.

Block Grants

Funds to support programs for the elderly are available through many federal agencies besides the Department of Health and Human Services. A large proportion of these funds are not specifically targeted for elderly groups but allow the elderly to be considered as an eligible population.

Decisions on allocation of these funds increasingly are made at the local level. This is characteristic of General Revenue Sharing, Community Development, and the new block grants enacted in fiscal 1982.

As opposed to categorical grants, block grants distribute funds directly to the state. States are allowed to utilize these funds for specific broad areas, but with little federal regulation and reporting. Among the initial block grants enacted in FY 1982, the Alcohol/Drug Abuse and Mental Health block grant, the Social Services block grant, the Energy Assistance block grant, and the Community Services block grant all contained funds that could be used to support programs for older persons. The Reagan administration expressed a strong interest in including other programs within the block grant framework.

In 1981–82, federal regulations for block grants specified only that a public hearing be held concerning the allocation of block grant funds and a report be sent to the federal government explaining how the block grant funds would be targeted on the basis of need. No specific evaluation on the effectiveness of distributed funds was planned. In specific programs, some "strings" were attached to the block grants by Congress. In the Alcohol/Drug Abuse and Mental Health block grant, states were expected in FY 1982 to continue to fund mental health centers at a "reasonable" level, and the funds could not be shifted among the three programs of this block grant until 1982. The block grants thus offered the states and local communities increased flexibility to determine program and population priorities, that is, whether the elderly are a group requiring special attention and funding.

The Social Services block grant is a replacement for Title XX of the Social Security Act. In 1974, Title XX was included in the Social Service Amendments to the Social Security Act, replacing Titles IVA and VI. Title XX funds were distributed according to the size of the state's population. The state was required to design a package of services and define the eligible population. Among the services for the aging that received funding in various states under Title XX were adult daycare, foster care, homemaker services, nutrition programs, senior centers, protective services, services in long-term care residences, and funds for comprehensive community mental health centers.

Despite the seeming extensiveness of this list, the number of programs and services for the elderly funded under Title XX was limited. This limitation resulted from federal requirements that states fund at least a specific group of "mandated services" and a ceiling that Congress placed in Title XX allocation.

Federal mandated services included adoption, daycare for children, early periodic screening, diagnosis and treatment of chronic and potential illnesses, employment counseling, family planning, foster care for children, information and referral, protective services for abused and neglected spouses and children, and services to the disabled, elderly, and blind. These required services were deleted from the block grant, but there is still a strong feeling in many states that Title XX was originally designed to provide services to children because of its origins in Titles IVA and VI of the Social Security Act.

Title XX had five goals:

1. To help people become or remain economically self-supporting
2. To help people become or remain self-sufficient
3. To protect children and adults who cannot protect themselves
4. To prevent and reduce inappropriate institutionalization

5. To arrange for appropriate placement and services in an institution when this is in an individual's best interest (State of Maryland, 1978)

In order to avoid rancor in distribution of block grant funds, many states have chosen to maintain these goals. Funds to help older people pay home energy bills are available through the Low Income Energy Assistance Program. Individuals are eligible if their income does not exceed 150% of the federal poverty level of 60% of the median income of the state. Of the $1.4 billion which Congress appropriated for this program in FY 1991, 41% was distributed to households with a resident over 60 years of age.

The Community Services block grant replaces the programs formerly operated under categorical grants by the Community Services Administration and allows the states to allocate funds to Community Action Programs in local areas or fund other agencies for poverty programs. The Community Services Administration also administered the Energy Assistance Program designed to help low-income individuals "weatherize" their homes and obtain financial assistance for high energy costs. Under the block grant approach, this money will also be distributed to the states for allocation to local communities and administrative agencies. Community Development Block Grants (CDBG) are earmarked for improvement of substandard physical facilities and housing. Of these funds, 75% must be spent by the local community in low- or moderate-income deteriorated areas. CDBG funds are being used to rehabilitate housing, set up community centers, or build storm drains and sewers. In FY 1992 CDBG funding was $3 billion.

Congress appropriated $349 million for the Community Services Block Grant (CSBG) in FY 1991. The CSBG can provide education, employment and housing assistance and emergency food assistance for individuals, including older persons. As is true of a number of block grants, data on the number of older persons served through the CSBG is unavailable.

The additional services in Title III, and the Title IV demonstrations, reflect the burgeoning number of issues currently under discussion in the field of aging, particularly caregiving issues, legal rights, and elder abuse. One important change is the perceived need to not only provide services to older people but also to individuals who assist them. The increased specificity about greatest needs and the requirement that the Commissioner of AoA approve the intrastate funding formula indicate a concern that programs and services are not equitable in their distribution. Whether the new specificity will guarantee more equitable distribution of funds and services is a task for the evaluation of the 1992 amendments.

REFERENCES

Butler, R. (1975). *Why survive: Being old in America*. New York: Harper and Row.

Congressional Record. (1992). *Older Americans Act*. Washington, DC: U.S. Government Printing Office, September 22, Part II.

Gelfand, D., & Bechill, W. (1991). Older Americans Act: A 25 year review of legislative changes. *Generations, 15*(3), 19–22.

Gold, B. (1974). The role of the federal government in the provision of social services to older persons. In F. Eisele (Ed.), Political consequences of aging. *Annals, 415*, 55–69.

Kutza, E. (1991). The Older Americans Act of 2000: What should it be? *Generations, 15*(3), 65–68.

State of Maryland, Department of Human Resources (1978). *Proposed FY 1979 Title XX Comprehensive Annual Services Plan*. Annapolis, MD.: Author.

United States General Accounting Office. (1990). *Older Americans Act: Administration on Aging does not approve intrastate funding formulas*. Washington, DC: U.S. Government Printing Office.

U.S. House of Representatives. (1978). *Conference report No. 95-1618: Comprehensive Older Americans Act Amendments of 1978*. Washington, DC: U.S. Government Printing Office.

Part II

Income Maintenance Programs

The system of income maintenance in the United States is a complex, fragmented one. Responsibility is divided among all the units of government and the private sector. The system—if it can be called one—was created step by step over a period of many years. Programs were created or modified and occasionally abandoned, as circumstances arose or changed. A prime example of incrementalism, the system is an illustration of block-by-block building to meet recognized need, often without careful consideration of the impact of the new developments upon existing programs.

A complete inventory of the existing U.S. system of income maintenance has rarely been attempted. The inventory list becomes long and includes a large variety of programs that provide some degree of income or other support, often as incidentals to other program objectives. Although these inventories are useful as a reminder of what is encompassed in the total system and of what a fragmented system it is, they wander too far astray from the narrow concept of income support to be helpful here.

The present system of income maintenance is characterized by program distinctions made on the basis of:

- *Governmental responsibility*. Some programs are federally operated, others by the states, and some privately.
- *Financing*. Appropriations from the general revenues of government, both federal and state, finance some programs. Others are financed out of reserve funds created by insurance premiums.

- *Relationship to the work force.* Some programs are limited by those who have an attachment to the work force, while others are available without such connection.
- *Eligibility.* There are some universal programs with no means test. Others are limited to those who pass a means test, with the test varying from program to program.
- *Participant contribution.* Some income maintenance programs are financed in part from contributions or taxes imposed upon the individual. Others are financed by payments made by the employer or from governmental tax revenue.

The consequences of the interplay of these factors are not only confusion in grasping what the system includes but also revelation of the weaknesses in the system. There is some duplication of coverage, and there are also gaps and omissions. There are serious variations in the level of adequacy of payments among the programs. Although some elements in the overall system are well financed, others are less securely financed. A number of programs operate in obscurity, thus limiting their utilization by many potential clients.

Elements in the U.S. income maintenance system will be reviewed in this part from the point of view of the resources available to help older people. The programs will be considered in terms of governmental response to the risks to which people—especially older people—are exposed, which are:

- Growing old without adequate income
- Being unemployed and without income
- Being ill and unable to work in order to support oneself and dependents
- Being ill and unable to pay for medical care

In Chapter 3, the risks of inadequate income will be the focus. The role of income maintenance programs in periods of illness and existing medical care coverage programs will be the focus of Chapter 4.

3

Age, Employment, and Income Maintenance*

GROWING OLD WITHOUT ADEQUATE INCOME

The risk of becoming old and being unable to work is one of the most serious situations that people face. While many older people retire from employment voluntarily, the tendency is for people to remain employed for as long as possible. Older workers who become unemployed because of obsolete skills or because companies go out of business or consolidate very often do not find another job. These workers are thus less able to plan their entry into retirement than those who have been steadily employed.

Historically, the aged have been recognized as in need of help, as evidenced very early by the enactment of poor laws. In the 1920s the impact of the rigorous poor law was eased by the introduction of the Old-Age Pension, a means-tested program of aid usually available at age 70. These programs were liberalized and incorporated into the Social Security Act (SSA) of 1935 in the form of grants to the states for old-age assistance. The SSA also established the Old-Age Benefit Program. Since it was apparent that it would be several years before that program would actually provide benefits, the means-tested program was the major source of income for the elderly.

Progressive liberalizations in the retirement provisions of the Social Security Act have resulted in that being, since 1951, the primary source of income for the aged. The old-age assistance program gradually dimin-

*This chapter and chapter 4 were written for the 1st and 2nd edition of *The Aging Network* by Jules Berman, Professor Emeritus, School of Social Work, University of Maryland. He previously worked at the Department of Health, Education and Welfare in a variety of legislative and policy positions.

ished in size, to the point that it provided assistance for only a small proportion of the aged. In 1974, the old-age assistance program was federalized and merged with similar programs for the blind and disabled as part of the SSI program.

Even though pension programs of private industry have, over the years, contributed to the provision of retirement income, a succession of favorable actions by the Congress combined with the growing interest of industry have resulted in an enormous growth in private pensions. Today they play a significant part in the retirement plans of a large number of people.

Before these programs are examined in greater depth, it is important to view them in relationship to each other. The old-age benefit program under the SSA is generally considered the basic program. By now, nearly every employed person is covered and will eventually receive Social Security benefits. Not only is the program broad in its coverage, but the rights that are accumulated under the program are "portable." That is, the rights are cumulative throughout one's lifetime and are carried from one employer to another. Social Security has become the cornerstone of protection in old age. Although benefits are increasing in adequacy and will assure future beneficiaries of about 41% of their preretirement income (based upon earnings which are subject to tax—a point which is discussed later), the amount will inevitably fall short of what many people will need or want in their retirement years. It is at this point that the private pension system enters the picture.

The government has acted to encourage the growth of private pensions with a view toward provision of income in addition to Social Security benefits. Social Security was never intended to provide benefits which were measurable against a specific standard of adequacy. The adequacy of Social Security income is obviously improved when combined with private pensions. Employers are now encouraged to establish private pension programs. Workers are given an opportunity to negotiate with employers in the establishment of such plans. Indeed, under rulings of the National Labor Relations Board, employers are required to bargain in good faith with their employees, not only over hours and wages, but also in regard to the pension plan.

In recent years, further steps have been taken by the Congress to encourage the growth of private pensions. The self-employed have been able, since the 1950s, to establish their own retirement plan, the so-called Keogh plans. Even persons working for others have been able to set up their own Individual Retirement Accounts (IRAs) to supplement Social Security benefits in retirement. The tax reform legislation of 1981 made it possible for any person, whether or not included in private pension plans of an employer, to set up on IRA.

With the establishment of the SSI program the federal government has finally tackled the difficult problem of minimum adequacy. In 1988 the federal government assured the aged of $354.00 income per month ($532.00 for a couple living together). This amount could consist of an SSI supplement to Social Security or other income, or it could all be the SSI payment. The figures given above are indexed to the cost of living and are adjusted annually, as are basic Social Security benefits.

In summary, Social Security remains the basic retirement plan. The private pension programs add to the benefit at the top, and the SSI program adds to Social Security or other income to create a floor. Thus there is some coherency to the retirement income planning of the federal government.

Old-Age Benefits

The entire Social Security program is work related. That is, individuals are eligible for benefits only if they have been in employment (or self-employment) or are dependent upon one who has been so employed. There are specific requirements concerning the length of employment and the kind of work in order to qualify for benefits.* The basic requirement involves 40 quarters, or 10 years, of work in "covered employment." Until 1979, the law provided that in order to receive credit for a quarter of work, individuals had to earn at least $50 in one quarter. Self-employed persons had to earn at least $400 in a year in order to receive a year's credit. Effective January 1979, employers were required to report earnings on an annual basis, and in 1992, $570 income earned an employee a quarter's credit Social Security. Employers must still identify the quarters in which the work occurred. This makes it slightly more difficult to obtain credit for work performed at low wages.

The 40 quarters that are needed in order to be eligible can be accumulated over a period of a lifetime. "Covered employment" has been

---

*The basic requirements for Social Security are the same for all programs—old-age benefits, survivor's benefits, and disability benefits—and are only slightly modified for medical benefits. When these additional programs are discussed in this chapter, basic eligibility information will not be repeated.

Social Security is a highly complex program with numerous detailed eligibility and benefit provisions, which are only summarized in this chapter, as is the content of other programs discussed. For technical details or the need to apply these provisions against a particular situation, consult with the nearest District Social Security Office, or the state offices which deal with unemployment insurance, welfare programs, workmen's compensation, and medical assistance.

broadly defined to include all work as an employee in commerce or industry or in self-employment. Work in certain government operations or nonprofit organizations is also included, if a particular agreement has been made between the federal government and these other levels of government or the nonprofit employers.

The eligibility requirement of 40 quarters was written into the law as a minimum period of time in order to qualify and assumes that the individual entered the labor force after the Social Security system was established. Millions of Americans were already well into their work life when Social Security was established in 1935, or before it became inclusive in coverage. Because of this situation, older people can qualify for benefits with fewer than 40 quarters of coverage. An individual who became age 62 in 1983 is eligible with only 32 quarters of covered employment. This eligibility minimum has increased gradually, and by 1991, everyone was required to meet the 40 quarters of employment.

Workers covered by Social Security pay a tax on their earnings, and employers add a like amount. The size of the ultimate benefit is based upon a calculation which takes into account the total of such taxable earnings. When the system was first initiated in 1936, the maximum earnings subject to tax were $3,000 a year. Over the years, this amount has gradually been increased. In 1979, the taxable earnings base was $22,900. The ceiling on earnings subject to tax was $55,500 in 1992. People whose annual incomes are in excess of these amounts pay taxes only on that portion of their annual earnings as specified in the law for that year. When the taxable base is increased, if affects only those workers who have been earning more than the previous year's taxable base.

The tax rate is also fixed by law, and it too has been steadily moving upward. In 1992 the tax rate was 7.65% of the taxable income base. Of this amount, 6.2% is allotted for Social Security and disability insurance. The remainder is for Medicare. The tax rate for the self-employed is now equivalent to that paid by the salaried worker and employer. This change, however, did not come fully into effect until 1990. Self-employed persons pay their Social Security tax each year at the same time they pay their federal income tax (U.S. House of Representatives, 1991). The taxable base for the Medicare portion is $130,000.

Veterans receive gratuitous credit for military service between September 1940 and December 1957. When veterans apply for benefits, it is assumed that they earned $160 per month during the years of military service. After 1957, servicemen paid the Social Security tax on their military earnings and therefore are eligible for benefits the same as any other employed person.

The size of the benefits reflects the level of earnings during the wage earner's working years. Upon application for benefits, lifetime earnings, that is, earnings from age 21 until the time of application, are totaled. The five lowest years of earnings are excluded, and the number of months—less the excluded five years—is divided into the total earnings. The resulting amount—the Average Monthly Earnings—is then used against a table provided in the law to determine the monthly benefit which will be received. The table of benefits reflects some favorable treatment for low-paid workers in that they receive more in benefits as a proportion of previous earnings than higher paid workers. In 1979, the law also incorporated a new principle, which is to adjust previous earnings to upgrade them to more nearly reflect current wage levels. Wages paid 25 or 30 years ago seem completely unrealistic by today's scale; yet their small amounts depress the Average Monthly Earnings figure, which is crucial to the size of the benefit to be paid. The goal has been included in the law of having benefits replace, for average earners, about 41% of previous earnings, that is, that portion of earnings which had been subject to the Social Security tax. This provision has the effect of increasing the size of some benefits while keeping new awards from exceeding this level of replacement.

Benefits are automatically adjusted annually, without any action by the Congress, to reflect changes in the cost of living. Inasmuch as Social Security benefits are only partially subject to income tax, this adjustment enables beneficiaries to maintain their purchasing power under the pressures of upward movement of prices. Until this procedure became automatic, an act of Congress was necessary to adjust benefits. This adjustment procedure was carried out on a regular basis, but some of the increases voted by the Congress exceeded the cost of living figures. Since this is now accomplished automatically, beneficiaries will be assured of maintaining the purchase power of their benefits but will not receive any upward adjustment in their living standards.

A minimum benefit of $122 per month had been provided under the law for wage earners whose lifetime earnings, which were covered by Social Security, were low. The $122 was provided no matter what the formula would yield in benefits. The minimum benefit was discontinued by Congress in 1981 except for beneficiaries already on the rolls.

There is another form of minimum benefits which helps persons who have worked many years in covered employment, yet at wages so low that they will enter retirement with very small benefits. The law now provides that long-term low-paid workers will receive benefits larger than they would under the normal formula incorporated in the law. This provision was added to the law in 1972 because the minimum benefit discussed earlier was found to be aiding many persons who were not long-term workers but who had been in other retirement systems and for whom the Social Security benefits were only supplementary. Even so, the workers who were in real need of some protection against a low benefit were not being sufficiently aided by the old minimum benefit.

Until the year 2000 the normal age for retirement is 65. Provision is made, however, for workers who have the required number of quarters of coverage to retire at an age as low as 62. The benefits for these earners are reduced on an actuarial basis so that their early retirement does not cost the system any money. This reduction is 20% for those retiring at age 62, proportionately less as the individual is nearer age 65 when applying for benefits. More than half of current applications for retirement benefits are being made by persons who are below 65 years of age.

The benefits of a retired wage earner may be increased if his or her spouse is of the appropriate age. This provision was added to the law in 1939 at a time when the pattern of family living was for the husband to be in gainful employment and to support his spouse and children. Thus the increase in the wage earner's benefits—usually the husband—of 50% was in behalf of the wife who had not been employed outside of the home. That addendum is paid in the instances of wives who have no earning records of their own, or if a wife's earning record would yield a benefit of a lesser amount than she would receive as a dependent spouse. The Social Security Administration will make comparison at the time of application for benefits and award the larger of the two amounts. While the addendum is added to the wage earner's monthly check, the wife can receive a separate check if she requests it. An addendum is also allowable if the retired wage earner has dependent children living at home. In this instance, benefits are payable on behalf of such children up to the age of 18, unless the children are full-time elementary or secondary students.

The addendum covering the spouse of a retired worker is available for both a husband and wife. That is, the wife can be the wage earner to whom a 50% increase will be granted in behalf of her husband, if the husband had no wage earning record or if his wage record will yield benefits smaller than 50% of his wife's. The law provides, however, that if the husband or wife who is claiming benefits on the basis of the earnings of the other is also receiving benefits from any governmental program, the spouse's benefits will be reduced by the amount of the additional benefit being received. The purpose of this provision is to disallow the Social Security benefits claimed by a spouse who is covered by the U.S. Civil Service retirement system or a comparable state system and who consequently is not in any way dependent upon the spouse who is covered by Social Security.

Benefits are payable to retired wage earners if they meet the retirement test as stated in the law. The test of retirement is put in terms of annual earnings. An individual receiving Social Security benefits but also earning an annual amount higher than the amount stated in the law may lose part or, if the earnings are sufficiently large, all of her or his benefit. This is an often misunderstood provision. Strictly speaking, the Social Security program is not an annuity program but a wage replacement benefit program. At age 70, the retirement test no longer applies, and wage earners can earn without limit and still receive full benefits. Income other than earnings is not counted for a retirement test, which means that individuals may have unlimited income from investments, rents, and the like without any impact on their Social Security benefits. The earnings limit for the retirement test has been raised in recent years. For 1992 it was $10,200 for persons age 65 and over and $7,440 under age 65. Earnings above the amounts stated reduce the monthly benefits on the basis of a $1 reduction for every $2 in earnings, but beginning in 1990 benefits were reduced $1 for every $3 earned. The point at which an individual's benefits are phased out because of earnings varies and depends upon the size of the benefits and the amount of earnings.

The retirement test is the most unpopular provision in the Social Security Act. It has been criticized as a discouragement to work and a denial of essential supplementary income to people whose basic benefits are insufficient. Counter to this are the arguments that Social Security is not designed as a pension but as a wage replacement benefit and that the elimination of the retirement test would increase the cost of the system, with the additional money going to people who are the least needy—those whose incomes are above $60,000.

A common problem experienced by older people concerns the death of a spouse and the remarriage of the surviving spouse who receives Social Security benefits. Often the remarriage is to a person who also receives benefits. A spouse who receives survivor's benefits could lose them upon remarriage. As a result of amendments in the law which became effective in 1979, the remarriage of a surviving spouse after age 60 will not reduce the amount of benefits.

Another problem occurs in the breakup of a marriage which leaves a divorced mate without any marriage ties to a retired worker and thus unable to claim the spouse's 50% addendum. Other recent changes in the law state that a divorced spouse who was married for 10 years may claim benefits based upon the former spouse's earning record at the time of retirement. The fact that the wage earner may have remarried does not affect the benefits to the divorced spouse. Prior to 1983, the divorced spouse was in a difficult position if he or she did not have an earning record and the former spouse chose to continue working. Under the 1983 amendments to the Act, the divorced spouse can now collect Social Security benefits at age 62 regardless of whether or not the former spouse applies for his or her own benefits.

The system also includes a death benefit of $255, which is payable to the estate of the deceased wage earner. Since 1981, this has been limited to deceased wage earners who have close family survivors. For those who do not retire—although eligible—and who have no dependents, such as spouse, children, or dependent parents, the death benefit may be the only payment out of the system.

FINANCING SOCIAL SECURITY

The financial integrity of the Social Security system is of crucial importance to the 34 million beneficiaries. All costs of the program, including the cost of administering it, come from a tax imposed on employers and employees. This tax money is identified separately in the U.S. Treasury and is available for appropriation to pay benefits and the cost of administration. Although most wage earners believe the Social Security tax is a single figure—7.65% for 1991—it is actually a series of smaller tax sums designed to reflect the cost of the various elements of the system. These include the retirement program, disability, survivors, and health insurance. In recent years, it has become apparent that some of these so-called trust funds for individual program purposes were running short and soon would be in deficit. The disability fund was in the deepest trouble and, were it not for the Social Security Amendments of 1977, would have already run out of money. The 1983 amendments, which increased both the tax base and the tax rate, rescued the Social Security system from imminent deficit. The amendments increased the flow of money into the Treasury from wage earners and employers and thus gave assurance that, for at least a time, the income was equal to the outgo.

Since the Social Security system is financed solely by the tax on employers and employees, there is no other money from the Treasury going into the basic system. Unless the nation should decide to allocate some general revenue funds to pay at least part of the costs, the benefits will continue to be paid for by the payroll tax.

The problems of Social Security are short range and long range. In the short range, sluggish economic activity (which reduces the number of employee contributors as a consequence of unemployment) and inflation (which requires an upward adjustment in benefits) put a strain on the money needed now for payments to beneficiaries. In the long run, the growing number of aged in the population and the reduction in the population of working age means that a reduced proportion of younger people will be supporting an increasing proportion of older people.

All recent presidents of the United States, Nixon, Carter, Ford and Reagan, have called for studies of the program to see what could be done. Proposals which are distasteful to nearly everyone have emerged to deal with the short- and the long-run problems. Under the pressures of keeping the Social Security system solvent, a bipartisan commission developed proposals that were signed into law in 1983. As already noted, the 1983 amendments set new tax rates and salary bases. These raises in rates and salary base are designed to bring additional money into the system and offset the increasing number of beneficiaries and the cost of living adjustments to which they are now entitled.

Besides requiring individuals already paying Social Security taxes to pay more, the 1983 amendments also tried to use two other strategies to shore up the Social Security trust fund: (1) increase the number of individuals paying the taxes; and (2) encourage people to retire later and thus continue to pay into the system for a longer period.

For the first strategy, the 1983 amendments required all new federal workers to pay Social Security taxes. This change adds a significant pool of new taxpayers who formerly paid into a separate federal civil service system. Any local and state government currently covered by the Social Security system is now forbidden to withdraw from the system in order to set up its own retirement plan.

One element of the strategy to encourage people to work longer was the already discussed liberalization of the retirement test in 1990. Even more important is raising the age of retirement with full benefits from the current 65 to 66 in 2009 and 67 in 2027. This means that individuals who retire at age 65 in 2009 will receive only 93% of the benefits to which they are entitled. In 2027, when the age of retirement for full benefits is 67, individuals who retire at 65 will receive only 86.7% of their benefits. In contrast, individuals who do not retire at 67 but continue to work will receive 8% more benefits for each year they work (e.g., 108% at age 68, 116% at age 69) (Cohen, 1983).

Social Security beneficiaries are now also guaranteed to receive increased benefits even in periods of low inflation. In 1986, Congress abolished the requirement that the yearly rate of inflation must be at least

3% before any cost of living adjustment is triggered. At least one group of beneficiaries, however, has found that the 1983 amendments did not necessarily provide them with any increase in their total income. Half of Social Security benefits are now counted as taxable income for individuals whose gross income combined with Social Security benefits exceeds $25,000 ($32,000 for a married couple). The counting of Social Security benefits as taxable income is a major departure from past practices. Importantly, the funds derived from these taxes are contributed to the Social Security trust funds as a means of further ensuring its solvency.

None of the proposals, either short-term or long-term, was easily enacted. The Social Security constituency is composed of middle-class people who are articulate and politically active, and they resist major changes. Congress and the President are hesitant to offend this group. In all of the discussions of Social Security financing, it is clear that Congress has a strong commitment to the Social Security system. The financing problems, however, will require continuing attention as the ratio of active workers to retirees continues to shrink.

SURVIVOR'S INSURANCE

Benefits for survivors of deceased wage earners under the Social Security system are available to the survivors (wife or husband and young children) of a prematurely deceased wage earner. These benefits are also available to the surviving spouse (age 60 or older and younger children if any) of a wage earner who was either retired or had been eligible for retirement. For purposes of this chapter, only the latter group of survivors—the older people—will be discussed.

As explained earlier, an addendum will be added to the benefit of a spouse if he or she is at least 60 years of age. (As noted earlier, this benefit can be reduced by the receipt of a public pension.) This benefit is paid, not only in behalf of spouses who have had no employment record of their own that would qualify them, but also to those who have a record of work in covered employment but for whom the earned benefit is less than 50% of the wage earner's Primary Insurance Amount (PIA). The survivor's benefit will be 100% of the wage earner's PIA. Thus it is possible that a women whose earned benefit was less than 50% of her husband's will, upon the death of her husband, receive a larger benefit— her husband's PIA—not an uncommon occurrence.

A benefit of the same size will also be paid to the widow or widower of a wage earner who had been eligible for a retirement benefit but who had not claimed it because of continuing employment, assuming the survivor meets the usual age requirement. In the event the aged survivor also has responsibility for young children of the deceased, the benefit will be 75% of the PIA plus a payment made in behalf of each child equal to 75% of the PIA. Benefits are also payable to dependent parents of deceased wage earners.

Beneficiaries of survivor's benefits are subject to the same earnings test as are retired people. Therefore, if a widower or widow is employed and receiving an income, the survivor's benefit might be reduced or even eliminated, depending upon the amount of the survivor's earnings.

SUPPLEMENTARY SECURITY INCOME

The SSI program was established in 1974 on the basis of legislation enacted in 1972. It provides for federalizing the former grants-in-aid programs of old-age assistance, aid to the blind, and aid to the permanently and totally disabled. These programs—except the disability program—had been administered by the states since 1935, with states administering grants for the disabled since 1950. Under the 1972 legislation, the federal government provides assistance to the aged, blind, and disabled who qualify under the specific provisions of the law. National standards are used both for eligibility and for payment. The payment level in 1991 was $407.00 for an eligible individual living alone and $610.00 for two eligible individuals—husband and wife. The odd amounts derive from a provision added to the original law that indexes the payment level to the cost of living, which is adjusted annually as with Social Security.

There are several major differences between the SSI program and the comparable programs in the Social Security system. (Comparable programs would be old-age and disability benefits.) The major difference is that the SSI program is means-tested, while Social Security benefits are not. Funds for the SSI program come from the general revenue of the Treasury, while Social Security is financed by a payroll tax on employers and employees. The SSI program is available to anyone who meets the proper qualifications—age, blindness, and disability—without regard to their participation in the work force. The Social Security program is directly related to employment, either by the beneficiary or by his or her dependents. Although both Social Security and SSI are administered by the Social Security Administration of HHS, a distinction is maintained between the two programs by printing the checks on a different color of paper.

National eligibility requirements for SSI are:

- No one is eligible who is an inmate of a public institution.
- If an otherwise eligible person is in a medical institution (public or private), the payment to that individual is reduced to $30 per month.
- No one is to receive an SSI payment if she or he is eligible for, but has not applied for, another kind of benefit payment, such as workmen's compensation or Social Security.
- Anyone who is otherwise eligible but who has been medically established to be a drug addict or an alcoholic will receive payment only if undergoing appropriate treatment for the condition at an institution approved by the Secretary of HHS and if she or he demonstrates compliance with the outlined treatment.
- Payment to eligible persons under SSI will not be made if those persons are outside the continental United States. If such persons have been so removed from the country and later return, they are required to wait 30 days before being reinstated for SSI payment.
- A disabled person under the age of 65 must accept a referral to the state vocational rehabilitation agency for a study of her or his condition and must accept a proposed plan of treatment in order to continue eligibility for SSI.
- Applicants must be either citizens or legally admitted aliens in order to be eligible for SSI.
- Persons who are age 65, or blind, or disabled are eligible. If the eligibility is blindness or disability, the individual must meet the test used in the Social Security program of disability insurance.
- The resources of an eligible individual must not exceed $2,000 for an individual and $3,000 for a couple.
- An individual's monthly income in 1991 had to be less than $427 and income of a couple no more than $630.

The system promises a certain level of income, which consists of SSI alone, if the individual has no other income, or a combination of SSI and other income to reach the established payment level. In determining the amount an individual or a couple will receive, some modifications are made in the treatment of income:

- Only net income from employment is counted. Income includes earnings, cash, checks, and in-kind income such as food and shelter.

- The first $240 per year of income such as from Social Security is not counted, but all income paid on the basis of need is fully counted.
- Earned income of eligible persons up to $780 per year is not counted.
- Casual and inconsequential income not to exceed $60 in a quarter is not counted.
- If the eligible individual is living in another person's household and is receiving support or maintenance in kind, the SSI payment is reduced by one-third.

A state may establish a higher payment level at its own expense but may not add eligibility requirements. The federal government will administer that payment at no administrative cost to the state. Many states have chosen to provide a state supplement, with some states administering it themselves. This means that the payment level varies around the country as individual states decide whether to add to the federal payment, how much to add, and to what extent these supplements should be increased as living costs rise.

Despite its importance, census data indicates that only about half of all persons eligible participate in SSI. Based on this data there are probably around two million older persons who could, but do not receive, SSI (Fretz, 1990). A number of recent outreach efforts have been mounted by the Social Security Administration in an effort to remedy this situation. The 1992 OAA amendments call for the identification of economically needy older persons who are eligible but do not receive public benefits (Title VII).

STATE GENERAL ASSISTANCE PROGRAMS

All the states have a program of general assistance which is the direct linear descendant of the old poor law relief programs. Like the earlier programs, they are largely local in character. Some states, however, help finance the program and may even set state standards. The primary eligibility provision is need, which often is severely tested. The program is available to persons who do not qualify for other programs such as Social Security, SSI, and the like. A likely candidate is a needy person age 60, for example. Unless such persons are disabled or blind, they would not be eligible for Social Security or SSI and could very well be in need. Inasmuch as there is no federal financial help in the state pro-

grams, the availability of benefits depends upon state eligibility requirements and often some local requirements. During the early 1990s, General Assistance programs in many states suffered major cuts as the
recession reduced state revenues.

PRIVATE PENSION PLANS

Private pensions are becoming an increasingly large part of the national
income support system. As noted earlier, the federal government has encouraged and facilitated their development. Although the government
has looked favorably on these programs, it is difficult for the federal
government to impose effective controls over them. The reason is that,
fundamentally, these are private programs, and the federal government
cannot readily make demands about what industry and commerce do
with their private programs. By 1974, however, several situations had developed in private pension plans which forced the federal government to
take action. Evidence was accumulating that there was gross inequity in
the benefits being paid. There were indications of corruption by managers of the plans. Plans were being set up which were poorly funded
and which, in all probability, would not be able to pay benefits. Mean-
while workers were making retirement plans on expectation of receiving
benefits from their private pension plans to supplement what they knew
would be inadequate Social Security benefits.

Although the action Congress took in 1974 was relatively strong—especially in light of its hesitation over the years to act decisively—one important characteristic of the system was not changed. That is, the private
sector has a choice of whether or not it wants to provide a pension plan;
and it retains the choice of discontinuing a plan, once one is set up. Further, it was impossible for the Congressional action to correct a major
weakness in private plans. That is, the benefit rights of an individual are
only rarely transferable—or portable, which is the technical word—when
the worker moves from one employer to another. Thus, Social Security
remains the only income support insurance program with that feature.

The main objective of the federal legislation was to assure the receipt
of benefits upon retirement after a period of service for an employer. A
further assurance is provided by setting up a reinsurance fund, similar to
the Federal Deposit Insurance Corporation, which insures bank deposits.
The reinsurance fund collects a small fee from all pension funds and
maintains a reserve to pay off accumulated obligations to beneficiaries
of any bankrupt fund.

The standards imposed by federal law on the private pensions operate separately for funds in which the employee has contributed as compared to those in which the employer makes all the contributions. There are more severe requirements for vesting (that is, the rights to a benefit) for the former than for the latter. The employee-contributed funds are in a small minority, however. For the employer-financed funds, vesting the benefits takes place following five years of service. After that time, the size of the benefit payment to which the employee is entitled grows in size as the number of years employed, when added to the employee's age, becomes larger. Conceivably an employee could work for several companies, working the minimum number of years for each in order to have vested rights and, upon retirement, receive several benefit checks, although each would be a small one.

Vesting can be accomplished in two ways. Under "cliff vesting" funds are 100% vested after 10 years. This is reduced to 5 years for individuals hired after 1989. Under "graded vesting" 25% of the funds are vested after 5 years. The percentage of the contributions vested increases until 100% is vested after 15 years. As is true of "cliff vesting," graded vesting for employees hired after 1989 begins at 3 years (25% vested) and is completed after 7 years.

There are several important characteristics of the private pension system:

- The payments are growing in adequacy although they do not equal Social Security. An exception is benefits to high-level executives, who often have a generous pension plan built into their remuneration.
- Benefits are payable to survivors of deceased plan members in a small but slowly growing number of plans.
- Few plans provide for adjustment to the cost of living, and if they do, it is not usually the full increase.
- The plans tend to favor the long-term employee who, by virtue of continuous employment by one employer, can become eligible for a more significant payment.
- In a few instances, an employee may carry over benefit rights to another employer in the same industry. An example is the trucker's pension fund, which operates across the industry.

Private pension funds share the same problem of nearly all retirement plans in the United States—that of being marginally secure financially. The insurance fund accumulates reserves very slowly and could be wiped out by a few large claims made simultaneously. The actuarially determined obligation for pension payments on some (even large) corporations is excessive. An issue which will gradually have to be faced is the extent of the corporate obligation for payment under terms of the plan versus the shareholders' rights to the assets of the company. As corporations encounter difficult economic times, such as the recession of the early 1990s, they may also reconsider their involvement in an extensive pension effort. The Insurance and Public Benefits section of the 1992 Older Americans Act amendments (Title VII) is supposed to help older workers evaluate the pension plans in which they are enrolled or for which they are eligible. The aim of the state run program is to help older individuals understand the ability of these pensions to meet their post-retirement needs and the relationship of these pensions to other public benefits and insurance plans. While it is likely that this will be resolved without reaching a crunch, it does suggest that the private pension system has to face the reality of financing troubles.

Individual Retirement Accounts (IRAs), in which the individual contributes up to $2000 annually, are one alternative for individuals who do not have private pension plans available. The interest on these accounts in banks, mutual funds, or insurance companies is not taxable until the individual withdraws the funds between the ages of 59 1/2 and 70. Earlier withdrawal is subject to major penalties on the interest. The tax reform legislation of 1986 restricted the deductibility of IRA contributions. Among persons whose employers also offer retirement programs, only those individuals whose adjusted gross income is less than $35,000 and couples whose adjusted gross income is less than $50,000 can deduct any IRA contributions from their income tax.

UNEMPLOYMENT AND INADEQUATE INCOME

The distinction between unemployment of an older person and retirement is often a thin one. An older person who loses his or her job may be vigorously looking for another one yet, since he or she needs income, may be forced to apply for and accept some income transfer benefits. Before moving on to the Social Security program—if he or she is eligible—the person may wish to exhaust his or her unemployment compensation rights. Many older persons receive unemployment compensation either before moving on to Social Security or simultaneously. It is possible for a person to receive both unemployment compensation and old-age benefits at the same time.

Unemployment compensation is a program of benefits for persons who were employed in specified fields of work but who have, not of their own choosing, lost their jobs. The program is administered by the states, who have considerable latitude in establishing eligibility standards, including the amount of the weekly benefit. Unemployment compensation is financed by a federally imposed tax, most of which is returned to the states by the federal government to pay the cost of the benefits granted and the cost of administering the program, which includes the operation of an employment service. States may add to the amount of the tax, making more funds available to support more generous benefits, both in dollar amounts and in duration of receipt of benefits, as well as to pay the cost of less onerous provisions for eligibility. Many states do this.

The number of workers covered by unemployment compensation has been increasing in recent years, until most workers in commerce and industry and many people in public employment and in teaching professions are now covered. Some progress has been made in incorporating casual employment into the system, such as domestic work and farm work. Even so, most people engaged in these kinds of jobs are still not covered, nor are self-employed persons. Benefits are payable only after a worker has been in employment for a specified period of time set by the states and therefore varying from state to state, with 26 weeks emerging as the most common length of time.

The trend has been for Congress to provide extended benefits in the course of an economic recession. The receipt of benefits has extended for as long as 15 months in recent years, but a duration of more than nine months is no longer likely. Many people question the wisdom of these extensions on the grounds that the availability of benefits tends to discourage diligent search for work. Also such a long period of unemployment strongly indicates that a work program is needed rather than an income transfer program. If benefits are to be extended, many observers contend, the recipients of such benefits ought to be means tested, which they are not now. Some unemployment benefits are subject to income tax. Some states include an addendum for dependents, but generally benefits are awarded to the worker without regard for family circumstances.

Eligibility for benefits hinges upon the unemployed individual being ready, willing, and able to work. Presumably illness or disability should exclude a worker, although in practice the unavailability of the worker for a job often is not known to the state. An unemployed person is not expected to take the first job that materializes without regard to experience or training; the system allows the worker to hold off accepting employment until a job becomes available in her or his line of work that uses her or his skills. As time passes, however, the unemployed worker is expected to lower his or her job expectations and accept less ideal work. Workers are not expected to take strike-breaking jobs nor ones that are below the usual wages paid.

Workers who wish to receive unemployment compensation are required to register for work with the employment service. If that office is successful in finding a job for the recipient of unemployment compensation, the unemployed person is expected to accept it unless she or he can show good cause for not doing so. Inasmuch as the employment service has few job openings for older workers, it is unlikely that an older person's willingness to work will be put to a test. Even if the employment office should refer the unemployment compensation beneficiary to a job, the employer may reject him or her, and of course this would not affect continued eligibility for benefits.

It has been a practice for older persons to apply for unemployment compensation as a prelude to retirement. Since the likelihood is very slight that they will be faced with a decision of whether or not to accept suitable employment which may be found by the employment service, the unemployment compensation program offers some additional tax-free income for the almost-retired person. While this appears to be legal, it is not within the spirit of the law and there have been discussions about making such persons ineligible for unemployment benefits.

The basic program of unemployment compensation benefits is sometimes supplemented by private funds created as a consequence of labor-management agreements. In the automobile, steel, and some of the other highly organized industries, management contributes toward a fund used to supplement the basic unemployment compensation program whenever needed. This supplement can take the form of continuing benefits after the regular program ends or more likely can supplement the size of the basic benefit. These funds are relatively new, having been established only in recent years. When put to a test, they were proven to be insufficient to last the duration of the unemployment period in the industries, although they were helpful to the workers who received them. These supplementary funds tend to provide more help to those with the greatest seniority.

REFERENCES

Cohen, W. (1983). *Social Security: The Compromise and Beyond*. Washington, DC: SOS Education Fund.
Fretz, B. (1990). Should the government and financing systems for deliver of services to the elderly be restructured? In P. Powers & K. Klingsmith (Eds.),

Aging and the law. Washington, DC: Public Policy Institute, American Association of Retired Persons.

U.S. House of Representatives, Committee on Ways and Means. (1991). *Background material and data on programs within the jurisdiction of the Committee on Ways and Means*. Washington, DC: U.S. Government Printing Office.

4

Illness, Medical Care, and Income Maintenance

Becoming ill or disabled creates two major problems for those affected. If inability to work cuts off income, the unemployed need some income transfers to support themselves and their dependents. The primary problem of the sick or disabled is providing income. The other major problem is paying for medical care.

RISKS OF ILLNESS, DISABILITY, AND INADEQUATE INCOME

Several programs, all of which depend on the particular status of the individual, address the need for income. The Social Security program includes benefits available to persons disabled on a long-term basis. Some states provide short-term disability benefits as an element in their unemployment compensation program. Workmen's compensation is available for those who have become ill or disabled on the job; this includes wage replacement and medical expenses. Many employers provide sick leave, which is a form of short-term disability benefit. The SSI program is available for the disabled who, for one reason or another, are not eligible for Social Security or any other income-producing programs.

Social Security Disability Benefits

Eligibility for these benefits follows along the lines of eligibility for Social Security in general, as described earlier. The major difference in eligibility, say, for old-age or survivor's benefits and disability benefits, is a requirement for a longer attachment to the labor force. Although disability benefits are available to younger workers who meet the test of severity of disability, the law requires that disabled persons have worked under covered employment for a proportionately longer period of time than is required of deceased wage earners who die prematurely and leave survivors. The intention is to emphasize that the worker to be covered has made a significant financial contribution to the system before becoming eligible.

For purposes of determining the amount of benefits after disabled workers establish eligibility on the basis of severity of disability and length of time in the work force, they are considered retired. That is, their lifetime wages in covered employment are totaled and divided by the number of months of work. For younger workers, the number of months of covered employment may be small, certainly when compared to the retired person. However, the average monthly earnings of the younger worker could be as high as those of a retired worker. Indeed, the monthly average might well be higher since the younger worker's wage history is more recent and covers a time when wages have been higher than those of a retired person whose wage history may go back 40 years. This peculiarity of the system has resulted in disability benefits generally running higher than those granted for retired persons. Legislation enacted in 1980 set some ceilings on benefits for the disabled to ensure that benefits do not exceed previous earnings but reduce the gap between retirement and disability benefits.

Benefits for disabled workers are increased if they have spouses and even more if they have dependent children. The procedure for determining the amount of these awards is similar to that used for retired workers, their spouses, and young children if any. Inasmuch as disabled workers are generally younger, very possibly with young children as well as spouse, the total benefits awarded have been higher than for other parts of the Social Security system. This has caused criticism, and efforts are being made to bring these benefits into line with survivor's benefits by limiting benefits to a fixed family maximum.

For claiming benefits, the definition of disability is a severe one. It attempts to limit the program to those persons with severe and long-lasting disabilities, mental or physical. The words in the definition, "inability to engage in any substantial gainful activity," suggest that a test is to be made of the individual's ability to engage in "any gainful activity," not just a test of whether or not there is employment in the community in which the individual lives. This definition could conceivably result in the denial of benefits to people who might be able to do certain kinds of work even if there is no possibility of any work of that nature showing up.

The individual applicant is responsible for presenting proof of disability and, if medical examination or testing is involved, must pay for that cost. If the Social Security Administration is not satisfied with the proof offered, it will pay for additionally required examinations and reports. When the program began in the 1950s, it was small and grew very slowly. In recent years it has expanded broadly, with some disagreement over the reasons for the growth. Some observers feel that the administrators of the program have relaxed some of the standards. Others feel that applicants have become more knowledgeable about the various benefit programs and that they have been helped by experienced lawyers and encouraged by recipient advocate groups. Many instances of denial by the Social Security Administration have gone to appeal within the organization and, if that failed, to the courts. A surprisingly large number of adverse administrators' decisions have been reversed by the courts.

Although the definition speaks in terms of long and severe disability, from the very beginning the assumption was that some beneficiaries might be rehabilitated. For this reason, provision is made for the state vocational rehabilitation agency to review all applications with a view toward identification of potential cases for vocational rehabilitation. The applicant who is recommended by the vocational rehabilitation agency for rehabilitation must accept the plan of that agency or forfeit rights to disability benefits. In some instances the rehabilitation plan is financed by the Social Security Administration as a charge against the Social Security funds. Those who are rehabilitated and who go off the program save the program a great deal of money over the years. Thus the cost of rehabilitation is regarded as a prudent investment. The actual record of rehabilitation cases shows that comparatively few are able to be fully rehabilitated and return to work. Legislation under consideration would encourage beneficiaries to undertake work by assuring them of quick reentry to the program if the work does not prove feasible.

Under heightened review processes an increased number of individuals receiving disability payments were terminated during the early 1980s. This included many older individuals who had received disability payments for many years. In fiscal 1983, the benefits of 182,074 workers were terminated as compared to 80,956 in 1981 (U.S. House of Representatives, 1986). In response to mounting complaints about unjust terminations, the law now provides the individual with the right to a face-to-face hearing before benefits are terminated. Appeals procedures have also been clarified. The Disabilities Reform Act of 1984 specified the grounds on which disability benefits could be terminated, including standards of medical improvement.

Supplementary Security Income

The SSI program provides assistance to persons who are disabled or blind, which is the federalization of the old grant-in-aid program for the needy disabled or blind which was adopted by the Congress in 1972 and became effective in 1974. When the program was operated by the states with federal financial support, each state set its own definition of disability and blindness within the broad guidelines of the federal law. When the program was taken over by the federal government, a national definition was introduced for both disabilities—a definition which follows along the concepts of the disability insurance program under Social Security. A grandfather clause was included to make it possible for those already certified by the states in 1974 to continue eligibility. Since the definition is now similar to that for the Social Security program, the SSI program qualifies only the long-term, severely disabled.

At the time the program was federalized, the minimum age of 18 was eliminated, thus allowing young children to qualify for benefits if they are severely disabled and, of course, if they are needy. The benefit payment for the disabled is the same as for the over-age-65 group, as noted earlier. The eligibility requirements relating to resources, citizenship, or legal status and the like are the same as under SSI old-age assistance provisions. In 1990, out of 4.8 million SSI recipients, 3.3 million were disabled and 84,000 were blind. It is estimated that approximately 40% of disabled SSI recipients are mentally impaired (U.S. House of Representatives, 1987). Among the blind and disabled SSI recipients, 601,000 were over age 65. There were an additional 1.5 million aged SSI recipients (U.S. House of Representatives, 1991). SSI has thus become a major financial component of the community-based mental health programs now developing for the chronically mentally ill in many areas.

Sick Leave

Important but often overlooked resources for providing income to people who are temporarily sick or disabled are the provisions many employers make for sick leave. Employers that provide sick leave tend to be those that employ white-collar workers—office, sales, and similar work. However, manufacturing companies have begun to provide this benefit as well. Government work of all kinds includes this form of illness protection.

Workmen's Compensation

Programs of workmen's compensation are operated by the states or private insurance companies under state supervision. Typically, benefits include both financial assistance in lieu of lost wages and payment for medical bills. The illnesses and disabilities covered by this program are those incurred on the job, under the concept of *no fault*; that is, no test is made to determine whether employees were careless or otherwise contributed to their own accidents. Benefits are often time-limited and are usually related to the severity of the disability. For the severely disabled, benefits include some form of rehabilitation, often in conjunction with the state vocational rehabilitation agency.

Not all employees are covered by workmen's compensation. Since these are state programs, eligibility provisions differ around the country. In some states there are exemptions of small employers, those with five or so employees. Typically, others not covered are domestic, casual, and farm workers. Because of these variations among the states and omissions from the program, there is some interest in enacting a federal law which would establish uniform standards for the nation.

Temporary Disability Insurance

Short-term disability benefits are available in about six states as an offshoot of the unemployment insurance program. These states include some of the large industrial states, such as New York and California, with the program providing coverage for approximately 25% of the national labor force in commerce and industry.

Benefits are available for workers who are covered by the state unemployment insurance law and who are absent from work because of illness or disability. These would be people whose illness or disability are unrelated to their work (otherwise they would be eligible for workmen's compensation) and whose absence from work will be temporary as contrasted with long-term absences as defined in the Social Security program. Workers covered by an employer's sick leave may not be excluded in some states; in others, disability benefits may be reduced or denied. Temporary disability benefits are not permitted to overlap unemployment insurance benefit payments.

All of the laws have minimum requirements for days absent or loss of wages before benefits will begin and, of course, limits on the duration of benefits being paid. Benefits are related to the size of previous earnings, as in unemployment compensation. The plans are financed by a state-imposed tax on employees and, in some states, on the employers. There is no federal financial support for these programs.

RISKS OF AGING, MEDICAL BILLS, AND INADEQUATE INCOME

Medical costs for the aged are increasing each year. This reflects not only the growing proportion of the gross national product devoted to medical care but also the proportionately higher medical costs of the aged as compared with the population as a whole. Health care expenditures increased 11% annually in the 1980s. The aging of the American population accounts for part of this increase. Overall, individuals over the age of 65 account for one-third of all personal health care expenditures in the United States (U.S. Senate et al., 1991). In addition, long-term care—a type of medical care needed almost exclusively by the aged—is costly and, by definition, long lasting. For these reasons, provisions to help the aged meet medical costs have been in the law for many years. From the earliest history of government and through the years, welfare programs have provided some medical care and some payment for medical care for poor people, especially the aged. That practice is now being carried out through the Medicaid program (Title XIX of the SSA).

Private insurance for health care costs has been available for decades but has been especially prominent since World War II. The Blue Cross plan for hospital insurance was begun during the Depression and has had many individual subscribers as well as group subscribers. Private health insurance has become a fringe benefit of employment. While Blue Cross—as a nonprofit community plan—had a large number of old persons as subscribers, other private plans (especially the profit-making ones) shunned the elderly because of their poor risk record and conducted all of their business through employers. Thus, if older persons remained in employment, they would have some financial help for medical expenses in this manner. There have always been questions about the extent to which private health insurance continues to be available to workers once they leave the work force and whether this form of insurance help is equitably available to people of all income groups—not just the aged, but all people.

It became obvious over time that private health insurance could not be depended upon to provide protection for the aged. Indeed, there was doubt that private profit-making health insurance companies wanted a major role in insuring the aged. The high incidence of illness among the aged made them a poor risk for private health insurance. Although private Blue Cross plans have been an exception to this rule, even this group of nonprofit private insurers began to be concerned about the stability of their financial position, especially as the cost of hospital care began to escalate dramatically in the 1960s. Even though the private health insurance industry and private medical practitioners were opposed to further government involvement, the public interest and demand for hospital insurance for the aged prevailed, and Medicare was enacted in 1965.

There are now three broad protective devices for the aged in meeting their medical costs, one being private health insurance, which is a major factor in payment of medical bills. Private programs vary widely in the protection offered, provisions for coverage, and circumstances of enrollment but provide considerable protection for many elderly persons, especially those under the age of 65. For those over age 65, private health insurance is widely available to supplement the Medicare program.

Medicare—a second element—covers nearly all persons age 65 and over, those receiving disability benefits under Social Security, and a few other small and highly exceptional groups. Eligibility and benefits will be discussed below. Although this program is universally available and at low cost to the aged, the result of exceptions and omissions is that Medicare is meeting less than 40% of the medical costs of the aged.

Despite its deficiencies, the growth in Medicare expenditures has been dramatic. Between 1988 and 1989 Medicare expenditures increased by 10%. Medicare expenditures in 1990 increased 13% from the previous year (U.S. House of Representatives, 1991). As the older population continues to increase and the number of workers decreases, the problem of financing Medicare looms larger. One projection is that the hospital trust fund for Part A of Medicare will be insolvent by 2005 (Broder & Rich, 1991) but earlier dates have also been mentioned. There are also projections that unless birth rates change, only two workers will pay into Medicare for every beneficiary by the year 2050. To combat this likelihood, changes can be expected to occur over an extended period in taxes paid for Medicare, deductibles, and premiums paid by beneficiaries as well as reimbursements to hospitals and physicians.

To control hospital costs, a new system of *prospective* payment for hospital care has been introduced. This Diagnostic Related Group system uses standardized payments for particular conditions. The results of this system have been controversial. Some critics have argued that older patients are being discharged prematurely. The Medicare Quality Protection Act of 1986 required hospitals to prepare discharge plans for patients who might be adversely affected by discharge. Patients must also be informed of their rights to in-patient hospitalization and have the right to appeal a decision for discharging them. By 1989, hospital stays for persons over age 65 had declined to 8.9 days. (National Center for Health Statistics, 1991). A Rand corporation study undertaken in 1985–

86 does not indicate any reduction in the quality of care after the introduction of the DRG system or a major increase in mortality as a result of the new discharge policies (Kahn et al., 1990).

A third element in this fabric of protection is the Medicaid program. This is a grant-in-aid program which is operated by the states and provides protection for some of the poor population. Coverage varies from state to state, and benefits also vary but are broader than those of Medicare. Each of these programs will be discussed.

Medicare

The Medicare program (Title XVIII of the SSA) is an integral part of the Social Security program. Generally speaking, eligibility for Medicare is determined by eligibility for Social Security; that is, Medicare benefits will be provided to persons who have established eligibility for old-age benefits or disability benefits. No separate eligibility determination is made except for disabled beneficiaries, who must have been in receipt of cash benefits for two years prior to Medicare eligibility. However, individuals are eligible for Medicare who, although eligible, are not actually receiving old-age benefits because they are earning more than the retirement income level, as discussed earlier. Medicare is not available to persons who are below the age of 65, except for individuals suffering from endstage renal disease.

The Medicare program is divided into two parts: Part A—hospital insurance—and Part B—medical insurance. All persons eligible for Medicare receive Part A benefits without any additional cost to them. Part B benefits are available only to persons who "join," that is, agree to pay a certain amount each month. This monthly fee is deducted from the check of persons who receive Social Security cash benefits. For persons who are eligible for Social Security benefits but who do not receive a check because they are earning above the retirement level, a bill from the Health Care Financing Administration is sent for subsequent payment. In both parts deductibles and coinsurance payments are required (discussed below).

Part A

Under Part A, persons with medically established need for hospitalization are entitled to 60 days of hospitalization. As a condition of eligibility they must pay for the first day of the care. That amount is raised annually as the cost of hospitalization increases. It was $652 in 1992. If additional days of hospital care are needed, 30 more days are available upon the payment of a daily coinsurance fee, which in 1992 was $163. This is also raised annually. There must be a short period of time between hospitalizations before the 60-day and 30-day periods become applicable again. If additional hospitalization is needed beyond the 60- and 30-day limits, an individual can draw upon a lifetime reserve allowable for each eligible person. That life-time reserve is 60 days, with a daily coinsurance fee of $326 (in 1992). The services provided by the hospital are those usually included within a hospital's per diem charges but not including the services of the anesthesiologist, pathologist, and radiologist. These services are charged separately by the doctors and are considered a Part B expense.

When patients have been hospitalized for at least three days and are found to be in need of medical care which cannot be provided in the home but which is not as medically sophisticated as that offered in the hospital setting, they may receive care in an extended care facility (ECF). These facilities are high-quality nursing homes which must be closely related to or have working agreements with a hospital and be able to provide the kind of care the patient needs. Without additional charge, patients may receive up to 20 days of care in an ECF. An additional 80 days of care will be provided upon payment of a daily fee of $81.50 (in 1992). The service of an extended care facility shortens the stay of patients in hospitals; it is not intended to be long-term nursing home care. Indeed, the Medicare program as a whole does not respond to the need for long-term care.

Home health care is available, with no ceiling on days, if needed, and at no additional charge. Home health care must be medically ordered and must be of a medical nature, not homemaker service. The daily skilled care must be for a relatively short period of time or be seen as having an end within a predicted period. Medicare will reimburse hospices for the care they provide individuals with a terminal diagnosis of 6 months or less life expectancy. The beneficiary may reside in a hospice for two 90-day periods and one subsequent 30-day period.

Part B

Part B of Medicare is called Supplemental Medical Insurance. As mentioned earlier, Medicare-eligible persons do not automatically participate in Part B. They agree to this insurance and pay $31.80 per month (in 1992) or accept that deduction being made from their Social Security checks. Nearly everyone receiving Social Security belongs to Part B. This plan provides partial payment for physicians for medical services. There is an annual deductible amount which, in 1992, was $100. That is, in order to be eligible for help from Part B, participants must first pay at least $100 for the kinds of medical services covered by Part B. Expenditures for drugs, dental services, and the like are not included in Part B. Individuals who have joined Part B, have paid their deductible amount of medical expenses, and have maintained monthly payments into the Part B fund will then be able to receive 80% reimbursement for reasonable charges for medical services received. Outpatient psychiatric care had been reimbursed at a 50% rate with a $1,100 limit. This limit has now been removed. Medicare also now covers flu shots and routine mammograms every 2 years for women over age 65.

Physicians can be paid in either of two ways. They can agree to make a direct charge to the Health Care Financing Administration, through a system of intermediaries which have been set up to deal directly with doctors. If they follow this route, they will receive 80% of the fee which the intermediary has set, following the rules and directives of the Health Care Financing Administration. These rules, reflecting the concern in the Congress over the rise in medical costs in general and physicians' charges specifically, are directed toward keeping the Medicare payment in the general range of average payments and not the higher charges made by some doctors. The doctor must look to the patient for the remaining 20% of his charges. In fiscal 1989 81% of all Medicare claims were paid through this "assignment" method (U.S. House of Representatives, 1990). The government is actively attempting to increase this percentage by allowing only physicians who accept assignment to bill at increased Medicare rates.

Physicians must now submit their bill to Medicare, regardless of whether they do or do not accept assignment. In 1991 physicians who did not accept assignment ("non-participant") were permitted to bill their patients for only 140% of the approved Medicare fee. In 1993, the allowable figure will be only 115% of the approved Medicare fee. Physicians must accept assignment for individuals who are eligible for both Medicare and Medicaid.

In the past the fee was based on "reasonable and customary charges" in the community. As of 1992 the rates are based on a fee schedule developed through the Department of Health and Human Services. The fee schedule covers 7,000 services, and reimbursement will be based on "value units" assigned to each procedure or medical service. These value units take into account the doctor's time, overhead, and risk of malpractice suit and are then multiplied by a conversion factor in dollars. The resulting amount will be the Medicare approved rate. Health and Human Services secretary Louis Sullivan termed the fee schedule, "the most wide-ranging and fundamental change in Medicare's physician payment since the creation of the Medicare program in 1965" (Rosenthal, 1990).

Medicare is now encouraging older persons to join Health Maintenance Organizations (HMOs) that provide a wide range of care to their members on a prepayment basis. Under the Tax Equity and Fiscal Responsibility Act of 1982, older individuals who join HMOs continue to pay their Medicare Part B payments, and the HMO receives payment from the federal government for each member equivalent to 95% of the average Medicare costs in that state. A range of services equivalent to that provided by Medicare must be provided by the HMO. By September 1986, 3% of Medicare beneficiaries had enrolled in HMOs. The federal government is also experimenting with Social HMOs which provide additional social services to older recipients. The demonstration was originally started in four sites and was expanded to four more in 1991. The benefits provided by the S/HMO include home health care, homemaker services, respite care, day care, and chronic care benefits for skilled nursing. The premium for the enrollee is between $24 and $49. Medicare and Medicaid reimburse the S/HMO at a per capita rate (Newcomer, Harrington, Yordi, & Friedlob, 1988). Those individuals who do join the S/HMO appear to opt for more extensive benefits and less out-of-pocket expenses, particularly expenses for drug, dental care, and eyeglasses (Newcomer, Harrington, & Friedlob, 1990).

As noted earlier, more than approximately 60% of medical care costs of the aged are not being covered by the Medicare program. The remaining 60% represents the various deductibles and coinsurance charges in Medicare (as described above) and payments for services not covered. Notable among these are drugs and dental services, although other services are also excluded. It is estimated that 25% of all older persons spend more than $500 a year on prescription drugs. This figure is increased by the cost of over-the-counter drugs. A major element in excluded costs is long-term care. As stated earlier, the Medicare provisions for institutional care are time-limited. Medicaid (discussed below) picks up some of these charges.

Long-term care is not included under Medicare because of its high costs but also because it is a combination of both medical and domiciliary costs. The growth of expenditures for these services nationally reflects not only the rising cost of medical care in general but the fact that intergenerational families have diminished in number. Provisions are not always available in the homes of children for older parents who need custodial-medical care. Planners of medical insurance programs hesitate to assume a cost under the heading of medical care which is only partially medical in nature and which is a reflection of societal changes. The result is that in 1990 almost 54% of total Part A and Part B Medicare expenditures were accounted for by inpatient hospital care, 1% by nursing homes, 3% by home health services, and less than 1% by hospices. The greatest proportion of Part B benefits were paid for physician services.

Medicaid

This program, known officially as Medical Assistance, is authorized by Title XIX of the SSA. Given all of its complications, Medicare is much easier to understand than Medicaid. The reason is that Medicaid is a grant-in-aid to the states and is not a national program like Medicare. The federal law offers states the choice of, first, whether they wish to have a Medicaid program and, second, a variety of options on the breadth of eligibility and services covered as well as the fees to be paid. The result is considerable variation in the kinds of programs which have evolved in the states. The last state developed a Medicaid program in 1981.

Once a state decides to have a Medicaid program, it must first decide whether the program is to be available only to people receiving money payments from welfare programs or whether the program will also include some of the medically needy. The welfare groups are those recipients of Aid to Families with Dependent Children (AFDC) and SSI. With the expansion of eligibility in 1974 through the inauguration of SSI, states were given a further option of excluding persons eligible under the expanded SSI program or including them. The "medically" needy are those people who would qualify for the money payments programs except that their incomes or resources exceed the stated limits for eligibility. This is a very important distinction to understand because it accounts for the large number of medically needy people who are not included in the Medicaid program. Among the excluded groups are those below the age of 65 who are not disabled. Those over age 65 would qualify for SSI, as would those who are under 65 and disabled. The lack these people have of a tie to the SSI program, in these examples, accounts for their exclusion from Medicaid. Another example is the intact family in which the father is employed but earns very little. Since such a family is not eligible for AFDC, the family is also not eligible for Medicaid.

About half of the states include some medically needy. In each of these states, a decision had to be made concerning the income level to be regarded as qualifying. Although federal law prevents states from being too liberal in making this decision, most states that include the medically needy have eligibility points below the federal maximum.

States must use Medicaid funds to pay for all Medicare premiums, co-payments, and deductibles for Medicare beneficiaries who are below the poverty line and have less than $4,000 in liquid assets. Beginning in 1991 the states were required to pay the premiums (but not other costs) of older persons whose income is below 110% of poverty and who have less than $4,000 in liquid assets. The income limit rises to 120% of poverty in 1995. The immediate cost to the Medicaid program is expected to result in significant savings in the long run.

The federal law sets up the classifications of services which states must or can offer to pay for. States must offer some institutional and some noninstitutional services. In addition, states must offer:

- Inpatient hospital services
- Outpatient hospital services and other X-ray and laboratory services
- Skilled nursing home services for adults
- Early periodic screening services for children
- Physicians' services in the home, office, or hospital

An appropriation of $580 million for 5 years beginning in 1991 will provide Medicaid "assisted living" services to frail elderly in their homes. This assistance will include meals, and visits by social workers and nurses. For the medically needy, the states may offer a smaller range of services. In addition to those required services, there is a long list of other optional services, which includes drugs, home health care, dental services, and the like. A major optional service which the states may offer is intermediate care facility (ICF) care. An ICF provides services that range somewhere between those of a domiciliary facility and a nursing home. This obviously includes many nursing homes which offer only minimal services and often charge fees which, although hard pressed, the state Medicaid agency will pay.

The federal law imposes a series of requirements on the states, most of which are designed to ensure efficient administration and continuous effort to weed out overutilization and ineligibility and also to make sure that applicants and recipients receive fair consideration by the state agency.

The federal share of Medicaid cost ranges from 50% in states with per capita income equal to or greater than the national average, to 83% for the state with the lowest per capita income in the United States. For those states with below-average per capita income, the federal medical percentage will range from 50 to 83%, depending on their rank in the states by per capita income.

By far the largest sums expended by the states for Medicaid are for hospitals, skilled nursing homes, and ICFs. Medicaid is the major source of public funds for long-term care. In 1989, 69% of the Medicaid expenditures for older persons went to nursing homes. Inasmuch as all Medicare institutional services have time limits and the institutional services under Medicaid generally do not, many older persons find themselves receiving care in various kinds of nursing homes which are Medicaid eligible. The federal law prohibits states from requiring that children be responsible for supporting parents. Even if older persons have resources in their own names—even considerable resources—many months of care in a nursing home will exhaust them. Thus, when the resources of the older persons diminish to the eligibility level for such resources as set by the state, they then become eligible for Medicaid.

Once a Medicaid recipient is institutionalized, States can place a lien on property to recover their Medicaid expenses but not on the home of a spouse, children under the age of 21, or a blind or disabled child of any age. In addition, a lien cannot be placed on property where a brother or sister of the Medicaid recipient has equity if this sibling lived for at least one year in the home before the individual was institutionalized.

Provisions for financing long-term care are greatly deficient. Medicare is weak in this regard; private health insurance policies rarely cover this need; and individual resources are—except for the very rich—inadequate to cover this care. Families who feel responsible for older members and their resources can, often at personal sacrifice, provide such care if needed. Proof that these resources are inadequate is suggested by the fact that over half of all nursing home patients are recipients of Medicaid.

The Medicaid program has been engulfed in the rapidly rising cost of medical care. States have taken some steps to protect themselves, but even these measures have not been sufficiently effective to prevent the costs from becoming burdensome. In response to this, states have tended to trim services as best they can and have attempted to keep fees which they pay from rising too rapidly. The consequence is that many medical practitioners have refused to treat Medicaid patients, and the level of

ICF service has diminished as states have been unable to raise the amount of payments they will make for this care.

To some observers, the only answer to this problem of providing medical care for low-income people is national health insurance. To some degree, all national decisions made around Medicaid have been regarded as temporary, made in the belief that national health insurance will surely come to be and will help solve the problems. Even as proposals continue, the prospects of such a national health plan still seem to be in the future.

Private Health Insurance

A major force for paying medical costs in the United States is private health insurance. Public policy has supported the notion of a strong private sector for paying for medical care. Medical practitioners have encouraged it; industry has looked to the private sector to provide help to employees with their medical bills; and tax laws have encouraged the development of private health insurance plans. Consequently, private health insurance pays about 27% of the medical costs in the nation, while government—mainly through Medicare and Medicaid—pays about 42%. Direct payments made by individuals amount to about 27%. (Philanthropy accounts for the remainder.)

Significant as private health insurance is, its impact is much less for the aged than for younger workers. Since so few of the aged are employed, they tend to have less private health insurance than do younger people. With the advent of Medicare in 1965, the private health insurance industry was pleased to assume a smaller role for the aged for obvious reasons. There is great risk that the aged will become ill and will need costly medical services. Private insurance provides policies that supplement Medicare. These policies pay for some of the deductibles and coinsurance charges (discussed earlier) and may provide payment for some additional hospital days, but they rarely cover long-term care. Thus even the combination of Medicare and supplemental private health insurance does not provide the aged with full coverage.

Many older people purchase more than one "Medigap" policy. The result is extra expense without additional coverage. One estimate is that 25% of older persons with Medigap coverage have at least two policies. A reduction in these duplicate policies would save the older individual from $350 to $1250 per year, depending on the number of duplicate policies (Sinclair, 1990). Federal legislation now forbids the sale of duplicate policies and requires the salesperson to inquire whether the older person already has any medical policies. The salesperson must also list on the insurance application any other health insurance policies they have already sold to the older person and the policies must return to the consumer at least 65% of what they bring in to the company.

Regulations adopted by the National Association of Insurance Commissioners will help to standardize Medigap policies. Under these regulations, ten plans will be offered. The basic plan will offer "core" services. These core services include the co-insurance for Medicare Part A, 365 days of hospital coverage after Medicare benefits end, the 20% of doctor's fees not covered by Medicare and the first three pints of blood a patient needs each year. The more extensive plans will cover a variety of options including coverage during foreign travel, home care, preventive care, and prescription drugs. Consumers will thus be able to make comparisons of the costs of each of these plans as offered by different insurers (Crenshaw, 1991). If it is effectively implemented, the State Insurance Assistance Program, initiated through the 1992 OAA (Title VII), should also help older individuals compare Medigap policies as well as obtain benefits.

Long-term care insurance that covers skilled nursing home and in-home care is now offered through a number of private insurers. The number and purchasers of these policies increased dramatically during the last part of the 1980s. Although only 17 companies offered long-term care insurance before 1985, this number had grown to 130 by 1991. These policies had been purchased by 1.6 million people (Blum, 1991). There has been strong criticisms of many of the policies offered because their benefits are inadequate and they do not adjust for inflation. Without an inflation clause, the policy may continue to reimburse $100 per day for nursing home care in 1990 as well as in 2020 when nursing home costs may have risen substantially. Many policies have also contained clauses excluding individuals with preexisting conditions.

An example of a long-term care insurance policy is the one available to state employees in Maryland through Travelers Insurance company. This policy allows the individual to choose a benefit of $50, $70, or $100 per day. For nursing home care the whole benefit is paid. For home health care, adult day care, and homemaker services such as meal preparation, laundry, and shopping, one-half of the daily benefit is paid. The policy will also pay up to 20 times 100% of the daily benefit for respite care, including a stay by the patient in a custodial care facility or a visit from a companion who serves as substitute caregiver. An assessment that the individual had a preexisting condition 6 months before enrolling in the plan could delay payment of benefits for 6 months.

For an individual aged 40 the cost of a $50 daily benefit in 1990 was $7.05 per month and $14.10 per month for a $100 daily benefit. The costs are higher if an inflation factor is built into the policy. Instead of a $7.05 monthly premium for a $50 daily benefit, the premium is $12.80 and double this figure for a $100 benefit. These premiums do not increase with age. If the long-term care policy is purchased at age 65, the monthly premium for a $50 daily benefit without an inflation factor is $62.90 and $86.30 with an inflation factor. The individual enrolling in the plan or for whom the policy is purchased must be less than 80 years old.

Long-term insurance remains a new, important but basically untested approach to long-term care. The payment of more than $1000 per year for this insurance may deter many 65-year-old persons from enrolling. A recent study indicates that 84% of older people between the ages of 65 and 79 cannot afford the policies currently offered by nine insurance companies (National Council on the Aging, 1990). Even the $150 cost per year may seem high to the 40-year-old who cannot envision the future need for this type of benefit. The ability of the premiums to adequately cover the cost of long-term care for both the enrollee and the insurance company is as yet unclear, but it is expected that this type of insurance policy will continue to grow.

A combination of public and private long-term insurance may become more prevalent in the 1990s. A plan adopted in New York and a number of other states allows individuals who purchase long-term care insurance to keep a dollar in assets for each dollar of insurance they purchase. This proviso reduces the assets that must be spent to qualify for Medicaid. The equity of this type of plan for older people of different incomes has been contested as well as its ability to adequately pay for nursing home care (estimated at $62,000 per year in New York) (Freudenheim, 1992).

Health insurance for older persons has become a complex, widely debated aspect of the American social welfare system. Clearly the existence of Medicare and other programs has provided a level of health care for older people that would formerly not have been possible. Despite the existence of all of these programs, however, the out-of-pocket medical expenses for older persons continues to be high. Per capita, these individuals spend 15% of their income on health care and this figure has not decreased despite the introduction of Medicare in 1965 (U.S. Senate, 1990).

REFERENCES

Blum, D. (1991). Insurance for long-term care offered by TIAA in effort to provide options. *The Chronicle of Higher Education, 37*(20), A15, A18.

Broder, D., & Rich, S. (1991). Social Security earns a mixed review. *Washington Post*, May 20, A9.

Crenshaw, A. (1991). Relief for Medigap confusion. *Washington Post*, October 16, Family and Retirement Section, 6.

Freudenheim, M. (1992). Medicaid plan promotes nursing-home insurance. *New York Times*, May 3:1:1, 20.

Kahn, K., Rubinstein, L., Kosekoff, J., Rogers, W., Keeler, E., & Brook, R. (1990). The effects of the DRG based prospective payment system on quality of care for hospitalized patients. *Journal of the American Medical Association, 264*, 1953–1955.

National Center for Health Statistics. (1991). *1989 summary: National hospital discharge survey*. Hyattsville, MD: Author.

National Council on the Aging. (1990). LTC insurance out-of-reach. *Networks, 2*(2), 5.

Newcomer, R., Harrington, C., & Friedlob, A. (1990). Awareness and enrollment in the Social/HMO. *The Gerontologist, 30*, 86–93.

Newcomer, R., Harrington, C., Yordi, C., & Friedlob, A. (1988). *Social/health maintenance organization demonstration evaluation: Summary*. University of California, San Francisco: Institute for Health and Aging.

Rosenthal, E. (1990). Medicare fee plan sent to Congress. *New York Times*, September 1, 1, 9.

Sinclair, M. (1990). Fear of costly illness fuels 'Medigap' waste. *Washington Post*, November 10, B1.

U.S. House of Representatives, Committee on Ways and Means. (1986). *Background material and data on programs within the jurisdiction of the Committee on Ways and Means*. Washington, DC: U.S. Government Printing Office.

U.S. House of Representatives, Committee on Ways and Means. (1987). *Background material and data on programs within the jurisdiction of the Committee on Ways and Means*. Washington, DC: U.S. Government Printing Office.

U.S. House of Representatives, Committee on Ways and Means. (1990). *Background material and data on programs within the jurisdiction of the Committee on Ways and Means*. Washington, DC: U.S. Government Printing Office.

U.S. House of Representatives, Committee on Ways and Means. (1991). *Background material and data on programs within the jurisdiction of the Committee on Ways and Means*. Washington, DC: U.S. Government Printing Office.

U.S. Senate, Special Committee on Aging. (1990). *Developments in Aging: 1989: Volume 1*. Washington, DC: U.S. Government Printing Office.

U.S. Senate, Special Committee on Aging, American Association of Retired Persons, Federal Council on the Aging, U.S. Administration on Aging. (1991). *Aging America: Trends and projections, 1991 edition*. Washington, DC: Authors.

Part III

Programs for the Aged

Existing programs and services can be classified according to the dependence of the individuals assisted. Programs and services can also be classified in a format utilized by the Government Accounting Office (Comptroller General of the United States, 1977*): home help, medical, financial, assessment, referral, social-recreational, and transportation.

Many of the programs and services included in this list have common elements. Adult daycare centers and multipurpose senior centers both utilize transportation and have major social components. Although this volume often discusses providing "services" or "serving" the elderly, the attempt is to differentiate between programs and services, terms often used synonymously. As defined, programs contain individual elements; services include many of these same elements combined under a larger umbrella. These programs and services are discussed as they are most commonly organized, but the existence of state-by-state variations means that descriptions of a program or service may be more applicable to one area than another.

In this part will be discussed individual programs vital to the well-being of the elderly: information and referral, health and mental health programs, transportation, crime prevention and legal assistance programs, employment, volunteer, and educational programs, and nutrition programs.

*Comptroller General of the United States. (1977). *Report to the Congress: The well-being of older people in Cleveland, Ohio*. Washington, DC: Government Printing Office.

5

Information and Assistance

GOALS

Creating an extensive network of services has no benefits for the older person unless he or she is informed about the availability of these services and how to make use of them. Information and assistance programs are thus a natural outgrowth of the tremendous increase in public and private programs for the general population and specifically for the elderly. The size of the agencies giving services, the size of the population being served in a given geographic area, and the number of different services available determine the extent of need for an information exchange system that can both identify appropriate services for those expressing a given need and collect and identify information on services being given.

> For the population at large, including the elderly, information and referral is a social service in its own right: an activity by which a person in need is made aware of, and connected to, a service or resource which can meet the need. However, the simple concept of establishing a link between need and resource becomes complex as one takes a closer look. It is a means to an end—an intermediate service which is determined by the final outcomes it attempts to facilitate. (Schmandt, Bach, & Radin, 1979, p. 22)

The functions of information and assistance for the elderly are essentially the same as the functions for the general population except for the focus on the specific needs of the elderly:

1. The assemblage and provision of information to link older persons with the opportunities, services, and resources designed to help them meet their particular problems
2. The collection and reporting of information about the needs of

older people and the adequacy of resources available to them as aids to the evaluation, planning, coordination, and resource development efforts required of state and local agencies

Information and assistance systems thus link individuals to services and services to each other in an effort to provide individuals with greater access to programs and services that can meet their needs. The 1992 OAA amendments also emphasize follow-up to ensure that individuals receive the services they need.

HISTORY

Information and assistance programs began in the 1960s when moneys were increasing for social programs. Some large federal and state agencies offered information and referral to the public in response to an expressed need. Information was provided in booklets and over the telephone as the need arose.

Official federal interest in information and assistance began in 1971, with the passage of legislation authorizing the Social Security Administration to provide information to wage earners who would soon be retiring. In 1973, under the Comprehensive Service Amendments to the Older Americans Act (OAA), priority was to be given to the development of information and assistance programs for the elderly. Similarly, the information and assistance needs of the general welfare population, including the elderly, were addressed under the 1974/1975 Title XX social services regulations, which made these optional services that states could elect to provide. However, information and assistance services were mandatory for SSI recipients. Title II of the Community Services Act of 1974 provided for urban and rural community action programs. Under a special section for senior opportunities and services, provisions were made for information and assistance programs. Information and assistance programs could also be operated under the National Health Planning and Resources Development Act of 1974 and the Community Mental Health Centers Amendments of 1975. In addition, a series of interagency agreements have been developed at the federal level to promote coordination of information and assistance services through joint efforts at the federal, state, and local levels.

Information and assistance has grown in importance with each reauthorization of the Older Americans Act. The 1992 amendments require the AoA Commissioner to establish information and assistance as a priority service. In Title III, plans submitted by an Area Agency on Aging must not only discuss the establishment of information and assistance programs but they must also emphasize the linkage of isolated elderly suffering from Alzheimer's disease or related disorders to programs and services. Demonstration grants related to information and assistance are also included in Title IV and many of the components of the new Title VII involve information and assistance. A major example is the Outreach, Counseling, and Assistance Program.

OPERATION AND FUNCTIONS

A truly productive information and assistance system not only will be able to generate and respond to questions of need but will be constantly testing the degree to which the belief that adequate services exist is based on fact. Information and assistance systems thus appear to have the potential for generating beneficial changes in the service system. An effective information and assistance system cannot work outside the service system. The success of an information and assistance program is dependent, at least in part, on the extent and quality of the service system to which it refers.

Not only does information and assistance provide information acquired both formally and informally, about the service system; it must generate that information through active and relatively frequent contact with the services available. Information and assistance programs can be helpful to clients only if the service agencies have a clear understanding of what they are actually providing. Because the information given by agencies is not always an accurate rendition of what is available, some information and assistance programs use client-supplied data to regenerate their descriptions. In addition, once the information about the agencies is in storage, it can be used as important data for planning and development purposes. Follow-up on clients receiving information from the information and assistance program can indicate how effective the service response has been—information important for future service planning.

ORGANIZATION

Scope

The diversity of information and assistance programs almost matches the number of information and assistance services available throughout the country, a number difficult to identify because information sharing takes many forms. In order to identify a minimum requirement for an adequate information and assistance program, the U.S. Administration on Aging (1977) prepared policy guidelines to state agencies administering plans under the provisions of the OAA. Issued in August 1974, these guidelines also discussed long-range goals for the development of comprehensive information and assistance programs. The nine service components were designed to build uniformity and comprehensiveness into the information and assistance programs and to give some measurability of adequacy. The service components emphasized (1) having an adequate facility to serve those seeking information, (2) making continuously updated resource files available to agencies needing service information, (3) making the service easily available to older persons, (4) providing outreach to those not familiar with using such a service, (5) following up on referrals, and (6) providing transportation when necessary to help the older person reach a service identified through information and assistance. The individual who calls or walks into an information and assistance service is assured of anonymity, and usually no names are recorded on data forms. A casework approach is often utilized in which the information and assistance worker explores the individual's problem and the alternative services available. As needed, the older person is referred to a specific service.

Schmandt et al. (1979) attempted to bring some clarity to the wide range of efforts that fall under the information and assistance label. Their attempt again indicated the complexity of the seemingly simple function of information and assistance. An information and assistance program may define its clientèle on the basis of age, income, or specific problems. The program may confine itself to telephone assistance or move into extensive outreach including contact with individuals in their own homes. Limited research on the needs of the population within the community may also be undertaken. Within a defined city or metropolitan area, the agency offering the information and assistance program may adopt a posture which emphasizes a personal type of relationship with clients or a relatively impersonal and highly professional one.

One of the difficulties in identifying and maintaining a minimum standard for information and assistance programs is the pressure to have these programs reflect the style, service system, and needs of the locale in which they are located. Schmandt et al. (1979) argue for both the standardized and localized programs. This would include a centralized telephone center as well as decentralized walk-in centers in local neighborhoods. A two-part system of this type can effectively respond to the multifaceted needs of a variety of clients in the local community.

Because of their diversity, there are a wide range of institutions involved in the planning and delivery of information and assistance programs. As indicated earlier, at the federal level, information and assistance responsibilities for the elderly are shared among the Administration on Aging, the Social Security Administration, and the Community Services Administration. State and county social service departments represent a second layer of organizations responsible for information and assistance functions. At the community level, a variety of public and private organizations dispense information and assistance, generally to populations that include the elderly as well as other groups.

Types of Programs Available

An extensive study by Battle and Associates (1977) for the Administration on Aging found that 85% of information and assistance programs were part of public agencies, about half of which were operated by state or area agencies on aging. In addition, the geographic area covered by the programs ranged from small communities to entire states. Age-segregated information and assistance programs tended to have more linkages to a variety of programs and services including nutrition, recreation, health, transportation, and counseling. Information and assistance programs under the auspices of Area Agencies on Aging were also more likely to have linkages to a greater variety of programs and services than independently operated programs.

The types of information generation, storage, and retrieval systems used are essential to determining the success of information and assistance. When local structures and community needs are taken into consideration when choosing a type of system, the system has a greater chance of success. A local walk-in information and assistance program has different information needs than one that serves a large region and supplies data for planning. The service, then, that can clarify its informational goals can be more effectively evaluated.

It has been suggested that the availability of late-hour and toll-free telephone lines would increase the success of information and assistance efforts. In 1990 the Administration on Aging awarded a grant to the National Association of Area Agencies on Aging to develop a toll-free 800 number which would refer callers to services in their area. The project began operation in a limited number of Northeastern states in 1991.

The basic purpose of information and assistance programs is to provide information to individuals. The ability of these services to fulfill this function is difficult to evaluate from the perspective of users because "many users do not conceptually separate the information and referral service from the actual service provider" (Burkhardt, 1979, p. 30). Individuals tend to call an information and assistance service when faced with an immediate problem. In the vast majority of cases they are referred to an agency or specialized service for assistance. Thus clients' perceptions of the effectiveness of information and assistance may be intertwined with how well they felt the agency to which they were referred dealt with their needs.

Information and assistance programs can, however, increase their perceived effectiveness by taking the necessary measures to insure that those clients who call actually make contact with appropriate services; that is, those who call an information and assistance program would have a better chance of getting the services they need if the program plays a linkage and advocacy role. To facilitate referral, information and assistance can refer a client directly to one or more agencies; arrange for transportation or escort to insure that the client can reach the referred service; go to the client's home to provide direct assistance; call the service provider directly, giving information about the client and then tell the client that the necessary contact has been made; or persuade a provider to handle a unique or difficult problem.

According to the information and assistance program, the problems of the elderly most often requiring referral include the following individual and related problems: income, money, Social Security; transportation; health problems and care—home health care; housing—home maintenance/repair; food and nutrition; homemaker services; employment; consumer needs and problems; legal problems; companionship; and nursing home care (Battle & Associates, 1977).

One of the big problems of information and assistance programs, as with any program available to the elderly, is accessibility to anyone who needs the service. The information and assistance program has the potential of being the most widely available of any service for the elderly because by nature of its service it is relatively inexpensive and equally accessible to everyone. However, despite their relative accessibility, information and assistance programs are used by a disproportionate number of people who are already connected into the system in some way. The isolated and unattached remain unattached to this service, as they do to most other services that are potentially available to them. Unfortunately, direct outreach is expensive, and many such programs do not have adequate funds. When funds are limited, extensive use of the media appears the best way to reach isolated elderly populations. In Detroit, an ambitious information and assistance program begun in the 1960s had to be cut back when it was found that outreach to and follow-up on individual clients were beyond the limited resources the agency (United Community Services, 1965) could make available for the information and assistance program. It is thus likely that most information and assistance services will not undertake the wide range of follow-up and client advocacy functions that are possible for information and assistance programs.

Several programs have been established in recent years to decrease the number of steps required before an individual obtains appropriate assistance from a variety of organizations. These programs utilize information and assistance programs as their base but go further in their assistance. In Maryland, the Gateway I program is designed to provide a "single point of entry," usually through intake at senior centers. During fiscal 1985, the program served 14,260 older persons and provided information on Social Security, housing, income/financial assistance, health care, transportation, legal assistance, employment, nutrition/food support, home repair, and leisure activities (Bechill, 1987).

As the Maryland Office on Aging (1984) notes:

Generally, each local site offers: toll-free (or collect) telephone service, in-person, walk-in service, full service five days a week, a coordinated system to provide information and assistance in obtaining available benefits and services, follow-up action to ensure that available assistance has been rendered, arrangements for comprehensive assessments of impaired elderly persons and current resource inventory files on aging services on local, state and federal levels in each local jurisdiction. (p. 30)

The National Long Term Care demonstration begun in 1980 was designed to test the ability of a single point of entry system and case management approaches to identify and provide services to frail elderly. Based on 10 sites and over 6,300 clients, the evaluation team reported in 1986 that the "channeling" approach identified a very vulnerable older population. Among this group, over 22% were unable to perform the major activities of daily living such as eating, getting out of bed, or dressing (Mathematica Policy Research, 1986). An effective single point of entry system could also be combined with a case management unit within the information and assistance agency. As Applebaum and Austin (1990) suggest, the case management unit could receive referrals directly from information and assistance workers who would assess the clients to ascertain whether they would benefit from case management.

Funding

Funding for information and assistance programs comes from a variety of federal, state, local, and private sources, although state and area agencies contribute a larger percentage of funds to more information and assistance than other types of contributors. Major federal resources available include the Administration on Aging, or the Community Services block grant.

Additional sources of funds include state and county taxes; civic and religious groups; private, nonprofit sources such as United Way and Community Chest Agencies; private groups such as local foundations, corporations, and unions; and income from the project itself through the sale of items such as brochures, directories, and planning information.

IMPORTANCE

Information and assistance programs can be the link between the individual needing some type of service that can best meet that person's needs. According to the National Council on the Aging (1982), the effective information and assistance system must be:

- confidential
- accessible to all older persons
- sensitive to feelings and problems of older persons
- friendly to older clients
- reliable and accurate in the information it provides
- accountable and responsive to older persons and families
- neutral and nonpartisan in its referrals
- broad in the range of information it provides.

Many older people are unaware of the kinds of services available and how they can be found and, in many cases, are approaching the thought of professional assistance for the first time in their adult life. A well-implemented information and assistance program can make older people aware of services, help them formulate their problem in the context of available services, and assist them in actually making the contact with the appropriate service. Organizing the maze of possible service systems, regulations, and eligibility requirements into a package of information, the information and assistance program is essential for responsive service delivery to the elderly, regardless of the size of the community. Just as information and assistance cannot be effective without a good service delivery system, service delivery systems cannot be effective without an efficient information and assistance program, one that reaches to everyone in need of problem solving.

REFERENCES

Applebaum, R., & Austin, C. (1990). *Long-term case management: Design and evaluation*. New York: Springer Publishing Company.

Battle, M., & Associates. (1977). *Evaluation and referral services for the elderly*. Washington, DC: U.S. Government Printing Office.

Bechill, W. (1987, March 9). *The reauthorization of the Older Americans Act*. Paper presented before the Subcommittee on Human Resources, Committee on Education and Labor, U.S. House of Representatives, Washington, DC.

Burkhardt, J. (1979). Evaluating information and referral services. *Gerontologist, 19*, 28–33.

Maryland Office on Aging. (1984). *1984 annual report*. Baltimore: Author.

Mathematica Policy Research. (1986). *National Long-Term Care Channeling Demonstration: Final report*. Plainsboro, NJ: Author.

National Council on the Aging. (1982). *Comprehensive service delivery through senior centers and other community focal points: A resource manual*. Washington, DC: Author.

Schmandt, J., Bach, V., & Radin, B. (1979). Information and referral services for the elderly welfare recipients. *Gerontologist, 19*, 21–27.

United Community Services of Metropolitan Detroit. (1965). *Information and referral services*. Detroit.

U.S. Administration on Aging. (1977). *Program development handbook for state and area agencies on information and referral services for the elderly*. Washington, DC: U.S. Government Printing Office.

6

Health and Mental Health

As noted in Chapter 1, the elderly suffer from a variety of chronic illnesses. Medical problems of the older adult are not so much the common cold as they are arthritis, the effects of strokes, and vision and hearing problems. Medical care for a population with these types of problems must stress not only efforts to cure but treatment that allows the individual to adjust to living with a condition that may vary in intensity but will always be present.

Attempts to provide medical care for the elderly have met a variety of roadblocks: (1) the lack of interest by physicians in treating individuals whose conditions are not "curable," (2) the high costs of medical care, and (3) the inaccessibility of medical treatment. These problems are also endemic in mental health treatment of the elderly.

Medicare and Medicaid have helped to reduce the cost of medical care for many older adults, although the out-of-pocket share of medical expenses incurred by the elderly has been increasing consistently. Specialized transportation programs for older adults have also targeted medical appointments as a top priority. The major problem that remains to be addressed is the recruitment and training of professionals and paraprofessionals dedicated to providing medical care for seniors. Until the mid-1970s, there was little emphasis on geriatrics in American schools of medicine. The curriculum in most medical schools has only recently begun to include any appreciable content on the aging process.

Even if physicians show increased interest in treating the elderly, hospitals are oriented toward acute illnesses, and individuals who remain hospitalized for an extended length of time run up enormous costs. The alternative to acute care hospitals—a long stay in a nursing home—has not been attractive to the elderly or their families.

Only the introduction of in-home services and adult daycare centers (discussed in Part IV) has made care possible outside of long-term facilities such as hospitals and nursing homes. The majority of health care programs serving the elderly are part of the extensive range of home care services that are becoming available. In this chapter we will examine health care programs available through clinics, hospitals, and non-home-care agencies.

Despite the availability of Medicare, out-of-pocket costs for health care paid by Medicare beneficiaries have continued to rise. In 1975, Medicare beneficiaries share of acute health costs equaled 4.2% of their per capita income. By 1990, this figure had risen to 5.7% (U.S. House of Representatives, 1990).

With the elderly spending vast amounts of money on health care, the question has arisen as to whether separate services oriented to older adults should be developed. Separate services may require duplication of facilities and equipment already available. These facilities may be avoided by older individuals who feel stigmatized by attending special clinics. Alternatively, while encouraging the elderly to utilize existing services may avoid major capital outlays, older patients at large clinics often receive less attention from health professionals attracted to younger, more "curable" clients. With younger clients being assertive about the health care to which they feel entitled, the net result is that the elderly are relegated to long waits and poor care.

HEALTH CARE PROGRAMS

Geriatric Clinics

A geriatric health clinic in a medical center is a compromise service delivery system that avoids setting up new facilities but guarantees the elderly that their medical needs will receive attention. At Syracuse University, a geriatric clinic was integrated with other community health facilities. The clinic planners hoped that this integration would help to avoid ostracization of the elderly. Patients were assisted in establishing a relationship with a physician, but the clinic also maintained a referral service for specialized medical problems not treatable at the clinic (Syracuse University School of Social Work, 1971).

A similar model was utilized at the geriatric clinic opened in 1970 at Worcester State Hospital in Massachusetts. Patients were referred to the clinic by neighborhood workers. At the clinic, medical histories, physicals, and laboratory tests were undertaken. Based on the results of these tests, a decision was made by clinic medical personnel either to treat or to refer the client to other medical services. Clients with no regular physician were referred to an outpatient clinic or a local hospital, or they remained as patients of the geriatric clinic (Worcester State Hospital, 1972).

These screening programs are particularly common at senior centers and many are held in May during Older Americans Month. In a medically underserved rural area of southwestern Pennsylvania, the Area Agency on Aging uses a 35-foot van for mobile health screening (Goughler, Lange, & Broggi, 1986).

The Worcester clinic provided treatment, but other programs have been primarily oriented to either screening, publicizing medical needs of the elderly, or encouraging the elderly to obtain adequate medical care. In Hawaii, difficulties in reaching facilities and psychological fears resulting from limited fluency in English or low education resulted in underutilization of health services by the elderly. To meet this problem, a senior center health screening program was instituted. Conducted on a bimonthly basis in Honolulu, the program was able to screen 100 individuals in 3–4 hours. Counseling was provided to the individual about existing medical conditions and abnormal results. Abnormal results were also reported to the individual's primary care physician. In some cases where serious conditions were noted, the screening program instituted follow-up to insure that the individual obtained the necessary medical treatment (Hawaii Senior Services, 1975).

Health Promotion

The Worcester and Hawaii programs contain elements of both primary and secondary prevention. Local primary prevention programs have been built around educational programs informing the elderly about nutrition, care of chronic illnesses, correct drug usage, and a variety of other medical issues. These educational programs have been run at senior centers, nutrition sites, and adult daycare centers. Short television and radio announcements have also been utilized in efforts to alert the elderly to potential health problems and appropriate treatment. The expanded "Disease Prevention and Health Promotion" programs of Title III [Sec. 319] should make health promotion efforts available in a larger variety of settings.

In many localities health fairs have been inaugurated. These one-day fairs provide information on a variety of health conditions and programs and also conduct basic screening of blood pressure, vision, and hearing.

Exercise Programs

In recent years it has become evident that regular exercise is an important element of illness prevention for individuals of all ages. Increasing numbers of senior centers as well as daycare programs are offering exercise classes and activities for their clients. The President's Council on Physical Fitness and Sports has received funding from the AoA to develop and promote an "Active People Over 60" program. This program utilizes workshops and demonstrations to promote the goal of exercise for older adults (National Institute on Senior Centers, 1978). In West Virginia the Preventicare program offers three-day-a-week exercise sessions at senior centers, nutrition sites, churches, mental health centers, hospitals, and nursing homes in 51 of the 55 West Virginia counties (National Institute on Senior Centers, 1978).

The Adults Health & Development clinic at the University of Maryland offers older adults regular Saturday morning exercises and physical activities in which they are assisted by individual students. The relationships developed through this one-to-one contact often extend into close friendships between students and older persons. Similarly, the Senior Actualizations and Growth Exploration (SAGE) program begun in California works with small groups of older persons, who join together for an extended involvement. A variety of techniques are used including exercise, meditation, yoga, massage, and gestalt therapy. SAGE's efforts show that many of the newer growth and therapy techniques can be effective with any age group given the individual's willingness to undertake the intensive commitment required.

Dental Care

Dental problems increase with age, and a lack of visits to the dentist only exacerbates dental problems. In 1979, 33% of older Americans had not visited a dentist in the last year and 44% had not been to a dentist in the past five years. In 1985–86 37% of Americans aged 65–74 were without any natural teeth. While this figure may seem high, it is a significant improvement from the 55% found in 1957. Among groups such as native Americans, however, over half of the group age 65–74 were edentulous (Phipps, 1989). Dental care is not reimbursed through Medicare, and only eight states cover dental care through Medicaid. Other efforts are being fostered to make regular dental care affordable for older adults. In some states, the dental societies are beginning to work with senior centers and Area Agencies on Aging to offer dental care to elderly clients at reduced rates. This reduced-rate dental care may be provided at the dentists' offices, but some senior centers are incorporating dental suites into their facilities. These dental facilities also serve as training sites for dental students.

Drugs

As major consumers of both prescription and over-the-counter drugs, the elderly are faced with the problems of absorbing the enormous costs of these medications, even when assisted by Medicare and Medicaid. The shift in many states to utilization of generic rather than brand name drugs is helping to lower costs. Since 1958, the American Association of Retired Persons (AARP) has operated direct-mail pharmacies for its elderly members. In 1978, AARP pharmacies were located in eight cities and offered a full line of over-the-counter and prescription drugs.

Beyond providing drugs at lower costs, a number of programs are now directed to providing more consumer education about the potentials as well as the dangers of drugs. The Elder-Ed program at the University of Maryland pairs retired pharmacists and students in drug education efforts at senior centers and apartment complexes for the elderly. A corollary effort, Elder Health, uses students and retired pharmacists to train other caregivers who can provide drug education to older consumers. Through its pharmacies, AARP is providing more detailed leaflets with the drugs it sells (Lipton & Lee, 1983). In addition, increasing numbers of pharmacists are maintaining personal profiles that keep an inventory of the drugs the older consumer may be utilizing. This effort enables pharmacists to alert consumers when drugs, often prescribed by different doctors, may cause dangerous drug interactions.

All of these diverse efforts will need to be greatly expanded in the future if the requisite health care for the elderly is to be provided. As Shanas (1978) has noted, the proportion of elderly living in long-term facilities has not increased greatly since 1966. As the proportion of community-based elderly increases, a larger complement of health care programs will be needed to prevent and treat acute and chronic illnesses prevalent among older adults.

MENTAL HEALTH PROGRAMS

In the United States, mental hospitals have often functioned as quasi-homes for the aged. Although the number of patients in state mental hospitals has lessened dramatically in the past 30 years, many of the elderly released from the hospitals had been patients for 20 years or more. Community-based treatment programs, psychotropic drugs (Bloom, 1975), the tightening of legal grounds for commitment, and the growth of nursing homes has resulted in a reduction in the number of patients in state hospitals from a high of over 500,000 in 1955 to 125,000 in 1985.

Community Mental Health

The community mental health programs took root in 1963 with the passage of the Community Mental Health Centers Act. The intention of the act's supporters was to enlarge mental health expenditures at all levels and develop a network of community-based treatment facilities. These treatment facilities would be located in geographic areas that had a maximum population of 175,000. Each state, however, had to determine appropriate catchment-area boundaries. In each catchment area an organization was to be designated as responsible for providing community mental health services.

As originally specified in 1963, the services included five major components. In 1975, this list was enlarged to a total of 12 different services:

1. Inpatient care
2. Outpatient care
3. Partial hospitalization (daycare)
4. Emergency services
5. Consultation and education
6. Specialized services for children
7. Specialized services for the elderly
8. Screening of individuals considered for referral to a state mental hospital
9. Follow-up services for discharged inpatients
10. Transitional halfway houses for former mental patients
11. Programs for prevention and treatment of alcoholism if not already in existence in the catchment area
12. Programs for the prevention and treatment of drug addiction if not already available in the catchment area.

Under the block grant program initiated in 1981, the number of required services was placed at five: outpatient services, 24-hour-a-day emergency services, day treatment, screening of patients for state mental health facilities, and consultation and education.

The actual proportion of effort and funds allocated by a mental health center to any one of these components would be determined by the needs of the community. While 675 centers were in operation by 1979, the goals of having a center in all 1,500 catchment areas in the country remains a long way from being realized.

Primary prevention as embodied in the consultation and education programs was one of the major assumptions of this "bold new approach" (Kennedy, 1963) to mental health services. Treatments for individual mental health problems were supposed to be supplemented by primary prevention programs that located the sources of stress in the environment and worked with community groups to alleviate these negative influences. Primary prevention efforts focused on at-risk populations would include the elderly in many communities.

The 1987 OAA amendments explicitly add the term "mental health" at many points where formerly only the term "health" had been used. Any mental health services provided with AAA funds must be coordinated with community mental health center programs and those of other public and nonprofit agencies.

Mental Health Prevention Programs

Unfortunately, adequate appropriations to replace federal funding have not been forthcoming, and cutbacks in programing have been made at many centers. These cutbacks have often been at the expense of primary prevention programs. Primary prevention programs are often seen by traditional trained mental health professionals as irrelevant to therapeutic intervention with individuals.

One innovative approach that is becoming increasingly common is the development of peer counseling among older people. In Santa Monica, California, a peer counseling program was begun in 1977. Since that date, 121 counselors have been trained. Each counselor must volunteer for eight hours per week for one year after training (Brattler, 1986). Many older people are ambivalent about mental health services, and Medicare funding for formal mental health services is inadequate. Peer counseling may be a means of overcoming these two problems and meeting the mental health needs of older people.

Tertiary prevention programs aimed at reintegrating discharged patients into family and community life have also encountered difficulty in becoming well established and accepted. Part of this difficulty can be traced to the methods used by advocates of these programs in obtaining support for deinstitutionalization. During the 1960s, mental hospitals were derided not only for their effects on individuals and the lack of adequate treatment but for their supposedly high costs.

Deinstitutionalization

Proponents of community-based programs argued that individuals could be treated outside the state mental hospital without creating an "institutional personality" and at a lower cost. Actual experiences have not always shown these cost claims to be true. While state mental hospital costs are evident upon careful auditing, accounting for the costs of a community-based program are more difficult.

Mrs. S. provides a good example. A women in her early 70s, she had been in the state hospital for 20 years. Discharged under the new community approach of the 1960s, Mrs. S. has been living in an old hotel in a beachfront community in New York. Because of her lack of any other means of support, she receives financial aid from the state as well as casework services from the Department of Social Services. The mental health services she obtains are provided through the Department of Mental Hygiene. If any vocational training is included in the supports she receives, these will be provided by the Department of Vocational Rehabilitation.

Mrs. S. is thus receiving a variety of services, most of which are not provided under mental health auspices. Unless this is taken into account when cost-effectiveness studies of institutionally based versus community-based programs are compared, the figures will show that the costs of the community services are considerably cheaper. This may not be true given the number of paid professionals involved in assisting Mrs. S. to remain in the community. As the reality of the costs involved in providing quality aftercare services in mental health has become evident, claims about cost-effectiveness have become muted. The opening of new programs to serve released patients has also been retarded.

Discharged mental patients living in old hotels and domiciliary facilities operated by state mental health departments continue to make headlines as many communities protest these problems being "dumped" in their neighborhoods. As some communities pass zoning regulations making it difficult to open new facilities, the discharged mental patients become concentrated in areas such as Long Beach, New York; South Miami; or parts of Chicago. If the ex-patients themselves do not create problems, their assumed vulnerability attracts individuals who prey on them.

The promise of deinstitutionalization has not been fulfilled. As Curtis (1981) has commented, it was not unreasonable to think that community programs could replace state hospitals when the enrollment of these hospitals was shrinking. The resistance of communities to deinstitutionalized patients, the instability of many small community programs, and the preference of the private sector for working with less impaired individuals were not anticipated.

Aided by the impetus of the Community Support Program of the National Institute of Mental Health, community-based foster care and group homes have become available in many states. Many of the basic costs of housing and feeding individuals in these programs are met through the availability of federal SSI funds for disabled individuals. With this base of federal funds, states have been willing to provide the additional case management services needed to enable a chronically mentally ill older person to live in a community setting.

ELDERLY IN THE MENTAL HEALTH SYSTEM

There are now three major groups of elderly involved in the mental health system: (1) elderly who have been long-term residents of state hospitals and are attempting to live outside the controlled hospital environment, (2) elderly who have been utilizing mental health services for a period of time, and (3) elderly who begin to exhibit major mental health problems only as they become older. These problems may include depression, insomnia, hypochondria, paranoia, and organic brain disorders. We will examine the present condition of mental health services for former residents of state hospitals and for older persons exhibiting mental health problems often associated with aging.

Discharged Patients

Individuals who have been in a mental hospital for a long period of time may have major difficulties readjusting to any form of independent life in the community. As Kirk and Therrien (1975) have argued, family members are often opposed to long-term mental patients living in their home. An added complication is that mental patients often have few employable skills and minimal financial resources. Waston (1976) has shown, however, that the morale among elderly psychiatric patients being treated on an outpatient basis was significantly higher than among elderly inpatients. For elderly outpatients to function adequately in the community, extensive supportive services are needed, including a means for obtaining regular medications.

Mental Health and Nursing Homes

The hue and cry about the lack of aftercare programs would be even greater if the 1960s had not seen a major growth in the number of nursing homes. Nursing homes have now taken a major share of the burden of caring for the institutionalized elderly. The drops in individuals in state hospitals since 1960 was matched by an equivalent increase in nursing home patients.

The National Center for Health Statistics' 1973 survey of nursing home patients found that the largest percentage were labeled "senile," a label that now appears to be as vague as it is overused (Glasscote et al., 1976). Whatever the mental condition of nursing home patients, few are actively receiving psychiatric care. Glasscote et al. summarized a 1976 investigation of the mental health needs and treatment of nursing home patients:

> Our sample of nursing facilities estimated that about three quarters of their patients are either formally diagnosed with a psychiatric disorder or are "de facto psychiatrically impaired"; if this figure can be projected to the 1,100,000 population of all nursing homes, then there are more than three-quarters of a million nursing home patients with psychiatric disability, most of whom have had no contact at all with psychiatrists. (p. 71)

Elderly in Mental Health Centers

Fortunately, only 5% of today's elderly are in long-term institutional settings. For the majority of the over-60 population, mental health services must be obtained from community mental health centers. As already shown, services to the elderly were a requirement for federally funded mental health centers. Despite this mandate of 1975, mental health centers have still not shown a major interest in providing extensive mental health services for older adults. For the majority of mental health professionals, the most desirable clients remain youthful, attractive, verbal, intelligent, and successful individuals (Schofield, 1964). In contrast, the elderly are often perceived as depressed individuals whose problems are merely the product of "getting old." Whereas the younger persons have an extensive future ahead of them, mental health professionals may view older persons as having their "best years" behind them and thus as less deserving of attention.

The present generation of elderly may also fail to utilize mental health services because of their limited education and fluency in English. Other more complex reasons are that they may (1) not recognize some behaviors as mental health problems, (2) believe that many mental health problems are the responsibility of the family unless extremely serious (Fandetti & Gelfand, 1978), (3) stigmatize mental illness and be fearful of being labeled "crazy" if it becomes known that they are utilizing mental health services, (4) be unaware of the services available at mental health centers, or (5) have difficulty reaching mental health centers and clinics because of lack of transportation.

At present the mental health needs of the elderly are much greater than the services provided:

> The prevalence of mental illness and emotional distress is higher among those over age 65 than in the general population. Up to 25% of older persons have been estimated to have significant mental health problems. Yet only 4% of patients seen in public outpatient mental health clinics and 2% of those seen in private psychiatric care are elderly. (President's Commission on Mental Health, 1978, p. 7)

Widowed Persons Programs

The widowed persons programs are important efforts run independently of mental health centers. These programs provide counseling on an individualized basis to men and women who are recently widowed. These widows and widowers are paired with volunteers who provide support on emotional issues relating to the loss of a spouse and practical information about preparing to lead a life as a single person. This practical information may cover finances or even learning to drive for the first time. The AARP runs the largest widowed persons program in the United States. In 1987, the program was available at 190 locations.

SPECIALIZED AGING SERVICES

Flemming, Buchanan, Santos, and Rickard (1984) have examined the effects of the switch in mental health funding from a "categorical" system to the block grant system that removed specific requirements for mental health services for the elderly. Under the block grant system, decisions about specific priority groups for mental health services are now made at the state level. The data collected indicated a decline since 1981 in the specialized services available to older persons in 55% of the centers participating in the Flemming et al. (1984) study. It thus remains questionable whether the mental health services available to older persons from mental health providers have improved.

An encouraging sign is the integration of mental health services in services provided by Area Agencies on Aging. In Washington, a service agreement between the Spokane Community Mental Health Center and the Eastern Washington Area Agency on Aging has been based on the assumption that "mental health needs of the elderly, especially frail, vulnerable, or moderately to severely dysfunctional cannot be separated from physical, social and economic needs" (Raschko, 1985, p. 461). Among the older individuals participating in the program, 95% have received no prior mental health care.

The Michigan Office of Services to the Aging and the state Department of Mental Health have implemented a program (Building Ties) through which participating counties designate a liaison person to help coordinate mental health services for older persons. In Indiana, a mental health center staff person is placed for a half day per week at a senior center, nutrition center, or public housing project. This staff person conducts educational programs, in-service training on mental health, group discussions, case and program consultation, as well as reduced-fee individual counseling (*Older American Reports*, 1990). The Psychogeriatric Assessment, Treatment, and Teaching program in Baltimore utilizes two nurses and two psychiatrists to conduct mental health outreach efforts in public housing with a large population of older residents. The residents are referred to the PATCH team by building management (Roca, Storer, Robbins, Tlasek, & Rabins, 1990). A similar program in Ventura County, California, relies on an interdisciplinary mobile geriatric team. These mobile teams have had success in reaching minority elderly who feel unable to seek services at a mental health center or who have transportation problems (Hernandez & Sweon, 1989).

As the President's Commission on Mental Health (1978) emphasized, the lack of outreach to older persons is a major factor in their representation in mental health services. Medicare coverage for mental health services remains limited. Medicare provisions emphasize hospital treatment and nursing home care, with only limited coverage for outpatient mental health services. Changes in these provisions to emphasize community-based treatment might provide the transfusion necessary for financially strapped community mental health centers and clinics to turn their attention to the mental health needs of the elderly.

REFERENCES

Brattler, B. (1986). Peer counseling for older adults. *Generations, 10*(3), 49–50.

Bloom, B. (1975). *Community mental health*. Monterey, CA: Brooks/Cole.

Curtis, W. R. (1981). Commentary. *New England Journal of Human Services, 1*(4), 4–6.

Fandetti, D., & Gelfand, D. (1978). Attitudes towards symptoms and services in the ethnic family and neighborhood. *American Journal of Orthopsychiatry, 48*, 477–486.

Flemming, A., Buchanan, J., Santos, J., & Rickard, L. (1984). *Mental health services for the elderly*. Washington, DC: Action Committee to Implement the Mental Health Recommendations of the 1981 White House Conference on Aging.

Glasscote, R., Biegel, A., Butterfield, A., Jr., Clark, E., Cox, B., Elper J. R., Gudeman, J. E., Gurel, L., Lewis, R. V., Miler, D. G., Raybin, J. B., Reifler, C., & Vito, E., Jr. (1976). *Old folks at homes*. Washington, DC: American Psychiatric Association and the Mental Health Association.

Glasscote, R., Gude, J., & Miles, D. *Creative mental health services for the elderly*. (1977). Washington, DC: American Psychiatric Association and the Mental Health Association.

Goughler, D., Lange, B., & Broggi, A. (1986). Health screening van solves access problems for rural Pennsylvania elderly. *Aging, 353*, 33.

Hawaii Senior Services. (1975). *Health screening for the elderly*. Honolulu: Author.

Hernandez, A., & Sweon, C. (1989). Mobile mental health team reaches minorities. *Aging*, No. 359, 12–13.

Kennedy, J. F. (1963). *A message from the President of the United States relative to mental illness and mental retardation*. Washington, DC.

Kirk, S., & Therrien, M. (1975). Community mental health myths and the fate of former hospitalized patients. *Psychiatry, 38*, 209–217.

Lipton, H., & Lee, P. (1983). Innovative drug information sources for professionals and elders. *Generations, 8*(2), 54–56.

National Institute on Senior Centers. *Senior Center Report, 1978, 1*(4), 3.

Older American Reports. (1990). Michigan program links aging services with community mental health providers. December 7, 474.

Phipps, K. (1989). *Oral health status of native-American elders*. Washington, DC: Gerontological Society of America Fellowship Program in Applied Gerontology.

President's Commission on Mental Health. (1978). *Report to the President* (Vol. 1). Washington, DC: U.S. Government Printing Office.

Raschko, R. (1985). Systems integration at the program level: Aging and mental health. *Generations, 25*, 460–463.

Roca, R., Storer, D., Robbins, B., Tlasek, M., & Rabins, P. (1990). Psychogeriatric assessment and treatment in urban public housing. *Hospital and Community Psychiatry, 41*, 916–920.

Schofield, W. (1964). *Psychotherapy: The purchase of friendship*. Englewood Cliffs, NJ: Prentice-Hall.

Shanas, E. (1978). New directions in health care for the elderly. In I. Brookbank (Ed.), *Improving the quality of health care for the elderly*. Gainesville, FL: University Presses of Florida.

Syracuse University School of Social Work. (1971). *Concerns in planning health services for the elderly*. Syracuse, NY: Author.

U.S. House of Representatives, Committee on Ways and Means. (1990). *Background material and data on programs within the jurisdiction of the Committee on Ways and Means*. Washington, DC: U.S. Government Printing Office.

Watson, C. (1976). Inpatient care or outplacement: Which is better for the psychiatrically medically infirm patient? *Journal of Gerontology, 31*, 611–616.

Worcester State Hospital. (1972). *Two year activities of a geriatric clinic in the Worcester area*. Worcester, MA: Author.

7

Transportation

Transportation programs are a necessary support for community-based aging services, including daycare centers, senior centers, mental health centers, and nutritional and educational programs. Transportation is also a crucial factor in the elderly being able to obtain medical care and maintain relationships with family and friends or attend social and cultural events.

Many communities lack any transportation system designed to serve the general public. This lack of public transportation programs will be a more significant problem in the future as the elderly population living in suburban communities increases. Dependence on the automobile is difficult for many older persons, who feel a lessening sense of security behind the driver's wheel as their reflexes slow. Visual problems also preclude many elderly from driving at night, limiting the social events they can attend. For the elderly on fixed incomes, the cost of purchasing and maintaining an automobile may also prove to be too burdensome. At present, reports indicate that the majority of elderly living in urban areas depend on walking to reach their destinations. The mobility problems of the isolated rural elderly are intensified because of inadequate and often poorly maintained road systems.

A variety of approaches to the transportation needs of urban, suburban, and rural elderly are thus required. To place the present thrust of transportation programs in an appropriate framework, we need to examine the goals of these services and the factors that impinge on realization of these goals.

OPTIONS

Transportation systems can vary in their extensiveness, their frequency of operation, and their ability to meet the individualized interests of potential consumers. In the language of transportation planning, these systems can be "demand responsive," "need responsive," or "desire responsive," While demand-responsive systems respond to calls for service on the part of individuals, need-responsive systems attempt to service transportation requirements felt to be important to the individual's maintenance of a satisfying life. The demands placed on transportation services by elderly individuals may be less than what they "need" for an independent, healthy life-style. Need-responsive systems are close to desire-responsive systems, and planners usually confine their analyses to these two groups.

The optimal transportation system for the elderly and the handicapped would be need-responsive, increasing their options for interactions with a range of individuals and programs. In densely populated areas an inexpensive, properly designed mass transit system may enable the older person to reach a variety of important destinations. In suburban and rural areas with low density and dispersed services, a system responsive to the older person's needs is more difficult to implement.

MODELS

The major variables in transportation systems are routing, schedules, and loading points. Four major combinations of routing and scheduling are possible: (1) fixed-route services with fixed scheduling, a model corresponding to mass transit; (2) fixed routing with varied scheduling; (3) variable routing with fixed scheduling; and (4) variable routing with variable scheduling. As we examine in-place and newly developing transportation systems, we will note examples of all four of these alternatives.

Aggregate trips taken by individuals to different sites and the costs or subsidization that must be borne for each trip taken are major factors in choosing transportation models appropriate to a community. As transit authorities around the country have discovered, public transit systems cannot be expected to run at a profit if fares are to be kept at a reasonable level. The growing understanding that public transit of any form needs to be subsidized has retarded its development in many areas. Unfortunately, many transit authorities attempting to stop the rise of deficits have become involved in a cycle of raising fares, resulting in a lower number of riders and subsequent fare increases. With each fare increase, the differential between the costs of mass transit and driving decreases, and increasing numbers of individuals therefore turn to their automobiles for commuting and pleasure trips. Transportation systems of all kinds must face the issue of the maximum subsidies that the community will tolerate and optimal methods for financing these subsidies.

FORMS OF TRANSPORTATION FOR THE ELDERLY

Mass Transit

During the 1960s and 1970s, an effort was made to encourage the elderly's use of existing mass transit facilities. Under the 1974 National Mass Transit Assistance Act, the Urban Mass Transit Administration was authorized to allot funds for capital and operating costs of mass transit systems. Communities attempting to qualify for these funds were required to institute programs for the elderly that reduced fares in non-peak hours to no more than one-half of peak-hour fares. A number of major cities had already instituted this approach before the federal legislation was enacted. By 1974, 145 cities had already instituted half-fare programs (U.S. Administration on Aging, 1975).

Cantor's (1970) interviews with a sample of New York City elderly indicated that they felt they used the subway and bus system more extensively because of the low-fare privileges. This increase in ridership creates some methodological problems in evaluating the costs of this type of program. Half-fare rides are obviously not matching the operating costs for each ride. If, however, the ridership increases at nonpeak hours, even at half-fare, is this increase reducing the subsidization? Alternatively, have some of the individuals now riding at off-peak hours switched their riding patterns from peak hours, reducing the number of full fares collected by the system and thus increasing the number of heavily subsidized rides?

Answers to these questions have been difficult to obtain, but the positive effects of the program for elderly riders have been demonstrated. This includes increased use of the mass transit systems by the elderly to attend social activities and programs and to obtain medical care. Unfortunately, available studies do not reveal the reasons many elderly still refrain from using the transit system. The stress of the elderly on convenience and accessibility rather than costs of transportation may account for reduced ridership among older people who have to walk long distances to reach transit stops or take buses even to reach the subway. Having accomplished this task, they then must surmount obstacles posed by steps on buses or stairways in subway stations.

The Urban Mass Transportation Act (UMTA) specifies that elderly and handicapped persons have the same rights to utilize mass transportation facilities and services as other individuals. In 1975, regulations were issued requiring recipients of UMTA funds to build their facilities in a manner that would not create physical barriers for the elderly and handicapped. Installation of elevators at all new subway stations has been one major outgrowth of this requirement.

The physical barriers on buses are more difficult to overcome. In East Orange, New Jersey (Rinaldi, 1973), an escort service was provided during the early 1970s to help elderly individuals negotiate the steps of buses and other public transit barriers. In 1973, a negative report on this effort was issued. Despite the assistance made available by the escorts, the costs of this service were prohibitive. Costs were doubled since fares were required for both the elderly person and the escort. The service was also not found to promote new trips by elderly individuals.

Regulations issued by the Department of Transportation required all new buses purchased with UMTA funds after September 1979 to have boarding ramps or hydraulic lifts, floor heights no more than 22 inches off the ground, and an ability to "kneel" to 18 inches. The regulations were rescinded in 1981, and local communities were allowed to demonstrate that they had made reasonable efforts to meet the needs of the elderly and the handicapped. Under the Americans with Disabilities Act passed in 1990, all new buses ordered after August 26, 1990, must be accessible to people with disabilities.

New Transportation Systems

Building public transportation systems is an extremely costly process, and these systems do not always provide the most direct route to a destination. In some cases a bus trip to a medical center may require 50 minutes, a transfer of buses, and cost $1.00. A taxicab ride to the same destination might occupy 10 minutes, cost $1.50, and be door to door.

The problems involved in creating new transportation systems for the elderly are more complex than reductions in fares on existing mass transit facilities. Critical examination of the potential of new systems is necessary because of the increasingly decentralized living patterns of Americans. In 1974, it was estimated that 5.5 million of the 54 million rural American residents had mobility problems (McKelvey & Ducker, 1974). The Federal Aid to Highways Act of 1973 emphasized the need to take the mobility needs of rural elderly and handicapped into account in highway planning and improvements (U.S. Department of Transportation, 1976).

Financial assistance for transportation programs has been available under Section 16(b)(2) of UMTA grants to assist nonprofit organizations in providing services to the elderly and handicapped when mass transit systems are unavailable, insufficient, or not appropriate (U.S. House of Representatives, 1976). In 1990, 1400 vehicles were purchased with these UMTA funds. Under the UMTA program, 20% of these vehicle costs must be contributed by the local agency or transit authority. Supplementing the UMTA funds in many communities are funds from Title III of the OAA (which as noted in Chapter 2 now places a strong emphasis on issues of access), revenue sharing funds, and purchase of care arrangements among individual social service agencies.

Substantial amounts of Title III funds have been channeled into transportation programs, although testimony in 1977 made it clear that the AoA discourages the use of these moneys for the purchase of vehicles. AoA officials fear that many agencies will not be able to afford the expenses of maintaining and operating these vehicles after using Title III funds to purchase them. The difficulties of meeting operating expenses is a common theme among organizations running extensive transportation efforts and facing mounting repair costs for heavily used vehicles. The costs of repairs plus high gasoline prices continue to make transportation an expensive service. Transportation funding may be aided by the 1987 OAA amendments, which authorized funding to states for older people with "special needs" such as transportation.

Obtaining adequate insurance at reasonable rates was previously a major headache for agencies attempting to implement transportation services for the elderly. In 1980, this major block to the expansion of transportation programs began to be resolved by new insurance ratings agreed upon by the federal government and the insurance industry. Under this new grouping, insurance ratings for vehicles owned by a program, or owned by employees or volunteers who transport the elderly, were placed midway between school buses and city buses. The new rates also provided excess liability insurance for the agency and the owner of the vehicle when transportation was provided for clients of a program. The excess liability was set at a low premium (*Older American Reports*, 1980). These new rates were the result of work by the federal government and community groups to convince the insurance industry that the elderly were not more prone to injury when transported than other groups. In Janesville, Wisconsin, a transportation program staffed primarily by volunteers over the age of 55 uses a combination of the driver's own insurance (usually $300,000) and a blanket policy purchased by the program (Green Associates, 1984).

A large number of diverse transportation systems began during the 1970s. The Older American Transportation Service (OATS) in Missouri began in 1971 with $30,000 from Title III. In 1978, 125 vans and buses (25 wheelchair-equipped) were being utilized in the program, which serves 89 counties. The OATS budget for 1979 was $125,000. Deficits in grant funding are made up by a variety of dinners and sales. OATS is a variable-route, variable-schedule program but requires that users send in a postcard or call for a reservation one week in advance. Medical trips are given priority (Pierce, 1979). In Nebraska, a similar Senior Handi-Bus program dispatches six passenger vans on 24-hour advance reservation, and similar efforts are underway in St. Petersburg, Florida, and Rhode Island.

In Cape May County, New Jersey, fixed-route, fixed-schedule dial-a-ride vans with seats reserved a week ahead make weekly trips to Atlantic City and Philadelphia. Trips to Philadelphia, the closest city, are usually in connection with medical treatment. Drivers working in this program must complete a National Safety Council defensive driving course and other safety requirements. All of the vans carry emergency first-aid equipment. The vans are also used during the week to transport seniors to Title III nutrition sites (Jones, Rott, & Murphy, 1976).

School Buses

Beside vans and minibuses, school buses would appear to be the vehicle most available for elderly transportation services, since these buses are usually utilized only to transport school children at early morning and late-afternoon hours. Unfortunately, only 16 states have legislation permitting school buses to be used for nonschool purposes. During summer months, when the weather allows many older individuals to attend activities, school buses are often being rotated in and out of repair shops for yearly maintenance. If state legislation permits the utilization of school buses for any purpose, the ultimate decision on their disposition usually rests with local communities. In some localities, parents have opposed additional use of school buses, fearing that this extensive use will create additional wear and tear and make the buses unsafe for their children (U.S. Department of Transportation, 1977). School buses also present the physical obstacles of high steps, making them inaccessible for wheelchair-bound individuals.

In Klamath, Oregon, school buses are being used to transport the elderly on a fixed-route, fixed-schedule basis. The Cape May County program already mentioned uses school buses to provide extensive services for its 15,000 elderly residents. The county estimates that each ride costs $1.55, of which the county contributes $.43. Running on a fixed route with fixed schedules, four buses travel through each town and village in the country at least once a week and stop at major shopping centers. At the shopping centers the buses wait 1 1/2 hours before returning to their original departure points. On Saturdays the buses are used for recreational trips for the elderly (U.S. Department of Transportation, 1975).

RIDERSHIP PROBLEMS

Encouraging frequent utilization of these transportation services is important in reducing the average cost per ride. A shuttle system developed in Washington, D.C., in 1978 to transport the elderly to shopping on Thursdays found it difficult to attract new riders to the 13-passenger wheelchair-accessible vans. As the director of the program commented: "So far, I think we haven't been reaching the people. Many of them remain isolated in their apartments, so how can we reach them?" (Bernhardt, 1979, p. 15). Cantor (1970) found the same problem in New York, where a sample of elderly indicated a mistaken belief that the available Dial-A-Ride systems were to be used only for medical purposes.

Faced with the problems of financing $15,000 vans and then obtaining sufficient numbers of riders to keep subsidization at a reasonable level, it would appear that taxicab usage would be more economical and more convenient. Taxicab-based systems might also reduce any negative feelings that elderly residents have about riding special buses and would make use of existing dispatching systems.

In the early 1970s, a shared taxicab service was implemented in Arlington, Virginia. By 1975, this system had been abandoned on the basis of excessive costs. Each passenger paid $.15 for the taxicab, but the actual cost per taxi trip was $2.74. Although 45% of the eligible elderly were using this service. it was hard to persuade passengers to share the taxis or that a reservation two hours in advance was not an arbitrarily imposed requirement. As the program reached its final stages, only 1.4 passengers were being transported in each taxicab ride (Kast, 1975). Aside from cost problems, many cab drivers may not want to pick up elderly passengers who live in poor inner-city or rural areas. The flexibility and convenience of the taxicab has thus been difficult to match with a program that is economical and efficient. "User side" subsidies do, however, appear to have strong support among older persons. Montgomery County, Maryland, has instituted taxi vouchers that older persons can purchase at a rate based on their income. Depending on its length, these vouchers can substantially reduce the cost of the ride.

Teal, Rooneys, Mortazari, and Goodhue (1983) found the average cost per ride in a special taxi-based program was $4.52, as compared to $2.87 for general transportation. Analyzing alternative approaches to special transportation programs, the researchers found shared-ride taxi systems the most effective. Fostering cost-effective shared-ride systems would require the abolition of existing strictures on ridership. Abolishing these strictures, however, would double the costs of the program. In the middle 1980s, the authors estimated the increased costs at from $50,000 to $150,000.

COORDINATION OF PROGRAMS

Many of the transportation programs for special groups are mandated under federal legislation. Title XIX specifies that each state plan must include provisions for assuring the transportation of Medicaid recipients to and from medical services. This provision can be satisfied by reimbursement of recipients for their transportation costs. Title III of the OAA requires the provision of transportation for clients to and from nutrition sites if transportation is otherwise unavailable.

An indication of the proliferation of transportation programs was provided by a study in Chattanooga, Tennessee, where 40 agencies were found to be operating transportation programs in 1975 (U.S. Department of Transportation, 1975). Coordination of these individual agencies' efforts in order to pool resources for capital outlays and operating costs is one step that promises to reduce the constantly increasing financial burdens of these programs. In Roanoke, Virginia, a nonprofit transportation agency was formed in 1975 in pool all the transportation resources and needs of individual agencies. Funds received by the transportation agency (Roanoke Dial-A-Ride) are then distributed to the participating organizations. In California, the local Transportation District provides 64% of the expenses for transportation programs in Marin County. The Transportation District also coordinates transportation programs for senior citizens, a medical transportation program, and a system of transportation for service and charitable organizations. Cleveland, Ohio, has acted to create a more efficient transportation system for older people by consolidating four providers into one system that offers both fixed route and demand services (*Older American Reports*, 1990).

FUTURE TRENDS

The transportation needs of the older person will continue to increase as the proportion of older persons living in suburban communities also increases. The emphasis on outpatient treatment for many health problems means that older persons will need to be able to reach their health providers on a regular basis. Many communities will attempt to provide fixed route transportation systems, but a more common model will be similar to that instituted in 1990 by Waynesboro, Virginia. In this rural area, for 50 cents a van is available on a one day advance reservation to transport individuals over the age of 60 who are visually and physically handicapped to doctors, the hospital, and shopping.

The passage of the Americans with Disabilities Act also has the potential to improve the mobility of older persons. Under the impetus of the act, efforts may be made to replicate initiatives such as the "Red Mitt" program of the Southeastern Michigan Rapid Transit District. This program permits a disabled person to hold up a red mitt and have a bus stop for them, regardless of whether they are at a bus stop or in their driveway (U.S. Senate, 1990).

Buses being utilized by two passengers an hour are more expensive than cabs, especially when the taxes and depreciation are figured into the total cost per ride. The coordination of programs being attempted in Delaware, California, and Virginia, as well as intensive efforts to inform the elderly of transportation services now available, are vital to counteract such high costs.

Aging programs are constantly proclaiming the provision of adequate transportation to be one of their major headaches. The expenses associated with this service will not decrease, although the spiral in insurance premiums noted in the late 1970s has largely abated. Transportation will continue to consume a major portion of the budget of service agencies even with proper coordination, and program planners must be aware of the costs and difficulties of providing adequate transportation.

For the elderly we can expect transportation programs to remain demand-responsive rather than need-responsive. Although flexible schedules and route services may be officially available, priorities of shopping and medical trips may consume most of the van and bus capacity available in many areas. It is thus doubtful that any new public transportation system will be able to open up major new opportunities for elderly individuals to expand their range of activities. The realistic goals of transportation services in the 1990s would appear to be to enable (1) formerly isolated elderly to reach the variety of agencies and programs now available, (2) elderly individuals to obtain the medical and mental health care they require, and (3) the elderly to undertake the necessary shopping trips to avoid doing without important goods or becoming dependent on any local store and its possibly inflated prices. Visiting or attendance at cultural events requires a flexible and individualized service not within the resources of transportation systems presently in operation. Rural elderly and the increasing numbers of frail individuals over the age of 85 are two groups for whom specialized transportation services will need to be directed.

The goals mentioned are major, and their fulfillment will not be a simple task. Their attainment promises an improvement in the isolating conditions under which many elderly and handicapped now live, but it will remain an expensive effort. Subsidization of transportation services will always be necessary. Providing adequate transportation services may prove to be a major test of the general public's commitment to maintaining the network of services needed by older individuals.

REFERENCES

Bernhard, M. (1979, January 8). Giving a lift to the elderly. *Washington Post*, p. A15.

Cantor, M. (1970). *Elderly ridership and reduced transit fares: The New York City experience*. New York: New York City Office on Aging.

Green, D., Associates. (1984). Use of volunteers in the transportation of elderly and handicapped persons. Washington, DC: Urban Mass Transit Administration.

Jones, P., Rott, E., & Murphy, M. (1976). *A report on services to the elderly (Part 1). Transportation: A low-cost fair-fare transportation program for the elderly and disadvantaged*. Washington, DC: Aging Program, National Association of Counties Research Foundation.

Kast, S. (1975, January 2). Arlington elderly about to lose those free rides. *Washington Star-News*, p. B-2.

McKelvey, D., & Ducker, K. (1974). *Transportation planning: The urban and rural interface and transit needs of the elderly*. Iowa City, IA: University of Iowa Institute of Urban and Regional Research.

Older American Reports. (1990). Three Ohio AAA's use state funds for local initiatives. *14*, 399.

Older American Reports. (1980) Vehicle insurance rates lowered for elderly programs. 4(9), 4.

Pierce, N. (1979, January 5). Elderly freedom is riding on OATS. *Washington Post*, p. A-16.

Rinaldi, A. (1973). *Aid to senior citizens' mobility in East Orange, New Jersey: An escort service*. Millburn, NJ: National Council of Jewish Women.

Teal, R., Rooney, S., Mortazari, K., & Goodhue, R. (1983). *Taxi-based special transportation studies*. Washington, DC: Urban Mass Transit Administration.

U.S. Administration on Aging. (1975). *Transportation for the elderly: The state of the art*. Washington, DC: U.S. Government Printing Office.

U.S. Department of Transportation. (1975). *Transportation for the elderly: The state of the art*. Washington, DC: U.S. Government Printing Office.

U.S. Department of Transportation. (1976). *Rural passenger transportation: Technology sharing*. Cambridge, MA: Transportation Systems Center.

U.S. Department of Transportation. (1977). *Transportation and the elderly: A literature capsule*. Cambridge, MA: Transportation Systems Center.

U.S. House of Representatives, Select Committee on Aging. (1976). *Transportation: Improving mobility for older Americans*. Washington, DC: U.S. Government Printing Office.

U.S. Senate, Special Committee on Aging. (1990). *Developments in aging: 1989, Volume 2—Appendixes*. Washington, DC: U.S. Government Printing Office.

8

Crime and Legal Assistance Programs

While programs related to crime attempt to protect the older adult from victimization by others, many of the legal services being stressed in aging attempt to protect the elderly from themselves. Legal services have increased since they became the focus of attention at the 1971 White House Conference on Aging and in the 1975 amendments to the OAA. Their appropriateness and the manner in which they are administered remain a point of contention.

Legal programs are diverse in nature. As we shall see, even the laws on guardianship and protective services differ from state to state. While it is impossible to cover all of these rapidly growing and changing programs, this chapter will provide an overview of the types of programs now in existence. It will also outline the legal issues involved in programs designed to protect the elderly from doing harm to themselves, either physically or financially.

THE ELDERLY AND CRIME

Concerns and Figures

Concern about crimes against the elderly has intensified in recent years. Reports of elderly people being mugged and murdered have made front-page headlines. In 1977, the report of a Brooklyn, New York, couple who committed suicide after leaving a note stating that death was better than living in continual fear received major coverage throughout the United States. A recent volume on crime and the elderly utilizes a cover made up of headlines and articles describing crimes against the elderly that have occurred throughout the country. In New York State, attempts were made in 1976 to enact legislation that would have mandated treating juveniles as adults if they committed crimes against the elderly. While public outrage against the victimization of the elderly mounts, it remains unclear whether the reality of the crime rate matches this concern.

Data collected on crimes committed against elderly victims are imprecise, as are criminal statistics in general, The FBI compiles its widely relied upon statistics from figures based on reported incidents of crime provided by local police departments, which have varied reporting requirements. There is also widespread belief that because older individuals may fear dealing with the police or retaliation by attackers who live in the neighborhood, they often do not report crimes of which they have been the victims. If a crime is reported to the police, the age of the victim is not always recorded.

Patterns of Crime

Utilizing survey data, Antunes, Cook, Cook, and Skogan (1977) attempted to provide some definitive answers to the confusion about the rate of crime against the elderly. Their investigation covered a number of issues: the likelihood (1) of an elderly person being a victim of violent crime, (2) that an older person will be in or near home when the crime is committed, (3) that elderly individuals will be attacked by youth gangs, (4) that the attackers will be strangers, and (5) that the attackers will utilize weapons. The researchers found that attacks on the elderly were in proportion to those committed on people in other age groups. The elderly were more likely to be attacked in or near their homes. Elderly individuals with limited access to transportation may develop life-styles that do not involve traveling great distances; the likelihood of any attacks occurring in or near home is therefore increased. Although attackers were often youths who were unarmed, no indication was found that older persons were more likely to be attacked by gangs.

A Justice Department study released in 1987 indicated that violent crimes against the elderly had declined 50% since 1973 and that older people still had the lowest victimization rate of any group over the age of 12 (Associated Press, 1987). In crimes of violence, robbery, assault, and theft, the rates of victimization of the elderly in 1987 were dramatically lower than other age cohorts. In the category "Personal Larceny with Contact" the rates of victimization of the elderly were the same as individuals in the age 12–16 category and higher than the 25–34, 35–44, or 50–64 cohorts (Jameson & Flanagan, 1989). Overall, these figures indicate an inverse relationship between the risk of personal and household victimization and age. The major exception to this is in the category of personal theft, which maintains a more stable rate across age categories than other categories of crime (Laub, 1990). It can be argued that the crimes against older persons would be more extensive if many elderly did not remain at home in the evening, thus also restricting the activities available to them.

Vulnerability

Do special legal programs need to be developed to protect the elderly against potential victimization? This question can be answered only by examining the effects of crime on people in different age groups. As an official of the Justice Department testified to the U.S. House of Representatives Select Committee on Aging (1976a):

> While there may be some uncertainty about crime victimization among senior citizens, there is, I believe, little question about their vulnerability— physical, psychological and financial. Take, for example, the instance of the theft of a television set. The effect on a younger person does not carry the same impact as it does upon a person who is 65 years and older and of limited means. Take the instance of physical violence. It has a particularly debilitating effect on the older person. The theft of a social security check has a tremendous impact upon a person of lower income. (p. 5)

This testimony points to a number of factors that make the elderly especially vulnerable to crime. A low income makes it difficult for many older persons to recoup from robbery, and it also makes them susceptible to confidence games that hold out the promise of quick wealth. Older individuals faced with the threat of violence may not have the physical strength to fight off a potential attacker and thus may be viewed as easy victims. The elderly also tend to reside in changing areas of the city where unemployment and general social problems abound. Many of these elderly residents receive their checks for Social Security, SSI, or pensions on fixed dates of each month. These dates are often common knowledge in the neighborhood and become red-letter days for attackers. The development of a system of direct deposit of checks is helping to reduce this problem. The elderly are also easy prey for attackers because they often live alone and go out shopping by themselves rather than in groups.

Effects of Victimization

The Justice Department official's comments on the financial and psychological effects of crime on the elderly can be supplemented by the

Cook, Skogan, Cook, and Antunes (1978) investigation of the physical effects of victimization. An examination of the 1973 and 1974 LEAA data indicates that individuals 40–49 are the group most likely to be injured in criminal attacks; the second most likely are the elderly. While the elderly suffered fewer broken bones or teeth when attacked, they were more liable to internal injuries and became unconscious more often than other age groups. Few of the elderly who reported these injuries required medical treatment, and the authors hypothesize that this may be due to a lesser amount of force being used against the elderly by their assailant. An amount of force equivalent to that used against younger adults might be extremely harmful to the older person, whose susceptibility to complications from broken hips and falls is greater.

Confidence Schemes

While the debate about the degree of violent crime against the elderly continues, there is less controversy about the special susceptibility of the elderly to confidence games. In addition to the physical weakness and living habits that increase the vulnerability of the elderly to violent crime, the American aged have a number of other characteristics that make them "marks" for consumer fraud. Especially important are their fear of growing older and the loss in functioning they assume aging will include. Devices that promise to prevent or repair losses in hearing or vision may be especially attractive to older adults, and those who suffer from chronic illnesses frequently jump at the opportunity to purchase medications that promise to relieve their pain. All of these factors are most at play among less educated elderly. Older individuals with more education show less interest in overpriced merchandise and less susceptibility to fraudulent schemes.

The most common of confidence games is the "pigeon drop." In this scheme, an elderly person is approached by someone on the street who informs him or her that a bag of money has been found. The money will be shared if the older person shows good faith by going to the bank and withdrawing some funds, which will be held by an attorney until the bag of money is legally released to them. The con artist, once given the money, disappears. Other con games are variations on this theme, which promise the elderly person some easy reward for providing some of her or his funds as a sign of good faith or as security.

A second form of fraud is engaged in by unscrupulous retailers and salesmen who encourage the elderly to buy items that are unnecessary, inadequate, or overpriced. The most common consumer frauds perpetrated against the aged involve hearing aids, eyeglasses, funeral arrangements, dentures, and health insurance. In many cases, the elderly are encouraged to buy prosthetics, such as hearing aids that will not make up for their auditory losses, or they are encouraged to buy overpriced aids. In 1978 there were reports of individuals selling the elderly overpriced health insurance.

CRIME PREVENTION AND ASSISTANCE

Robberies, attacks, consumer frauds, and confidence swindles can beset the elderly individual. Because victimization can take so many forms, the programs that have been devised to protect the victims are also extensive. They are run under a variety of auspices, including general or special units of the police department. Some programs are operated by the local Area Agency on Aging or a social service agency.

Educational Programs

A report by the Select Committee on Aging of the U.S. House of Representatives (1977b) emphasizes the need for crime-related educational programs for the elderly. These educational programs focus on informing older residents about how to avoid street crimes and recognize confidence swindles. A second type of program related to crime prevention encourages increased cohesion in the community and the implementation of support services, such as an escort service. Finally, most areas now have some form of "victim assistance" program that provides both financial compensation and counseling to victims of crime.

At the national level, the AARP has worked to develop a training program that is available to senior citizen organizations. In four two-hour sessions, this program informs the elderly about methods of avoiding street crime and burglary, about the most common types of confidence schemes, and how to work with the police to reduce crime. In Evansville, Indiana, the police department holds a two-day symposium every year for the elderly which is geared to common crime problems (International Association of Chiefs of Police, n.d.). In Cottage Grove, Oregon, the police department has developed a program that trains senior citizens to be crime prevention specialists. Having completed training, they contact other elderly residents in the community, informing them about building security and how to mark their valuables for identification. In Jamaica, New York, the Jamaica Service Program for Older Adults has formed a safety committee. This committee has established a liaison with the local police precinct and sponsors a variety of programs directed at senior citizens, including a safety fair, monthly programs on safety, and a project designed to encourage older persons to report crime. In Baltimore, Maryland, the mayor's office has developed videotapes dealing with assault, robbery, and burglaries. These tapes concentrate on techniques that can be used when the individual is confronted with these crimes. In Kansas City, Missouri, the Mid-America Regional Council began a national demonstration program, including educational components designed to "decrease unrealistic perceptions and fears of crime of the elderly in specific areas" (U.S. House of Representatives, Select Committee on Aging, 1977b, p. 51).

In Los Angeles, the Interagency Task Force on Crime against the Elderly has been formed from the law enforcement agencies, the Area Agencies on Aging, social service agencies, libraries, and educational institutions in the area to design educational programs dealing with victimization of the elderly. The task force's efforts have included the use of television and radio announcements. California has also attempted, through its Consumer Information and Protection Program for Seniors, to provide education for the elderly on prevalent types of consumer frauds.

Security Programs

In many areas with a high concentration of elderly, educational efforts have been combined with increased security measures. LEAA funded a project in Syracuse, New York, to establish security units in eight low-income-elderly housing projects. In Plainfield, New Jersey, a $6,000 program was developed to control access into senior housing units through the use of closed-circuit TV systems. In South Bend, Indiana, $3,000 was spent for the installation of door locks for elderly residents who could not afford them. This project was operated by the South Bend police.

The federally funded Blow the Whistle on Crime program made efforts to provide whistles to individuals in over 300 cities. In the Crown Heights section of Brooklyn and in high-crime areas of Milwaukee, Wisconsin, and Wilmington, Delaware, "security aides" provided escort services for the elderly. The Wilmington program utilized both older individuals and teenagers as escorts. With funding cuts in fiscal 1982 and the disappearance of LEAA as an independent agency, the emphasis became focused on technical assistance through dissemination of materials rather than direct program funding.

Victim Assistance

A final group of programs is aimed at providing assistance to individuals who have been the victims of crime. The previously mentioned Jamaica, New York, effort provides sessions for elderly crime victims and attempts to help them cope with their "reactions," which are often more severe than among younger victims (Lurgo & Resick, 1990). In March 1976, the New York City Department of the Aging began a program to assist elderly people in obtaining the social and financial services they would need to overcome the strains of crime. In both New York and Kansas City, crime victims are contacted by social workers and informed of the services available to them. By taking the initiative, these programs attempt to prevent the elderly from feeling isolated and ineffective in dealing with the problems created by a crime. "Victim centers" in major cities serve all age groups and are often located within police departments. As officials describe them,

> specially trained officers concentrate on the allied offenses and try to relate to the victims and provide the type of direct assistance the victim often needs. In certain instances, the victim centers attempt to restore to the victim any property or resources which have been lost. In other cases the centers are geared to meet the needs of special classes of victims such as rape victims or elderly persons who have been victimized. (U.S. House of Representatives, Select Committee on Aging, 1977a, p. 11)

Many of the elderly who become crime victims are reluctant to serve as witnesses. There are also "witness centers" in conjunction with the local courts. The witness is informed about court procedures as well as provided with necessary services, such as transportation. The centers will provide protection for witnesses if necessary.

As Jaycox (1981) notes, it was difficult to evaluate the victim witness programs beyond an expression of satisfaction by clients and observers, some time savings for witnesses and "modest improvements in the witness appearance rates" (Jaycox, 1981, p. 4). The Victims of Crime Act, passed in 1984, has helped to fund state compensation and victim assistance programs throughout the country. In 1986 the funds collected from fines and distributed to states supported 1500 programs. Besides this federal legislation, since 1980 35 states have passed legislation related to victims (Davis & Henley, 1990).

Unfortunately, many elderly people find that they are not reimbursed by insurance for what they lose as a result of victimization. A study by Marquette University (U.S. House of Representatives, Select Committee on Aging, 1977a) found that the average nonreimbursed costs for medical injury to the elderly were $200. The noninsured property damage and loss was $432. Loss of income averaged $373. Many states have not instituted victim compensation laws which provide reimbursement for the costs sustained by all individuals.

The state-by-state variation in these victim compensation laws is great. The maximum amount of compensation for medical expenses or loss of earnings and the maximum time within which a victim may file a claim vary. A sample case in Wilmington, Delaware, illustrates the principle of victim compensation. The victim, a 72-year-old woman, was assaulted. She paid $102 for medical expenses. Since she cooperated with the police, was a victim of a violent crime, and was a resident of Delaware, the compensation board also reimbursed her for other out-of-pocket expenses related to the crime for a total of $350 (U.S. House of Representatives, Select Committee on Aging, 1976b). In Baltimore, the Commission on Aging has established a victim's assistance unit composed of a director, attorney, and counselor. The unit works with elderly individuals who have been victimized. The majority of these elderly victims are referred to the unit by the police.

As people have become aware of the existence of the compensation programs, the time lag between claim filings and awards has often increased. In 1977, New York state officials testified that the volume of cases needing action had resulted in a 10-month interval between submission of claims and reimbursement (U.S. House of Representatives, Select Committee on Aging, 1977a).

Despite all of this activity, the effectiveness of these programs is not yet clear. The loss of a feeling of community and the general fear that pervades many American cities is still strong. This fear can also be found among suburban elderly even if they have not personally experienced criminal victimization (Cantor, Brook, & Mellor, 1986). In the 1980s, the emphasis was on long jail sentences. Whether a punitive approach toward offenders will reduce crime rates or the fear of crime remains to be seen.

LEGAL REPRESENTATION

As services have increased, the elderly have become more involved with a variety of public and private bureaucracies which determine their eligibility for these programs. Disputes about eligibility may necessitate legal representation. For older people, legal issues which most often arise are questions about Social Security and SSI benefits, landlord-tenant disputes, Medicare claims, food stamp certification, and wills and probates.

There is little doubt that the elderly have not received adequate legal assistance, partially because lawyers are not likely to earn high fees working with the elderly. Many older persons also remain unaware of their legal rights or are afraid of dealing with lawyers, just as they do not report crimes out of fear of dealing with the police. Elderly individuals who do possess higher educational backgrounds and are more confident about legal transactions may lack the transportation necessary to reach a lawyer's office.

Legal Services Corporation Programs

Legal representation for the elderly has begun to improve in recent years, mainly through the efforts of the Legal Services Corporation (LSC) authorized under federal legislation in 1975. This corporation is an independent successor to the poverty law program that existed within the now-defunct Office of Economic Opportunity. The LSC has lawyers in offices throughout the country and services all individuals who fall below the federal poverty level, including the elderly. Specialized programs for the elderly have been supported by funds from Title III of the OAA, revenue sharing funds, and Title XX of the Social Security Act. Title III funds for legal services increased in 1975 as a result of 1975 amendments to the OAA, which specified four priority areas for state and community programs: transportation, home services, legal and other counseling services, and home repair and renovation programs. In Memphis, Tennessee, $220,000 from revenue sharing funds was allocated by the city for a legal program for the elderly, and $150,000 was set aside in Sacramento, California, for a similar program. In San Diego, California, the Bank of America has supported a program to increase legal representation for the elderly. The LSC and the AoA have provided support to the National Senior Citizens Law Center (NSCLC) and Legal Counsel for the Elderly at the American Association of Retired Persons.

As Stephens (1977) notes, a large percentage of the legal problems presented by the elderly fall under the heading of public benefit claims. In some cases obtaining benefits may be merely a matter of obtaining important information. A major case cited by the LSC was the refusal of the Social Security Administration to release the official SSI manual, which contained vital information on emergency benefits. The threat of a lawsuit from LSC resulted in 1,000 of these manuals being distributed around the country (Nathanson, 1977).

The threat of legal action is also helpful in situations where private pension plans contain major loopholes and possibilities of abuse by employers. In one case, a truck driver for a major supermarket chain retired after 34 years of work, expecting a pension of $300 a month. When his first check arrived, he found that it was for only $250. The employer informed him that his pension had been reduced because he retired a month too early, even though his date was advised by an official of the firm. A student at the Protection for Elderly People program of the George Washington University Law School wrote to the supermarket chain informing them of the problem. After two months, the retired driver received a check for $1,200, an apology from the company for the mistaken advice, and credit for the additional month (National Law Center, 1976).

In FY 1982 funding for LSC was cut substantially, reducing the availability of LSC personnel and the type of cases the agency could handle. The class action suits that LSC had undertaken had also created resentment that threatened the continued existence of the agency.

While the efforts of the LSC, the NSCLC, and Legal Counsel for the Elderly are admirable, these three organizations alone are unable to provide sufficient legal representation to serve the multiple needs of the elderly. Some law schools have set up special clinics to serve the elderly, but it is unlikely that in the upcoming years we will see any rush on the part of lawyers toward major private practice with older populations. A number of other approaches to utilizing lawyers are now being tried. In Tennessee a legal aid program sends lawyers on a regular circuit of three to 15 counties in the state. On these trips, the lawyers visit senior centers and run seminars for the elderly on important legal issues. In addition, the NSCLC provides "support and information" for lawyers representing elderly clients. The NSCLC will provide information on previous cases of draft pleadings for legal aid lawyers who request this assistance. NSCLC also provides technical assistance to states on a variety of issues including housing for the elderly and formulations of pension plans.

One innovative approach to meeting the legal representation needs of older persons are Legal Hotlines. The first hotlines were developed in 1985 by the Legal Counsel for the Elderly. These hotlines are now available to callers in Pennsylvania, Florida, Texas, Ohio, and Washington, DC. The hotlines utilize attorneys who are paid a per diem rate. The attorneys can offer legal information or advice to a caller. They can also refer the caller to a publicly funded legal program or a program that offers services for a reduced fee. If the attorney decides that the caller's problem is not a legal problem, he or she may refer the older person to a local social service agency (Kolasa & Soto, 1990). Legal hotlines may be funded through organizations such as AARP or through community organizations using AoA funding.

As Kolasa and Soto note, the hotlines overcome transportation problems facing the elderly and help the older person define the problem more carefully without facing major legal fees. (Kolasa & Soto, 1990). There have been some problems with the hotlines. Most prominent has been high turnover rates among the staffing attorneys. Hotlines have also had difficulty working with hearing impaired older callers (Porter & Affeldt, 1990).

Pro bono representation is now a policy of the American Bar Association, but attempts to specify the amount of time lawyers should donate to clients have been resisted. While efforts are being made to increase lawyers' gratis representation of the elderly, it is likely that much of the increased legal counseling will be undertaken by paralegal counselors.

Paralegal Assistance

As of 1977, over 100 paralegal programs existed in the United States, with many focusing attention on the legal problems of the elderly. The common definition of a paralegal as "any person who deals with the products of the legal system, that is statutes, regulations administrative agencies and court" (Buford, 1977, p. 109) has been objected to by Buford. This definition, he contends, is vague and omits the crucial fact that the "paralegal is an employee of an attorney who has been trained to work on tasks formerly done by attorneys" (Buford, 1977, p. 109). Although paralegals are not licensed by bar associations, they are allowed by federal regulations to handle cases of individuals seeking such public benefits as Social Security, SSI, welfare, public housing, and food stamps. In cases where a lawyer is required, paralegals may prepare the briefs for lawyers.

A second group of individuals who can provide assistance to the elderly are what the Paralegal Institute has termed community services advocates (CSA). CSAs may be individuals with backgrounds in many other fields. The common denominator is that they come into frequent contact with the elderly. Caseworkers or home health workers may thus play an important role as CSAs, and the National Paralegal Institute has made efforts to train social service workers as CSAs. Not employed by an attorney, CSAs are limited in the legal representation they can provide the elderly in actual hearings. However, they can be strong advocates for the elderly who are having legal problems, particularly in relation to public benefits.

In the 1978 OAA amendments, legal services were classified as one of the three priorities. As part of its plan for the aging, each state was required to show that the Area Agencies on Aging (AAAs) were contracting for legal services while making efforts to involve private bar organizations in legal services at reduced rates or for free. The emphasis on legal services was deleted from the 1981 amendments to fit the approach that localities should exercise control of programs.

Data from 1980 reveal that the average AAA spent 6% of its Title IIIB funds on legal services. Under the 1987 OAA amendments, state units on aging must require AAAs to expend a specified percentage of their funds on legal services and document that the actual providers of legal services are attempting to meet the needs of low-income minority elderly (Section 306). Although no data have been collected since 1980, the percentage of AAA funds spent on legal services is presumed to have declined (American Bar Association, n.d.).

Some of the funds for legal services have been allotted to the ombudsman programs. In fiscal 1983, ombudsman programs funded by $12 million of federal and nonfederal funds were operational in 54 states and territories. Although there were 1,000 staff involved in the program, the ombudsman program relies heavily on the 5,000 volunteers. As the number of ombudsman programs has grown, the number of complaints have also grown: In 1982, 29,000 complaints were investigated; in 1984, 46,000 (U.S. House of Representatives, 1985). The 1987 OAA amendments included a specific authorization of $20 million for the ombudsman program and specific guidelines for establishing a long-term care ombudsman program with the State Offices on Aging. The State Office on Aging, or contractor, is charged with using the ombudsman program to investigate complaints by residents of long-term care facilities and establish procedures for access by the ombudsman to the long-term care facility. The amendments also prohibit retaliation by a long-term care facility against an individual or employee who files a complaint or provides information to an ombudsman.

PROTECTIVE SERVICES

While in many cases legal representation of an elderly person can increase the person's self-sufficiency, protective service measures remove many of the rights an individual has to make his or her own decisions:

Elderly persons who are thought to be unable to manage their personal or financial affairs in their own best interests are subject to the imposition of protective services designed to protect them from themselves and from unscrupulous third parties. (Horstman, 1977, p. 227)

Elements of Protective Services

Protective services have two major components: (1) intensive services provided with the individuals' consent to those who appear to need major supportive assistance, and (2) services provided for individuals without their consent after a hearing, which involve "legally enforced supervision of guardianship which, temporarily depriving the client of certain rights, enables an agency to assist the person" (Regan & Springer, 1977, p. 4). These services and guardianship may be imposed on individuals of any age, but the concept of protective services has been most widely applied to individuals over 60.

Recipients

We can define the type of person for whom protective services might be appropriate by examining an individual case.

Mr. E., seventy-three, a tall powerfully built man with no surviving family, formerly a skilled iron worker, had become settled, but not rooted in one area of town after an early adulthood of country-wide transiency. He had never married but was proud of earlier feminine conquests. Inarticulate, having had a large investment in his body image, he now lacked the kind of strengths which formerly had helped him achieve his goals. With a foreign childhood rearing and little formal education, Mr. E. was now frustrated by the ravages of illness and old age. He reacted behaviorally with extreme intolerance of others, suspicion, and severe verbal abusiveness. At the point of referral, Mr. E. was in grave danger of dying and was thwarting efforts of interested agencies to induce him to accept proper medical attention through hospitalization. Despite his cleanliness of person, his disabilities had affected the maintenance of his small apartment which was cluttered and dirty. A friendship of twenty years with a male friend indicated some underlying capacity for human attachment. The grave medical problems were compounded by the limitations of an income of $105 monthly from social security. (Wasser, 1974, pp. 103–114)

Mr. E. can obviously benefit from many forms of assistance, including a variety of personal services. He may also be one of the 25% of the elderly often estimated to have major mental health problems.

During the famous social experiment in protective services at the Benjamin Rose Institute of Cleveland, individuals such as Mr. E. were provided with intensive casework assistance from experienced social workers with master's degrees in social work. These social workers functioned under one overriding directive: do, or get others to do, whatever is necessary to meet the needs of the situation (Blenkner, Bloom, Nielsen & Weber, 1974, p. 68). In order to be effective, the social workers had to utilize a variety of concomitant services needed by clients of the protective services program. These included financial assistance, medical evaluations, home aides, and psychiatric consultation. In 20% of the cases, legal consultation was utilized; and in 12%, guardianship proceedings were instituted and completed. The Benjamin Rose program provides a model for the types of assistance that protective services might supply, its basic assumption being that clients of the program require more intensive assistance than is normally provided by most agencies.

GUARDIANSHIP

Contemporary legal guidelines for guardianship and commitment are inadequate. The complex questions raised by protective services have been outlined by Blenkner et al. (1974):

1. If the services provided to an individual such as Mr. E. are inadequate and are resisted by Mr. E., who should have the right to define Mr. E. as a problem and deprive him of his ability to make decisions?
2. If older persons resist services, does provision of services against their will provide them with assistance or merely satisfy the "psychological discomfort" of the social worker?
3. Is providing protective services the answer to the problems of Mr. E., or is the real issue for the elderly the conditions that are imposed on them, and under which they are forced to live?
4. If the proposed solution to Mr. E.'s problems is placement in a long-term care setting, will this solve the problems for the family and neighbors upset by his behavior but be destructive to his own personal functioning?
5. Can any services, whether voluntary or imposed, help many of the individuals who come under the wing of protective services improve to a "normal" functioning level?

Even if answers to these questions affirm the need for protective services, there remains the necessity of careful criteria for legal intervention models. There are increased signs of an understanding of the complexity and importance of guardianship. Among the eligible supportive services included in Title III of the 1992 OAA amendments are "representation in guardianship proceedings by older individuals who seek to become guardians. . ." and "information and training for individuals who are or may become guardians. . ." [Sec. 312].

Consequences of Guardianship

An individual placed under "guardianship" can suffer a variety of losses. These include the right to sue, charge purchases, engage in contracts, deed property, marry, divorce, open a bank account, or vote. In some states, the individual's eligibility for program benefits including Medicare and pensions will come under scrutiny when a guardian is appointed.

> An incompetent is defined traditionally as one who by reason of mental illness, drunkenness, drug addiction, or old age is incapable of self care, of managing business or of exercising family responsibilities or as one who is liable to dissipate an estate or become the victim of designing persons. (Regan & Springer, 1977, p. 36)

In most states the individual must be declared incompetent for a guardian to be appointed. Vague bases for declarations of incompetence such as "old age" have contributed to the abuses now associated with the protective services approach.

Despite these changes there are still variations across states in the procedures required in guardianship hearings. In 15 states the presence of the older person being considered for guardianship is mandatory. Many other states dispense with the older person's attendance in the "best interest of the clients." On a national basis only 8% of older people actually attend the guardianship proceedings in which they are involved.

A 1978 examination of state statutes reveals that 34 states had public guardianship legislation (Schmidt, Miller, Bell, & New, 1981) and that considerable progress has been made toward defining the grounds for guardianship and the public entities' responsibility in the guardianship process. In contrast to "plenary" guardianships, which award all decision-making rights to the guardian, limited guardianships are possible in many states but are not frequently used. Under limited guardianship, the guardian's "ward" retains some authority over decisions. Temporary guardianships can also be used in emergency situations.

Incapacity (the inability of the person to care for his or her person or property or the imminent danger to the person of physical harm or material waste) is the standard for making decisions about the need for guardianship. The criteria for determining incapacity range from "clear and convincing" evidence to vaguer standards that stress the "best interests of the ward." In over half of the 34 states, a medical examination is required, and 14 states include a psychological examination. Minnesota employs a more comprehensive approach, requiring a separate evaluation by a physician, a psychologist, and a social worker with recommendations about the type of guardianship best suited for the individual.

In some states, this interdisciplinary approach has been formalized through the development of Geriatric Evaluation Services (GES). The GES evaluates clients being considered for commitment to a mental hospital, appointment of a conservator, emergency protective services, or protective placements.

In many of the states, the terms *guardian* and *conservator* are used interchangeably, and only careful reading of the statutes indicates the responsibility of the individual appointed by the court. One-third of the states initially prefer to utilize an adult child, parent, or relative of the person as a guardian. If none of these choices is available, then a public guardian is called upon. In 20 states, a specific state or county agency is designated in the legislation as the public guardian of the older person. In seven states, the ward has an opportunity to participate in the selection of the guardian.

In the view of Schmidt et al. (1981), those states that appoint a public agency providing services to the ward as a guardian are developing a conflict of interest. The agency's priority may be efficient and low-cost service delivery rather than protection of an individual. Seventeen states have the same agency providing services and acting as a guardian. Few of the states explicitly mention the funding of the guardian, and 20 of the 34 states make some provision for review of the guardianship. These alterations, while not sufficient, are clear evidence of changes in philosophy concerning protective services and guardianship.

The guardianship-conservator model is long-term in nature. There is, however, a rationale for an emergency intervention model for individuals whose needs are immediate or expected to be temporary. In most states individuals believed to be dangerous to themselves and others may be confined for a period which averages 72 hours. After that time, a formal hearing must be held to determine whether an individual should be committed for a longer period. In Maryland, three criteria must be evident before individuals can be committed to a state mental facility: the individuals must (1) be dangerous to themselves or the community, (2) require inpatient treatment, and (3) be mentally ill.

Alternatives to long-term commitment have not existed until recently and have not always been explored by protective service workers. Alternative settings were a major point in the landmark *Lake v. Cameron* (1966) decision, in which the D.C. Court of Appeals ruled that Mrs. Lake could not be held in St. Elizabeth's Hospital unless all other possible less restrictive alternatives were explored. Unfortunately for Mrs. Lake, no alternatives available at that time (1966) were deemed appropriate, and she was remanded to St. Elizabeth's.

Changes in Protective Services

The potential for abuses in protective services is obvious, and a number of major changes are being promoted throughout the country to prevent undue restriction of the elderly's civil rights. These include: (1) changes in the law to redefine competency according to the level at which an individual is capable of functioning, rather than by a vague medical diagnosis; (2) requirements that the individual be informed of the importance of guardianship hearings, the right to counsel, and the right to cross-examine witnesses (it is interesting to note that one study in Los Angeles found that in only 2% of the guardianship hearings was counsel present for the subject; in Ohio, a negative correlation of .94 was found between representation by counsel and decisions to commit an individual to a long-term care institution); (3) legislation to authorize a full range of protective social services throughout the country; and (4) establishment of a system of public guardianship for people without private guardian resources.

Horstman (1977) has argued for a "bill of rights" for all aged people which would define their constitutional rights in relation to confinement. Under his plan, confinement would be utilized only when the following five conditions were present:

1. The individual had been declared mentally incompetent to determine the viability of seeking or refusing treatment, and
2. Less restrictive alternatives to total institutionalization have been fully explored and found to be inadequate to protect and maintain the individual, and
3. The individual is unable to live safely in freedom either by himself or with the assistance of willing and responsible family members or friends, and

4. The individual is untreatable, and
5. Institutionalization is in the individual's best interest. (p. 288)

It could be argued that a nationwide development of protective services might cut down the need for guardianship or commitment hearings. The Benjamin Rose Institute study stressed caution in aggressively expanding protective services. The research did not show significant differences on a number of measures between individuals in the experimental and control groups. As summed up by Blenkner, Bloom, Wasser, and Nielsen (1971):

> For the participant, himself, however, there was no significant impact with respect to increased competence or slowed deterioration and greater contentment or lessened disturbance. Furthermore, although he was more "protected," the participant was no less likely to die when given protective services than when left to the usual and limited services of the community. In fact, the findings on functional competence together with those on death and institutionalization force consideration of the hypothesis that intensive service with a heavy reliance on institutional care may actually accelerate decline. (p. 494)

This negative evaluation placed a brake on the development of protective services and raised important questions in many social workers' minds about the degree to which the development of extensive services promoted dependency of the aged on the worker. A reanalysis by a new group of researchers at the Benjamin Rose Institute (Bigot, Demling, Shuman, & Schur, 1978) indicates, however, that the original staff may have underestimated the positive effects of the intensive social work services. The federally funded "channeling" demonstration provided a single point of access to coordinated services. Reports on the effects of this project were released in 1986. These data raise again the issue of whether extensive services to older persons may not produce dependency and reduce functioning levels (Mathematica Policy Research, 1986).

The positive and negative effects of protective social casework services offered by agencies remains unclear. The effects of legal procedures for the elderly that remove their rights are much clearer in their negative implications. Legislative enactments as outlined by Regan and Springer (1977) will afford due process for the elderly and restrict the power to unduly remove the civil liberties of the elderly. These legislative revisions should be a prime concern for advocates of aging programs and practitioners in aging.

Elder Abuse

In recent years abuse and neglect of older persons has become a major topic of concern for protective service workers. The 1984 amendments to the OAA required AAAs to assess the need for elder abuse services in their jurisdictions, and the 1987 amendments authorized a $5 million program of grants for elder abuse services and education. Title VII of the 1992 OAA amendments authorizes at least $15 million for elder abuse programs. These funds are to be used for education about elder abuse, receipt of reports about elder abuse, outreach to older persons who may be the victims of elder abuse, and referrals of complaints about elder abuse to law enforcement agencies [Sec. 705(a)(6)].

Partly because of the stigmatized behavior it represents, the actual prevalence of elder abuse and neglect remains in question. A Massachusetts study based on a random sample found a prevalence rate of 32 cases of elder abuse per 1000 individuals (Pillemer & Finkelhor, 1988). Nationally, one estimate is that 1.5 million older people have been abused in their homes. If these national figures are accurate, they represent an increase of 50% since 1980 (NARCEA Exchange, 1990).

In response to this indicated major increase in elder abuse, the Department of Health and Human Services implemented a task force to examine the development of standards for defining and reporting elder abuse, as well as to examine optimal methods to combat this problem. The Administration on Aging also initiated an agency-wide effort to focus on elder abuse not only at home but in institutions.

It is likely that many states will follow in the steps of Mississippi, which passed a law in 1990 making elder abuse and neglect in nursing homes and hospitals a felony offense (NARCEA Exchange, 1990). Pennsylvania has enacted a law providing legal protection for individuals who report suspected elder abuse. This diversity in response across states remains one of the major problems in combating elder abuse. By 1989, 41 states had passed legislation requiring professionals to report all suspected cases of abuse, neglect, and, in some cases, self-neglect (Hommel & Lisi, 1989). Wolf's (1988) list of problems at the state level include: "no consistency with regard to groups covered, definitions, mandatory reporting, investigation procedures, penalties, immunity, confidentiality and services" (p. 12).

Although this legislation has an important protective function, it may also lead to more guardianship cases. Guardianship results if a public agency required to investigate report of abuse or neglect finds that the older person is uncooperative with the investigation, refuses to accept the services the agency recommends, rejects a recommended move to a nursing home, or opts to stay in an environment where he or she is being abused. If there are inadequate services available in the state to help the abused older person, then guardianship may be seen as the only alternative.

A number of programs around the United States can serve as models for elder abuse initiatives. In New York, Mt. Sinai Medical Center has developed a comprehensive assessment and treatment program for abused elderly. Besides providing the treatment available in the hospital, the program helps abused older persons learn about their legal rights. A Madison, Wisconsin, program takes a different approach by training volunteers who can serve as advocates for abused or neglected elderly. The New Ventures program teaches volunteers to assist in managing finances and negotiating the health and human services system. In San Francisco, Community Agencies Serving the Elderly has developed a consortium of 55 community agencies that provide extensive services in cases of elder abuse (Models from Manhattan to Oahu, 1991).

REFERENCES

American Bar Association. (n.d.). Committee on Legal Problems of the Elderly. *White Paper: Legal assistance under the Older Americans Act: Current status and recommendations*. Washington, DC: Author.

Antunes, G., Cook, F., Cook, T., & Skogan, W. (1977). Patterns of personal crime against the elderly: Findings from a national survey. *The Gerontologist, 17*, 321–327.

Associated Press. (1987, November 23). Crimes against the elderly down 50% since 1973. *Washington Post*, A18.

Bigot, A., Demling, G., Shuman, S., & Schur, D. (1978). *Protective services for older people. A reanalysis of a controversial demonstration project*. Paper presented at the annual meeting of the Gerontological Society, Dallas, TX.

Blenkner, M., Bloom, M., Nielsen, M., & Weber, R. (1974). *Final report: Protective services for older people*. Cleveland, OH: Benjamin Rose Institute.

Blenkner, M., Bloom, M., Wasser, E., & Nielsen, M. (1971). Protective services for older people: Findings from the B.R.I. study. *Social Casework, 82*, 483–522.

Buford, A. D., III. (1977) Non-lawyer delivery of legal services. In M. Rafa (Ed.), *Justice and older Americans*. Lexington, MA: Lexington Books.

Cantor, M., Brook, K., & Mellor, M. J. (1986). *Growing old in suburbia: The experience of the Jewish elderly in Mount Vernon*. New York: Fordham Univ., Third Age Center.

Cook, F., Skogan, W., Cook, T., & Antunes, G. (1978). Criminal victimization of the elderly: The economic and physical consequences. *The Gerontologist, 18*, 338–349.

Cravedi, K. (1986). Elder abuse: The evolution of federal and state policy reform. *Pride Institute Journal of Long Term Health Care, 5*(4), 4–9.

Davis, R., & Henley, M. (1990). Victim service programs. In A. Lurgio, W. Skogan, & R. Davis, (Eds.), *Victims of crime: Problems, policies & programs*. Newbury Park, CA: Sage Publications.

Hommel, P., & Lisi, L. (1989). Model standards for guardianship: Ensuring quality surrogate decision making services. *Clearinghouse, 23*, 433–443.

Horstman, P. (1977). Protective services for the elderly: The limits of parens patriae. In J. Weiss (Ed)., *Law of the elderly*. New York: Practicing Law Institute.

International Association of Chiefs of Police, Technical Research Services Division. (n.d.). *Crime prevention programs for senior citizens*. Gaithersburg, MD: Author.

Jameson, K., & Flanagan, T. (1989). *Sourcebook of criminal justice statistics, 1988*. U.S. Department of Justice, Bureau of Justice Statistics. Washington, DC: U.S. Government Printing Office, 1989.

Jaycox, V. (1981). *Creating a senior victim/witness volunteer corps: An introductory brochure*. Washington, DC: National Council on Senior Citizens.

Kolasa, M., & Soto, M. (1990). *Legal hotlines to serve older people*. Third Annual Joint Conference on Law and Aging. Washington, DC: October.

Lake v. Cameron, 364 F. 2d 657 (N.C. Cir. 1966).

Laub, J. (1990). Patterns of criminal victimization in the United States. In A. Lurigo, W. Skogan, & R. Davis, (Eds.), *Victims of Crime: Problems, policies & programs*. Newbury Park, CA: Sage Publications.

Lurigo, A., & Resick, P. (1990). Healing the psychological wounds of criminal victimization: Predicting postcrime distress. In A. Lurigo, W. Skogan, & R. Davis, (Eds.), *Victims of crime: Problems, policies & programs*. Newbury Park, CA: Sage Publications.

Mathematica Policy Research. (1986). *National long-term care channeling demonstration: Final report*. Plainsboro, NJ: Author.

Models from Manhattan to Oahu. (1991). *Aging Today, 12*(5), 15.

NARCEA Exchange. (1990). Legislation and Policy Notes.

Nathanson, P. (1977). Legal services. In M. Rafa, (Ed.), *Justice and older Americans*. Lexington, MA: Lexington Books.

Older American Reports. (1987). Few states fund services on elder abuse, report says. 11(4), 6.

Pillemer, K. (1985). The dangers of dependency: New findings on domestic violence against the elderly. *Social Problems, 33*, 146–158.

Pillemer, K., & Finkelhor, D. (1988). The prevalence of elder abuse: A random sample survey. *The Gerontologist, 28*, 51–57.

Porter, D., & Affeldt, D. (1990). Legal services delivery systems: An overview of the present and a look at the future. In P. Powers & K. Klingensmith,

(Eds.), *Aging and the law: Looking into the next century*. Washington, DC: Public Policy Institute, American Association of Retired Persons.

Regan, J., & Springer, G. (1977). *Protective service for the elderly: A working paper prepared for the U.S. Senate Select Committee on Aging*. Washington, DC: U.S. Government Printing Office.

Schmidt, W., Miller, K., Bell, W., & New, B. (1981). *Public guardianship and the elderly*. Cambridge, MA: Ballinger.

Stephens, W. (1977, November–December). Legal aid programs in Tennessee. *Aging*, pp. 16–17.

U.S. House of Representatives. (1978). *Report No. 95-1618, Comprehensive Older Americans Act of 1978*. Washington, DC: U.S. Government Printing Office.

U.S. House of Representatives, Select Committee on Aging. (1985). *The long-term care ombudsman program: A decade of services to the institutionalized elderly*. Washington, DC: U.S. Government Printing Office.

U.S. House of Representatives, Select Committee on Aging. (1976a). *Elderly crime victimization (Federal Law Enforcement Agencies—LEAA and FBI)*. Washington, DC: U.S. Government Printing Office.

U.S. House of Representatives, Select Committee on Aging. (1976b). *Elderly crime victimization (Wilmington, DE, Crime Resistance Task Force)*. Washington, DC: U.S. Government Printing Office.

U.S. House of Representatives, Select Committee on Aging. (1977a). *Elderly victims crime compensation*. Washington, DC: U.S. Government Printing Office.

U.S. House of Representatives, Select Committee on Aging. (1977b). *In search of security: A national perspective on elderly crime victimization*. Washington, DC: U.S. Government Printing Office.

Wasser, E. (1974). Protective service: Casework with older people. *Social Casework, 97*, 103–114.

Wolf, R. (1988). The evolution of policy: A 10-year retrospective. *Public Welfare, 46*(2), 7–14.

9

Employment, Volunteer, and Educational Programs

For many elderly, retirement is a long-awaited event that promises to allow them to engage in long-postponed activities. Retirement may also mean relief from the drudgery of a job that has been endured but never enjoyed. For other older workers, retirement is a dreaded moment, a termination of a career with its attendant status, a loss of important collegial relationships, and a future that promises to consist of hours of unfilled time. Activities for the elderly must therefore include both paid jobs and volunteer opportunities. Jack Ossofsky, former Executive Director of the National Council on the Aging, attempted to place the issue of employment and volunteer activities in a framework that transcends purely economic issues:

> Maintaining options for the older American is the heart of the issue. . .
> The greatest loss among the elderly is not economic status, income or
> health, serious as these may be. It's the loss of options, the opportunity to
> stay employed, volunteer for social work, start a second career. (Cattani,
> 1977, p. 13)

In this chapter we will examine both paid employment programs and volunteer opportunities available to the elderly.

EMPLOYMENT LEGISLATION

Age and Retirement

In 1900, two-thirds of the men over 65 were still in the labor force. In fact, until 1950, over one-half of the men over 65 were still working (Na-

tional Council on the Aging, 1978). While many workers elect early retirement, others feel forced out of jobs without any considerations being
given to their experience and competency.

Social Security regulations have restricted the work options of the elderly since benefits have been reduced in proportion to earned income
for persons aged 65–69. The removal of any Social Security limitations
on earned income might encourage more older individuals to seek employment. The problem of employment for the elderly has thus been
twofold: (1) finding employers who did not discriminate against them
and (2) finding sufficient numbers of part-time jobs which provide additional money without exceeding the limit allowed by Social Security
regulations.

Age Discrimination Legislation

The major ally of the elderly in their effort to obtain employment has
been the Age Discrimination Employment Act of 1967 (ADEA), which
outlawed discrimination based on age (unless age was a bona fide requirement of the job), and the Age Discrimination Act described in
Chapter 2. Originally the provisions of the ADEA covered employees in
private firms, public agencies, and labor organizations who were between 40 and 65. In 1977, 86 suits were filed under this act; but in 1978
and 1977, over 5,000 complaints were registered with the Department of
Labor, the agency formerly responsible for enforcing the act's provisions
(U.S. Department of Labor, 1977).

For the elderly, the most important changes in the ADEA took place
in 1978. The 1978 amendments increased coverage of the act to individuals up to 70 years of age in private and nonfederal employment. Mandatory retirement for most federal employees was abolished. The 1986
amendments to the ADEA outlawed mandatory retirement at the age of
70. It is estimated that there will be 195,000 more older workers by the
year 2000. In 1986, 1.1 million workers were over the age of 70 (Durso,
1986). Since 20.9 million workers have been employed under compulsory
retirement provisions, the effects of these changes will need to be carefully observed. Regulations accompanying the passage of the 1978
amendments to the ADEA transferred the enforcement of the act from
the Department of Labor to the Equal Employment Opportunities Commission. This shift brought the ADEA enforcement under the wing of
the agency charged with overseeing all other antidiscrimination
activities.

EMPLOYMENT PROGRAMS

Attaining part-time and full time jobs requires well-coordinated placement services that match skills of the worker to possible positions. Efforts in this direction are underway. Much less common are efforts to retrain older workers for new positions which require the attainment of extensive new skills.

Counseling

The first stage of the employment efforts in many areas entails helping older workers gain a better understanding of their skills. This type of counseling has been part of the programs of voluntary agencies in Cleveland and Baltimore dating from the middle 1960s (Health and Welfare Council, 1965; Occupational Planning Commission of the Welfare Federation of Cleveland, 1958). The counseling clinics attempt to provide the worker with supportive help, foster the development of self-assurance, and help with occupational adjustment. Meeting these goals involves attempting to overcome some of the common problems found among older individuals interested in working. These may include poor motivation or poor work histories, a long lag period since their last job, and a lack of appropriate skills for a changing labor market. Added to these deficits may be physical or emotional problems. Once counseling has helped to overcome these problems and enabled workers to achieve a realistic understanding of their own work potential, adequate placement becomes critical.

Using a variety of federal and local funds, placement programs are operating in a number of states and localities. This number could easily be expanded. In 1978, 100 nonprofit placement centers were estimated to be in operation, but the number of centers that could be utilized nationally has been estimated at 268 (Cattani, 1977). Many of these programs are funded through provisions of the OAA, but a number of the most well-developed programs predate AoA's funding for employment programs. In 1959, the Atlanta Branch of the National Council of Jewish Women (Cattani, 1978) started a program that now places 500 older workers per year. In Evanston, Illinois, Senior Action Services operates a storefront and places 120 seniors each year. This placement record represents one out of every three applicants. These workers hold jobs as typists, house sitters, companions, and chauffeurs. Locally funded, Senior Action Services' efforts are coordinated through Operation Able, a coordinating group for all Chicago-area senior programs (Cattani, 1978).

Older Americans Act Employment

On a national scale, the largest provision of funds for the older worker stems from Title V (formerly Title IX) of the OAA. Prior to the emphasis on employment in the OAA, Title X of the Public Works and Economic Development Act of 1965 provided some job opportunities for the elderly. This program, targeted for high-unemployment areas, made some funds available for older workers. By 1975, approximately 4,800 seniors had obtained employment under this funding mechanism (Braver & Bowers, 1977).

The original Title IX of the OAA authorization of 1975 was aimed at helping needy older persons obtain a higher income level. It was also hoped that employment would provide these workers with a renewed sense of involvement with the community while they acquired new skills or upgraded existing ones. The 1992 OAA amendments emphasize older persons with "the greatest economic need" "who have poor employment prospects" [Sec. 502].

The OAA also saw older persons as resources able to provide communities with needed additional human service workers, especially to fill major gaps in providing services to the elderly. The Senior Community Service Employment Program (SCSEP) of Title V has been contracted by the Department of Labor to a number of major organizations including the National Council on the Aging (NCOA), the National Farmers Union, the National Retired Teachers Association/American Association of Retired Persons, the U.S. Forest Service, the National Council of Senior Citizens, three minority organizations, and individual states. In 1975, 22,440 slots were authorized under the program (U.S. Department of Labor, 1977), but this figure had risen to 64,933 by 1990 and the total budget to approximately $367 million. Funds are distributed to allow the national organizations that participate in the program at least to maintain the same level of activities they had in 1978. The 1987 OAA amendments called for new national contractors: national Indian aging organizations and national Pacific Island and Asian American aging organizations. Individual states receive funds in accordance with the percentage of state residents over age 55 and the per capita income of the state. A major concern of the program is to avoid political problems that would result if SCSEP workers filled job classifications normally held by full-time employees and were seen as competitive with these workers (National Council of Senior Citizens, 1978).

The SCSEP program grew dramatically in the last part of the 1970s. There were nearly 12 times as many participants enrolled in 1980 as compared to 1976. Approximately half of all of the workers were in jobs providing services to the general community. This breakdown parallels the types of jobs being emphasized in other elderly employment programs. A concrete example of these efforts is the assistance seniors in Los Angeles have provided elderly Filipinos in obtaining citizenship. In Hoboken, New Jersey, elderly workers have been spending four hours a day with the children of recent Italian immigrant families, teaching them math and phonetics (Taylor, 1979). The SCSEP administered through the AARP provides similar opportunities for 8,000 individuals in public or private nonprofit organizations and is now in operation in 107 locations (American Association of Retired Persons, 1987). The National Council on Senior Citizens Senior Aide program provides limited employment in 53 areas for older persons working in community service organizations for the elderly. This includes activities such as delivering meals to the homebound or providing shopping services (National Council of Senior Citizens, 1978). In all SCSEP efforts, the older adult has been limited to a maximum of 1,300 hours of work per year, averaging 20–25 hours per week, and payment of either the federal or state minimum wages, whichever is higher.

While these programs are administered through agencies oriented to the elderly, additional efforts are being undertaken by the Department of Labor and the Department of Agriculture. The Green Thumb program operated by the National Farmers Union with funds from the Department of Labor administers activities in mostly rural areas in 43 states and Puerto Rico, Begun in 1965 to do highway beautification, it now arranges for 18,000 older men and women to serve in host agencies. About 70% serve the community at large and 30% target services to the elderly. Focusing on intergenerational involvement, 3,964 enrollees served young people through assignment in the field of education, mostly in small rural schools. In 1985, almost 6,000 Green Thumb participants were 70 years of age or older (National Farmers Union, 1987). The U.S. Forest Service utilized over 6,000 low-income individuals over 55 in a variety of projects in National Forest lands in 1990.

The Job Partnership Training Act (JPTA), which replaced CETA, earmarks 3% of its funds for poorer workers over the age of 55. The Act provides training and remedial education as well as counseling and job search assistance. The training and assistance are oriented to private businesses. Title III of JPTA offers job search assistance to workers about to be laid off or at the end of their unemployment compensation eligibility. In the 1989–90 program year, over 38,000 older participants

Table 9-1. Characteristics of 1990 Participants in SCSEP Program (%)

Sex	
Male	29
Female	71
Educational status	
8th grade or less	26
9th–11th grade	22
High school graduate	35
1–3 years college	12
4 years or more college	5
Ethnic background	
White	62
Black	24
Hispanic	9
American Indian/Alaskan Native	2
Asian/Pacific Islander	3
Poverty level or less	81
Age	
55–59	17
60–64	26
65–69	27
70–74	17
75 and over	13

Source: U.S. Senate, Special Committee on Aging (1991).

were served through the set-aside and 9,500 workers over age 55 were involved in Title III services.

Meeting Employment Needs

As is evident from Table 9-1 SCSCEP participants are primarily women. There is substantial participation of minority elderly, particularly black elderly. Although 30% of the participants are over age 70, the majority are in their sixties. Unsubsidized job placements accounted for 23% of all placements. This percentage is higher than for many previous years.

Despite an inability to overcome the problem of obtaining unsubsidized jobs, the self-esteem and well-being attested to by SCSEP participants has been seen as a testimony to its importance. The demographic profile of the United States is shifting, and fewer younger workers are available. Increasing numbers of employers may soon move on their own volition to hire older workers to meet their labor force needs. An interest in hiring older workers is in evidence among fast-food and retail outlets and is expected to increase during the remainder of the century. Hirshorn and Hoyer's (1992) research confirms the interest of private sector firms (with more than 20 employees) in hiring retirees. Regardless of the new interest among employers in older workers, there is no indication that the majority of older Americans are interested in working. In its national study of retired Americans, the National Health Interview Survey found only 12% who wanted to work, and the figure was lower among those individuals who had retired for health reasons (Kovar & LaCroix, 1987).

Many older people may welcome the opportunity to develop new skills and talents if the working conditions are not onerous or the employment opportunities are interesting. One example of this type of effort can be found in Chicago, where Roosevelt University has trained older Hispanics to work in bilingual day care for children. This program meets the need of community programs for bilingual workers. The program also provides older adults with opportunities for advanced education, since the prospective workers are enrolled in the university for courses (Winkelstein & Olson, 1985).

VOLUNTEER AND INTERGENERATIONAL PROGRAMS

There are numerous opportunities available to older people who wish to serve as volunteers. The emphasis on older persons as volunteers has increased as the pool of women outside the paid labor force has shrunk. Older persons are thus recruited to assist museums and community organizations as well as traditional volunteer organizations such as the Red Cross. In addition to these general voluntary efforts, there are a number of programs oriented specifically to recruiting older persons as volunteers. At the federal level, the most important efforts are those administered through ACTION—a federal agency that includes the Peace Crops. ACTION also administers three programs more directly oriented toward the older person: the Retired Senior Volunteers Program (RSVP), the Foster Grandparents Program, the Senior Companions program, and the Service Corps of Retired Executives (SCORE). These programs are administered through ACTION's Division of Older Americans Volunteer Programs. RSVP was authorized under the 1969 amendments to the OAA. When ACTION was formed in 1971 as the federal volunteer agency, the program was transferred to this new organization.

RSVP

RSVP roots can be traced to a pilot program developed by the Community Service Society of New York in 1965. This project attempted to enlist older adults in volunteer work in the community and make use of their neglected talents and experience. The planners of project SERVE (Serve and Enrich Retirement by Volunteer Experience) hoped that the involvement of the elderly in the program would provide them with a renewed sense of self-esteem and satisfaction as well as filling important gaps in community resources.

The present RSVP program continues this tradition. Programs are locally planned and sponsored. Local communities must also provide 10% of the costs of the projects for the first year, 20% the second, and 30% for the third year. Individuals enrolled in RSVP work in "volunteer stations" which include courts, schools, libraries, nursing homes, children's daycare centers, and hospitals. Volunteers in the program include a retired minister who operates a commissary cart at a local nursing home and a retired lawyer who works one day per week at an Indian community center providing legal advice. Many volunteers are reimbursed for transportation to and from their assignments and for out-of-pocket expenses. The programs also provide the volunteers with accident and liability insurance. In FY 1991 RSVP projects were utilizing 427,000 volunteers (Older American Reports, 1991).

Foster Grandparents

The Foster Grandparents Program is designed to provide low-income elderly with important social experiences while they assist children who have special physical or psychosocial needs. As ACTION notes, "Foster Grandparents do not displace salaried staff, but complement staff care to special children with the love and personal concern essential to their well-being" (ACTION, 1979). Foster Grandparents work four hours a day in a variety of settings including correctional facilities, pediatric wards of general hospitals, homes for the mentally retarded or emotionally disturbed, schools, and daycare centers. In 1989, Foster Grandparents received a nontaxable stipend of $2.35 per hour in compensation for their efforts, reimbursement for transportation and meals, and accident insurance. To participate in Foster Grandparents the older person's income must be no greater than 125% of the federal poverty level. The recruitment and training of Foster Grandparents is the responsibility of the individual program. The local programs also provide the older individual with counseling and referrals on personal matters. In FY 1990, the Foster Grandparents Program budget of $60 million enabled 23,000 volunteers to be recruited to work with approximately 77,000 children around the country. Because of its emphasis on assisting poverty-level elderly, ACTION has concentrated on working with local agencies to develop Foster Grandparents programs in low-income areas.

Senior Companions

The Senior Companion Program, which was authorized in 1973, is modeled after the Foster Grandparents Program except that its stress is on low-income elderly working with other elderly. "Senior Companions may provide services designed to help older persons receiving long-term care, deinstitutionalized persons from hospitals and nursing homes, and others with special needs for companionship" (ACTION, n.d.). The main emphasis of the program is on chronically ill homebound elderly. The volunteers must agree to serve at least 20 hours per week and at least 10% of project funds must be obtained from non-federal sources. By FY 1990, over 27,000 elderly were being assisted by 12,000 Senior Companion volunteers in 142 projects. Legislation enacted in 1986 now makes it possible for older individuals who exceed the income limits of the Foster Grandparents or Senior Companion program to join the program under certain conditions (U.S. Senate, 1991).

SCORE

The fourth program for older Americans is the Service Corps of Retired Executives (SCORE). Sponsored by the Small Business Administration, SCORE places retired executives in small businesses such as groceries, restaurants, bakeries, pharmacies, and other organizations which can benefit from their managerial experience. In Wharton, Texas, a SCORE volunteer is helping a bottling company revise its accounting system. In Chicago, a SCORE volunteer helped a small supermarket qualify for a Small Business Administration loan. As in the other ACTION programs, SCORE volunteers are reimbursed for out-of-pocket expenses (ACTION, n.d.). In FY 1990 almost 13,000 older persons were serving as SCORE members. These members provided services in a variety of formats which included 164,000 one-time counseling sessions, 30,000 follow-up counseling sessions, and 3,000 workshops to 102,000 clients. In addition, SCORE volunteers gave 3,400 speeches around the country to civic groups. Overall volunteers donated about 721,000 hours of service (U.S. General Accounting Office, 1990).

Besides the efforts undertaken through ACTION, intergenerational programming is now being implemented under the auspices of numerous agencies. Some of this programming is based on the premise that younger as well as older people benefit from intergenerational contact. Some of the increase in intergenerational programming is also due to the difficulties community programs have in obtaining adequate funds to pay staff.

Intergenerational programs can utilize youth to assist older people, as in the service-learning efforts on college campuses undertaken by the National Council on the Aging in the early 1980's (Firman, Gelfand, & Merkel, 1983). A more common approach is the utilization of older adults in programs for children, as in the Foster Grandparents model. In San Francisco, the Seniors Enriching Educational Roles brings older retirees into local schools as tutors and instructors in a variety of courses (Siegel, 1985). One of the most well-known intergenerational efforts is the Teaching-Learning Communities program in Ann Arbor, Michigan (Tice, 1985). Since the 1970s, older volunteers have been brought together with children with learning and emotional problems in the Ann Arbor schools. The range of intergenerational programs is already impressive and these programs can be expected to increase during the decade.

In order to assist in the recruitment and recognition of volunteers, the 1992 OAA amendments permit Area Agencies to hire a volunteer services coordinator. If more than 50% of the AAAs in a state develop a volunteer services coordinator position, the State Office on Aging must also develop a volunteer coordinator position. Expanded intergenerational programs in schools are also supported by a new section in Title III. The intent of this authorization is to provide intergenerational school-based programs oriented to students with limited capacity in English and at risk of either leaving school, drug abuse, remaining illiterate, or living in poverty. At the same time, by locating intergenerational programs in schools, older persons can obtain access to school facilities such as libraries, gymnasiums, theatres, and cafeterias (Congressional Record, 1992).

EDUCATIONAL PROGRAMS

Educational opportunities for seniors have increased as institutions of higher education have recognized the potential for having adults of all ages on campus and the need to move some of their educational programming into the community. As the cohort aged 18–24 decreases, the opportunities for adults to fill their places in the classroom become more apparent.

Community Colleges

Community colleges have become community educational centers not only for people seeking Associate of Arts degrees but for individuals wanting to upgrade skills and explore new areas of learning. Responding to this interest, many colleges have developed extensive noncredit programs that are offered both at the college and at sites in the community. For example, reading, literature, history, and art classes are often taken into nursing homes, senior daycare centers, and nutrition centers. Many of these noncredit programs, freed from semester structure, can be offered on a flexible time schedule. They are geared to the older person and often designed in conjunction with groups of seniors.

Community colleges have also encouraged older persons to take courses on campus through tuition wavers, precampus counseling, and remedial supports. Dundalk Community College in Maryland offers a full semester of orientation for older persons. During the orientation, each department is visited, time is spent in the labs and with the faculty, and remedial materials are made available. The campus-based courses include some geared particularly for the elderly as well as regular offerings which can be taken for credit or audit. The tuition waver can come either through the decisions of the college itself or as part of a city, country, or statewide program of tuition waivers. Because of the unique nature of the community college, it has done more to encourage older persons to become involved in education than any other educational group.

College and University Programs

Universities and four-year colleges have also expanded their participation in educational programming for older persons. The most common way to expand opportunities is through tuition and fee reductions or waivers. Universities have provided everything from a minimum reduction in fees for audit only to full waiver of tuitions and fees for any course or program of study. This latter approach usually offers all courses, degrees, and recreational facilities without cost to any state resident aged 60 and over. The first two years of the program often offer a full range of courses with the strongest emphasis in languages. Evaluation of these programs is showing that seniors who participated in these programs integrated themselves into the overall student body and did not ask for any special orientation, group meetings, or activities at the time they enrolled or at any later time. The university programs also appear to be attracting primarily older adults with previous college experience.

The extent to which a college or university can offer free programs is dependent upon the size and status of the institution. For large state universities, the effect of 300 tuition-free students on the overall class structure will be minimal. For a small college or university, 300 students could make a significant difference in the course offerings and the size of classes. It is partly for this reason that educational opportunities for older persons vary greatly.

ElderHostel

ElderHostel is a national educational program that is gaining in popularity among older persons and educational institutions. This educational program sponsors one-week courses on college campuses during the summer months. ElderHostelers interested in participating in the program stay in dormitories with other summer students on the particular college campus during the week of courses. The purpose of the program is to create opportunities for elderHostelers to live with other students, participate in campus activities, and take courses from regular campus faculty. The courses, designed for the one-week program, are similar to those that would be offered to full-time undergraduates during the school year and may include an introduction to music, special history courses, flora of New England, or introduction to astronomy. Three courses are offered in each of the one-week segments. A campus can offer as many weeks as it wishes for Elderhostelers, depending on the resources available.

The Elderhostelers come from throughout the nation and can go from campus to campus across the country. Each ElderHosteler must pay his or her own transportation and toward the costs of the course, room, and board; there are no additional charges for the program. By 1990 there were already 200,000 ElderHostelers participating in programs on over 200 campuses throughout this and other countries. The enthusiasm among seniors for ElderHostel should not be surprising. As the numbers of older adults with extensive educational backgrounds continues to grow, there will be more demands on their part for advanced educational opportunities.

REFERENCES

ACTION. (1979). *Senior Companions Program history.* Washington, DC: Author.

ACTION. (n.d.). *Service Corps of Retired Executives.* Washington, DC: Author.

American Association of Retired Persons. (1987). Personal discussion with staff.

Braver, R., & Bowers, L. (1977). *The impact of employment programs on the older worker and the service delivery system: Benefits derived and provided.* Washington, DC: Foundation for Applied Research.

Cattani, R. (1977). The elderly: Fight for job rights. *Christian Science Monitor,* January 9, 12–13.

Cattani, R. (1978). Government job programs provide limited help to elderly. *Christian Science Monitor,* January 11, 15.

Congressional Record. (1992). *Older Americans Act,* September 22, Part II, H8969–H9006.

Durso, L. (1986). Reagan expected to support mandatory retirement ban. *Older American Reports, 10*(42), 3.

Firman, J., Gelfand, D., & Merkel, K. (1983). Students as resources to the aging network. *The Gerontologist, 23,* 185–191.

Health and Welfare Council. (1965). *Older workers project: A demonstration on the job training program for workers over 50.* Baltimore: Author.

Hirshorn, B., & Hoyer, D. (1992). The private sector employment of retirees: The organization experience. Wayne State University: Final report to the Andrus Foundation. Detroit, MI: Wayne State Univ. Institute of Gerontology.

Kovar, M., & LaCroix, A. (1987). Aging in the eighties, ability to perform work-related activities. *Advance Data,* No. 136. Hyattsville, MD: National Center for Health Statistics.

National Council of Senior Citizens. (1987). *Senior aides: A unique federal program.* Washington, DC: Author.

National Council on the Aging. (1978). *Fact book on aging.* Washington, DC: Author.

National Farmers Union. (1987). Personal discussion with staff.

Occupational Planning Commission of the Welfare Federation of Cleveland. (1958). *Measuring up: A career clinic for older women workers.* Cleveland: Author.

Older American Reports. (1992). *Success of older American volunteers documented in annual report, 16*(April 17), 157.

Siegel, E. (1985). Intergenerating in San Francisco's Public Schools. In Struntz, K., & Reville, S., (Eds.), *Growing together: An intergenerational sourcebook.* Palm Springs, CA: American Association of Retired Persons, The Elvirita Lewis Foundation.

State programs vs. senior companion models. (1978). *Prime Times, 1*(2), 9.

Taylor, W. (1979). *The September 1979 profile of the senior community services project*. Washington, DC: National Council on the Aging.

Tice, C. (1985). Teaching-Learning Communities: An investment in learning and wellness. In Struntz, K., & Reville, S., (Eds.), *Growing together: An intergenerational sourcebook*. Palm Springs, CA: American Association of Retired Persons, The Elvirita Lewis Foundation.

U.S. Department of Labor. (1977). *Age Discrimination in Employment Act of 1967*. Washington, DC: U.S. Government Printing Office.

U.S. General Accounting Office. (1990). *Small business: Efforts to improve activities of the Service Corps of Retired Executives*. Washington, DC: Author.

U.S. Senate. (1982). *Developments in aging, 1981: Volume 2, Appendix*. Washington, DC: U.S. Government Printing Office.

U.S. Senate. (1987). *Developments in aging, 1986: Part I*. Washington, DC: U.S. Government Printing Office.

U.S. Senate. (1991). *Developments in aging, 1990*. Washington, D.C.: U.S. Government Printing Office.

Winkelstein, E., & Olson, G. (1985). A community/university day care training model: A bilingual intergenerational approach to adult learning. In Struntz, K., and Reville, S., (Eds.), *Growing together: An intergenerational sourcebook*. Palm Springs, CA: American Association of Retired Persons, The Elvirita Lewis Foundation.

10

Nutrition Programs

The nutrition program, formally authorized under the 1973 amendments to the OAA, provides at least one hot meal a day, primarily in a congregate setting, for those age 60 and over. Originally criticized by some as a new version of the Depression soup lines, this program ultimately became the most popular and universally well-received program of the 1970s. Its success can be attributed, at least in part, to the fact that it provides a measurable service (namely, the preparation and serving of a meal) in a setting that brings people together informally while integrating its efforts with other available services in the community.

The goals of the program identified in 1973 by the AoA illustrate the dual emphasis of the program:

1. Improve the health of the elderly with the provision of regularly available, low-cost, nutritious meals, served largely in congregate settings and, when feasible, to the homebound.
2. Increase the incentive of elderly persons to maintain social well-being by providing opportunities for social interaction and the satisfying use of leisure time.

These first two goals also provide a summary of the success of the program. Nutrition is essential to good health but is greatly affected by the social situation. Eating is a social activity, and regardless of other resources, the older person is less likely to prepare adequate meals when eating alone. The other goals of the program are:

3. Improve the capability of the elderly to prepare meals at home by providing auxiliary nutrition services, including nutrition and homemaker education, shopping assistance, and transportation to markets.

4. Increase the incentive of the elderly to maintain good health and independent living by providing counseling and information and referral to other social and rehabilitative services.
5. Assure that those elderly most in need, primarily the low-income, minorities, and the isolated, can and do participate in nutrition services by providing an extensive and personalized outreach program and transportation service.
6. Stimulate minority elderly interest in nutrition services by assuring that operation of the projects reflects cultural pluralism in both the meal and supportive service components.
7. Assure that Title VII (changed to Part C under Title III in 1978) program participants have access to a comprehensive and coordinated system of services by encouraging administration coordination between nutrition projects and Area Agencies on Aging (AAAs).

This latter goal was strengthened in the 1978 OAA, which brought the administration of the nutrition program under the direction of the AAAs for the first time. Before 1978, the formal links with the AAAs were optional.

THE CONGREGATE NUTRITION PROGRAM

History

Although there has been conflicting data on the nutritional deficiencies of older Americans based largely on the differences among urban, rural, ethnic, and economic variables, some general patterns of deficiency have emerged (Rawson, Weinberg, Herold, & Holtz, 1978):

> Calcium appears as the most common denominator, noted as deficient in most of the studies cited. Iron and Vitamins A and C are the next most commonly identified deficiencies . . . within the elderly, the problems of nutrition intake increase as the individuals grow older and are based as much in quantitative dietary shortcomings as in qualitative deficiencies. (p. 27)

Although the elderly malnourished have been a part of our society for a long time, formal, sustained programs to provide for those who do not have personal or financial resources are relatively new. The most significant research prior to the planning and development of a national nutritional program was the 1965 National Study on Food Consumption and

Dietary Level sponsored by the Department of Agriculture. This study showed that 95 million Americans did not consume an adequate diet; 35 million of these had incomes at or below the poverty level. Subsequent analysis indicated that 6–8 million of those age 60 and over had deficient diets. These data laid the foundation for a federal nutrition program for the aged (Cain, 1977).

A task force set up to develop recommendations based on the results of the national study recommended demonstration projects for a three-year period to determine the best mechanisms for delivering nutritional services. Demonstration projects were needed because of the lack of information on how such programs should be designed and, more important, the extent of their effectiveness (Bechill & Wolgamot, 1972). The purpose of the demonstration projects was to "design appropriate ways for the delivery of food services which enable older persons to enjoy adequate palatable meals that supply essential nutrients needed to maintain good health . . . in settings conducive to eating and social interaction with peers" (Cain, 1977, p. 142).

While this overall goal seems straightforward, the demonstrations were expected to examine multiple issues. Besides the major effort to improve the diet of older adults, the meals were to be served in social settings which would allow for the testing of the effects of different types of sites. These sites would be evaluated in terms of their ability to promote increased interaction among the older clients. The effects of a nutrition education program on the eating habits of the elderly would be evaluated as well as the general ability of the congregate meals approach to reduce the isolation of older persons. Of course, the AoA was also concerned about the comparative costs of different methods of preparing and delivering meals and the problems that were entailed in any effort to increase the nutritional quality of the older person's diet (Cain, 1977).

The AoA funded 32 demonstration and research projects under Title IV. An intensive evaluation of the demonstrations produced the support for the national nutrition program first authorized in the 1973 OAA Amendments. The 32 demonstration projects were designed to control for variations in income, living conditions, ethnic background, environmental setting, staffing, and record keeping. This intricate design allowed national guidelines to be developed that would incorporate the successful components of each project. More important, the Title IV projects indicated to the AoA and the U.S. Congress that the proper provision of congregate meals for groups of elderly people fostered social interaction, facilitated the delivery of supportive services, and met emotional needs while improving nutrition.

Program Operation

Under the provisions of the OAA, the AoA is mandated to develop a nutrition program for older adults

1. which, five or more days a week, provides at least one hot or other appropriate meal per day and any additional meals which the recipient of a grant or contract may elect to provide, each of which assures a minimum of one-third of the daily recommended dietary allowances as established by the Food and Nutrition Board of the National Academy of Sciences. . .
2. which shall be provided in congregate settings; and
3. which may include nutrition education services and other appropriate nutrition services for older individuals. (Title III, Part C)

Because the nutrition program was developed at the federal level under the authorization of the AoA and was, thus, ultimately administered through a single agency, the guidelines for operation have been clearer than in other programs (such as home-delivered meals) which have developed out of different local and national program units.

Each state is allotted funds in proportion to the number of older persons in the state as compared with the older population nationally. However, each state is guaranteed a minimum of .5% of the national appropriation. The federal government pays 90% of the cost of establishing and operating nutrition services. The nutrition program is administered by the state agency on aging, unless another agency is designated by the governor and approved by the Secretary of HHS. Based on a previously approved state nutrition plan, the moneys are allocated to AAAs or public and nonprofit agencies, institutions, and organizations for the actual provision and delivery of meals. Before the 1978 amendments, one-half of the local nutrition programs were under the sponsorship of the AAAs, the other half under the local sponsorship. Within two years of the 1978 amendments, all nutrition programs were to be administered through the local AAAs to ensure service delivery coordination. However, AAAs are authorized to contract the nutrition programs to other local groups as appropriate.

The state units on aging and local nutrition administrative units must provide for advisory assistance that includes consumers of the service at the state level, members of minority groups, and persons knowledgeable in the provision of nutrition services. Nutrition advisory groups can advise on all aspects of the program as well as play an advocacy role for the continuation and growth of the program. Programing, allocations, recruitment of participants, meal sites, and service linkage are common areas of concern for nutrition advisory committees.

All persons age 60 and over and their spouses are eligible for services under the nutrition program. Special emphasis is placed on serving the low-income and disadvantaged elderly. This is achieved by locating nutrition centers, when possible, in areas that have a high proportion of low-income elderly. Through this system, any variation of a means test is avoided, thus increasing the general acceptability of the program to the elderly, who often avoid programs that appear to be "charity."

Actual centers or sites are located in any space appropriate for the serving of congregate meals. The centers can serve as few as 5 or as many of 250 participants on a given day; however, the average center serves between 20 and 60 participants each day. Church basements, schools, highrise apartments, senior centers, and multipurpose centers are the more common locations for nutrition sites. Because transportation is so important to the success of the program, centers are usually located in high-density areas, where walking is possible, or on bus or subway lines. In suburban and rural areas, the centers are located in areas where some form of transportation to and from the center can be provided by the site. Unless the nutrition program is incorporated into senior centers that offer all-day programing, nutrition sites or centers are open up to four hours a day. The location of the center, transportation available, and additional resources affect the length of time of the daily operation of the program. For example, those programs in school cafeterias are often sandwiched between student lunch programs.

Location also affects the type of programing developed by the site. Sites that are not used for other purposes allow greater freedom for alterations, decorating, and storage space than locations that have other activities scheduled in the same space. Shared space has posed a hardship for many nutrition programs in meeting the national guidelines for program development.

The meals themselves are either prepared on site, delivered to the site in bulk, or delivered to the site in individual trays or containers. Because of cost and health code regulations, the on-site preparation is the least popular form of meal preparation. Catering services contracting with many nutrition sites in a given area can provide six- to eight-week-cycle menus that both meet the nutritional requirements of the program and are interesting to the participants. Private firms, hospitals, and long-term care institutions are the most likely sources for meals because they can incorporate special diet meals into the program and already have an understanding of the nutritional needs of older persons. School cafeterias and restaurants are less successful meal sources. Catered meals arriving in individual trays provide the most flexibility for nutrition center locations, as health code requirements are minimal.

Eating and Socializing

Because the purpose of the nutrition program is to provide both meals and socialization, programing is an important part of the services offered. When the nutrition site is incorporated into a high-rise for the elderly, a senior center, or a recreation center, programing is usually part of the additional available resources. When the nutrition site is its own center, programing responsibility rests with the nutrition site managers under the direction of the nutrition project director for the region. Programing is diverse and related to the interests and backgrounds of the participants. The programing available is similar to that found in senior centers but with special emphasis on nutrition education, meal preparation, buying practices, health maintenance, and physical fitness. Not all participants become involved in the programing. An example of what appears to be most popular (based on a personal survey) is programing which requires self-selective active participation, menu swapping, food demonstrations, exercise programs, and handcrafts. Lectures, movies, and other passive activities are less successful at nutrition sites.

Eating and Needs

People who attend the nutrition centers very often have other service needs. Because of this, the nutrition program has had to reach out and develop linkage with other community services in order to respond to the needs of the participants. The nutrition programs have not built a duplicate service system but have, instead, integrated other agency services into their programs. Visits by Social Security representatives, health department officials, and recreation leaders are part of nutrition programing. The limit on service funds has also been a factor in the location of nutrition sites. Many times priority is given to sites located in existing community programs. For example, the nutrition program has led to the expansion of the multipurpose senior center system and has made possible many geriatric daycare programs. County departments of recreation have been able to expand their programing because of the available lunch program. Housing developments for the elderly have also been able to build around the lunches being served.

The same limit imposed on funds for services was imposed on funds for personnel staffing, with the same result. Project directors have reached to other programs to supplement nutrition center staffing needs and have, in some cases, used senior aides and RSVP volunteers to provide support staff. Guidelines indicate that staffing preference should be given to older persons. In locations where the nutrition center or site is separate from other services. the staff usually consists of one part-time site manager assisted by volunteers. In this manner, the participants themselves become involved in the actual operation of the program and see it as "their program" for which they feel responsible.

Funding

Funding for the basics of this program came from the federal government, with an initial outlay fund of $98 million. In 1975 and 1976, the amount was raised to $125 million and has continued to grow dramatically since then. The nutrition program is now the largest single component in AoA funding and served almost 2.7 million people in FY 1990. Because of inflation, the increases have not allowed for a substantial growth in the number of elderly served per day. To help compensate for the funding limitations, sites are requiring reservations, advance notice of cancellations, and in some cases, a three- or four-day rotating system of attendance, all of which create hardships for older persons who have become dependent on these programs for an adequate diet.

Participants are encouraged to contribute something for the meal. The guidelines provide that individuals, from their own consciences, shall determine how much they should and can afford to pay (Cain, 1977). Nutrition centers furnish envelopes or have similar systems in which participants pay what they feel is appropriate. The 1984 OAA amendments forbid programs from charging for their meals. Voluntary contributions, however, accounted for $179 million in FY 1990. Some congregate nutrition programs have adopted the use of posters to encourage older people to contribute for their meals. Others, such as the Columbus County Office for the Aging, in New York State, have a suggested contribution scale. State offices on aging also receive surplus commodities or cash to supplement the cost of the meals they provide. The funding provided by the Department of Agriculture is based on the number of meals served with Title III funds. With the limited funding in some local areas in relation to the participant demand, participants have decided among themselves to contribute higher amounts in order that more people can be served. This, then, provides an opportunity for the participants to see the direct result of their contributions.

As funding becomes more restricted, the question of eligibility will become more important. With limited resources, can everyone continue to be eligible? Should outreach be eliminated? Should it be available on a first-come, first-served basis or restricted to the low-income, minority, isolated, and handicapped?

The OAA nutrition program serves basic physiological and social needs, is measurable, and is relatively inexpensive. For these reasons, it has become one of the most successful programs of the last 10 years.

HOME-DELIVERED MEALS

Home-delivered meals ("Meals on Wheels") are provided to homebound persons, and enable those persons who cannot buy food or prepare their own meals to have good nutritional meals on a regular basis. Approximately 90% of all those receiving homebound meals are 60 and over. The purpose of the program is to provide either one or two meals per day, five days a week. Being able to obtain these delivered meals may enable many of these aged to remain living in the community.

History

Programs of home-delivered meals began in England immediately following World War II. The first program in the United States began in Philadelphia in 1955. The longest continuously operating program is "Meals on Wheels" of Central Maryland, Inc., which began in 1960 in Baltimore and was modeled after the English programs.

The early models of home-delivered meal programs were operated locally and largely by volunteer organizations. Originating in a church kitchen, these programs would serve from 15 to 100 clients, generating payment from clients either through a fixed fee or on a sliding scale. From 30 to 300 volunteers would be involved in any given local program. Referrals would come from friends, families, professionals in the field, or the elderly themselves. Whether one or two daily meals were delivered and the costs of the meals both depended on the facilities available for meal preparation. Menus, number of meals served, amount, and cost were determined by the local organization sponsoring the program. Volunteers were primarily retirees and nonworking women, each of whom volunteered approximately two hours a week. The hot meal was delivered at noontime, and if a second meal was provided, it was a cold evening meal delivered at the same time as the hot meal.

The early programs were sponsored by local churches, community groups, or nonprofit organizations and were largely self-sufficient based on the fees charged the participating clients.

In the early 1970s, as more government funds became available, either new programs under government sponsorship or links between nonprofit local programs and government agencies began to emerge. With the introduction of these new support mechanisms, uniform standards, quality control, and uniformity began.

In the early 1970s, moneys for social services under Title XX of the Social Security Act community action funds were the prime support for home-delivered meals efforts. In 1973, under Title III of the new amendments to the OAA the congregate nutrition program had formally begun. In the guidelines, up to 10% of the meals served could be home delivered. Later, the 10% ceiling was eliminated. The figure has risen to 15–20%, depending on the congregate program and the needs of the participants. The 1978 amendments to the OAA for the first time designated a separate authorization for home-delivered meals. This program was to be administered through the nutrition program; and now federally sponsored, locally run home-delivered meal programs are added to the preexisting community-based programs. In some situations, there were no preexisting home-delivered meal programs; in other communities the two existed. AoA-funded home-delivered meal services served primarily clients who were congregate-site participants, while locally funded programs served other eligible clients. Because congregate nutrition participants often pay only when they feel they can while those being served by a locally self-supporting home-delivered meal program pay a fixed fee, the meals-on-wheels cost to a client is often as much as five times higher. In the Maryland suburbs of Washington, DC, the actual cost per day for the one hot meal and one cold meal food delivered through the meals on wheels programs is $4.56. Recipients who can afford the top fee are charged $4.00. This can cause confusion when a client moves from one program to the other.

The 1978 legislation with separate authorization for home-delivered meals—funded for the first time in 1979—brought the issue of privately operated, largely volunteer groups vis-a-vis federally sponsored programs to a head. The authorizing legislation states that home-delivered meal programs under the separate authorization were to be administered through the federal nutrition program with preference for funding given to local preexisting voluntary home-delivered meal programs. Since 1978 OAA funding for home-delivered meals has grown dramatically, accounting for $88 million in FY 1991 (Government Information Service 1990).

Program Operation

Basically, in a home-delivered meal program, two volunteers—one acting as a driver and one as a visitor—visit eight to 10 different clients each day, spending five minutes with each while delivering the meal. The home-delivered meal program's primary function is to prepare and deliver the meals, but it also provides a few minutes of friendly visiting. If additional services are needed, the client is referred to other support systems.

The meals are prepared by volunteers in church kitchens or are catered by private services, hospitals, long-term care institutions, schools, or colleges. When catered, the meals are either packaged by volunteers (delivered in bulk) or packaged by the meal-producing agency. The extent to which special-diet meals are available is determined by the amount of funds available and the source of the meal preparation. Low-salt and diabetic diets are the more common special diets available. The development of better serving boxes for keeping food warm and of better individualized food-storage containers have improved the system of food delivery. Because of the importance of keeping food above 120° or below 45° until reaching the point of individual delivery, appropriate delivery equipment is essential to an effective program. Either a six- or eight-week-cycle menu ensures the variety necessary in such a program while guaranteeing that the one-third required daily allowance is met in each meal.

For many of the home-delivered meal programs, the volunteer aspects of the program are themselves a service to older persons. In a study of the volunteers in "Meals on Wheels" of Central Maryland (Olsen, 1979), one-half were over 60 years of age themselves and indicated that being able to serve in this program gave meaning to their lives; 29% of the volunteers were widows and living alone. Although primarily for the homebound, the program obviously also provides a service to those preparing and delivering the meals.

There has been some experimentation with dehydrated, dried, and frozen food, but such alternatives have not yet been readily accepted by the programs or the elderly. These alternatives have been under experimentation for the purpose of providing meals to those clients for whom daily visits are impractical, especially the rural elderly (Rhodes, 1977). Some of these alternate methods of food preparation have been evaluated; and preliminary result indicate that the food itself, preparation, and cost are competitive with current situations.

When the home-delivered program is attached directly to the nutrition congregate site, the nutrition participants themselves often package and deliver the meals. In this way, those that are attending can keep in touch with participants who are unable to attend. As was pointed out in Congressional testimony (Cain, 1977), the longer the congregate nutrition program is available, the greater potential for home-delivered meals as part of the program. One project found that after three years, up to 30% of the participants were now receiving the home-delivered meals because of changes in their physical condition. The interrelation of the two programs is important in order that those who are eligible for the nutrition program can have an opportunity to continue, even when physical limitations temporarily make visiting the center impossible. The home program can speed recovery and perhaps, in many situations, make a return to the congregate site possible.

Under the 1978 amendments, for the first time those under 60 years of age became eligible for a service under the OAA. Because home-delivered meal programs have served anyone homebound, this legislation allows the younger homebound to continue to be eligible for the programs.

Funding

Funding for home-delivered meals has always been diverse. Either a fixed fee based on the cost of the meal or a sliding scale that averages the cost of the meal has been the common method until recently. Eligible clients have been able to use food stamps in most locations to supplement the cost of the meals. Currently, funds from Title III of the OAA are the key sources for revenue. These funds can be used not only for the cost of the meals themselves but to pay those who prepare, package, and deliver the meals. Because of the availability of federal funds, there is a shift from volunteer to paid help for meal preparation and delivery. Local United Way, church, community service, and neighborhood groups also contribute money, equipment, or transportation to the program. With the inclusion for the first time of home-delivered meals into the OAA and the separate authorization for funding, the home-delivered meal program continues to expand its important role in the community service delivery system. Overall, funds from Title III and other sources enabled

102 million meals to be delivered to older persons in FY 1990 (Older American Reports, 1992).

A comprehensive evaluation of the nutrition program has not been undertaken in recent years. The 1992 OAA amendments require AoA to conduct an evaluation on a large number of criteria, including the effectiveness of the program in serving "special populations" of older persons and the impact of the program on participants [Sec. 206]. At the same time, the amendments also authorize funds for meals within schools for older volunteers.

REFERENCES

Bechill, W. B., & Wolgamot, I. (1972). *Nutrition for the elderly: The program highlights of research and development nutrition projects funded under Title IV of the Older Americans Act of 1965, June 1968, and June 1971.* Washington, DC: U.S. Government Printing Office.

Cain, L. (1977). Evaluative research and nutrition programs for the elderly. In *Evaluative research on social programs for the elderly.* Washington, DC: U.S. Government Printing Office.

Government Information Service. (1990). *Local/state funding report, 18*(45), 5.

Older American Reports. (1992). AoA releases FY '90 data on Title III state programs. *16*, April 17, 152.

Olsen, J. (1979). *The effect of change in activity in voluntary associations on life satisfaction among people 60 and over who have been active through time.* Unpublished doctoral dissertation, University of Maryland, College Park, MD.

Rawson, I., Weinberg J., Herold, J., & Holtz, J. (1978). Nutrition of rural elderly in southwestern Pennsylvania. *Gerontologist, 18*, 24–29.

Rhodes, L. (1977). NASA food technology, a method for meeting the nutritional needs of the elderly. *Gerontologist, 17*, 333–340.

Part IV

Services for the Aged

In contrast to programs, the existing services in aging offer a large number of components and always seem to be under pressure to expand. Since these services are community-based, these expansionist pressures often come from seniors in the community and their families. Pressures for expansion are increasingly being generated by a federal government that is demanding more accessibility to services for seniors and more accountability on the part of service providers.

This part will examine some complicated and vital service delivery systems including multipurpose senior centers, housing services, in-home services, adult daycare centers, and nursing homes. As is evident, these services are being presented in an ordering that relates to their orientation to elderly with differing levels of need. Multipurpose senior centers serve ambulatory elderly, while housing services may be oriented to ambulatory elderly with some housekeeping and personal needs for which they require assistance. In-home services and adult daycare centers serve seniors with more extensive physical or emotional problems. Finally, nursing homes are oriented toward a population which cannot survive in the community even with the provision of extensive services.

It should be noted that although these services are discussed individually, they are not mutually exclusive. Seniors may be taking advantage of more than one service. Ambulatory elderly who attend a senior center may also be living in elderly housing and receiving some homemaker assistance. Clients of adult daycare centers may also be recipients of extensive in-home services.

11

Multipurpose Senior Centers

The multipurpose senior center is probably the most diverse service now available to the elderly. This diversity is emphasized in NCOA's definition of a senior center:

> a community focal point on aging where older persons as individuals or in groups come together for services and activities which enhance their dignity, support their independence and encourage their involvement in and with the community. (National Council on the Aging, 1978, p. 15)

This definition emphasizes the senior center as a community focal point, the key ingredient of present senior center philosophy. Senior center programs operate from a separate facility, serve as a resource for information and training, and promote the development of new approaches to servicing the older adult.

The OAA emphasizes the multipurpose senior center's role as a community facility for the organization and provision of a broad spectrum of services for the older person. The success of senior centers, however, lies not only in the breadth of services they provide but in the voluntary participation of the users in center activities. Seniors can choose not only whether they want to participate in a center program but in what way they want to become involved. Individuals thus maintain their independence while reaching out to others and to the community in a variety of activities.

HISTORY AND LEGISLATION

Associations of peers have always been sources of support for individuals. Clubs organized for older people only can be traced as far back as 1870. However, centers for older people began with a program in New

153

York City in 1943. The idea came from workers in the New York City Welfare Department who felt that the older people with whom they were working needed more than a club.

> The organizers of the project, besides securing a meeting place, had contributed games, had suggested the serving of refreshments to foster sociability, and having gathered the old people together, expected that they could manage by themselves. They had in this way provided them with a more sociable means of passing time, which then seemed adequate provision. No one had thought beyond this point. (Maxwell, 1962, p. 5)

The idea of this form of association quickly spread, as private groups began setting up centers throughout the country. The San Francisco Senior Center, begun in 1947, was created through efforts of the United Community Fund, the American Woman's Volunteer Services, the Recreation Department, and individual local citizens (Kent, 1978). In 1949 the new "Little House" in suburban Menlo Park, California, was able to attract while-collar and professional clients (Maxwell, 1962). The centers in New York and Menlo Park became the prototypes for the two conceptual models of the senior center that are now dominant. One conceptual approach embodied in the social agency model views senior centers as "programs designed to meet the needs of the elderly and postulates that the poor and the disengaged are the more likely candidates for participation in senior centers." The alternative "voluntary organization model hypothesizes that the elderly who are more active in voluntary organizations and who manifest strong attachments to the community are also the ones who make use of senior centers" (Taietz, 1976, p. 219).

Senior centers grew primarily as locally supported and directed institutions. Established either by local nonprofit groups or by local units of government (departments of social service or departments of recreation), centers were designed to be primarily responsive to local needs. However, most of the growth in senior centers has occurred since 1965. Before that time small clubs were the most common form of social organization. Even in 1970, there were only 1,200 centers as opposed to 10,000 in 1985 (Krout, 1987).

In the 1970s, federal legislation made more funds available for the development of senior centers. The most important piece of authorizing legislation was Title V of the OAA. The 1973 amendments, Section 501, inserted into the act the new "Multipurpose Senior Centers" title. Although not funded until 1975, this title identified senior centers as a unique and separate program. Because Title V provided funds for "acquisition, alteration, or renovation" of centers but not for construction or operation of centers, Title III made it possible to fund senior centers for the development and delivery of a variety of specific services. Title V provided resources for the facilities, while Title III provided operational moneys.

The 1978 amendments to the OAA consolidated the Title V program into Title III, repealing the Title V. With this change, Title III can "provide for acquisition, alteration, renovation, or construction of facilities for multiple purpose senior centers as well as provide for the operations of these centers." This consolidation provides for a greater opportunity to organize senior centers under the direction of the AAAs. The new Title III also allows the AAAs to fund senior centers from the beginning to the fully operational stages.

A number of other legislative enactments provide mandates for senior centers:

1. The local Public Works Development and Investment Act of 1965 provided funds which may be used for the development of multipurpose senior center facilities. Under Title I of this act, funds may cover 100% of the cost of construction, renovation, and repair of buildings to be used as centers.
2. Title XX of the Social Security Act, authorized in 1974, provided funds for group services for older persons in senior centers. Many of the programs offered through senior centers were eligible for funds under Title XX, because Title XX's purpose was the provision of social services for low-income persons. Only individuals who met the eligibility requirements could receive services. Because of this requirement, it was often difficult to coordinate Title XX programs with those funded through the OAA, which had no eligibility requirements other than the age of the recipient.
3. The Housing and Community Development Act of 1974 provides funds for the expansion of community services, principally for persons of low and moderate income. Construction funds are available through this act (U.S. Administration on Aging, 1977).

CHARACTERISTICS

Senior Center Users

By 1990 the senior center concept had grown to a point where between 5 and 8 million older persons were participating in 10–12,000 centers around the country (Krout, Cutler, & Coward, 1990). In 1984 senior center participants represented 15% of the population over age 65. The attendance at senior centers represents a usage rate 4 to 12 times greater than at any other community-based programs for older persons.

There has been a strong interest in differentiating users from non-users of senior centers. Krout's (1988) review of research on this issue does not provide any definitive answers. The variables that did **not** differentiate users from nonusers of senior centers include sex, age, marital status, degree of loneliness, and lack of transportation.

Studies of the effects of race and ethnicity on senior center usage have produced mixed findings. Other variables that have produced mixed findings include occupation, income, educational differences, health status, and degree of social contact with others. While these reported studies were based on local samples, an analysis of national data (Krout et al., 1990) found senior center participation related to "higher levels of social interaction, lower income, increasing age up to 85, living alone, fewer ADL and IADL difficulties, higher education up to post-high school, being female, and living in central city or rural nonfarm areas" (p. 79).

Importantly, race was not a predictor of senior center usage. As Ralston (1989) points out, however, there are major gaps in data on the use of senior centers by Asians and native American elderly. Nationally, 11% of the participants are black elderly and 3% Hispanic. Ralston and Griggs (1985) also found a significantly higher commitment to senior center programs among blacks than among whites. Although blacks may have more difficulty in getting to the centers, black women were more encouraged by children to attend the senior center than were white women.

Models

There are several alternative models for senior centers. As indicated earlier, Taietz (1976) clarified the basic conceptual difference between the social agency model and the voluntary organizational model. These two models evolve out of the support system on which they are based. Early research identified the social agency models as the most commonly developed. As Taietz notes, the social clubs for the elderly have been most meaningful to individuals who are isolated from social relationships, the clubs helping to relieve the older person's loneliness. For the older person who is active in a number of informal and organizational roles, the existence of age-graded social clubs may not seem an exciting opportunity.

The voluntary organizations are usually groups that have many social activities but also possess regular memberships, have organizational by-laws, and conduct scheduled meetings of the members on a variety of topics (Taietz, 1976). In a study of senior centers in 34 communities, Taietz noted the similarities between senior centers and other voluntary organizations which include both service components and professional staff. One major difference, however, was that, while veterans and fraternal groups tend to be sex-exclusive, senior centers provide men and women with equal access to programs. However, because the centers under this model are similar to formal voluntary organizations, their major clientele will tend to be active elderly rather than the more isolated senior.

In *Alternatives to the Single Site Center* (Fowler, 1974), three different mechanisms for categorizing senior centers were developed. The first defines centers in terms of activities generated. The center can be identified by whether it provides primarily services, activities, individual services and casework, or a combination of the three. The second mechanism for categorizing centers is by administration. The center administrative core may be either centralized (everything in a central facility), decentralized (located in several neighborhood facilities), combined (central location, with satellites), or a multiplicity of operations with some linkage. Finally, centers can be classified by the origin of their services. The services can be offered exclusively by center staff, by center staff and community agencies, or by community agencies with the center staff providing coordination. The descriptions of the models themselves show how complex and diversified the structure can be and still come under the rubric of senior centers.

As part of the NCOA study of centers, another model emerged, one based on size and complexity of operation and including four levels:

1. Multipurpose senior center
2. Senior center
3. Club for older persons
4. Program for all persons, with special activities available for elderly

The differences between centers and clubs do not rest solely in their activities or membership but rather in the breadth of services available to clients, the permanent nature of the physical facility, and the numbers of unpaid staff. Many senior centers are also incorporated entities. In the NCOA survey, 51% of the responding organizations were centers, 46%

clubs, and 3% could not be placed in any existing category (Leanse & Wagner, 1975).

Cohen (1972) attempted to further delineate the center from the club. The center he viewed as having the following five characteristics:

1. Community visibility based on a good facility and easy identification
2. A central location for services, through either central site or satellites
3. An ability to serve as a focal point for concerns and interests
4. An ability to serve as a bridge to the community
5. A program purpose that focuses on the individual, family, and community

The diversity of structure, size, and functioning capabilities are a result of the origins of senior centers. The centers have emerged from the community; are sponsored primarily by voluntary, nonprofit, or public community-based organizations; and still receive a substantial percentage of funding from locally determined sources.

PROGRAMING

Although center programing is diverse, it falls into two basic types: recreation-education and service. The programing provided is most likely to be successful when it is built as part of the larger community structure and under the direction, or at least with the support, of the older people who will be served by the center.

Recreation and Education

Recreation-education is the type of programing most commonly conceived as the central component of a senior center. It is this that sets it apart from other service delivery agencies in the community and builds the center as a neighborhood focal point for seniors. The development of activity and the selection of the activities to be offered are related to the target group identified by the center. If the center plans to serve everyone within a given geographic area, the programing should reflect the diversity of the population served. Whether clients are men or women, people of high or low income, people of various ethnic backgrounds, or from urban or rural settings should be reflected in the activities designed for the center. If not, unrepresented components of the population potentially served will not utilize the center because their activity needs are not being met. Taietz (1976) warned program directors of the danger of neglecting the special efforts required to attract isolated and alienated elderly to the centers. Hanssen et al. (1978) add another cautionary note with the identification of another subgroup for whom activity programing is not always available:

> The senior center does not consistently accommodate those seniors with perceived physical limitations and those who are mildly depressed. This finding highlights a critical problem for senior centers. If they are to provide services beyond recreation, they must help those persons with greater perceived health problems and that have other limitations. (p. 198)

Many senior centers are beginning to make special efforts to serve elderly with special needs. These elderly may have serious chronic illnesses and physical impairments. In Detroit, senior centers are cooperating with the Metropolitan Society for the Blind to co-sponsor a program which brings blind elderly into senior center activities. In Springfield, Illinois, a senior center is conducting a lip-reading program for older persons with hearing problems (National Institute of Senior Centers, 1979). With increased emphasis in federal programs on the "frail elderly," we can expect these programs to expand.

A center can choose as a target population a particular subgroup of the seniors eligible within a certain geographic area. In making this decision, however, the center staff needs to work with the larger community to be assured that there are similar resources available for the other components of the population group.

The recreation-education component of center programing can be as varied as the community resources allow and as the participants' interests indicate. Common activities include arts and crafts, nature, science and outdoor life, drama, physical activity, music, dance, table games, special social activities, literary activities, excursions, hobby or special interest groupings, speakers, lectures, movies, forums, round tables, and community service projects. When center participants themselves identify their interests and plan the activities with expert assistance from staff, there is a greater chance of adequate participation and success.

Services

The services component of programing is the other essential ingredient for a successful senior center. What identifies the senior center as the community focal point for older people is the combination of both activity and service in one location. The availability of a lecture on horticulture, dental screening, or square dance lessons along with Social Security advice at the same site and with the same friends makes the senior center a unique community resource.

The services available through a senior center depend on the facilities, the resources, and the community supports available. These services can be provided directly by center staff, by agency staff assigned to the center, through satellite centers close to the agency, or by the agencies themselves rotating through the center.

Services likely to be available through senior centers fall into a number of categories (Cohen, 1972):

1. Information, counseling, and referral, including general information, intake and registration, personal counseling, referral resource files, and special group education around special problems.
2. Housing and living arrangements and employment, including helping the older person locate appropriate housing situations, job referral and counseling programs, and job retraining.
3. Health programs, including screening clinics for a variety of health problems; pharmaceutical services; specialty services, such as dentistry, podiatry, hearing, and speech; and health education programs. These programs are most likely to be developed in conjunction with county health departments, doctors, nurses, extended-care facilities, hospitals, and outpatient clinics in the area.
4. Protective services, including preventive services such as planning for the appropriate use of funds, securing safe living arrangements, supportive services to help enable the older person to be as self-sufficient as possible, and intervention services including assistance in gaining access to such legal resources as commitment or guardianship.
5. Meals, such as those provided through the OAA nutrition program. The development of the nutrition program since 1973 has been the single biggest contributor to the development of senior centers. Since the nutrition program needed sites for the congregate meals and senior centers needed a meal program in order to continue adequate daily programing, the nutrition program has given the centers a much-needed resource.
6. Legal and income counseling, including helping determine eligi-

bility for Supplemental Security Income (SSI) and the preparation of wills.

7. Friendly visiting as an outreach program, with the participants of the center providing the visiting and outreach services.
8. Homemaker assistance.
9. Telephone reassurance and buddy programs.
10. Handyman and fix-it programs.
11. Daycare services.
12. Transportation programs.
13. Nursing home resident activities within the senior center facility.

In the NCOA study, the majority of self-identified multipurpose centers were found to be at least offering educational, recreational, and either information and referral or counseling services. Many multipurpose centers were also providing health services and opportunities for volunteers. Specifically, the most frequently offered services were transportation to the center, arts and crafts, lectures, employment counseling, health screening, friendly visiting, and health counseling.

The programs garnering the greatest participation of elderly were meals, information and referral, and sedentary recreation. However, the activities that generated the most enthusiasm were tours and trips, particularly among women and blacks. Some members joined the center in order to be eligible for the outings that were planned. Overall, participants indicated that their reasons for attending the centers were to meet others and for opportunities to use leisure time. Thus participants are able to select activities and programs based on individual preference and to participate in evaluations on how well the expectations are met (Leanse & Wagner, 1975).

It is clear that effective programing is essential for a senior center to fulfill its role as community focal point. Because senior center participants are more likely to attend by choice or at least see themselves as first coming to the center by choice rather than need, the importance of relevant programing determines the continued attendance of older community residents.

Programing Examples

Perhaps the best way to gain an overview of the multipurpose senior center is to examine some examples of centers that illustrate the wide range of programs that can be offered in these facilities. The senior center in Franklin County, New York, is run under the auspices of the county's office on aging. Because the office serves a rural population, the primary service of the eight senior centers is transportation—12- and 20-passenger vehicles provide 9,000 rides a year to the center, stores, and health facilities. In addition, the centers provide full-time nutrition, education, physical fitness, and craft programs. Assistance is also provided to seniors who are applying for special government programs. In the smaller communities in the county senior citizen clubs meet monthly for social purposes. The clubs' membership links up with the senior centers for trips and other cooperative events.

The Waxter Center in Baltimore provides one of the most comprehensive services in the country. Built as a result of a $4 million bond issue, the center now has over 11,000 members. Housed in a large, specially designed three-story building, Waxter offers a range of activities including swimming, language classes, crafts, a library, lectures, and trips. Because a large number of separate rooms are available, 15 to 20 different activities can be carried out at the same time, giving each member a wide choice of individual or group settings. The center also operates an extensive health screening clinic, an adult daycare program, and a special program to integrate nursing home patients with center members. Representatives from Social Security, SSI, Legal Aid, home care agencies, and other public agencies are at the center on a daily basis. The center, including the nutrition program, is open seven days a week.

The Hudson Guild–Fulton Senior Center in New York City has a membership of 1,300, with 300 members present on any given day. An advisory committee helps to make decisions affecting the staffing operations of the center and to initiate programs that respond to their own interests and talents. The center views itself as a supermarket, with members selecting what they need from the center's offerings. The center's classes include crafts, exercise, drama, music, discussions, and languages. Tickets are available through the center to the wide range of concerts, theater, and opera offerings that are available in New York throughout the year.

The Hudson Guild–Fulton center provides assistance to its members for Medicaid, Medicare, Social Security, and other public-assistance problems. Personal and housing problems as well as legal concerns also receive attention from the center staff and volunteers. Clients are assisted in finding jobs and volunteer placements. Health screening programs and a telephone reassurance program help to maintain the health of the elderly and keep them in contact with the center. A minibus is utilized to transport members to health care appointments. The center also provides breakfast to about 30 seniors and lunch to an average of 200 older adults at the center and to 75 in their homes.

Although this description of senior centers concentrates on concrete services, the center can also be seen as having an important role in maintaining the self-esteem and integration of the older person in the society (Gelfand & Gelfand, 1982). Intergenerational programing can help to break down age segregation, and membership in the center can help foster identity of the older person with an organization at a time when their organizational affiliations are diminishing.

The center can also provide an opportunity for older individuals to develop new roles that may have been stymied by the demands of their daily work patterns. Perhaps most important of all is the opportunity that the center gives to older persons to develop friendships. These friendships may result from the general socializing that older persons engage in at the center. Indeed, there are indications that it is this opportunity for socializing, rather than specific programs, that attracts many older people initially to senior centers (Gelfand, Bechill, & Chester, 1991; Ralston, 1987). These opportunities to socialize may, in turn, lead to the enlargement of the older person's support network. The new members of the network may become confidants. In some centers, "quasi-formal" support groups have developed among members who are friends and keep tabs on important events in each other's lives. When some negative event occurs such as the loss of a spouse or family member, they help by sending cards or visiting and gradually bringing the person back into center activities.

Senior centers can also provide support to family members, including members who are caregivers to older relatives. This support may only be educational in nature or it may take the form of groups that allow the caregivers to share feelings and problems. Viewing the center as not merely a service delivery operation but a facility that has the potential to meet some of the important emotional and social needs of the older person can make a major difference in the attitudes and programing of the staff.

FACILITIES

Because senior centers can present an image that encourages older persons' participation in center programing, the choice of a facility has always been a very important part of senior center development. The fact that under the old Title V of the OAA moneys were available only for the development of the center's physical plant underscores the importance of appropriate facilities:

> A senior center should be a place in the community which is attractive and makes older people feel that it is a place where they want to come. In addition, an attractive facility represents to the community that older people are valued by both the community and themselves. (U.S. Administration on Aging, 1977, p. VI-1)

In order to maximize opportunities for securing a wide range of clients, attempts are always made to locate a senior center in an area convenient to transportation. This location should also be in a neighborhood that is accessible to the target population of the center. Adequate parking facilities, outside activity spaces, and easy accessibility for the handicapped are also vital elements of the center's physical plan. The interior of the center should provide a variety of room sizes including private areas for counseling, a kitchen-dining area, and adequate space for staff and supplies.

A national study (Krout, 1990) indicates that three-quarters of senior centers are housed in separate facilities. Among centers that are combined with other types of settings, 33% are included as part of recreation/community centers, 20% are in multi-service agencies, 12% in churches, 7% in housing facilities/projects, and 6% in schools. An additional 20% are housed in a variety of settings.

With the rising costs of building, rehabilitating, and renovating facilities, it is anticipated that development of adequate facilities could continue to be a barrier to expanding the senior center programs. Fortunately, in many communities, unused schools have been changed to senior centers. The recycling of buildings that had related purposes can help keep down costs.

FUNDING

Funding mechanisms for senior centers reflect the importance of integrating the center into the community. There is rarely a single source of support for all the activities that a center may wish to inaugurate. Instead, funding from a variety of sources is utilized to cover different components of the center's activities. The auspices under which the center is operated may thus be a crucial determinant of the sources of funds a center is able to tap, since the perspective various resource groups have of the center's sponsor will affect their willingness to make funds available for the senior center program.

A number of federal funding sources are available to centers including:

1. Title III of the OAA, which authorizes funds for multipurpose senior center construction, operation, nutrition services, and special programing. Title IV authorizes training and research funds as well as model projects. Title V of the OAA can fund senior community service employment programs through senior centers.
2. Block grants from the Department of Housing and Community Development can be utilized for developing, improving, and coordinating senior center activities and facilities.
3. As determined by the locality, General Revenue Sharing funds could be allocated to senior centers.
4. The volunteer programs of ACTION can provide additional personnel resources for the senior center.
5. If deemed a priority, a state may allocate funds from the Social Services block grant.
6. Funds from the Higher Education Act can assist centers in developing funding for educational activities and for the training of center staff to implement a variety of learning projects.

In addition to federal funds, state and local funds are also available. Centers have been funded through legislative appropriations in many states, and several centers have been financed through a bond issue, either city or state supported. Civic and religious organizations often make contributions to senior centers. Because the center is visible, contributions by these groups not only provide needed resources to the centers but bring some visibility to the contributing organization. These groups can most easily donate labor, space, materials, and equipment for the center. Private philanthropists and nonprofit groups also are likely to make contributions; and United Way, as well as local private foundations, can be a source of annual support. Finally, the center itself can generate some income from either membership dues, fund raising projects, or the sale of center-generated products.

Most centers attempt to combine moneys from a variety of sources, with the primary source being Title III of the OAA. However, significant support has been made available by ACTION, the Department of Labor, state and county funds, state and local revenue sharing, in-kind contributions, United Fund, religious organizations, foundations, membership fees, civic groups, and project income. Because in-kind contributions account for a substantial amount of support, center budgets are difficult to estimate. Free space, volunteers, and service agency personnel are all important but hard to evaluate in dollar-and-cents terms.

The senior center has been seen by its advocates as the most likely candidate for the "focal point" of services outlined in the OAA. The centrality of the senior center as a service provider was underscored by its usage in the "channeling" demonstration to provide assessment and case management services for older persons.

In order to be effective as a focal point, however, the senior center needs to maintain its identity as a place where all older individuals come. Recent indications are that some older persons are beginning to view the senior center as a place exclusively for the frail elderly, but a majority of senior center directors questioned in Maryland (60%) stated that their participants begin to attend the center between the ages of 61 and 69 (Gelfand, Bechill, & Chester, 1989). Nationally, 41% of center participants are between the ages of 65 and 74, 37% between 75 and 84. Smaller percentages are over 85 (10%) or between 55 and 64 (11%). (Krout, 1990). Unless senior centers are effective in attracting the "young-old" as participants, the median ages of the participants will continue to rise. Senior centers thus need to avoid being characterized as facilities with programs that exclusively focus on the frail elderly. The ability to maintain a position, not only as a multiservice provider, but as a provider for all diverse groups of older persons, is a major challenge for senior centers.

REFERENCES

Cohen, M. (1972). *Senior centers: A focal point for delivery of services to older people*. Washington, DC: National Council on the Aging.

Fowler, T. (1974). *Alternatives to the single site center*. Washington, DC: National Council on the Aging.

Gelfand, D., Bechill, W., & Chester, R. (1989). *Maryland senior centers: Programs, services and linkages*. Baltimore: School of Social Work, Univ. of Maryland.

Gelfand, D., Bechill, W., & Chester, R. (1991). Core programs and services at senior centers. *Journal of Gerontological Social Work, 17*, 145–161.

Gelfand, D., & Gelfand, J. (1982). Senior centers and support networks. In D. Biegel & A. Naparstek (Eds.), *Community support systems and mental health*. New York: Springer Publishing Co.

Hanssen, A., Meima, N., Buckspan, L., Henderson, B., Helbig, T., & Zarit, S.

(1978). Correlates of senior center participation. *Gerontologist, 18,* 193–199.

Krout, J. (1987). Rural-urban differences in senior center activities and services. *Gerontologist, 27,* 92–97.

Krout, J. (1988). The frequency, duration and stability of senior center attendance. *Journal of Gerontological Social Work, 13,* 3–19.

Krout, J. (1990). *The organization, operation and programing of senior centers in America: A seven year follow-up.* Fredonia, NY: Final report to the AARP Andrus Foundation.

Krout, J., Cutler, S., & Coward, R. (1990). Correlates of senior center participation: A national analysis. *The Gerontologist, 30,* 72–79.

Leanse, J., & Wagner. (1975). *Senior centers: A report of senior group programs in America.* Washington, DC: National Council on the Aging.

Maxwell, J. (1962). *Centers for older people.* Washington, DC: National Council on the Aging.

National Institute of Senior Centers. (1979). Senior centers and the "at risk" older person. *Senior Center Report, 2*(5), 1, 2, 7–8.

Ralston, P. (1987). Senior center research: Policy from knowledge. In E. Borgatta & R. Montgomery, (Eds.), *Critical issues in aging policy: Linking research and values.* Newbury Park, CA: Sage Publications.

Ralston, P. (1989). *Senior centers and minority elders: A review.* Paper presented at the Annual meeting of the Gerontological Society of America, Minneapolis, MN: November.

Ralston, P., & Griggs, M. (1985). Factors affecting utilization of senior centers: Race, sex, and socioeconomic differences. *Journal of Gerontological Social Work, 9,* 99–111.

Taietz, P. (1976). Two conceptual models of the senior center. *Journal of Gerontology, 31,* 29–222.

U.S. Administration on Aging. (1977). *Program development handbook for state and area agencies on multipurpose senior centers.* Washington, DC: U.S. Government Printing Office.

12

Housing

HOUSING CONDITIONS OF THE ELDERLY

Housing is a crucial aspect of the social environment. The type and quality of housing available to an older person has an impact on their general level of satisfaction, as well as on their ability to live in the community. Retired older persons also spend more time in their homes than younger, working individuals. A 1989 national survey found that 87% of older respondents want to remain in their own homes, even though two-thirds of them anticipate needing help with the maintenance of the outside of their house. Over half of the respondents also think they would need help in the future with heavy housework. Although 13% of these older people would like to move, a larger percentage (22%) saw a move as a future likelihood (American Association of Retired Persons, 1990).

Households headed by elders live in somewhat more modest dwellings, both in terms of size and quality, than American households at large. Elderly couples have the highest-income households, followed by older individuals living alone. The poorest is the multiperson household headed by a person 65 and over. Among the 17 million households headed by older persons, 75% owned their own homes (Newman, 1986). Although 80% of these homeowners have paid off their mortgages, many elderly find it difficult to maintain their homes. This is particularly true in rural areas. Data on housing conditions among older rural homeowners indicate that only 29% of farm homes and 46% of nonfarm homes had no deficiencies (Lee, 1986).

Economically, the elderly tend to pay more for housing than do younger age groups; 38% of all elderly-headed households spend more than 35% of their income on housing. However, within this group, 43% of single individuals and 50% of renters pay over 30% of their income for housing. Rural elderly households spend substantially less on housing, and husband-wife households have the lowest economic burdens for shelter. Unfortunately, low-income older adults comprise the largest proportion of elderly spending more than they should on housing: over 55% of low-income households spend over 35% of their income on housing (Newcomer & Weeden, 1986).

The diversity of needs and resources among older people has begun to produce diverse forms of housing. Many older persons are living in rental or owned units where they have lived for many years. Other older individuals with limited incomes have taken advantage of the subsidized housing made available through the Department of Housing and Urban Development or local state agencies. More affluent elderly have increasingly shown interest in retirement communities with specific age limits for residents or new continuing care ("life care") communities. In this chapter, the major specific housing services available to the elderly—those which are both publicly and privately sponsored—will be discussed.

History

The concept of federally supported housing began in the 1930s with the National Housing Act of 1934 and the United States Housing Act of 1937. The 1934 act inaugurated the first home mortgage program—a restructuring of the private home financing system—under the Federal Housing Administration (FHA). Under the 1937 act, the government offered subsidized housing to low-income families. Although the primary purpose of this latter legislation was to clear slums and increase employment, new housing resulted.

Under the Housing Act of 1949, the national goal of "a decent home and suitable living environment for every American Family" was first stated. The act also included programs for urban renewal, increased funds for subsidized housing, and new programs for rural housing. During the 1950s, housing programs were more directed toward rehabilitation, relocation, and renewal.

Section 202 began under the Housing Act of 1959. The program provided low-cost loans to developers of private housing. It was the forerunner of later mortgage subsidy programs. In the Housing Act of 1961, below-market interest rate mortgages were begun to assist rental housing for moderate-income families through section 221(d)(3). In 1965, two rent subsidy programs were begun. In one program, residents would pay 25% of their income in privately owned housing units built with FHA financing. Under the Section 23 leasing program, the government would lease regular units for low-income families.

In 1968, Congress found that "the supply of the nation's housing was not increasing rapidly enough to meet the national goal of 1949" (U.S. Department of Housing and Urban Development, 1973). Congress then established a production schedule of 26 million housing units—6 million of these to be for low- and moderate-income families over the next 10 years. One of the programs of this act was Section 236—a program that provides a subsidy formula for rental housing. In 1969, the Brooke Amendment was passed, which limited the amount of rent that could be charged by local housing authorities to 25% of adjusted tenant income.

In September 1973, President Nixon halted all housing programs, except the low-rent public-leasing program, in order that a thorough review could be accomplished of what was then viewed as a spendthrift and inadequate program (U.S. Department of Housing and Urban Development, 1973). Following a study, during which no new federally subsidized housing starts were approved, the Housing and Community Development Act was signed into law in August 1974. The act removed the suspension that had been placed on construction and required contracts annually of at least $150 million to help finance development or acquisition costs of low-income housing projects. Because most of the money was to be channeled through the new Section 8 program, which was authorized under this act, funding was slow to begin. Administratively, at least two years elapsed before the Section 8 program was fully operational (U.S. Senate, 1975).

Public Housing

Although a term often assumed to relate to all forms of subsidized housing, "public housing" was the earliest means of providing adequate housing for low-income elderly. Public housing was established under the Housing Act of 1937. Funds for these complexes are appropriated by the Department of Housing and Urban Development (HUD). The 480,000 units now in existence are managed by local housing authorities who maintain the buildings and ensure that low-cost rentals are available to poor families. Rentals are set at 30% of the family's income. In addition HUD provides funds for maintenance of the buildings while other agencies may provide staff for special programs for older persons.

It is often difficult for older persons to live in public housing units, since many local housing authorities require that older residents who need supportive services arrange to have these needs met if they are to remain in the complex. A small percentage (10%) do not allow older persons who are not independent to live in the public housing complex.

Currently 40% of public housing units are occupied by older people and many of these tenants have "aged in place." In recognition of the needs of this population, the National Affordable Housing Act of 1990 allows local housing authorities to charge HUD for the inception of "service coordinators" positions and for 15% of the cost of services to older tenants. These services may include meals, chore services, transportation, personal care, and health-related services. Approximately half of all public housing units are over 20 years old. The federal budget for FY 1992 provided enough money to build 7,500 public housing units. In recent years the Federal emphasis in the field of housing has shifted to other programs such as Section 8 and Section 202.

The Section 8 Existing Housing Program

Authorized under the Housing and Community Development Act of 1974, this program filled the void of the 1973 moratorium. It provides no direct funding to the developer but instead pays monthly rent so that housing can be developed on the private market. As of 1992, of the 2 million units completed, 50% were occupied by older persons (Retsinas & Retsinas, 1992).

Section 8, or subsidized rent, is the rent for a unit in a development which is receiving federally subsidized Section 8 housing assistance payments. The Section 8 rent differs from the market rent in that it depends strictly on the amount of income of the tenant. Tenants pay 30% of their adjusted income for rent, with the Section 8 housing assistance payment making up the difference between tenant-paid rent and the full market rent. Tenants are now allowed to pay more than 30% of their income for rent if the public housing authority agrees that the rent is reasonable for both the unit and the family (U.S. Senate, 1991). The tenant could pay as little as $40 or $50 per month or nearly as high as the market rents, depending on the monthly adjusted income. Rents under Section 8 cannot exceed the fair market rent for the area as established by HUD. Rents are reviewed annually, and the tenants must move if 30% of their adjusted income meets the fair market rent for that particular housing project. Fair market rents are reviewed annually and take into account construction costs and maintenance fees for individual locations. In order to qualify for Section 8 subsidies, the income of a family of four could not be above 80% of median income in their area of residence. Congressional action between 1981 and 1984 reduced Section 8 eligibility to 50% of median income, thus making many families ineligible for Section 8 subsidies.

Projects with Section 8 rental units are owned by private parties, profit and nonprofit, and by public housing agencies. Under Section 8, HUD has made 15- or 20-year contracts with private parties for the rental units unless the project is owned by or financed with a loan or loan guarantee from a state or local housing agency, in which case HUD will guarantee the rental units for 40 years. Efforts have been made to increase the private guarantee time of 20 years because, in some situations, it is a disincentive for private parties to become involved in the program. Any type of financing may be used for the purchase or rehabilitation of a project which houses Section 8 rental units, including HUD-FHA mortgage insurance programs, conventional financing, or tax-exempt bonds.

Under Section 8, the owner handles the whole program and is responsible for leasing at least 30% of the subsidized units to very low income families (families whose income is 50% or less of local median income). Under the Section 8 legislation, priority is given to projects with 20% of their units in Section 8 only to guarantee an income mix in the housing project. However, if the rental units are to be used for the elderly, there is no restriction on the number of Section 8 rental units per project.

The purpose of the Section 8 program is to develop rental housing for medium- and low-income families within the structure of the private housing market. Section 8 units can exist in houses, small apartment buildings, or any other location that has units to rent. Suburban, rural, and urban areas are equally eligible. However, HUD determines how many Section 8 rental units can be awarded to a given area in each state. Usually, applications far exceed the units available for the specific areas in question.

The Section 8 housing program had a slow beginning after it was authorized in 1974. In 1975, there were 200,000 applications, but only 30 new units actually materialized (U.S. House of Representatives, 1976). The cumbersome application and administrative procedures were blamed for the delay. In addition, because it was an entirely new program involving low-income families, the private financial community—the group that had to generate the construction moneys—did not appear ready to fund the building of units which would house Section 8 families until the program had grown to become one of the key housing programs for the elderly. Section 8 covers only the actual rental units but is most successful when combined with other housing construction and service programs.

Concerns about cost appeared to create questions about the development of any large number of Section 8 units in the 1980s. By 1989, 46% of Section 8 housing was occupied by older persons. Between 1981 and 1987, funding for housing assistance dropped 67%. Section 8 rent subsidies are now available only for existing housing. Subsidies for new housing were eliminated in the Housing Act of 1983.

As a possible alternative to the Section 8 Existing Housing Program, the Reagan administration instituted housing vouchers. These vouchers allow individuals to find their own housing in the private sector. Funds for 33,000 certificates were appropriated in FY 1991. In the Voucher Program the tenant also contributes 30% of his or her income to the rent. A Payment Standard based on fair market rents is determined for the local area. If the rent of the tenant's unit is less than the Payment Standard, the tenant's contribution is reduced by the difference. If the rent exceeds this Payment Standard, the tenant must make up the difference. There are no limits in the rent the tenant can pay under the Housing Voucher program (Leger & Kennedy, 1990). Housing vouchers have been authorized for only 5 years. By FY 1989, approximately 229,000 vouchers had been "reserved."

An evaluation of the experiences of a large number of enrollees indicates that the housing voucher program has been successful (Leger & Kennedy, 1990). Questions have been raised from the onset of the program as to whether enrolles will be able to find housing they can afford and landlords who will accept the vouchers. In areas with tight housing markets these two factors could pose a major hurdle. The average success rate for finding housing was 65%. There were, however, three areas with lower success rates and one area where the success rate was only 33%. The reasons for these differences could not be clarified. Overall, Housing Voucher recipients were slightly more successful in obtaining qualifying housing than recipients in the Existing Housing Certificate programs.

Over one-third of the recipients were able to stay in their existing apartments while obtaining vouchers. Housing Voucher recipients who moved paid rents that were 6.7% higher than recipients in the Certificate program. This difference may, in part, reflect "higher prices for higher quality units" (Leger & Kennedy, 1990, p. xii). Older persons had better success rates than younger age cohorts and single person older households had the highest success rate of any group. The success rate of older persons in the voucher program was somewhat higher than in the certificate program. There was a significant reduction in rent burden of elderly in the voucher program. The elderly were the only population group for which a significant difference was found.

The Section 202 Program

Authorized under the Housing Act of 1959, Section 202 provides federal loans at a maximum of 8.38% interest (in 1990) directly to nonprofit sponsors. Rental housing can be provided for the elderly through new construction or rehabilitation of existing structures. The loans are repayable over a 40-year period. The property should include needed support services and can have such rooms as dining halls, community rooms, infirmaries, and other essential services. Many of the non-profit homes for the aged, such as Cathedral Residences in Jacksonville, Florida—a large housing complex which serves over 700 elderly—were partially constructed with money under Section 202.

The Section 202 program was very successful throughout the 1960s but was phased out after that time in preference to Section 236, another federal loan program. However, Section 236 was frozen in 1973 when all federal housing programs were halted to allow for review. Section 202 was reinstated as part of the Housing and Community Development Act of 1974, but it did not return to full activity until the summer of 1975. Under the 1974 act, a $215 million borrowing level was approved for FY 1975, but it was not used until the following year. Regulations in 1976 reaffirmed the importance of the program in providing both construction and long-term financing for housing projects. By 1980, 734 projects had been approved and 247, containing 262,000 units, actually constructed (U.S. Senate, 1981). Funding for Section 202 programs has been markedly reduced during the 1980s. In the budget for FY 1987, funds for only 12,000 units of Section 202 housing were included.

As of FY 1990 it was estimated that 54,000 projects were waiting to be built. Many of these were stalled because of problems in financing created by the regulations in the housing program related to financing and cost containment. Efforts were made in 1990 to reduce this backlog. In contrast to the 1970s, when more than 20,000 units were built each year, only 8,000 units of Section 202 housing were constructed in FY 1990. Because of this limited funding, waiting lists for these units have become common in many communities. On average there are six 202 housing units available for every 1,000 elderly (U.S. Senate, 1991).

Private nonprofit corporations and consumer cooperatives are eligible for Section 202 financing. Loans can carry the average market yield plus 1% during construction and .5% thereafter for administration and program losses. Housing developments under Section 202 cannot exceed 300 units. Section 8 participation is required, and approval of Section 202 loans is based on the feasibility of getting Section 8 financing. In other words, if the number of Section 8 units for a section of the state have already been obligated, Section 202 construction financing cannot be granted.

Section 202/8 allocations are made in accordance with Section 213, a fair share needs formula. The formula, which determines the number of eligible units for a given geographic area, is based on the following criteria:

1. The number of households with the head or spouse age 62 or older
2. The number of such households which lack one or more plumbing facilities
3. The number of such households with incomes less than the regionally adjusted poverty level
4. The prototype production costs for public housing units as adjusted by average cost factors within the loan region

The 1974 Housing Act also specified that 20–25% of funds for Section 202 housing must be awarded in rural areas. The residents of the housing must also reflect the racial population of the community. This provision was meant to ensure that minority elderly obtained housing. The projects are required to either have an adequate range of necessary services or to facilitate the access of residents to social services. The application process for Section 202/8 housing is extensive and consists of five stages. It usually takes three to five years from the time of idea to actual implementation, and approval is given only to those developers with a proven track record.

Although Section 202 projects continue to be built, the size of these projects has dropped substantially from 153 units in projects built and occupied before 1975 to 47 units in projects awarded in 1988. Some of this reduction in size is related to the growth of 202 projects outside of central cities: 22% of the projects occupied after 1984 were built in areas with less than 10,000 residents, a figure that is in stark contrast to the 2.2% of the projects occupied before 1975. As in previous years the largest proportion of projects are sponsored by religious groups (50%).

Over the years the residents of Section 202 housing reflect changes in the aging population. The average age of residents rose from 72 years in 1983 to 75 years in 1988. There was a 4 to 1 ratio between women and men and 20% of the residents were from minority backgrounds. The managers of the projects reported an increased proportion of residents they would regard as frail. The highest percentage of the frail residents were in older projects, a reflection of these residents growing older in the 202 housing (U.S. House of Representatives, 1989).

Other Federal Housing Initiatives

Section 231 insures lenders against losses on mortgages for construction or rehabilitation of unsubsidized housing for the elderly. This program is available to both profit and non-profit developers. By FY 1989, 67,000 units of housing for older persons were insured under this program. Although not specifically targeted for the elderly, Section 221(d)(3) and (4) play a larger role at present in insuring multi-family housing for the elderly. These two sections permit the inclusion of congregate programs in the developments they insure. One of the innovations of 221(d)(4) was Retirement Service Centers, which provide rentals at the market rate for older persons but also include congregate meals, housekeeping, and laundry services. Although the program had completed 128 projects providing almost 19,000 units by 1990, it was suspended by the Department of Housing and Urban Development. The decision to suspend this program was based on a default rate in excess of 35%.

Section 223(f) provides mortgage insurance for existing multifamily housing units for the elderly where the repair needs are not extensive; this program is available in connection with refinancing or purchase of a project (United States Senate, 1990). Section 236 authorizes interest-reduction payments on behalf of owners of rental housing projects designed for occupancy by lower income families for the purpose of reducing rentals for such tenants. In recent years units built through 221(d)(3) and 236 financing have become unavailable to low-income tenants as landlords have prepaid their mortgages and raised the rents. The 1990 National Affordable Housing Act allowed landlords to sell the property. If a nonprofit group interested in purchasing the property cannot be found, the property can be sold. Older or disabled tenants, however, must be given three years to find another apartment. The displaced tenants will be given vouchers to subsidize their housing and the former landlord will pay 50% of the moving costs (Retsinas and Retsinas, 1992).

The 1990 Housing Act also contains two important new initiatives. The HOME Investment Partnership provides block grants to localities with the expectation that most of these funds will be used to renovate existing homes. The Home Ownership and Opportunity for People Everywhere (HOPE) reflects national support for an idea that originated with a public housing complex in Washington, DC. HOPE provides funds that allow public housing tenants who would not receive mortgages from banks to purchase their units. The implementation of all these programs will be dependent on the state of the federal budget during the 1990s. The HOME initiative is expected to make up for the termination of the Rental Rehabilitation program in 1992. This program financed the rehabilitation of 188,000 rental units, 12% of which were occupied by older persons.

State and Local Housing Programs

State and local housing agencies have become an important source of financing for the actual building or rehabilitation of housing units. These agencies provide mortgage money directly to developers through sale of notes and bonds. Construction financing may be provided through the sale of notes, and permanent loan funds are provided through the sale of long term bonds. The bonds sell at an interest rate of 1–2% below that of conventional sources of real estate financing, allowing housing agencies to pass on the savings on the notes and bonds to developers in the form of lower interest rates, which result in lower rents and mortgage carrying charges for market rate tenants and home buyers.

The purpose of the housing agency programs is to attract private developers to the low- and moderate-income housing field with the aim of providing housing for a broad range of income levels. The programs usually place a limit on equity return to developers.

Services

The various HUD programs and state housing agencies support housing that ranges from public ownership and complete public financing to private financing, building, and renting, with federal insurance on the mortgage only. The upper-income limits allowed vary by program, with the most stringent limits being placed on the direct public housing (up to $9,000) and the least stringent limits on the mortgage insurance only program (up to $19,000).

As indicated earlier, nonprofit developers are free to design as much additional space as they wish and are encouraged to add supportive services to the housing units financed under Section 202. However, because of the income limitations placed on those living in federally financed housing, the developer has to keep the rents within the fair market rates and within the rates that the limited-income residents can pay. This, in turn, places limits on the amount of additional support services which can be provided. For example, a high-rise for the elderly in Baltimore, financed under Section 202/8, has the entire top floor overlooking the city as a carpeted and draped multipurpose room. The cost of building as well as maintaining this large, well-equipped, and well-used room must be absorbed in the rental fees allowed for each individual apartment. With the rental ceilings being determined by the government, the room can be only marginally maintained.

Amenities built into the housing programs depend on finances available and on the cost of these amenities in relation to the cost of the overall building. The support from the community in maintaining additional housing facilities and regional preferences will also be determinants of a final design package. The potential resources that can be included in elderly housing are extensive, ranging from transportation, nutrition, and health screening programs to craft rooms, groceries, and even small restaurants.

Elderly housing projects can thus be part of the larger service delivery system of the community. Because federal housing funds are limited, services run under outside auspices may need to be incorporated into the housing units. Two excellent examples of a housing complex with integrated services are Worly Terrace, Columbus, and Glendale Terrace, Toledo, Ohio. Geared to the elderly who are returning from mental hospitals and to low-income community residents—many of whom were losing their homes through urban renewal—these housing developments operate a unique series of integrated financing and service systems. While HUD paid for the basic construction of the units, the state of Ohio paid for the rooms not eligible under federal regulations (in this case, dining room, community building, clinic, and craft room); and the local housing authorities manage the completed housing units. Worly Terrace is located near public transportation, shops, and several churches. The complex has a six-story high-rise building with 106 living units, four one-story buildings with 120 units, and a centrally located community building. There are furnished and unfurnished quarters for as many as 270 residents, with apartments for single persons, couples, or two unrelated single persons to share an apartment. Available services include hot meals; beauty and barber services; preventive health services including health screening, services of a full-time registered nurse and licensed practical nurse, part-time physician, and podiatrist; social activities; and recreation (U.S. House of Representatives, 1976).

The services available in publicly financed or insured housing depend on the developer, the sponsor, the interest of the residents, and the community resources available. Early planning and community support for the project enhances the chances for adequate support services.

Beginning in 1988, the Robert Wood Johnson Foundation and the Administration on Aging conducted a series of demonstration grants to ten state housing finance agencies. Using these funds, supportive services (primarily non-medical in nature) were developed for older residents living in housing financed by these agencies. Title IV of the 1992 OAA authorizes demonstration programs for services in federally assisted housing. State Units on Aging and AAAs are eligible for these grants. Title III also mandates a leadership role for Area Agencies on Aging in coordinated development and provision of supportive services for older persons in non-profit housing.

Home Repair and Renovation

Many older homeowners find it necessary to seek alternative housing because of their inability to carry out the maintenance necessary to keep their home in good condition. They also may lack the funds to hire contractors to perform necessary repairs. As homeowners quickly learn, minor repairs that are delayed for a substantial period of time can easily become major costly repairs. In 1975, a report prepared by the state of Michigan commented:

> Many seniors reside in structures which are in desperate need of repair. Often a senior will relocate to a new structure when repair to his former living unit would have been more cost-efficient to the government. (Charter Township of Meridian, 1975, p. 4)

The Michigan investigators found that 40% of the single-family homes owned by the elderly in the state needed minor or major repairs.

Home repair programs aimed primarily at low-income elderly have now been organized around the country. Many of these programs have dual purposes: (1) bringing substandard homes up to local code levels and (2) providing supplemental income by hiring older persons to work on these projects. In Meridian Township, Michigan, $42,000 was spent repairing 26 homes between 1975 and 1977. Much of the work on these homes was done by workers over 55 who were paid $4–5 per hour for part-time labor. In the Virgin Islands, homemakers refer clients to the home repair program. Repairs were carried out by a variety of individuals including CETA workers (King, 1976). On the Navajo reservation, efforts to upgrade the housing of the elderly have been cooperatively undertaken, with younger workers contributing their time.

In Evansville, Indiana, a major repair program for elderly residents was carried out in a number of neighborhoods. As in other geographic areas, the repair efforts were concentrated on functional aspects of the home including wiring, vermin control, replacement of broken window panes, and new plastering. The hope of the project coordinators was that instituting the repair program would produce a ripple effect which would encourage the elderly to continue making their own repairs and also encourage other neighborhood residents to undertake long-needed repairs. One of the reasons this ripple did not occur was because a majority of the elderly did not even tell their neighbors about the program. This silence was attributable to their ambivalent feelings about accepting aid. In order for the program to be more visible within the community, the evaluators argued that the repairs would have to be undertaken on a continuous basis rather than bringing repairmen into the individual home for an intensive but brief period of time (Abshier, Davis, Jans, & Petranek, 1977).

Home repairs that are to be anything more than cosmetic are also costly. In Michigan, the Meridian Township program spent $6,500 per house to bring these homes up to code standards. As labor costs continue to increase, we can expect that this figure will be appropriate to similar efforts around the country, although volunteer labor can reduce costs significantly. In one community, a neighborhood corporation provides regular home repair and renovation services for over 2,000 enrollees (McCleary, 1986). Older individuals comprise 60% of the households receiving Community Development Block Grant (CDBG) funds for home repairs (Weeden, Newcomer, & Byerts, 1986). In 1990 the Section 312 Rehabilitation Loan Program made loans for rehabilitation available to 1,250 individuals for important repairs to their homes. Among these loan recipients, approximately 22% were over 60 years old. Funding for these home repair programs can also be developed from a variety of possible sources including Title III of the OAA, the Social Services block grant, or local appropriations. In rural areas, low-interest home repair loans are available through the Farmers Home Administration Section 504 Program. Under the Department of Energy Weatherization Assistance Program, low-income elderly can also apply for funding to help them purchase energy-saving aids such as storm windows or insulation.

Congregate and Assisted Housing

Housing for the elderly should respond to the wide variation in the needs of older persons. The growth in the interest and availability of assisted or congregate housing is a response to the need for housing among those elderly who cannot continue to maintain full independent living and yet are not in need of some form of full-service institutional setting. The increase in need for this type of housing is related, at least in part, to increased average longevity, a phenomenon in which a greater proportion of the total population is over 75 years of age and has conditions that require some forms of care in addition to basic housing needs.

In addition, there is a commonly occurring pattern in housing for the elderly, federally assisted as well as private. That is, service needs increase as the tenant ages. Tenants who entered the housing program as healthy, independent persons find they need additional service supports with advancing age. New, unanticipated services are then required. Congregate housing is a housing environment which provides enough services to enable many impaired elderly to remain in a community-based residential situation. Lawton (1976) focuses more precisely on the services that might be available in such a congregate housing situation:

> Congregate refers to housing that offers a minimum service package that includes some on-site meals served in a common dining room, plus one or more of such services as on-site medical/nursing services, personal care, or housekeeping. (p. 239)

In contrast, assisted or "sheltered" housing as operated in many states offers a more extensive package of services with an emphasis on meals and personal care. Some states are instituting subsidized assisted housing in single-family homes. Assisted housing helps with personal needs but is not a care facility. The individual residents remain responsible for their own care with support services available as needed. Assisted housing does not have ongoing health services.

The growth in congregate housing has come long after the availability of both independent-living housing situations and institutional settings. Congregate housing was authorized in 1970 in the congregate housing provision of the Housing and Urban Development Act. By 1990, almost $50 million had been appropriated for congregate services. These funds supported services for approximately 1,900 residents living in 60 projects. Between 5 and 6 million dollars has been awarded in each recent fiscal year to support the congregate program.

Given the increasingly older population of the 202 units, it is not surprising that 28% of the projects are providing either congregate meals or housekeeping services for residents. More extensive services will also be required in Section 202 housing for residents. Under the 1990 National Affordable Housing Act, a meal that meets daily nutritional requirements will be required. In addition, other services such as housekeeping, transportation, personal care, and chore services that meet the needs of the residents of the complex must be offered (Older Americans Report, 1990a). As part of this increased emphasis on maintaining older persons in their community, a 5-year demonstration project was approved to combine Section 8 certificates and housing vouchers with supportive services such as meals, housekeeping, transportation, personal care, and health services. This demonstration is limited to 1,500 certificates and vouchers.

The idea of locating extensive services in 202 housing is not new. Projects in some communities include a variety of services operated and financed by state or local agencies. Operating funds can now be used to hire service coordinators. In Section 202 projects with Congregate Housing Services Programs, the salary for the services coordinator must be taken from operating funds rather than the congregate service budget. The service coordinator provides referrals, supports, and linkages for tenants with needs (Older Americans Report, 1990b). HUD allows service coordinators in certain elderly housing projects.

Despite the need for congregate services in many housing facilities, caution has been recommended in their development. As Lawton (1976) points out,

> Maintenance of independent function is facilitated by an environment that demands active behavior from its inhabitants, and conversely, the presence of too easily accessible services will erode independence among those who are still relatively competent. (p. 240)

Whatever the validity of this belief, providing additional services does require additional money which cannot be fully recouped from fees charged the residents. Further, the provision of additional services could possibly duplicate other community resources available.

Foster Care

For many years, the concept of foster care has been familiar to those who work with children, but the service has been made available to the elderly only since the early 1970s. However, even 10 years later, the foster care program is not as readily available a resource as it should be.

Foster care focuses on a population that cannot sustain full independence. It thus attempts to prolong independence and delay institutionalization. Foster care is a specialized form of sheltered housing whereby the client is placed in a new setting which has family supports. Foster care "is for persons in need of care and protection in a substitute family setting for a planned period of time" (Newman & Sherman, 1977, p. 436). Its uniqueness lies in its family setting and its size. In most foster care programs, the number of older persons per family unit is not more than four.

Foster care programs are generally administered by local departments of social services and have relied heavily on Title XX funds for operation. Strict income limitations were attached to the Title XX funding, which made moderate- or high-income elderly ineligible for foster care through Title XX funding. Although more limited, moneys are also available through state departments of health or mental health and through the Veterans Administration. More liberal income policies are in effect when funds from these sources are being used. In some programs, the foster family is paid a percentage of the SSI check directly by the recipient of the foster care. In these cases, the foster family does not always break even on the costs.

Eligible homes are usually solicited through appeals to the general public. After eligibility is determined, the family is paid a fee, plus certain expenses, for the care of the older person in foster care. According to a study of the New York Foster Homes program, 93% of the caretakers—those providing the foster home care—were female, and only 58% of them were married (Newman & Sherman, 1977). Less than one-third of the home situations provided the participants with involvement in family that included a husband, wife, and at least one child. In Baltimore, the majority of caretakers were women age 55 and over, black, on pensions, living alone, who had held service-oriented positions (personal data, 1978).

One of the limitations to expanding the foster care program is in the recruitment of families. In some cases, the demand is double the number of homes available. Most recruitment comes from friends and families who have had experience as caretakers (Newman & Sherman, 1977).

One-fourth of the New York state participants in foster care programs were between 60 and 65 years old; 75% were women. Of the foster care residents, 33% had never been married, but 50% were widowed and 5% were divorced. Most of the foster home residents who had worked had held unskilled or semiskilled positions (Newman & Sherman, 1977).

Three-fourths of the caretakers said they included the resident in their family activities and felt she or he was a member of the family. Three-fourths of the residents took walks or in other ways interacted in the neighborhoods where they lived, while two-thirds participated in community activities. As noted in the report, the sense of family is created even when the caretaker is the only member other than the residents. Being a caretaker can provide meaningful roles to older people as well as provide family situations for those who need some type of sheltered care.

Foster care has been found to be especially effective for older discharged mental patients. The largest foster care program in the United States is run by the Veterans Administration. In a study of foster residences operated by five VA hospitals (Linn & Caffey, 1977), both younger and older patients were found to have improved after placement in foster care residences. Despite evidence that well-operated foster care is effective for older mental patients, it remains an "appropriate and underutilized resource" (p. 345).

An important test of the utility of foster care for individuals who would otherwise be placed in nursing homes has been conducted in Massachusetts and in Maryland since 1978. In this program, individuals being discharged from the hospital are assigned randomly either to foster care homes or to nursing home care in order to assess the relative social and cost effectiveness of these two service modalities. Caretakers are paid $350–$500 per month. The cost of the Community Care program has been 32% below that of nursing home care.

The participants in the program showed better or improved functioning on the Activities of Daily Living and better mental status scores than controls in nursing homes. The Community Care program participants also were more likely to achieve the nursing goals set for them. In contrast, nursing home residents were more involved in a variety of social activities and had higher life satisfaction scores at the end of one year (Oktay & Volland, 1987). A state-run foster care program in Massachusetts, Adult Family Care, matches older people with families in communities. As part of this effort, a Massachusetts Council for Adult Foster Care has been organized. As Oktay and Volland (1981) note, foster care cannot be used for all patients, some of whom are too hostile, demanding, or ill to be placed with a non-family caregiver. In some cases, patients or their families resist the idea of foster home care either because it is new or the family feels that the care provided cannot be intensive enough to meet their relative's needs. Given the findings on social activities, it is also important to consider whether foster care results in social isolation of older persons in communities where social activities and transportation are not adequate.

Board and Care and Domiciliaries

Board and care homes are widely available but there has been little information available about these facilities. Because there are no national regulations governing this level of care, each state has adopted its own terminology and regulations which govern the type of care given. Probably the best definition for this general level of care is contained in the Colorado regulations:

> An establishment operated and maintained to provide residential accommodation, personal services and social care to individuals who are not related to the licensee, and who, because of impaired capacity for self-care, elect or require protective living accommodations but who do not have an illness, injury, or disability for which regular medical care and 24-hour nursing services are required. (Glasscote, et al., 1976, p. 58)

In summary, this level of care is primarily personal and custodial. Usually regulations for board and care homes require that:

* Local and fire safety codes be met
* There be a full-time administrator responsible for the supervision of staff, residents, and safety
* Nursing personnel be on call most of the time
* There be facilities for occasional distribution of medication

Residents are usually required to arrange for their own medical care and, in many instances, provide for their own social activities. In effect this level of care provides a protected environment, meals, and some personal care services but does not restrict or organize the activities of the residents. Many low-income board-and-care residents are able to pay for care through their SSI checks. In some states, board-and-care homes are licensed by the local Department of Social Services. It is believed, however, that the number of unlicensed board-and-care homes is far greater than the number of licensed homes.

A study of board-and-care homes in Cleveland provides important information about the characteristics of these homes (Eckert, Lyon, & Namazi, forthcoming). Most of the 177 homes studied were private residences. The owners and operators were middle-aged or older women, two-thirds of whom had previously worked in a health care setting as aides or nurses. Residents were charged an average of $450 per month for their care, which included at least three meals a day, laundry service, and round-the-clock supervision. The residents of the homes had an average age of 77 and were predominantly female. The proportion of black residents (15%) was higher than the representation of this group in the American population and 16% of the residents had never married. The residents expressed positive feelings about the homes. The researchers warn against "overzealous" action that would regulate these types of living environments and reduce their ability to meet the needs of physically impaired and economically limited elderly. Reports to Congress about overmedication of board-and-care residents by untrained caregivers has prompted calls for further investigation of the quality of board-and-care homes. Title II of the 1992 Older Americans Act requires AoA, in cooperation with the National Academy of Sciences, to commission a study of the quality and safety of board-and-care homes.

Domiciliaries and homes for the aged are primarily non-profit and often church-sponsored homes that provide personal care but require that persons entering be healthy. These homes go well beyond the standards which are set by the various states in that they usually provide comprehensive activities, social services, and personal care programs. Many of the residents have private rooms, and rarely are there more than two people in each room. Residents can select activities that are offered and are free to come and go from the facility as desired. These facilities can be small, often accommodating as few as 50 residents, and in some cases large enough to accommodate as many as 300. Attached to many of these homes for the aged are intermediate care or skilled care nursing units to provide appropriate medical treatment for those who need such care. Depending on the size of the facility, the home will either be able to continue to care for a resident that needs medical care on a regular basis or will transfer that person to a regular skilled or intermediate care facility.

Single-Room Occupancy Hotels

Housing situations that are often neglected in discussions of this topic are single-room occupancies (SROs). SRO housing is primarily cheap hotels and rooming houses located in commercial areas adjacent to the downtown business district and operated through the private market. There is no licensing of SRO housing beyond the local fire and safety codes imposed by individual local jurisdictions.

Many of those living in SRO hotels do so by choice:

The avoidance of intimacy and the routinization of suspicion that are endemic features of the SRO can be seen to be compatible with the voluntary
self-isolation of these elderly residents. They are life-long isolates and for
them, the SRO is a familiar environment. (Stephens, 1975, p. 231)

Residents of SROs are likely to show long histories of being independent, self-reliant, and socially isolated. They are more likely to have histories of time spent in mental hospitals, jails, and prisons and in unskilled work situations (Erikson & Eckert, 1977; Stephens, 1975).
Importantly, residents have usually avoided any dependency on government income programs but instead show a work history, even though it is
likely to be unstable.

Most residents of SROs remain isolated from each other, only talking
in the public spaces and conducting conversations that are primarily su-
perficial in nature. Deep friendships almost never emerge. However, as
pointed out by Stephens, this pattern is a continuation of a lifetime pattern, rather than a change with age. The SRO provides an opportunity to
continue the isolated pattern within a framework of affordability, and
for many who live in such situations, it is a conscious choice. The most
effective supports to these people are from the hotel staffs and nearby
shopkeepers (Erikson & Eckert, 1977). It is important to formalize and
strengthen these already existing informal support systems as well as to
bring in nonprofessional outreach workers to help the residents connect
with more formal service systems. However, the choice of isolation that
this living style affords can preclude successful response to available programs and services.

Retirement Communities

One of the more recent phenomena developing as a result of the large
number of people who are retiring, particularly with good retirement incomes, is the retirement community. Retirement communities can range
from small mobile home subdivisions to sizable communities like
Youngstown and Sun City, Arizona. The latter had, in 1969, an estimated population of 37,000 (Anderson & Anderson, 1978). The communities can include apartments, semidetached houses, and units that can
be purchased or rented. Beyond the living units themselves, varying
forms of recreation and supportive services can be offered. The country's first development for senior citizens—Youngstown, Arizona—was
founded in 1954 and incorporated as a retirement community in 1960.
Currently, it has $2 million in recreation facilities alone; nearby Sun City
has $12 million in recreation facilities.

Most retirement communities have age requirements as the key entrance requirement. In Sun Lakes, Arizona, only people over age 40 can purchase property, and no one under age 19 can be a permanent resident. The age limit for buying a home in Sun City is 50, and children of residents must be at least 18 years of age. Residents of any of the Rossmoor Leisure Worlds must be at least 52 years old, and the same age requirement holds for five retirement communities in New Jersey (Heintz, 1976).

"Retirement communities are planned, low-density, age restricted developments constructed by private funds and offering extensive recreational services and relatively low cost housing for purchase" (Heintz, 1976). The general characteristics of retirement communities include entrance requirements, complete community planning, and relatively low-cost housing coupled with high levels of amenity. The concept of low-cost housing, however, is not universal in retirement communities. The two bedroom homes in retirement communities in southern New Jersey averaged around $60,000 in price in 1990 with a $150 monthly maintenance fee paid to the cooperative association.

In a study of five retirement communities in New Jersey, Heintz identified characteristics of people who elected to join such communities. She found that residents were primarily Caucasian, retired, and semiaffluent, between 65 and 74 years old. Families in retirement communities had the same household size as the national average, but there were more male-headed households (82.3%). The retirement community population was better educated and more likely to have worked in a high-status or highly skilled occupation. Even though the average age for entrance was only 52, 86% of the residents were actually retired. The satisfaction of residents with the retirement communities was expressed in the fact that there was an annual turnover rate of only 2–5%. Only 6% of the residents expressed a desire to move from the community.

The communities themselves devoted 80–95% of the acreage to housing, with the remaining land being used for recreation. The usual construction pattern is of single-family attached and detached houses in cul-de-sac arrangements, with the community focal point being the clubhouse.

An example of a successful retirement community is Leisure World in Laguna Hills, California. Begun in 1963, by spring 1977 it had nearly 12,000 residences and a population of 19,000. "Leisure World was designed to provide security, quick accessibility to good health care, good nearby shopping, good transportation, excellent facilities for recreation and adult education and additional activities to ensure freedom from boredom" (Leisure World Brochure, 1977).

The importance of security in a retirement community is illustrated in the efforts Leisure World has made:

> Hundreds of Leisure World residents say one of the principle reasons they came to live in Leisure World is security. . . . The entire residential area is surrounded by about 8.5 miles of six-foot wall or fence. In some places the wall is topped by barbed wire. Entrance to the residential areas is only through one of eleven guarded gates. Cars of residents have a special symbol attached to the front bumper; all others are stopped for identification and for permission by a resident to pass through . . . a security force of 255 officers is backed up by full-time, armed officers who have specific police training. (Leisure World Brochure, 1977)

The facilities in Leisure World are extensive. Minibuses circulate over 11 routes, fare-free, carrying 88,000 passengers a month. There are five clubhouses, concerts, movies, stage presentations, and 167 clubs and organizations. The enormous sports and recreational opportunities range from swimming pools and horseback riding to a variety of crafts facilities. All of the activities offered by Leisure World are free to residents except golf and horseback riding. Health facilities are available but on a fee-for-service basis. The success of Leisure World in Laguna Beach is evidenced by the fact that the houses are sold by lottery drawn from the extensive waiting list.

Despite potentially large purchase costs and monthly maintenance fees, retirement communities are growing in popularity, particularly because they offer security, recreation, good housing, and social opportunities with neighbors of a similar age. Researchers commenting on a survey of residents in a number of retirement communities note: "Most persons living in a retirement community have weighed the advantages and disadvantages of this life style. The evidence gathered on thirty-six communities suggests that there is a high amount of satisfaction with their choice. Despite problems or uncertainties about land ownership these communities deliver the kind of environment that their residents desire" (Streib, LaGreca, & Folts, 1986, pp. 101–102). Although the pattern may change as the residents age, many retirement communities do not provide extensive services for their residents. The CARES volunteer organization in Crestwood Village, New Jersey, provides transportation and free medical equipment to residents when needed.

"Continuing care retirement communities" or "life care communities" are more oriented to service provision for residents. These communities guarantee to provide care for residents throughout the remaining years of their life, regardless of their physical condition. In many cases, residents pay a large entrance fee, ranging from $20,000 to $100,000, and a monthly charge based on the size of the apartment and number of individuals. In many life care communities, these monthly charges do not cover most nursing home costs. Some life care communities guarantee to return a specific percentage of the entrance fee to the individual's estate, while others retain the whole fee.

Because of the long-term care nature of the services guaranteed, financial demands on life care communities are extensive. Some life care communities have failed because of inadequate financial resources, and some have had to raise the monthly resident charges drastically to meet their operating costs. In response, states have begun to scrutinize the economic resources of proposed life care developers and 30 states now regulate these communities. Life care communities based purely on rental payments are also now becoming available. In general, the resident population of life care communities tends to be over 75 years of age.

One example of a continuing care retirement community in Columbia, Maryland, offers two options. Under the first option 90% of the entrance fee is refunded if the resident leaves or dies. Studio apartments cost $62,950, the least expensive one-bedroom apartment, $73,000, and two-bedroom apartments begin at $150,000. The second option offers lower entrance fees but the amount refunded to the resident if he/she leaves or dies declines by 2% for each month the resident lives in the housing. Under this plan studios cost $54,000, one-bedroom apartments begin at $63,000, and two-bedroom apartments, $128,000. For individuals living in a studio, the monthly fee (that covers one meal a day, utilities, housekeeping, linen, transportation, community activities, and building maintenance) was $1100 in 1990. For a couple living in a one-bedroom apartment, the monthly fee was $1900. With the payment of the monthly fee, the resident is also entitled to lifetime nursing care services that include home health services and short- and long-term care in the community's Health Center. Non-nursing medical services must be paid for individually (Greater Washington Senior Beacon, 1990).

By 1990 there were approximately 700 continuing care retirement communities with approximately 210,000 residents. Nationally, the entrance fees ranged from $30,000 to $100,000. Recently, in order to broaden the market for these communities, there has been a movement away from entrance fees to communities that only charge monthly fees, and these are adjusted according to the service needs of the residents. Under this plan an individual who requires nursing care pays a higher monthly fee than other residents. As continuing care communities have grown in number they have also begun to vary in what they offer. While some provide nursing care on the premises, others are linked to nursing homes or guarantee a resident priority in obtaining a nursing home bed (Lewin, 1990). While these communities are expected to grow in number, the development by hotel chains and nursing home firms clearly targets an affluent segment of the older population.

Shared and Accessory Housing

One seemingly simple approach to meeting the housing needs of older people is the "matching" of individuals who have similar housing needs. While this may include a diverse group including single younger individuals, this type of effort may enable older persons who require housing to find individuals with whom they can share homes. As housing costs continue to escalate and rental housing becomes scarcer, these types of matching efforts by local social services agencies have proliferated. Over 200 are now estimated to be in operation in the United States (Schreter & Turner, 1986). Shared housing can run into problems with zoning regulations which may restrict housing in an area to "families." Individuals living in shared housing are now eligible for the Existing Housing Certificate program.

Accessory housing utilizes parts of single-family homes as separate apartments for older relatives. "Granny flats," or Elder Cottage Housing Opportunities (ECHO) units, have been adopted from Australia. These freestanding units are adjacent to existing single-family units, usually homes owned by children of the older individual living in the ECHO facility. Although ECHO units can be very cost-effective, they also raise zoning issues in many residential communities zoned exclusively for single family homes. ECHO housing units are now eligible for Section 202 financing.

Home Equity Programs

Many older people are "house rich and cash poor." That is, they have a great deal of money invested in their homes. This is true of older persons at all income levels: 23% of elderly homeowners below the poverty line have over $50,000 equity in their homes (Fairbanks, 1990). Unfortunately, this money is not accessible unless the house is sold, a step that many older families do not want to undertake. Many older people also find rising property taxes a difficult financial burden to bear. Legislation that limits property taxes for older people can be vital in allowing home-owners to stay in their houses. One such program is a "circuit breaker" that prevents property taxes from rising above a percentage of the older person's income ("threshold programs"). Sliding scale programs rebate a percentage of property taxes to older persons, the percentage being determined by the older person's income. Thirty states have instituted some form of this tax relief. In addition, 17 states allow property taxes to be deferred until the death of the older person or the sale of their property.

Home equity conversion is a more ambitious effort to make available the equity older people have in their homes. Since 1980 a variety of programs, most commonly referred to as reverse mortgages, have become available. By 1988, a private Individual Reverse Mortgage Account was available in 11 states (American Association of Retired Persons, 1989). Public reverse mortgage programs also are available in Connecticut and Virginia. The federal Home Equity Conversion Mortgage Insurance Demonstration was enacted in 1987 and began operation in 1989. This legislation authorizes 2,500 insured transactions and insures the lenders against default by borrowers. In 1990 the demonstration was expanded to 25,000 loans to be available until 1995.

The reverse mortgage is what is termed a "rising-debt loan." In its simplest form, the lender pays a monthly amount to a homeowner based on the home's equity, the interest rate, the loan amount, and any lump sum initially distributed. The homeowner must pay the debt when he/she vacates the house or dies. In the latter case the funds are expected to come from the sale of the home. The homeowner maintains title to the house as well as responsibility for taxes and maintenance. Problems with these reverse mortgages stem primarily from a depreciation in home values, which could make it difficult to recoup the loan from the sale of the home. Even if the bank obtains and sells the property, there is no guarantee that there will not be net loss on the loan to the bank as a result of depreciation of the value of the home. Lenders are therefore wary of uninsured home equity loans.

REFERENCES

Abshier, G., Davis, Q., Jans, S., & Petranek, C. (1977). *Evaluation of the Cape-Smile home repair program.* Evansville, IN: Indiana State Univ.

American Association of Retired Persons. (1989). *Home equity conversion for the elderly: An analysis for lenders.* Washington, DC: Author.

American Association of Retired Persons. (1990). *Understanding senior housing for the 1990s.* Washington, DC: Author.

Anderson, W., & Anderson, N. (1978). The politics of age exclusion: The adults only movement in Arizona. *Gerontologist, 18*, 6–12.

Charter Township of Meridian. (1975). *Home repair assistance for low income senior citizens.* Okemos, MI: Department of Development Control.

Erikson, R., & Eckert, K. (1977). The elderly poor in downtown San Diego hotels. *Gerontologist, 17*, 440–446.

Eckert, K., Lyon, S., & Namazi, K. (forthcoming). Congruence between residents and the environment in small board and care homes: An exploratory study. *Adult Residential Care Journal.*

Fairbanks, J. (1990). Home equity conversion programs: A housing option for the 'house-rich, cash-poor," elderly. *Clearinghouse, 23*, 481–487.

Glasscote, R., Biegel, A., Jr., Clark, E., Cox, B., Elper, J. R., Gudeman, J. E., Gurel, L., Lewis, R. V., Miler, D. G., Raybin, J. B., Reifler, C., & Vito, E., Jr. (1976). *Old folks at homes.* Washington, DC: American Psychiatric Association and the Mental Health Association.

Greater Washington Senior Beacon. (1990). Continuing care retirement community opens in Columbia, MD. Washington, DC: Author.

Heintz, K. (1976). *Retirement communities, for adults only.* New Brunswick, NJ: Rutgers Univ., Center for Urban Policy Research.

King, G. (1976, November–December). Bugs, barrels and bush: Home repair in the Virgin Islands. *Aging,* 8–11.

Lee, G. (1986). Rural issues in elderly housing. In R. Newcomer, M. Lawton, & T. Byerts, (Eds.), *Housing an aging society.* New York: Van Nostrand Reinhold.

Leger, M., & Kennedy, S. (1990). *Final comprehensive report of the freestanding housing voucher demonstration: Volume 1.* Washington, DC: U.S. Department of Housing and Urban Development.

Leisure World Brochure. (1977). Laguna Hills, CA: Author.

Linn, M., & Caffey, E. (1977). Foster placement for the older psychiatric patient. *Journal of Gerontology, 32*, 340–345.

Lewin, T. (1990). How needs, and market, for care have changed. *New York Times,* December 2, 1:36.

Local/State Funding Report. (1990). Housing conferees reach final agreement, 18(43), 1, 6.

McCleary, K. (1986). Minor repairs for older homeowners. *Aging, 352*, 2–5.

Newcomer, R., & Weeden, J. (1986). Perspectives on housing needs and the continuum of care. In R. Newcomer, M. Lawton, and T. Byerts, (Eds.), *Housing an aging society.* New York: Van Nostrand Reinhold.

Newman, S. (1986). Demographic influences on the future housing demand of the elderly. In R. Newcomer, M. Lawton, & T. Byerts, (Eds.), *Housing an aging society.* New York: Van Nostrand Reinhold.

Newman, S., & Sherman, S. (1977). A survey of caretakers in adult foster homes. *Gerontologist, 17*, 431–437.

Oktay, J., & Volland, P. (1981). Community care programs for the elderly. *Health and Social Work, 6*, 31–47.

Oktay, J., & Volland, P. (1987). Foster home care for the frail elderly as an alternative to nursing home care: An experimental evaluation. *American Journal of Public Health, 77*, 1505–1510.

Older Americans Report. (1990a). Conferees work out differences on section 202 housing bill, *14*, 375.

Older Americans Report. (1990b). HUD allows service coordinators in certain elderly housing projects, *14*, 432.

Retsinas, J., & Retsinas, N. (1992). Housing loophole may hurt elders. *Aging Today, 13*(6), 1, 2.

Schreter, C., & Turner, L. (1986). Sharing and subdividing private market housing. *Gerontologist, 26*, 181–186.

Stephens, J. (1975). Society of the alone: Freedom, privacy and utilitarianism as dominant norms in the SRO. *Journal of Gerontology, 30*, 230–235.

U.S. Department of Housing and Urban Development. (1973). *Housing in the seventies.* Washington, DC: U.S. Government Printing Office.

U.S. House of Representatives, Committee on Ways and Means. (1986). *Background material and data on programs within the jurisdiction of the Committee on Ways and Means.* Washington, DC: U.S. Government Printing Office.

U.S. Select Committee on Aging, House of Representatives. (1989). *The 1988 national survey of section 202 housing for the elderly and handicapped.* Washington, DC: U.S. Government Printing Office.

United States Senate, Special Committee on Aging. (1975). *HUD's response to the housing needs of senior citizens.* Washington, DC: U.S. Government Printing Office.

United States Senate, Special Committee on Aging. (1990). *Developments in Aging: 1989, Volume 2.* Washington, DC: U.S. Government Printing Office.

U.S. Senate, Special Committee on Aging. (1991). *Developments in Aging: 1990: Vol. 1.* Washington, DC: U.S. Government Printing Office.

13

In-Home Services

THE GROWTH OF IN-HOME SERVICES

Home care continues its development as a major program for the older American population and now accounts for 3.8% of Medicare expenditures. Despite this small number, in recent years home care has represented one of the fastest growing components in Medicare expenditures.

An individual's eligibility for home care depends on his or her degree of disability, but defining disability is difficult because of the various measurement standards that are used. The number of Activities of Daily Living that the individuals cannot do without assistance is becoming more utilized as a disability standard. Stone and Murtaugh (1990) have estimated the size of the disabled elderly population eligible for home care using various criteria. Using the criteria of needing help with three or more ADL's for at least 12 months, 4.1 million elderly, representing 15.5% of the elderly in the community, could be termed disabled and eligible for home care. With the most restrictive criteria, 400,000 older persons, representing 1.5% of the community based elderly, could be termed disabled enough to need home care. In 1987, 5.6 million elderly living in the community had difficulty with at least one ADL or Instrumental Activity of Daily Living, or some problem that affected their ability to walk (Short & Leon, 1990).

The National Medical Expenditure Survey (Short & Leon, 1990) indicates that 36% of people classified as having functional difficulties received services. Not surprisingly, home care was the most commonly used service. A study of 426 older residents in Philadelphia, who report one or more ADL limitations, revealed 23.5% received in-home health care services (Axler, Kotranski, & Olsen, 1990). Those older individuals not receiving adequate assistance may be forced to become part of an enlarged nursing home population.

Unfortunately, admission to nursing homes, chronic care hospitals, and other long-term facilities is often utilized as a solution to problems of impairment when all that the older person may need is limited periods of care during the day. Although institutionalization is costly, the existing funding systems encourage this approach rather than any possible alternatives (Robertson, Griffiths, & Cosin, 1977).

In-home services are provided to individuals who live in their own home or apartment. The hope is that these services can "through coordinated planning, evaluation and follow-up procedures, provide for medical, nursing, social and related services to selected persons . . . with a view toward shortening the length of hospital stay, speeding recovery, or preventing inappropriate institutionalization" (U.S. Senate, 1972, p. 25). These services have received a relatively low priority in the United States until the present time. Support for the development of viable home services has been minimal. The funding that has been available has been enmeshed in regulations that define in-home services so narrowly as to make their actual provision negligible in terms of meeting real need (U.S. Senate, 1972).

In-home services to the elderly are fairly evenly divided between health and welfare agencies, a phenomenon that has resulted from the parallel but relatively independent growth of social and health services to the homebound. Welfare agencies were the first to offer in-home services. In the early 1900s, private charitable family agencies provided homemakers to care for children whose mother was sick. During the 1930s, poor and unemployed women were hired as housekeepers for other poor persons who were in need of the service. By 1958, 145 agencies offered homemaker or home health aid services, of which one-half served adults (U.S. Administration on Aging, 1977).

After 1958, the number of agencies providing in-home services grew rapidly, with the percentage of public agencies comprising a larger portion each year until 1967. With the introduction of Medicare and Medicaid in the mid-1960s, the emphasis of service shifted from family and child care to serving the elderly. With this shift in recipient population came a shift in the type of care given, from home maintenance to personal care. The care of the sick, elderly person required an emphasis on personal care, and Medicare and Medicaid reimbursed only for the personal care aspects of in-home work.

The growth of agencies providing home health services has been remarkable. Medicare certified fewer than 2,000 home health agencies in 1967. By 1987, 5,794 agencies had Medicare certification. In addition to these agencies, an estimated 3,700 to 6,000 agencies were providing services, although not certified by Medicare. The diversity of services and service providers makes it difficult to guarantee the quality of in-home services. The 1992 OAA amendments require State Units on Aging to monitor the quality of in-home services. In addition, the amendments add a section to Title III that guarantees the rights of clients of in-home services. These rights include the right to be informed in advance about a service, participate in its planning, voice grievances about its delivery, be treated with respect, have records treated as confidential, and be informed of their rights under the OAA [Section 314].

Health agencies—long established to provide health services in community and institutional settings—started to add home health aid services to their in-home services when reimbursements through Medicaid and Medicare became available. Skilled nursing care had been available through health agencies for some time before the new funding became available. With the availability of new funding, welfare agencies offering homemaker services and health agencies offering home health aid services began offering the same or similar basic services. Both personal and homemaking services are required to enable persons to remain in their own homes. Because of overlapping of the services—personal and homemaking, by both social and health agencies—HEW developed in 1965 standards which established that a single person, a homemaker-home health aide, could provide both homemaking and personal care services. Unfortunately, some confusion still exists because some funds which pay for the services still retain the separate titles; that is, Medicaid and Medicare reimburse home health aides while Title XX reimburses homemaker services (U.S. Administration on Aging, 1977).

SERVICE PATTERNS

In-home services encompass several levels or types of services. However, the services and levels of services being given should be flexible and readily changed as the client's needs change. Because they are administered in the home of the client, in-home services are an extension of the individual's functioning ability—the ability that allows that person to continue to live in and be part of the community. Because they are personalized to individual situations, there is a potential need to change the service components as persons respond to the services being given. Thus, coordination of services is an integral element of successful in-home services. A smoothly functioning network of services must be available to ensure that the individual receives exactly what is needed at the time it is needed. Strong links and easy accessibility among the services are essential to ensure cooperation for the benefit of the client. For example, Baltimore recently began a coordination program involving 10 in-home service agencies, whereby, through a central intake system, the client could be matched with the most appropriate services. As service needs change, the central intake system can continue to reassign the appropriate services.

Available in-home services can be grouped into three general categories, based on the level of intensity of service (U.S. Senate, 1972).

1. *Intensive or skilled services*. These services are ordered by a physician and provided under the supervision of a nurse. Skilled care would be given to clients with such problems as cardiac difficulties, bone fractures, open wounds, diabetes, and terminal illnesses involving catheters and tube feedings. The services could require physician visits, regular visits by a nurse, and frequent physical and occupational therapy treatments in addition to less technical services such as nutritional services, delivered drugs and medical supplies, home health equipment, transportation, and other diagnostic and therapeutic services which can be safely delivered in the client's home.

    The intensive or skilled service level usually involves a complex grouping of services which themselves might not be needed for a long period of time but modified amounts of which would probably be part of client planning for an extended period of time. Coordination is particularly important for this level of in-home services because of the potential for change and probable number of different service components that could be needed.

2. *Personal care or intermediate services*. Those eligible for personal care services are clients who are medically stable but who need assistance with certain activities of daily living, such as bathing, ambulation, prescribed exercises, and medications. These services can be given to·persons who are convalescing from acute illnesses or to persons with temporary disabilities related to a chronic illness, or as part of a chronic illness. Personal or intermediate care services can be given independently or in conjunction with skilled care.

3. *Homemaker-chore or basic services*. These services involve light housekeeping, preparation of food, laundry services, and other maintenance activities that help sustain the client at home. In those circumstances where the clients can care for themselves but do not have the capacity to care for their personal environment,

these basic services help sustain the home situation for them. Basic or chore services can be given in conjunction with both intermediate and skilled services and usually are given on an ongoing basis.

The key in-home service worker, particularly for both personal and homemaker-chore areas of service, is the homemaker-home health aide. Homemaker-home health aide services comprise the personal and homemaking services needed to enable persons who cannot perform basic tasks for themselves to remain in their own homes. The basic duties performed include cleaning, planning meals, shopping for food, preparing meals, doing the laundry, changing bed linens, bathing, giving bed baths, shampooing hair, helping the persons move from the bed to a chair, checking the pulse rate, helping perform simple exercises, assisting with medications, teaching new skills, and providing emotional support. The homemaker-home health aide can perform primarily personal care services, homemaking services, or both, as the training usually involves skill development in both areas. The combining of these positions in recent years has allowed greater flexibility to respond to the specific personal and homemaking needs of the client through a single person (U.S. Administration on Aging, 1977).

Heavy house cleaning and simple home maintenance, such as painting and simple carpentry repairs, are usually performed by a person specifically employed for the purpose and are not included in the homemaker-home health aide functions. Special programs which match high school or college students with the chore needs of older persons have enabled this type of work to be done. Usually, the older person pays a minimum wage for the services, as such services are not covered under most funding programs.

An attempt to develop intensive services for seriously disabled older individuals without relocating them outside their own homes is exemplified by the Nursing Home Without Walls program. In New York State this program was begun in 1977 and designed to be an alternative to institutionalization (Cardillo, Horton, & Luther, 1988). Individuals accepted into the program are provided a wide range of services comparable to those offered in a nursing home. The services are available on a 24-hour, 7-day-a-week basis and are offered through hospitals, residential health care facilities, and certified home health agencies.

An older person assessed as needing skilled nursing care is also evaluated to determine whether he or she has a suitable living environment at home for the nursing home without walls program. If the environment is physically suitable, a plan is prepared. The costs of the program's services are capped at 75% of the average annual cost for nursing home care, although exceptions are made to this formula. By 1988, 86 providers were providing care to 7,700 patients at approximately half the cost of nursing home placements. A similar program is also in effect at the On Lok center in San Francisco. An evaluation of 16 community care demonstrations (including the New York and On Lok efforts) indicates a pattern of "higher life quality" for participants. The evaluators contend, however, that "expanding publicly financed community care does not reduce aggregate costs, and it is likely to increase them—at least under the current long-term care service system which already provides some community care" (Kemper, Applebaum, & Harrigan, 1987, p. 96).

SERVICE AGENCIES

In-home services are provided by a variety of agencies which are usually based in the community and defined by the source of the funding and the service specialty:

> An agency eligible to receive Medicare and Medicaid funds is a home health agency, a public or private agency which in addition to requirements for sound administration, adequate records, professional supervision, assessment and review, has as its primary function the provision of skilled nursing service and at least one additional therapeutic service. (U.S. Senate, 1972, p. 21)

Thus the agency is defined by the type of service that it provides.

Home health agencies can be both hospital and community based, public, private nonprofit, or proprietary:

- *Home care units of community hospitals.* These units have emerged as a part of the hospital program, primarily as a method of discharging patients as soon as appropriate. As a hospital affiliate, the patient can retain the same doctor and can move in and out of the hospital as needed for ongoing care. Hospital-based programs are particularly effective for terminally ill patients who can spend some time at home but who need a close affiliation with emergency health services. These home care units are staffed primarily with public health nurses and have on call the medical units from the hospital itself. These units provide primarily skilled-care services.
- *Departments of social services.* Local departments of social services usually provide intermediate- and basic-level in-home services under

their adult services units. Because their background is a welfare agency, these homemakers are more likely to be involved with household activities and to a lesser extent with personal care services.

- *Private nonprofit community agencies.* Included in this group are such agencies as Associated Catholic Charities, Jewish Family and Children's Services, Family and Children's Services, and Visiting Nursing Associations. These types of agencies provide homemaker-home health aides, nurses, and other in-home service workers as part of larger community-related programs. Each agency usually selects which specific service area it will provide, such as personal care services only or nursing services, and incorporates them into the other agency services being given.
- *Community health centers.* Community health centers can provide some in-home services as part of their community health services program. The in-home services are usually tied to those clients who are participating in the health center as an extension of services given.
- *Proprietary agencies.* Proprietary agencies, such as Upjohn, provide in-home services to the homebound on a fee-for-service basis. The services are usually at the skilled level of care and provided for short periods of time.

Between 1984 and 1985 the number of nonprofit and proprietary Medicare-certified home health agencies increased 60%. Hospital-based home health care agencies also increased 60%. Part of this growth has been attributed to the fact that Medicare certification is now allowed in states without laws for the licensing of home health agencies. Although 32 states require licensing, there is no uniform requirement for training, certification, and supervision of home health aides across the country (Leader, 1986).

Funding

The most difficult problem in the delivery of in-home services is that of funding. Because of current funding restrictions, the demand for services far exceeds the supply. Further, the demand is primarily for those types of services that are not readily reimbursable through the available funding sources. The community and institutional agencies which provide the services are available and prepared to deliver the services, if the repayment mechanism was available for reimbursement. The greatest unmet need for in-home services is for those with long-term disabilities and for the chronically ill whose conditions are not likely to improve quickly. There are approximately 2.4 million adults who require service intervention beyond that which is now available (U.S. Senate, 1987).

It is ironic that, in most situations, the cost of home health services is less than the potential alternatives for the eligible clients. A Senate Special Committee on Aging report (1972) showed that almost one-half of the patients admitted to home health services would have required hospitalization if the services had not been available. Early discharge programs to home care services in Denver and Philadelphia showed a reduction of 19.2 and 12.9 days, respectively, in average hospital days per patient.

There are five basic ways for payment of in-home services. The first—client fees—is used by most agencies that provide in-home services. The voluntary agencies are more likely to offer sliding-scale fee schedules because they are usually supported in part through contributions from individuals, religious groups community groups, disease-related groups, or United Way fund-raising organizations.

The second payment method—Medicare—is used by agencies which provide health-related services in situations when the client and the service meet Medicare eligibility requirements. In order to be eligible for Medicare reimbursement, the service must be given by a home health agency which has, as its primary function, the provision of skilled nursing service and at least one additional therapeutic service. The services that are reimbursable focus upon acute or short-term illnesses, not on chronic or custodial ones. In addition, there are varying interpretations as to what is appropriate for reimbursement, interpretations that might be applied after the service has been given. Because of the potential unpredictability of Medicare reimbursements, agencies are often reluctant to give Medicare-reimbursed services other than those specifically defined as eligible services. This makes it difficult for clients to receive appropriate services for their situations. A survey of all 50 states indicated that 35 permit family caregivers to be paid for their assistance to an older person. The majority of these states utilize Medicaid funds for these payments (Linsk, Keigher, & Osterbusch, 1988).

Actual services provided under Medicare are restricted to home bound patients (individuals unable to leave their home without the assistance of a person or a device such as a wheelchair or cane). Home care must be prescribed by the physician caring for the patient and the patient must require either intermittent skilled nursing care, physical therapy, or speech therapy (Leader, 1991). "Intermittent" care is defined as at least once every 60 days, but once a patient meets Medicare eligibility, the services can be provided as long as they are *medically necessary*. As already noted, despite these restrictions, Medicare expenditures for home care continued to grow throughout the 1980s.

Reimbursable services under Medicare include part-time or intermittent nursing care (under the supervision of a registered nurse); physical, occupational, and speech therapy; medical supplies; home health aide services; and counseling for social or emotional problems. The important services missing from this list are crucial personal and home maintenance services.

Medicaid is the third payment method and is used by agencies which provide health-related services in situations when the client and the service meet Medicaid eligibility requirements. Unlike Medicare, in which every person age 65 and over is potentially eligible for the benefits, Medicaid is available only to those who meet strict income requirements. Although the actual income limit is determined within each state because Medicaid is partially financed by the states, the usual income limit is set to coincide with the SSI limit, plus whatever state aid for income is being given.

Home health care became a required service under Medicaid in 1970 and could be given by the same agencies that are eligible for Medicare. Although the services provided under Medicaid vary among the states, basically Medicaid covers nursing services, home health aide services, and medical supplies and equipment. Medicaid benefits do not require that skilled nursing care or therapy be given. The potentially eligible persons do not need prior hospitalization nor is there a limit on the number of visits.

Unlike Medicare, there is no requirement for prior hospitalization and no limit on the number of visits that can be provided under Medicaid. Medicaid also allows personal care and nonmedical services related to activities of daily living to be reimbursed. However, many states restrict the home health services they will cover under Medicaid. Few states actually reimburse personal care and nontechnical services. Thus, despite its potential as a funding source, the state limitations on covered services have meant fewer programs being offered to chronically ill elderly at home than Medicaid provisions allow (Oktay & Palley, 1981).

In 1985, $21 billion was allocated from federal and state coffers for home health care benefits under Medicaid (Nassif, 1987). Despite this impressive figure, the preponderance of Medicaid funds are still oriented to institutional care. In 1984, 64% of federal Medicaid payments were allotted to nursing homes, 17% to hospitals, 33% to physician services, and slightly more than 11% for home health care (Newcomer & Weeden,

1986). It is thus clear that Medicare is more likely to pay for in-home services while Medicaid is used primarily for institutional care.

The former Title XX of the Social Security Act was a fourth source of funds for in-home services from public and private agencies. As already noted, Title XX monies were allocated on the basis of population to the state departments of social services. Unlike Medicare and Medicaid, the services were not reviewed on a service-by-service basis for reimbursement. Home-based services, such as homemaker, home health aide, home management, personal care, consumer education, and financial counseling, were eligible services under Title XX. These services could be ongoing and were not restricted to a limited amount per year. However, the program was limited by the income eligibility of the client and the amount of money available to the public and private agencies for personnel to provide the services. Despite the opportunities for funding of in-home services under Title XX, only limited amounts of funds have been addressed to the needs of older clients and home health.

The fifth payment source is Title III of the OAA, which provides moneys for in-home services through the local Area Agencies on Aging. The funds are made available to provide

> services designed to assist older individuals in avoiding institutionalization, including preinstitution-evaluation and screening and home health services, homemaker services, shopping services, escort services, reader services, letter writing services, and other similar services designed to assist such individuals to continue living independently in a home environment. (Older Americans Act as amended in 1978)

The funds can provide for a variety of services by both public and private agencies for both the chronically and acutely ill. The only eligibility requirement is that the recipient be 60 or over. Although there is no income restriction on the services, efforts are made to make most of the services available to low-income elderly. The service limitation under Title III programs is in the financial limits of the allocations themselves. Because eligible services are broadly defined under this act, efforts have been concentrated on using these funds and services for those people who are ineligible for services under the other funding programs—primarily those who were just over the scale for Title XX and those with chronic illnesses.

CASE MANAGEMENT SERVICES

Because of the variety of funding sources and varying eligibility standards, programs around the country have attempted to combine various sources of money with other local resources in order to be able to provide as broad a base of service as possible. In many areas this has blossomed into full-scale case management programs. A crucial component of case management is a careful in-home assessment to assure that an appropriate mix of services from a variety of agencies is secured for the older client. In some communities, some of the needed services may not be available locally, creating problems for the case managers. As the appropriate "packages" of services become more evident around the country, there has been increased effort to expand programs to enable case management to be effective in keeping the older individual in the community.

In Maryland, the Gateway II program serves moderately and severely health-impaired persons over 65. Comprehensive assessment of the older individual and assignment of a case manager to help coordinate services are the basic components of the program. Limited "gap filling" funds are available when other programs are not sufficient to meet the older client's needs. The program is means-tested. Only individuals within 80% of the state's median income and with assets of $11,000 are eligible for the program (Bechill, 1987).

The Triage experience in Connecticut indicates that a well-conducted case management approach can diminish the cost of providing service by reducing inappropriate institutionalization of the older person as well as the use of inappropriate community based services. As a federally funded demonstration, Triage was allowed to waive some Medicare requirements for clients. Triage cost estimates were well below those of long-term residential care (Quinn, Segal, Raisz, & Johnson, 1982).

In many areas case managers have no ability to affect the quality of a service except by refusing to refer individuals to a particular agency. Case management programs in Monroe County, New York, and in San Francisco employ an approach that enables them to control the quality of programs they utilize. In Monroe County, the ACCESS program controls funds for the purchase of services. The On Lok program in San Francisco offers comprehensive services for its clients (Grisham, White, & Miller, 1983). Case management services can also be an integral part of other programs such as adult daycare. In a national survey (Weissert et al., 1989), 79% of the daycare centers under the auspices of general hospitals and social service agencies offered case management services.

Case management and supportive services may be even more crucial where family members live at a distance from their older relatives. The Jewish Family and Children's Agencies around the country have developed an Elder Support Network. Family members are able to arrange for case management and supportive services to be provided to their relatives living throughout the United States. The services are provided through local Jewish Family and Children's Agencies. Charges are on a sliding scale based on the family member's income. Similar services are available through networks of private social workers.

RELATED SERVICES

There has been a growth in the number and types of formal support systems for the homebound that complement in-home services or even substitute for these services when regular contact and visiting are all that are needed. Two such programs, reassurance and friendly visiting, are most frequently available, primarily as adjunct programs within senior centers or agencies providing other programs and services to the elderly.

Reassurance Services

As the number of elderly maintaining independent residence in the community continues to increase, a method for ensuring their daily well-being becomes vital. In housing specifically designed for seniors, systems that require turning off a hall light outside the apartment each morning can be used to indicate that the resident has not suffered any mishap during the previous day.

For individuals living in other types of residences, telephone reassurance has been stressed as a means of maintaining daily contact with older individuals. The telephone reassurance systems can be traced to the efforts of Grace McClure during the 1960s. After attempting to contact an elderly friend for eight successive days, Mrs. McClure made a personal check of the friend's apartment and found her on the floor after having suffered a stroke. Mrs. McClure's subsequent efforts in Michigan resulted in a telephone reassurance service and replication of this type of service in many parts of the country.

In the typical telephone reassurance service, the individual is called twice a day. If there is no answer, a policeman with a house key is dispatched to make a personal check. The individual must also inform the police when they are leaving their home in order to ensure that calls are not made when the house is vacant. In New York City, a private service provides two calls a day and includes information about television listings, news, and weather (Conait, 1969).

Among publicly funded services a variety of volunteers have been used to do the telephoning, including residents of a nursing home in Nassau

County, New York, and multiple sclerosis patients in other programs in New York State. In rural areas, mail carriers are asked to alert a special office if they notice mail accumulating in an older person's mailbox (National Institute of Senior Centers, 1978).

One possible side effect of these services is the friendships that can form between volunteer callers and clients. This potential for friendships is being built into some services that utilize a buddy system. This approach depends on a team of approximately 10 people who utilize a daily round robin of calling. If the chain is broken on any day, the individual unable to make contact with the next person reports the problem to a central office, and a personal visit is made to the home (Match, 1972).

If well-run, these reassurance services are important links for the aging. More affluent elderly are now able to enroll in a service that enables them to hook their home into a central office. Failure to punch a code on a specially designed machine will result in a checkup visit to the home. Under these systems, central offices can be alerted to emergencies by either push-button codes or, in some cases, voice activation of the system. Social service agencies as well as hospitals are now making these automated systems available under a variety of fee schedules. The key link in the machine-based or telephone-based reassurance service is the reliability of the staff responsible for checking on the elderly client who fails to utilize the designated code or answer the phone. Because of this problem, few services are relying totally on relatives because of their possible unavailability at crucial times.

Visiting Services

Although they are now available in greater numbers, many cities have operated friendly visiting services for a long period of time. The visitors service in Chicago was begun in 1947. The friendly visitors services utilize volunteers to visit elderly individuals who are homebound. Visitors may chat with the older persons, read to them, help them with correspondence, or play chess and board games.

While they are most often oriented to community-based elderly, a friendly visitor service was begun in Maryland in 1977 to provide companionship for nursing home residents who did not receive regular visits by family and friends. One friendly visiting service utilized members of a senior citizens club as visitors, and programs around the country rely on volunteers of all ages to reach elderly who might otherwise be isolated from social contacts.

Expansion of effective in-home services still hinges on funding mechanisms being instituted to make these services more reimbursable. Under the 1987 Older Americans Act amendments, a program of grants to individual states was authorized. The services that can be provided under this program to "frail" elderly are extensive. They include homemaker and home health aides as well as nonhealth services such as choice services, telephone reassurance, respite care in the home for family caretakers, and minimal physical modification of the home. In FY 1990, 88,000 older persons were served under this program. Over half of these clients were from low-income backgrounds.

Even with their expansion, it is questionable whether in-home services from formal providers can substitute for emotional support from family and friends. In order to bolster the caretaking efforts of family and friends, Title III of the 1992 OAA amendments authorizes a program to offer training, technical assistance, and information to informal caregivers and frail older individuals (Part G).

REFERENCES

Axler, F., Kotranski, L., & Olsen, K. (1990). Home care for the impaired elderly: Factors influencing use of and access to formal and informal health care. Poster presentation at The Gerontological Society Annual meeting. Boston, MA: November.

Bechill, W. (1987, March 9). The reauthorization of the Older Americans Act. Paper represented before the Committee on Education and Labor, U.S. House of Representatives, Washington, DC.

Brody, S. (1974). Long-term care in the community. In E. Brody, (Ed.), *A social work guide for long-term care facilities*. Rockville, MD: National Government Printing Office.

Cardillo, A., Horton, R., & Luther, C. (1988). *Nursing Home Without Walls Program: A decade of quality care at home for NY's aged and disabled*. Albany: New York State Senate Health Committee.

Conait, M. (1969). *Guidelines for telephone reassurance services*. Ann Arbor, MI: Univ. of Michigan, Institute of Gerontology.

Cosmos, C., & Crawley, A. (1990). The wilderness of home health care. *Elder Law Forum, 2*(5), 1, 6.

Grisham, M., White, M., & Miller, L. (1983). Case management as a problem-solving strategy. *Pride Institute Journal of Long Term Home Health Care, 2*(4), 21–28.

Kemper, P., Applebaum, R., & Harrigan, M. (1987). Community care demonstrations: What have we learned? *Health Care Financing Review, 8*(4), 87–100.

Leader, S. (1986). *Home health benefits under Medicare*. Washington, DC: Public Policy Institute, American Association of Retired Persons.

Leader, S. (1991). *Medicare's home health benefit: Eligibility, utilization, and expenditures.* Washington, DC: Public Policy Institute, American Association of Retired Persons.

Linsk, N., Keigher, S., & Osterbusch, S. (1988). States' policies regarding paid family caregiving. *Gerontologist, 28,* 204–212.

Match, S. (1972). *Establishing telephone reassurance services.* Washington, DC: National Council on the Aging.

Nassif, J. (1987). There's still no place like home. *Generations, 11*(2), 5–8.

National Institute of Senior Centers. (1978). Senior center programming: Expanding services to the vulnerable elderly. *Senior Center Report, 1*(3), 4–5.

Newcomer, R., & Weeden, J. (1986). Perspectives on housing and the continuum of care. In R. Newcomer, M. Lawton, & T. Byerts, (Eds.), *Housing an aging society.* New York: Van Nostrand Reinhold.

Oktay, J., & Palley, H. (1981). A national family policy for the chronically ill elderly. In *The Social Welfare Forum,* 1980. New York: Columbia Univ. Press.

Quinn, J., Segal, J., Raisz, H., & Johnson, C. (1982). *Coordinating community services for the elderly: The Triage experience.* New York: Springer Publishing Company.

Rich, S. (1987, July 10). Daily needs not met for many elderly. *Washington Post,* p. 6.

Robertson, D., Griffiths, R., & Cosin, L. (1977). A community based continuing care program for the elderly disabled: An evaluation of planned intermittent hospital readmission. *Journal of Gerontology, 32,* 334–339.

Short, P., & Leon, J. (1990). *Use of home and community services by persons age 65 and older with functional difficulties.* National Medical Expenditure Survey Research Findings 5, Agency for Health Care Policy and Research. Rockville, MD: Public Health Service.

Stone, R., & Murtaugh, C. (1990). The elderly population with chronic functional disability: Implications for home care eligibility. *The Gerontologist, 30,* 491–502.

U.S. Administration on Aging. (1977). *Human resources issues in the field of aging: Homemaker—home health aide services.* Washington, DC: U.S. Government Printing Office.

U.S. House of Representatives, Committee on Ways and Means. (1991). *Background material and data on programs within the jurisdiction of the Committee on Ways and Means.* Washington, DC: U.S. Government Printing Office.

U.S. Senate, Special Committee on Aging. (1972). *Home health services in the United States.* Washington, DC: U.S. Government Printing Office.

U.S. Senate, Special Committee on Aging. (1987). *Developments in aging, 1986: Part I.* Washington, DC: U.S. Government Printing Office.

Weissert, W., Elston, J., Bolda, E., Cready, L., Zelman, W., Sloane, P., Kalsbeek, W., Mutran, E., Rice, T., & Koch, G. (1989). Models of adult day care: Findings from a national survey. *The Gerontologist, 29,* 640–649.

14

Adult Daycare

THE ROOTS OF DAYCARE

Dependency and Aging

It is unfortunate that daycare services for the elderly often seem to resemble similar programs for children. While the programs may be similar in some aspects, services for the aged should not be based on viewing the elderly as childlike. As one advocate for adult daycare urges:

> We object to the comparison to child care because it is inaccurate. We are not a place where people are left in safety as children are left, until someone is ready to "pick them up" again. Our services have an objective, and those who are consumers are not children. They are adults who may be limited for shorter or longer periods of time in their capacities for total self-care— but they are participants in their own care programs with everything that the term implies. (Lupu, cited in Trager, 1976, p. 6)

The common thread running through services for children and the elderly is that of dependency. Lupu argues, however, that dependency among the elderly and children stems from different sources. The elderly do not lack knowledge of "right from wrong" and have attained the skills necessary to conduct their everyday life. Dependency in the elderly usually stems from physical and mental impairments that make it difficult for them to continue to successfully accomplish routine tasks. These tasks may include what are labeled as "activities of daily living" such as dressing, bathing, using the bathroom, cooking, and self-feeding. The task of the daycare center is to assist the individual in functioning as independently as possible given his or her physical and mental status. A National Council on the Aging (NCOA) study defines daycare as a "community based group program designed to meet the needs of functionally impaired adults through an individual plan of care. It is a structured, comprehensive program that provides a variety of health, social, and related support services in a protective setting during any part of a day but less than 24 hour care" (Behrens, 1986, p. 5).

History of Daycare

Daycare is one possible response to the need for families to have a respite from caring for an impaired older person on a daily basis as well as providing them with some free time. Kaplan (1976) has summarized the basic assumptions about daycare as a belief in (1) "the intrinsic worth of living within one's community," (2) the merit in keeping the family together, (3) the beneficial nature of allowing a person to continue independent living, and (4) independent living as beneficial in the broader concept of social well-being for older persons and their families.

Daycare for adults originated in Britain during the 1940s, when outpatient hospital centers for psychiatric patients were set up. These centers, located in psychiatric hospitals, were designed to decrease the numbers of individuals who would require admittance to inpatient units. By the late 1950s, the British had extended daycare programs to geriatric patients; by 1969, 90 programs were already in operation.

In 1947, the first geriatric day hospital in the United States opened under the auspices of the Menninger Clinic, and in 1949, a similar operation was begun at Yale (McCuan, 1973). Bolstered by the increased interest and funding for aging programs in the 1970s, daycare programs have now begun in most states.

DAYCARE CLIENTS

Eligibility

Because of this short history, a variety of programs with varied focuses now fall under the daycare rubric. Federal guidelines have not yet been set up to determine eligibility for federally funded daycare programs. In 1974, Congress authorized demonstration daycare programs. In its guidelines for these demonstration programs, HEW defined daycare as a program "provided under health leadership in an ambulatory care setting for adults who do not require 24-hour institutional care and yet, due to physical and/or mental impairment, are not capable of full-time independent living" (U.S. Health Resources Administration, 1974, p. 1).

An individual with physical and mental impairment is further defined under these guidelines as a "chronically ill or disabled adult whose illness or disability does not require 24-hour inpatient care but which in the absence of day care service may precipitate admission to or prolonged stay in a hospital, nursing home or other long-term facility" (U.S. Health Resources Administration, 1974, p. 1). It is obvious that the major projected daycare population is an at-risk group whose involvement in daycare programs may provide enough support to enable them to remain out of long-term care institutions. Among existing programs, daycare is not often used for individuals discharged from nursing homes.

Present Users

In examining a number of daycare programs, Weissert (1975) commented on the participants: "Most are aged who need continuing support and will probably leave the adult day care program only to go into a nursing home or at death" (p. 14). The participants in Weissert's sample had between two and five diagnosed medical conditions. The same configuration of conditions was noted by Kaplan (1976) examining a daycare program in Ohio. Kaplan found that 75% of the participants had many of the same symptoms usually found among nursing home patients. As Gurian (1976) argues, daycare clients can thus potentially come from three major groups: (1) individuals enrolled in day hospital programs in mental hospitals which provide mental health treatment during the day, (2) nursing home patients, or (3) elderly living in their own homes or with their families. Interestingly, although the vast majority of elderly live independently, Weissert (1975) found that, on average, only 31% of the clients in the 10 programs studied by his researchers lived alone. In 1978, Mahoney found that only 26% of the daycare clients in three Connecticut centers lived alone. A study in Ohio compared daycare users and impaired elderly. Daycare participants were more likely to be unmarried, living with other individuals, and in a physically more dependent position than impaired community elderly not involved with the daycare program (Barresi & McConnell, 1984). The need for daycare thus may first be perceived by those who become caretakers as the elderly individual's physical or mental condition deteriorates. Referrals to daycare centers may be coming either from the families of elderly persons or from agencies or service providers who come into contact with the families and are aware of the centers rather than being initiated by the elderly themselves. In contrast, the literature on nursing homes indicates that the majority of long-term residents have previously lived alone. It is therefore possible that daycare clients differ from nursing home residents in the degree to which economic, social, and psychological support is being provided by family members.

As the possibility of federal reimbursements increases, the definitions of eligible daycare clients should become clarified. Although a number of models have been proposed (Robins, 1976), daycare programs will probably be increasingly categorized as maintenance rather than rehabilitative services. If individuals come into daycare programs from nursing homes, they will be those elderly whose conditions have improved and who are found not to be in need of the 24-hour nursing services offered by these homes. The daycare centers will be expected to provide a gamut of services necessary to maintain the participants near their present level of functioning.

Evaluating Benefit to Clients

The ambiguities that now exist in definitions of daycare create an initial difficulty in evaluating the effectiveness of these programs. If daycare centers are maintenance oriented, it still may be difficult to evaluate the centers that enroll large numbers of seriously impaired individuals. For these individuals it is possible that there will be deterioration, admission to nursing homes, or death despite the extensive care a center may provide. A broken hip, myocardial infarction, or organic brain syndrome may occur at any point in the impaired elderly person's day, and these occurrences may be unaffected by attendance at a daycare center. While it is possible that the day services may delay the onset of these conditions or deterioration in existing conditions, the use of adult daycare has not been shown to have an effect on the health or mental health outcomes of clients (Weissert et al., 1989).

Eligibility for daycare services as well as evaluation of the center's ability to meet its stated goals will be determined to a great extent by the range of services offered by the individual center. Thus the clients served and the criteria used for evaluation will differ between a center that is rehabilitation oriented and has multiple medical services, a maintenance-oriented center with many different services (not all offered on site), and a center that is socially oriented and has a minimum of medical services.

DAYCARE CENTER SERVICES

Program Outlines

The range of services that daycare centers currently provide to maintain impaired clients at their optimal level of functioning is clear: screening for physical conditions; medical care (usually by arrangement with an outside physician); nursing care; occupational, physical, and recreational therapy; social work; transportation; meals; personal care (e.g., assistance in going to the toilet); educational programs; crafts, counseling. In contrast to senior centers, daycare services are not available on a drop-in basis. Clients are scheduled, usually on a minimal two-day per week basis, but often on a full five-day basis. While many clients are ambulatory, daycare centers endeavor to provide transportation and appropriately designed space to serve individuals confined to wheelchairs.

Most daycare centers are small, typically serving 15–25 clients a day. This size helps to prevent the development of an institutional atmosphere. Centers are located in setting ranging from schools, apartments, and churches to hospitals and nursing homes. Clients usually arrive at the center between 9 and 10 A.M. and may have coffee before becoming involved in an individual or group project. A period of exercise matching the client's capability may be held before lunch, which is followed by a rest period and another group or individual project. The projects range from crafts and reading to dances and discussions. At any point in the day, appropriate counseling, nursing care, and medical-social services may be provided. Activities are conducted in accordance with the individual plan of care that the center develops for each client upon his or her acceptance into the program. Clients are transported back to their residence in the late afternoon (3–4 P.M.). This schedule would not apply to centers that run an extended-hours program in the morning and afternoon. As would be expected, the staff–client ratio necessary to provide the individualized attention described here is high, averaging around 1:5 or 1:7 at most centers. In order to maintain the client's relationship with the community, many centers make extensive use of volunteers and emphasize frequent outings, including picnics, shopping, and trips.

Program and Client Emphasis

The major disagreement among daycare advocates has revolved around the relative emphasis on particular services. This lack of consensus can be seen in the ambiguous guidelines for the 1974 HEW demonstration programs:

> The essential elements of daycare programs are directed towards meeting the health maintenance and restorative needs of participants. However, there are socialization elements which by overcoming the isolation often as-

sociated with illness in the aged and disabled are considered vital for the purpose of fostering and maintaining the maximum possible state of health and well being. (U.S. Health Resources Administration, 1974)

The relegation of "socialization" programs to the second sentence of these guidelines reflects uncertainty as to the importance of these elements in the daycare program. Padula (1972) has attempted to distinguish between "day hospital" programs, which are health related and service the disabled or ill elderly, and "day care," as a social program for "frail, moderately handicapped or slightly confused older persons" (p. 8). A report by the NCOA (National Institute of Senior Centers, 1978) on adult daycare distinguishes between daycare, in-home services, and senior centers: "Daycare differs from in-home services in that the therapeutic care is given in a group setting, which reduces loneliness and social isolation of the impaired older person and facilitates the delivery of multiple services."

Unless federal or state guidelines clearly specify the outlines of daycare services, the components emphasized will partially depend on the affiliation or sponsorships of the centers. Daycare centers sponsored by Area Agencies on Aging may have a greater degree of emphasis on social rather than health components, depending for their health services on linkages with medical and nursing schools. Programs such as the Mosholu-Montefiore program in New York place a heavy emphasis on health components because of their strong relationship to major hospital facilities and, in the case of this particular program, because it uses space provided by the hospital. The actual ratio of health to social services depends on the requirements of funding sources. Trager (1976) has succinctly summed up the problems that may result from viewing social and health components as distinct and separate daycare entities:

The development of centers which set policies and objectives in the context of treatment and physical restoration may tend to exclude those in need of some, but not all of these services. For those who are considered candidates for supervision and socialization, there may be a tendency to ignore essential health related services. Facilities which are treatment oriented may also tend to take on institutional characteristics and to make a "patient" of the participant—an aspect of institutional care which often is counterproductive in terms of the objectives of treatment. On the other hand, major emphasis on a supervision-socialization policy excludes consideration of restoration and rehabilitation possibilities which may appear to be relatively limited but are of great importance to the participant and such facilities might take on the characteristics of current institutions which are "holding facilities" and ignore essential health needs. (p. 16)

A national study of daycare centers (Weissert et al., 1989) indicates a lessened tendency during the 1980s to view health and social services as separate entities. Three center models were found. Model I includes centers under the auspices of nursing homes or rehabilitation hospitals. Model II includes centers affiliated with general hospitals or social service agencies. Model III centers are "special purpose" centers serving veterans, older persons with mental health problems, cerebral palsy, or the blind. Among these centers are some dedicated to older persons with Alzheimer's disease.

In Model I centers the clients are a primarily "physically dependent, older, white population, most of whom do not suffer a mental disorder" (Weissert et al., p. 648). In Model II centers the clients are "predominantly unmarried females, more frequently racial minority populations, most of whom are under 85, typically not dependent or only minimally dependent in activities of daily living, but more than 40% of whom may suffer a mental disorder" (Weissert et al., 1989, p. 648).

Despite their physical problems, the daycare participants in the survey differed from nursing home residents. Nursing home residents are, on average, more than 4 years older, and twice as likely to be over age 85 and to be unmarried and functionally dependent. Model II participants, however, are more akin to community based elderly than Model I participants.

In all three models a variety of services are offered. As expected, the centers under the auspices of nursing homes or rehabilitation hospitals (Model I) are more likely to have therapeutic or health related programs than Model II centers. Model II centers are more likely to offer social and supportive services. Despite these differences, Model II centers have enlarged the health services they offer since the 1970s.

RESPITE SERVICES

Closely related to daycare, respite services are strongly advocated but receive only limited financial support. Although there are questions as to whether the target of respite is a caregiver or care receiver, respite services usually offer relief to individuals who provide intensive daycare for older relatives or even unrelated individuals. A respite care program in Detroit, funded through the AAA, the Department of Social Services, and the United Way, offers 168 hours of respite per year or three hours a

week for the caregiver (Durso, 1986). In 1987, this program was also going to be made available on a fee-for-service option for higher-income
individuals. A respite program in California is devoted to family caregivers of older people with chronic brain disorders (Griffin, 1985). This
Family Survival Project included respite care as part of a full array of
services for caregivers.

FUNDING

As the discussion of funding sources in Chapter 2 indicates, services for
the aging are now being kept afloat through funds obtained from a number of sources. This is exemplified by daycare, where a variety of federal,
local, and private funds are used. At the federal level, Medicaid plays a
dominant role in funding adult daycare centers, but many centers also
rely on fees paid by participants or their families. Support from fees or
philanthropies was a primary source of income for the Model I centers
described above. Daycare centers also obtain funding from the Social
Services Block Grant as well as from Title III of the Older Americans
Act.

In 1976, the Medical Services Administration issued guidelines designed to assist states in preparing regulations for reimbursable daycare
centers. While the target population of these centers might not differ
from the centers already described, the medical service requirement
might be more extensive. Programs conducted by a hospital or programs
that are recognized as "clinics under state laws" are eligible for Medicaid
reimbursements. These reimbursements are authorized under the outpatient hospital provisions of Title XIX.

Under the guidelines, the reimbursable medical services that daycare
centers might offer include:

1. Medical services supervised by a physician
2. Nursing services rendered by a professional nursing staff
3. Diagnostic services in addition to initial screening
4. Rehabilitation services including physical therapy, speech therapy,
   occupational therapy, and inhalation therapy
5. Pharmaceutical services
6. Podiatric services
7. Optometric services
8. Self-care services oriented toward the activities of daily living
9. Dental services

10. Social work services
11. Recreation therapy
12. Dietary services
13. Transportation services

Although existing centers may provide many of these services, provision of all of them is probably beyond the resources of many. The guidelines specify that the packages of services available for any individual must be a combination of some or all of the elements listed. All of the services might be available in a center, but it is expected that the most complex medical services would be found in day hospital settings because of the close hospital-staff linkages. In all centers, the guidelines stress screening of clients by a multidisciplinary team and the development of an individualized treatment plan.

Based on the guidelines, each state has the responsibility to establish and approve a required package of services for reimbursable daycare and day hospital programs. Discussions about the degree of medical supports that will be required by the state to qualify a center for reimbursement are already becoming intense.

Under Title XX, many daycare centers were funded without the extensive medical services that may be required under Title XIX. Unfortunately Social Services Block Grant (Title XX) funds were limited and based on annual population figures for each state. Title XX funds are also allocated on the basis of public hearings and plans developed on a statewide level. Some states have not included day services for the elderly in their plans, while others have viewed block grant support as only seed money for programs. Programs that were instituted on the basis of Title XX allocations have now found that block grant funds are not always available to meet increasing inflationary costs or even that states are cutting back individual program funding in order to distribute small amounts of money to a larger number of centers. In this way the states hope to encourage a larger number of centers, but individual centers have had to scramble to meet the deficit imposed by the cuts in their funding.

COST EFFECTIVENESS AND BENEFITS

Even before their social and psychological benefits have been determined, daycare centers have had to face the question of their costliness. Unfortunately, the cost-effectiveness studies fail to provide enough clarity to allow for a final determination of the financial question. Because of variations in services, costs may differ widely among centers. The NCOA study of 847 centers found that the expenditures averaged $27 per day. When subsidies from a variety of funding sources were included, daycare expenditures rose to $31 per day. In 57% of the centers, fees charged to paying participants on a sliding scale ranged from $31 to $40 per day (Behrens, 1986). In some instances, costs borne by programs other than daycare centers are not included in these tallies. Space rental paid by other agencies is a major example. Weissert et al. (1989) found an average cost of $30 per day among daycare centers.

An additional cost factor that needs to be examined is the ability of daycare programs to provide the totality of services required by an elderly individual. In Connecticut, Mahoney (1978) found that 47% of the clients in three daycare centers also received assistance from other agencies. Clients who were receiving only daycare services were more likely to be living with their families and have fewer functional impairments.

A final problem in cost computations for daycare is that much of the presently available data are based on studies in centers soon after they had opened, when costs may have been higher than, or at least different from, what they would have been at a later point. It thus remains unclear whether a daycare center is more cost effective than a nursing home.

Holmes and Hudson (1975) have argued, however, that cost effectiveness is not the appropriate question to be asked about the daycare approach. Rather, they propose a cost-benefit formula in which the total benefits of participation in the daycare program for the client, family, and community might be explored. These benefits can be related to Kaplan's (1976) basic assumptions about daycare. Acceptance of these assumptions leads to a variety of questions which can be asked about daycare services:

1. Do daycare centers enable impaired elderly to maintain residence in the community?
2. Do daycare services improve or maintain their participants' level of physical or emotional functioning?
3. Do the centers increase the participants' independence on basic activities of daily living?
4. Do daycare services prevent or postpone institutionalization of participants?
5. Do daycare services improve or maintain the participants' interpersonal relationships with family and friends?

6. Do daycare services assist individual participants in reestablishing their desired life-style or increase their life satisfaction?
7. Do daycare services offer supports for family members involved in the care of an elderly individual?

These questions were examined by Weiler, Kim, and Pickard (1976) in a controlled study of a daycare center. Positive answers were found to a number of these questions. Most important, the researchers noted that the daycare participants were functioning at a lower level than the community control group when first examined in November but at a higher level than the control group five months later. A similar result was obtained by Weissert, Wan, and Livieratos (1979) in a controlled study.

Daycare has established itself as an important component of the continuum of services for the aged. With daycare programs available, the caregiver of an older person in the community has some alternatives to the often seemingly overwhelming burdens of care. The most appropriate model for daycare programs will probably remain an issue related to the availability of other services in the community, such as home care, and the characteristics of the older population for whom the daycare center is targeted. With better staff-client ratios and more health programs, Model I centers may be better suited to participants with special or severe health needs. Model II centers may be more appropriate to individuals who require extensive social services.

REFERENCES

Barresi, C., & McConnell, D. (1984). *Discriminators of adult day care participation among retired elderly*. Paper presented at the Gerontological Society of America Annual Meeting, San Antonio, TX.
Behrens, R. (1986). *Adult daycare in America*. Washington, DC: National Council on the Aging.
Durso, L. (1986). Respite care: Focus on caregiver needs. *Older American Reports, 10*(48), 5.
Griffin, K. (1985). Family Survival Project. *Generations, 10*(1), 57–58.
Gurian, B. (1976). Mental health model of day care. In E. Pfeiffer (Ed.), *Day care for older adults*. Durham, NC: Duke University Center for the Study of Aging and Human Development.
Holmes, D., & Hudson, E. (1975). *Evaluation report of the Mosholu-Montefiore day care center for the elderly in the northwest Bronx*. New York: Community Research Applications.
Kaplan, J. (1976). Goals of day care. In E. Pfeiffer (Ed.), *Day care for older*

adults. Durham, NC: Duke University Center for the Study of Aging and Human Development.

Mahoney, K. (1978). *Outside the day care center: Additional support for the frail elderly*. Hartford, CT: Connecticut Department of Aging.

McCuan, E. R. (1973). *An evaluation of a geriatric day care center as a parallel service to institutional care*. Baltimore: Levindale Geriatric Research Center.

National Institute of Senior Centers. (1978). Adult day care: An overview. *Senior center report, 1*(7), 3–8.

Robins, E. (1978). Models of day care. In E. Pfeiffer (Ed.), *Day care for older adults*. Durham, NC: Duke University Center for the Study of Aging and Human Development.

Trager, B. (1976). *Adult day facilities for treatment, health care and related services*. Washington, DC: U.S. Government Printing Office.

U.S. Health Resources Administration, Division of Long-Term Care. (1974). *Guidelines and definitions for day care centers under P.L. 92–603*. Washington, DC: U.S. Government Printing Office.

Weiler, P., Kim, P., & Pickard, L. (1976). Health care for elderly Americans: Evaluation of an adult day health care model. *Medical Care, 14*(8), 700–708.

Weissert, W. (1975). *Adult day care in the U.S.: Final Report*. Washington, DC: Trans Century Corporation.

Weissert, W., Elston, J., Bolda, E., Cready, L., Zelman, W., Sloane, P., Kalsbeek, W., Mutran, E., Rice, T., & Koch, G. (1989). Models of adult day care: Findings from a national survey. *The Gerontologist, 29*, 640–649.

Weissert, W., Wan, T., & Livieratos, B. (1979). *Effects and costs of day care and homemaker services for the chronically ill*. Hyattsville, MD: National Center for Health Services Research.

15

Long-Term Care Residences

NATURE AND HISTORY OF LONG-TERM CARE

Long-term care can be provided through in-home services or daycare centers. In this chapter, however, the focus is on residential institutions for the elderly. The forms of care provided can range from assistance in dressing, bathing, and ambulating to sophisticated medical life support systems. The uniqueness of long-term care facilities lies in their constraint on individual choice in everyday situations since the person living in these settings must adjust to being removed from "normal" individual or family living patterns. Existing long-term care residences include chronic care hospitals, private and public nursing homes, homes for the aged, psychiatric hospitals, and Veterans Administration facilities. All of these facilities provide varied levels of care ranging from extended, skilled, and intermediate care to a personal and boarding care. Long-term care facilities are run under a variety of auspices including public, private-nonprofit, or proprietary organizations.

History of Institutional Settings

The history of long-term care institutions in America began with the almshouses and the public poor houses of colonial America. When a family or individual could no longer care for the pauper, that person became the responsibility of the government. The disabled, aged, widowed, orphaned, feeble-minded and deranged, and victims of disasters were mixed together in almshouses, hospitals, workhouses, orphanages, and prisons. Officials made little distinction between poverty generated by physical disability and economic distress. Boarding out or foster care programs were not uncommon although often harshly administered (Cohen, 1974). Following the Revolutionary War, almshouses became increasingly popular, and in 1834, the Poor Law of England reaffirmed this approach. This philosophy of isolating the aged and infirm from society continued to be the predominant social policy throughout the nineteenth century.

Residents of almshouses were usually pressed into working for very low wages as a means of earning at least a meager salary. Any financing for the facilities was the responsibility of the towns and counties in which the facilities were located; all efforts at state or federal support were denied for three-quarters of a century. By the late nineteenth century, other resources were being located for some indigent populations, but the elderly were still relegated to the almshouses. In 1875, a New York State report noted:

> Care has been taken not to diminish the terrors of this last resort of poverty, the almshouse, because it has been deemed better that a few should test the minimum rate of which existence can be preserved than that many should find the almshouse so comfortable a home that they would brave the shame of pauperism to gain admission to it. (cited in Cohen, 1974, p. 14)

In the beginning of the twentieth century, the rise of private foundations and philanthropy began to expand the types of institutional care available. In addition, by 1929, the Old Age Assistance Act began to offer an alternative to institutionalization in most states. In the 1930s, new welfare, loan, housing public works, and rent programs, as well as the Social Security Act (SSA), provided a new concept of income support for the aged.

In the early versions of the SSA, there were prohibitions against federal financial participation in the cost of any relief given in any kind of institutional setting. Later this prohibition continued in relation to public facilities because public institutions were considered a state responsibility (Cohen, 1974). The intent of the legislation was to encourage the elderly to live at home or with foster families. However, the actual effect was the displacement of people from public facilities—particularly to boarding homes. As these facilities began to add nurses to their staffs, the name nursing home emerged (Moss & Halmandaris, 1977). Some people could not afford to move to the boarding homes—substandard as many were—and so continued in the public homes at state expense (Drake, 1958).

Since the 1930s, institutional long-term care has increased rapidly. In 1939, there were 1,200 facilities in the United States with 25,000 beds. In 1954, there were over 25,000 facilities with about 450,000 beds. In 1986, (excluding hospital-based facilities) there were 25,646 nursing and re-lated care homes with approximately 1,700,000 beds and 1,553,233 resi-dents (Sirrocco, 1988). These facilities were primarily homes for the mentally retarded, homes for the aged, or board-and-care homes. Three-fourths of the nursing homes were proprietary.

In 1953, federal participation in the cost of assistance for indigent per-sons in private institutions was first authorized, but the ban on payment to public institutions continued. However, if states wanted to participate in the federal program, they were required to establish some standards for the institutions. Also, in the 1950s, several federal acts authorized moneys through grants and loans for constructing and equipping long-term care institutions. The Hill-Burton Act, the Small Business Adminis-tration, and the National Housing Act provisions were the most prominent.

The passage of Title XVIII (Medicare) in 1965 and Title XIX (Medic-aid) in 1967 opened new and major funding sources for long-term care institutions. With this legislation, service delivery requirements were re-shaped and clarified. Prior to the enactment of Medicare and Medicaid, there was very little consistency among what were defined as institutions of long-term care. Nursing homes, homes for the aged, convalescent hospitals, and chronic care facilities were all defined separately by each state. The new funding sources set common definitions and basic na-tional standards for service delivery in this important area and long-term care (Winston & Wilson, 1977).

Dunlop (1979), however, has argued that the growth in nursing home beds was greater before passage of Medicaid than after. Indeed, Medic-aid replaced earlier forms of medical assistance and has enabled the con-tinuation of nursing home growth while developing a mechanism for en-forcing nursing home standards.

Extent of Long-Term Care Programs

Despite the extensive increase in the number of long-term care patients, only 4.3% of people aged 65 and over are residents in nursing homes at any one time (Sirrocco, 1988). As people get older, their chances of be-ing in a nursing home increase. Murtaugh et al. (1990) estimate that 43% of the individuals who are 65 in 1990 will spend some time in a nursing home during their lifetime. These estimates are based on life ex-pectancies as well as current usage patterns of nursing homes.

Not only has the number of beds increased, but the size of the homes has also, which reflects the change from family businesses to larger corporations. In 1963, the average nursing home had 39.9 beds, and this had increased to 84.7 beds by 1982 (Sirrocco, 1985). Despite this growth, nursing home supply has not kept up with demand. An examination of national data on nursing homes reveals that over 6,500 of the 16,388 nursing homes had more than 100 beds. Nursing homes under government auspices had an average of 126 beds, non-profit homes an average of 101 beds, and for-profit homes had an average of 87 beds (Sirrocco, 1988). Occupancy rates in nursing homes averaged 92% in 1985 and social workers had a difficult time finding beds for clients when needed (Rivlin & Weiner, 1988).

Long-Term Care Patients

There is an inverse relationship between age and nursing home residency: In 1985 45% of nursing home residents were over the age of 85, 39% were between the ages of 75 and 84, and 16% were between 65 and 74. With this age breakdown it is not surprising that three-quarters of the nursing home residents were women and that 84% of these women had no spouse (U.S. Senate, Special Committee on Aging, 1990). Black residents (over half residing in the South) comprised about 8% of nursing home residents. Hispanics (residing primarily in the West and South) accounted for 2% of the total nursing home population (Sirrocco, 1988).

Importantly, more than 50% of nursing home residents have no living close relatives, which may account for the fact that 60% receive no visitors. These figures indicate that one of the contributing factors to nursing home admissions is the lack of family support that might enable the person to continue living in his or her own home.

It is clear that long-term care residences are increasingly being used for the care of very old patients, most of whom have some physical or mental impairment and many of whom have no close family on whom to rely. Long-term care residences are closer to being chronic disease hospitals for physically and mentally impaired elderly than care centers and homes for ambulatory aged who are not self-sufficient (Tobin & Lieberman, 1976). This change has occurred in part because there are community and quasi-institutional options for those who are reasonably self-sufficient. Because of the change in the residential population of nursing homes, the care has become increasingly more medical, rather than social and psychological. However, "the loss of physical or psychological self-sufficiency does not automatically mean the loss of social needs; the consequences will indeed be dire if we retreat to warehousing these most

needy elderly and do not make every effort to provide life-sustaining social as well as physical supports" (Tobin & Lieberman, 1976, p. 236).

TYPES OF LONG-TERM CARE RESIDENCES

There are many different types of long-term care facilities for the elderly.
However, until the creation of national funding legislation in the mid-1960s,
there were no national standards governing the types of care in any given facility. As a result of the Medicare and Medicaid legislation, extended care facilities (ECFs), skilled nursing home services, and intermediate care facilities
(ICFs) were identified and defined in terms of standards of care. Since that
time, many of the long-term care institutions have adjusted their services to
meet the outlined criteria in order to be eligible for reimbursements. Even so,
both more extensive care (such as that provided in chronic care hospitals) and
less extensive care (such as that provided in domiciliary care facilities) are still
under regulations as defined by individual states and, therefore, are more difficult to define nationally.

Extended Care Facilities

ECFs are defined almost entirely in terms of Medicare reimbursement.
In actual operation, they differ very little, if at all, from skilled nursing
services:

> The extended care facility is a short-term convalescent care facility specifi-
> cally arranged to take care of carefully selected patients coming from hospi-
> tals. . . It involves aspects of rehabilitation, social work, high-quality medi-
> cal and nursing care, and supportive services—that is, those services usually
> associated with long-term care of high quality. (Cohen, 1974, p. 20)

Extended care is defined more in terms of the length of stay, origin of
the patient, and rehabilitative potential than in the type of services that
are actually given. Because Medicare defines eligibility for extended care
so narrowly, there are very few ECF beds actually in use, and the beds
that are available are usually in skilled nursing facilities. Currently, then,
almost all long-term nursing-related care falls into the other two categories: skilled nursing care and intermediate care.

Skilled Nursing Facilities

Skilled nursing facilities are required to provide certain services including
"the emergency and ongoing services of a physician, nursing care, reha-

bilitative services, pharmaceutical services, dietetic services, laboratory and radiologic services, dental services, social services, and activity services" (Glasscote et al., 1976, p. 34). Some of these services must be a part of the facility itself, but rehabilitative, laboratory, radiological, social, and dental services may be provided by formal contractual agreement with outside resources.

There must be visits by attending physicians every 30 days of the first 90 days of a patient's stay. After that time, if justified, the visits can be reduced to every 60 days. A patient care plan should also be prepared and reviewed regularly so that the patient is assured of receiving services that are needed and so that changing conditions are being translated into appropriate care. In 1986, a report of the National Institute of Medicine criticized the quality of care and life in nursing homes. The report stressed the need for greater federal involvement in the regulation of nursing home operation. In 1987 new federal rules strengthening inspection of nursing homes accepting Medicare or Medicaid funds were passed in Congress. Although the states can waive the rules in some cases, these homes must have a registered nurse on duty at least 8 hours each day and a licensed practical nurse on duty at all times. A social worker with a bachelor's degree in social work will also be required at all homes of over 120 beds. In addition, new training requirements for aides were instituted. Regular programs of activities, use and preparation of drugs, and physical facilities in relation to fire and safety codes are carefully delineated for skilled nursing facilities. In general, skilled nursing facilities can be characterized as medical institutions that care for patients who are severely ill.

Intermediate Care Facilities

ICFs were defined in conjunction with the Medicaid legislation of the late 1960s. The definition evolved from the recognition that a large number of poor people were not ill enough to require full-time professional staff attention but did need health supervision and access to various health and rehabilitative components (Glasscote et al., 1976). This level of care is defined in terms of Medicaid reimbursement only. Those patients who are paying privately pay a fee which is established by the nursing home and are not involved in the definitions of levels of care.

Intermediate care can be provided not only in facilities that are set up for that purpose but in skilled care facilities, homes for the aged, hospitals, or personal care homes. In other words—as with skilled care—the definition of intermediate care is of the level of care provided rather than the facility providing that care.

Many regulations are the same as for skilled nursing facilities:

Regulations for construction, sanitation, safety, and the handling of drugs are very similar. Theoretically and philosophically the difference is that the SNF is a "medical" institution and the ICF is a "health" institution. In the ICF, social and recreational policy is to be given near equal emphasis with medical policy. (Glasscote et al., 1976, p. 39)

In addition, there are lesser requirements for supervisory personnel. For example, on the day shift nursing services must be supervised full-time by either a registered nurse or a licensed practical nurse. This is a less sophisticated nursing requirement than that of the skilled nursing facility.

The federal regulations for both skilled nursing facilities and ICFs leave room for interpretation, new regulations, and elaboration (Glasscote et al., 1976). This is important because it allows the states, who administer, supervise, and control the nursing home program, to build an improved program based on their own particular needs and resources. It is also the states that set the criteria of who is eligible for which level of care. Potential patients who are eligible for Medicare must have their conditions reviewed by the locally designated authority to determine the appropriate level of care for each condition. The nursing home is then reimbursed for the designated level of care, with the intermediate level determination receiving less reimbursement than the skilled level. The levels of care must be separated, either by facility or by wings in a facility. Because of this requirement, if the condition of a patient already admitted to a nursing home should change to the extent that the required level of care changes, that patient will either be moved to another section of the nursing home or in some cases, be moved to another facility. A private paying patient who becomes eligible for Medicaid after admission will, at that time, be evaluated and assigned a level of care that might or might not require a physical change.

In 1986 half of nursing homes were skilled nursing facilities. Representing the largest facilities, these homes account for almost 65% of certified and uncertified nursing home beds in the United States (Sirrocco, 1988).

Mental Hospitals

Mental hospitals continue to care for the elderly but not in as significant numbers as before. Older persons now constitute 23% of the patients in state hospitals but accounted for only 5.5% of the admissions in 1983 (Lebowitz, 1987). Many of these older patients are among the long-term hospital population. Large numbers of older individuals were transferred out of state mental hospitals following the passage of Medicare and Medicaid legislation. Many of these former state hospital patients instead became residents of nursing homes. The number of older patients in state hospitals has also been restricted by decisions in state and federal courts, which have made grounds for involuntary commitment to mental hospitals much more stringent.

Since 1989 the federal government has attempted to restrict the use of nursing homes as substitutes for mental hospitals. At present, nursing facilities may not admit anyone with mental illness or retardation to a nursing home unless they are first evaluated by the state to determine whether they need the services of a nursing home and active mental health treatment. Once admitted to a nursing home, the resident's condition must be reviewed annually to assess if he or she still needs to be in the nursing home and needs active mental health treatment. If the answer on these two criteria is negative, the residents must be discharged from the nursing home. Anyone who has resided in the nursing home for more than 30 months has the choice to stay in the facility or move to another setting. The State must also provide treatment for those individuals in the nursing home whose assessment indicates it is needed. Importantly, Alzheimer's disease and dementia are not considered mental illnesses under Pre-Admission and Annual Resident Review. If this assessment and review process is enforced and substantial numbers of older persons are either kept out of nursing homes, hospitals, or are discharged, there may be problems related to finding appropriate placements for these individuals (Jones & Kamter, 1989).

FUNDING

The funding system of long-term care facilities has been a major influence on the development of types of facilities and care that are available. The two most important sources, in terms of shaping the long-term care industry, are Medicare and Medicaid.

As indicated earlier, Medicare legislation, which was passed in 1965, authorized care in a long-term care institution for those patients who were hospitalized for at least three consecutive days, who needed skilled nursing care, and who were to be admitted to a Medicare-certified facility within 14 days of their discharge from the hospital. The patient had to be evaluated regularly and could stay in the long-term care facilities for no longer than 90 days under Medicare. This new funding source made ECFs very popular in the last half of the 1960s, as it was an excellent vehicle for shortening hospital stays. In 1969, the rapidly rising costs for the program led to a change in the regulations. New administrative regulations required that participants in the program have rehabilitative potential. In addition, nursing care was defined in more narrow terms, which included only a very limited number of diagnoses and therapeutic situations. The effect of these new regulations was to virtually cut off Medicare as a vehicle for nursing home care for the elderly (Moss & Halmandaris, 1977). Because many nursing homes were caught losing thousands of dollars in disallowed costs at the time the regulations changed, the number of nursing homes that even wanted to participate in the Medicare program dramatically decreased. However, the precedent of reimbursement for medical long-term care was set.

Legislation establishing Medicaid—a system of medical cost reimbursement for the poor—opened the greatest opportunity for funding nursing home care. In 1988, Medicaid payments accounted for 90% of all public spending on nursing homes and 45% of all nursing home expenditures. An additional 48% of the costs are paid for by older persons or their families. Since Medicaid is a shared federal–state program, the federal government provides a basic set of requirements upon which the states build the program. The states determine their own definitions of needy; there is some flexibility from state to state as to who is eligible for Medicaid in long-term care institutions. States can include the categorically needy—those who are eligible for federally aided financial assistance—and the medically needy—those whose incomes are sufficient for daily living expenses but not enough to pay for medical expenses. Because of the nature of this definition, persons who might not be eligible while in the community could be eligible for Medicaid if entering a long-term care residence. Often the residential Medicaid eligibility factors for long-term care residences relate more to personal assets than monthly income, and so once the assets are liquidated, a person entering a nursing home can become eligible for Medicaid reimbursements.

Formerly, to achieve eligibility a married couple had to "spend down" almost all of their assets. One result was that the spouse who remained living in the community was reduced to impoverished conditions. Under the "spousal impoverishment" provisions of Medicaid, the spouse remaining in the community is now allowed to retain a maximum of up to one-half of $125,160 of the couple's assets and a minimum of $12,516 (in 1990). The states are allowed to raise this minimum. Raising the minimum to $20,000 for example, allows couples with assets of $20,000–$40,000 to preserve all of these funds for the use of the spouse living in the community. This new minimum would have no effect on couples with assets of $40,000 or more. By 1991, some states had raised the minimum to the maximum, a change that allows the older couple to preserve a good portion of their assets. In addition, the spouse in the community is allowed to have an income of 150% of the federal poverty level in 1992. The monthly income levels cannot exceed $1,500.

The couple's house can be transferred to the community based spouse without penalty. Other possible transferees include minor, blind, or disabled children living in the house or sons or daughters who lived in the home for 2 years as a caregiver prior to the institutionalization of the nursing home resident. Patients can also enter a home as private paying patients, and as their assets diminish, they become eligible for Medicaid.

Extensive publicity has been generated on potential abuses of Medicaid reimbursements. Nationally, 75% of all nursing homes are profit-making businesses, while 25% are nonprofit or public homes (Sirrocco, 1985). These figures represent a one-third increase in the number of profit-making homes during the last decade. As Moss and Halmandaris (1977) point out, conflicts between profits and quality of care are likely when services become a money-making operation. The conflicts will be greatest in firms that operate a number of homes, since they may attempt to maximize their profits by lowering the costs they incur at any one particular home.

State regulatory agencies, understanding the financial incentives of the nursing home industry, promulgate reimbursement regulations that are designed to encourage quality care and limit profits. There have been variations in the success of these regulations.

Under the Medicaid program, nursing homes are reimbursed in relation to their costs. All costs must be included in the reimbursement fee, and the patient is not to be charged extra for services given. The states must set their reimbursement rates to allow the nursing homes to operate efficiently and meet quality standards. In setting their cost rates, the states are also expected to take into account the special situation of nursing homes that predominantly serve low-income individuals. Medicare also uses a cost-related system for reimbursement, but allows a prospective reimbursement for some types of nursing homes. During 1987, approximately $73 per day reimbursement was being provided by Medicare for skilled nursing facilities. This figure represents a substantial increase from the $32 per day paid in 1977 (U.S. House of Representatives, 1987).

For all patients in nursing homes under Medicaid, each is eligible for at least $30 a month in spending money which can be spent for anything the patient wants, including cigarettes, haircuts, clothes, and magazines. This spending money is in exchange for the fact that any income the patient is receiving, such as Social Security, is to be paid to the home and subtracted from the amount of the Medicaid reimbursement. For those patients who can personally handle the money, the program is successful. However, for those patients who cannot manage their own resources, there has been potential for abuse in the use of the money, since it can come under the supervision of the nursing home administration.

Private Payments

A significant minority of nursing home payments come directly from the patients or their families. As mentioned earlier, a patient may have significant assets and enter the institution as a private paying patient. At a cost of $12,000 to $50,000 per year, payments for nursing home care can quickly deplete all of a resident's assets. Between 1986 and 1990, 54% of all individuals admitted to nursing homes during that period were forced to rely on Medicaid reimbursements to pay for their care. The percentage is higher among residents who remain in nursing homes longer than a year (Rivlin & Weiner, 1988). Unlike reimbursements under Medicaid, the home can charge the patient for extra services which may be required for care. For example, extra padding, extra toileting time, extra time for feeding, could all result in extra charges. Private paying patients usually cannot predict the exact costs of the home and have no recourse if they object to the prices charged except to find another nursing home.

Much of the care which is provided under board and care, personal care, and domiciliary care homes is paid directly by the residents of the facilities. SSI and Social Security checks are turned over to the facility in exchange for personal care services that are rendered.

State and Local Funding

State funding, which covers about one-half (it varies slightly from state to state) of the Medicaid reimbursement, reimburses the board and care, personal care, and domiciliary care facilities when personal income is inadequate to cover the allowed daily reimbursement rate. It also covers the costs of individual care in mental hospitals, and in these settings the total cost of patient care is paid. One of the reasons for the increase in the number of elderly who are being transferred to nursing homes and personal care facilities from state hospitals is the states' desire to develop a situation where the federal government is paying at least part of the cost of caring for the elderly.

Long-term care facilities provide an excellent example of how the funding mechanisms have shaped the types of services and the amount of service available for the elderly. In addition, long-term care is unique in that the majority of care is being provided by profit-making organizations—a factor that both influences and is influenced by the funding available for this particular type of service. Whatever the source, the cost of nursing home care is striking. In 1985, approximately $36 billion was spent on nursing homes.

PERSONNEL AND PROGRAMING

Staffing Patterns

Staffing patterns of long-term care residences are closely related to reimbursement rates. Homes attempt to meet state regulations regarding personnel while at the same time keeping costs in line with reimbursement allowances, including profit. Unfortunately, the end result is generally an inadequate and poorly trained staff. Of the over 700,000 nursing home personnel in this country in 1982, approximately 65,000 were registered nurses and 86,000 were licensed practical nurses. The rate of nurses per 100 beds ranged from a high of 12.0 in the Northeast to 9.3 in the North Central area of the United States. The nurse/patient rate increases with the size of the nursing home (Sirrocco, 1985). Aides and orderlies perform between 80 and 90% of all nursing care actually given patients (Horn & Griesel, 1977). Most aides and orderlies receive no training for their jobs. Of those applying for jobs in nursing homes 53% have had no previous experience and only half of them have completed high school. The turnover rate is 75% each year (Moss & Halmandaris, 1977). One important reason for the lack of trained and committed staff is the salary, which is usually at or just above minimum wage. This is a disincentive to produce a commitment to the job, to seek additional training, or even to stay on the job for any length of time beyond that of getting enough experience to get another, perhaps better paying, job. However, any job training beyond the minimal in-service programs required by the homes would up the demands for higher wages, which in turn would reflect directly on the Medicaid reimbursement figures. Community colleges are beginning to offer special training for aides, which in certain situations could help provide stability to staffing patterns.

The number of staff (including aides) actually on the floor of a nursing home influences the quality and amount of care given. The stated minimum requirement, which varies from state to state, usually says that a certain amount (two to three hours) of nursing care is required per patient per day. However, when this is translated to personnel, it could be actual on-floor nursing care, or on-floor care except for lunches and breaks, absences, and vacations. For the latter, the actual on-floor care is half an hour below that required. The interpretation affects the care, the cost, the reimbursement rate, and the profit margin. Some states have been reluctant to interpret such regulations precisely until they can generate a Medicaid reimbursement rate that can pay for actual staffing requirements.

In addition to the basic nursing and support staff, homes are required to have access to certain types of professional staff. The extent to which the home actually hires the professional person required as opposed to responding to the need through contractual agreements affects the quality of care in the home. For example, actually hiring a social worker, a dietician, an occupational therapist, and a full-time physician brings more services to the home than using these people a few hours a week on a contract basis. The size of the home, the relationship of the individual home to a larger organizational structure (the individual hired by a chain of homes can work in two or three facilities), and the type of reimbursement mechanism influence the extent to which the home actually hires the additional personnel required.

Programing and Advocacy

Beyond having an activity director whose responsibility is to provide some activity for patients, state regulations do not stipulate the types of programing for nursing homes. The result is that there is a tremendous variety of programed activities available in long-term care institutions. Some homes make only the minimum number of programs available, while others establish links with the community to ensure that those programs most appropriate to the patients' needs are presented.

Sensory training, reality orientation, and remotivation are essential components of nursing home programing. Reorientation of the patient to the larger world, heightening the patient's sensory sensitivity, and reestablishing earlier interests all help to improve the patients' daily functioning. As in other major services, the range of activities that may be well received by patients runs the gamut from picnics, dance, theater, and crafts to movies and guest speakers. Some nursing homes have links with senior centers, adult daycare centers, and nutrition programs in order to provide ways of getting patients into other settings and of bringing community people into the nursing homes. Volunteer organizations from the community also provide special services for patients in many community nursing homes.

Programing that has a purpose and recreates the interests and talents of the patients is the most successful. Many patients have little opportunity to share their experiences and even themselves with others when they enter a nursing home. Programing can create these opportunities if it is seen by the patient as being meaningful. In a study by Dudley and Hillery (1977), long-term care institutions had the highest scores on alienation and high scores on deprivation of freedom when compared to several other types of residential organizations. The level of alienation in part results from the practice of placing restrictions on the resident's ability to make decisions. Programing on a voluntary basis, with a variety of activities from which the patients may choose and which, from time to time, they suggest, can have the effect of reducing the sense of alienation that comes with the institutional process, particularly in nursing homes.

Families can also be built into the programing for the home. As Miller and Beer (1977) point out, familial friendships are the most meaningful and the most enduring of all preexisting resident relationships. There are no substitutes for positive family relationships. However, if a patient has only minimal family ties, the nursing home can create an atmosphere of the extended family through its programing by bringing in volunteers and using other patients, when appropriate.

Two advocacy programs in recent years have focused on the special needs of patients in long-term care settings, particularly nursing homes, and on how to get those needs vocalized in a way which produces a response. One, the patients' rights movement, began in the early 1970s when several states passed patients' rights legislation in response to the belief that the personal rights and liberties of patients were being lost with the institutional process (Wilson, 1978). In 1974, the federal government developed regulations which established a set of patients' rights for patients in skilled and intermediate care facilities. These rights, which relate to individual liberties and dignities, are readily displayed, explained to the patients, and assigned to nursing home personnel for enforcement. Some of the rights covered in the regulations include being informed of the services available in the facility, being informed of one's medical condition and the plan of treatment, being encouraged and assisted throughout the stay in the nursing home, being able to manage personal financial affairs, being free from mental and physical abuse, being assured of confidential treatment of personal and medical records, being able to retain use of personal clothing and possessions as space permits, and being assured privacy for visits by one's spouse. Unfortunately, there are conditional clauses that make enforcement difficult, and the only disciplinary tool available is decertification of the facility, a recourse that is too severe for individual violations. Despite the difficulties of enforcement, the federal government, working through the states, has made a firm commitment to enforce the patients' rights.

The second advocacy program created to respond to specific needs of patients is the ombudsman program, which is designed to examine complaints by patients and, through investigations, give patients a voice in determining their own individual circumstances. Begun in 1972, five ombudsman programs were funded nationally as models of the ways that the program could be most effective. Two more programs were added in 1973. Today, most ombudsman programs are affiliated with the State Units on Aging and work through the Area Agencies on Aging. They still retain the objective of being the focal point for complaints regarding nursing home care, but they also act as a nursing home referral service, an organizer of friendly visiting programs, and a center for educating patients and the community on the rights of nursing home patients (U.S. Administration on Aging, 1977).

In recent years the role of the ombudsman has been strengthened through both federal and state legislation. The nursing home reforms described below place an emphasis on the nursing home resident knowing about the ombudsman program. In New Jersey the state ombudsman is permitted to investigate complaints and hold hearings as well as subpoena individuals and records. In the District of Columbia the ombudsman serves as "resident's representative" and can file petitions for receivership, as well as complaints for civil damages and actions against the District (Schuster, 1989).

Despite these legislative enactments, representatives of ombudsman programs still encounter a number of difficulties. A survey by the National Association of State Long-Term Care Ombudsman Programs indicated funding problems that restrict the availability of ombudsman services and their ability to respond to complaints. In addition, the survey found a wide range in the frequency of services. Only 16% of the states in the survey report that an ombudsman pays more than one visit a month to nursing homes and the frequency of visits is even lower in board-and-care homes. In these facilities over 50% of the states reported no visits by the ombudsman. Overall, ombudsmen investigated 154,000 complaints in fiscal 1990 (*Older American Reports*, 1990; 1992).

Title VII of the 1992 OAA amendments defines the functions and duties of the ombudsman more extensively than in the 1987 amendments. The functions range from investigation of complaints to informing residents of long-term care facilities about means of obtaining services and ensuring that the residents obtain these services. The duties are similar to the functions but also include review and comment on proposed laws and regulations that may affect residents, facilitation of public access to review of these laws and regulations, and support for the development of resident and family councils in long-term care residences.

QUALITY IN LONG-TERM CARE RESIDENCES

How well the long-term care residence is carrying out its mandate, meeting requirements, and providing the level of care agreed to under its contract with the funding sources is evaluated through the inspection system. The federal government provides the regulative substructure on which the states build specific codes for operation. The states then divide the inspection responsibilities between local fire and safety agencies. The result is a series of inspections of the homes for different purposes, which are, at times, in conflict with one another. The two biggest problems with the current inspection systems are: (1) inspections are primarily to evaluate the physical plant rather than to evaluate the actual quality of care; because actual quality of care is very difficult to measure, long lists of physical requirements become the substitute; and (2) there is essentially no weapon for noncompliance except revoking the license to operate—a very difficult step, in many cases inappropriate to the situation, both because the need for nursing home beds is so acute and because shutting down a home and moving patients is traumatic; hence a state or local enforcement body will not usually impose such a step until after years of flagrant abuse.

Basically, most states have four components to their inspection systems: (1) sanitation and environment, (2) meals, (3) fire safety, and (4) patient care. This means that there is a visit by a sanitarian, a dietician, a professional review team, and a fire inspector (Moss & Halmandaris, 1977). In most states, at least two of the inspections are to be unannounced, although this is not always the case. Until the inspection procedures become better organized and develop more effective ways of measuring the actual quality of care, the inspection system will not be the best answer to improving the care in long-term care residences.

In 1987, a comprehensive set of nursing home reform amendments was passed and went into effect in October, 1990. Under the amendments, skilled nursing facilities and intermediate care facilities are termed "nursing facilities" and are held to a single standard of care. Within each of these facilities, a comprehensive assessment of residents must be undertaken at admission, when the residents physical or mental condition changes, and at least on an annual basis. These assessments form the basis of a care plan designed to help the resident maintain or attain the highest level of physical, mental, and psychosocial functioning possible given their condition.

Each facility must have a licensed nurse on duty at all times. A Registered Nurse must be on duty during at least one shift per day. The nurse aides who work at the nursing facilities must complete a 75-hour training course within 4 months of being hired. A physician must visit the home every 30 days during the first 3 months of a resident's stay and thereafter every 90 days. The amendments allow the visits to be conducted by a physician's assistant or nurse practitioner if they are supervised by a physician. A full-time social worker must also be employed in all nursing facilities over 120 beds in size.

All of the above changes are an effort to ensure quality of care in nursing facilities. In addition, the facilities must maintain a Quality Assessment and Assurance Committee which can identify the issues that need to be assessed and implement action designed to correct deficiencies. The facility must also offer an activities program and rehabilitative services. An independent consultant must be utilized to monitor all psychopharmacologic drugs. The amendments also include a clear statement of residents' rights in the home (National Citizen's Coalition for Nursing Home Reform, n.d.)

REFERENCES

Cohen, E. (1974). An overview of long-term care facilities. In E. Brody, (Ed.), *A social work guide for long-term care facilities*. Rockville, MD: National Institute of Mental Health.

Drake, J. (1958). *The aged in American society*. New York: Ronald.

Dudley, C., & Hillery, G. (1977). Freedom and alienation in homes for the aged. *Gerontologist, 17*, 140–145.

Dunlop, B. (1979). *The growth of nursing home care*. Lexington, MA: Lexington Books.

Glasscote, R., Biegel, A., Jr., Clark, E., Cox, B., Elper, J. R., Gudeman, J. E., Gurel, L., Lewis, R. V., Miler, D. G., Raybin, J. B., Reifler, C., & Vito, E., Jr. (1976). *Old folks at homes*. Washington, DC: American Psychiatric Association and the Mental Health Association.

Haber, P. (1987). Nursing homes. In G. Maddox, (Ed.), *The encyclopedia of aging*. New York: Springer Publishing Company.

Jones, E., & Kamter, A. (1989). Advocating for freedom: The community placement of elders from state psychiatric hospitals. *Clearinghouse Review, 44*, 444–449.

Lebowitz, B. (1987). Mental health services. In G. Maddox, (Ed.), *The encyclopedia of aging*. New York: Springer Publishing Company.

Miller, D., & Beer, S. (1977). Patterns of friendship among patients in a nursing home setting. *Gerontologist, 17*, 269–275.

Moss, F., & Halmandaris, V. (1977). *Too old, too sick, too bad*. Germantown, MD: Aspen Systems Group.

Murtaugh, C., Kemper, P., & Spillane, B. (1990). The risk of nursing home use in later life. *Medical Care, 28*, 952–962.

National Citizen's Coalition for Nursing Home Reform. (n.d.). *A brief summary of selected key provisions of the Nursing Home Reform Amendments of OBRA '87*. Washington, DC: Author.

National Institute of Medicine. (1986). *Improving the quality of care in nursing homes*. Washington, DC: Author.

Older American Reports. (1990). Ombudsman provisions need clarification during OAA reauthorization, Congress told. *14*, September 19, 263–264.

Older American Reports. (1992). AoA releases FY '90 data on Title III State programs. *16*, April 17, 156.

Rivlin, A., & Weiner, J. (1988). *Caring for the disabled elderly: Who will pay?* Washington, DC: The Brookings Institution.

Schuster, M. (1989). Legal support to the long-term care ombudsman program: A practical guide. *Clearinghouse Review, 44*, 418–421.

Sirrocco, A. (1985). *An overview of the 1982 national master facility inventory survey of nursing and related care homes*. Hyattsville, MD: National Center for Health Statistics.

Sirrocco, A. (1988). *Nursing and related care homes as reported from the 1986 inventory of long-term care places*. Hyattsville, MD: National Center for Health Statistics.

Tobin, S., & Lieberman, M. (1976). *Last home for the aged*. San Francisco: Jossey-Bass.

U.S. Senate, Special Committee on Aging. (1990). *Developments in aging: 1989, Volume 1*. Washington, DC: U.S. Government Printing Office.

U.S. Administration on Aging. (1977). *Nursing home ombudsman program: A fact sheet and program directory*. Washington, DC: U.S. Government Printing Office.

U.S. House of Representatives. (1987). *Background material and data on programs within the jurisdiction of the Committee on Ways and Means*. Washington, DC: U.S. Government Printing Office.

Wilson, S. (1978). Nursing home patients' rights: Are they enforceable. *Gerontologist, 18*, 255–261.

Winston, W., & Wilson, A. (1977). *Ethical consideration in long-term care*. St. Petersburg, FL: Eckerd College Gerontology Center.

16

The Future of Aging Programs and Services

Predictions about demographic terms and programs are dangerous to make because of their unreliability, but future directions for aging programs and services will probably rest on four major factors: changes in the numbers of elderly and their respective ages, political clout of the older population, attitudes toward aging services among the general public, and federal funding of aging programs.

As Chapter 1 indicates, the elderly are a growing segment of American society. Since all of the individuals who will reach 60 years of age in 1990 or 2000 have already been born, we can safety predict that this portion of the population will continue to increase. The only factors that could alter this expected growth are a drastic shift in mortality or fertility rates, a major disaster, or war. Barring these events, the rise in the older population will continue until 2030, when the adult population over 60 will approximate 20% of the total population. The growth of the older population and the stable numbers of younger groups during the last decade have already resulted in an increase in the median age of the American population from 28 to 32.6 in 1989 (U.S. Senate et al., 1991).

With this rise in the median age, we can expect a growing concern about aging. However, it is important that we constantly remember that the rise in median age of the American populace reflects a significant increase in the population at the extreme end of the age spectrum: an increase of those over the age of 85 by 50% (as happened between 1970 and 1980) is bound to generate larger numbers of individuals who are severely handicapped and need intensive programs and services of all types, including long-term residential care. Thus the need for programs and services will be intensified rather than reduced during the 1990s and beyond.

THE ELDERLY VOTING BLOCK

It is as yet unclear whether the older persons will support the growth of expenditures or even the maintenance of current levels of funding for these services. Data that attribute the growth of funding for programs to political activism of the elderly have been criticized. The basic problem with this approach is its tendency to characterize the elderly as a group with solidarity of concerns. Judging from the economic and social diversity within the over-60 population, there is little reason to expect the elderly to vote as a block. A more realistic view is that older adults form a large group whose views range from conservative to radical. Different age cohorts among the elderly have strongly differing values and political attitudes that were formed during childhood and carried into adulthood. The carryover of these attitudes into old age has now been amply demonstrated by research. The thesis that individuals become politically conservative as they grow older is basically unfounded. In some instances, such as the election of senators in Florida in 1972, older voters appear to have had an impact (Butler, 1975). Organized efforts by senior citizen groups in 1965 also helped to promote the long-delayed passage of Medicare legislation and in 1989 groups of older people were instrumental in the repeal of the Medicare Catastrophic Coverage Act. On the other hand, elderly voters in many states have shown that their negative feelings about expenditures of public funds for social and health services are deep seated, even when these expenditures are for programs that may benefit them at some later time.

The aged have yet to evidence a cohesive self-consciousness. Many elderly who correctly perceive "old age" as a stigmatized status in American society will continue to consciously avoid identification with their age peers. The efforts of organizers such as Maggie Kuhn are focused as much on changing the attitudes of the older person as they are on organizing. As Binstock (1972) has argued, it is not enough for a group to have an influence on the outcome of an election by balloting. Power at the polls must be translated into the types of lobbying and advocacy efforts that result in legislation and funds. The organizational coherence required for these efforts has only recently been shown by the aged.

ATTITUDES TOWARD AGING SERVICES

Even if the elderly have not been as politically effective as their increasing numbers would suggest, the changing shape of the American age pyramid has made it difficult for legislators to ignore the needs of older adults. An example of the responsiveness of legislators to the older population occurred in Virginia in 1981, when the state proposed cutting Medicaid benefits to older persons just above the official poverty threshold. These cuts were expected to discontinue benefits for 500 older people. These elderly would have been forced to relocate from nursing homes unless they or their families could produce the additional funds required to compensate for the Medicaid cutoff. In response to public outcry, a decision was made not to utilize this approach to compensate for the decline in federal contributions to Medicaid.

Besides general sympathy for the needs of older persons among the general public, the nature of services provided through Area Agencies on Aging and other programs helps to continue political support. Rather than dealing with issues such as self-esteem, the focus is on elementary survival needs: food, clothing, shelter, and companionship. Little emphasis has been placed on shaping the values of the elderly.

The types of basic programs offered to the elderly have two major advantages: (1) they provide tangible and accountable results; and (2) they allow the provision of programs to a group that is noncontroversial and provide a shift in public focus away from stigmatized "minority" populations. The number of meals served, the number of housing units built, and the medical services provided are easily quantified. Legislators needing evidence of their concern for constituents' needs relish the opportunity to point to these types of concrete services provided to the aged.

For the majority of the American public, the elderly represent a passive and undemanding group. They are thus viewed as a contrast to threatening ethnic and minority groups. Housing for the elderly has thus become a popular means for many white communities to deal with requirements that they place a specific proportion of their federal housing funds into low-income projects. Housing for the elderly enabled these communities to serve a low-income population with some assurance that the low-income elderly would also be white.

NONTHREATENING PROGRAMS

We have already noted that elderly housing is supported by many communities because of their feeling that the aged are tolerable, if not welcome, neighbors. Programs for the aged are also seen as non-threatening by legislators. Few aging services require major shifts in priorities. There are no demands for "community control" similar to those posed by residents in designated Model City neighborhoods of the 1960s. There are also no threats to businesses and agencies that now have a strong, if not controlling, influence in many local communities. In fact one of the major outcomes of the expansion of federal funding for the elderly has been the efforts by many established agencies to expand their programs and services for the aged. This expansion has helped to offset cuts in other programmatic areas.

NEW JOBS AND PROFITS

The nursing home industry provides a major example of a service delivery system that has expanded as financing mechanisms have been developed. With the passage of Medicare legislation in 1965, the numbers of nursing homes increased dramatically. Opportunities for nursing home proprietors and other providers of services for the aging were aided by developments in related fields, particularly the emphasis on moving individuals out of large long-term care settings such as mental hospitals. Because of a lack of adequate community-based alternatives, many of the elderly individuals discharged to the community became residents of nursing homes. This discharged population, along with a renewed emphasis on maintaining the individual in the community if at all possible, has helped to foster the growth of nutrition programs, daycare centers, and multipurpose senior centers that began to develop quickly after 1973.

As aging programs and services grew, a corps of individuals dedicated to providing the services associated with these programs and services naturally came into existence. Because of the basic nature of many aging programs and services, the ratio of service providers to elderly clients can be very high. This is especially true among programs and services for the aging which work with elderly who have difficulties in daily functioning. As the proportion of the service sector dedicated to working with the elderly enlarges, the interest group having a stake in the retention and enlargement of these services also increases. These interest groups are making the step from the ballot box to the halls of the legislature that is required for programs to be enacted and funds appropriated. Because of its community empowerment ideology, the War on Poverty never generated the professional and paraprofessional constituency that might have enabled poverty programs to resist dismantling. When either authorization or appropriation legislation is being threatened, members of the professional services delivery cadre are highly visible and emphasize their support for the legislation by stating that they represent the aged.

FAMILY CONCERNS

One of the growing bases of support for programs and services in aging are families faced with the responsibility of providing assistance to an older relative. Although the stereotype of "role reversal" in which the older person reverts to a child-like dependency on adult children has been discredited, many older individuals, especially those over 75, require some form of assistance from their adult children. This assistance ranges from help in shopping to assistance in reaching a clinic for a medical appointment. As three- and four-generation families become more commonplace, the concern over having services available to the older person has become greater.

Many families shoulder extensive burdens of care for older relatives, often on a 24-hour basis. At some point the lack of formal services to reduce the burden of providing this care may encourage family members to consider the use of a nursing home for their family member. In order to avoid this decision, many families have become enthusiastic supporters of senior centers, adult daycare centers, and a variety of new service initiatives. Indeed, demographic changes in the United States mean that it is possible for two generations of a four-generation family to be old enough to qualify for services under the Older Americans Act (Gelfand, Olsen, & Block, 1978).

THE 1990s AND BEYOND

Overall public support of programs and services for older people continues to be strong. There is, however, a growing perception that while many older people require extensive assistance from government programs, others use public programs and services for which they could afford to pay. The percentage of children living below the federal poverty level has tended to position the debate over adequate services as a contest between programs for children and programs for older people.

Organizations such as Generations United now attempt to bring together advocacy groups for both the aged and children and to defuse any real or perceived conflict in goals. The 1989 controversy over the Medicare Catastrophic Coverage Act set back these efforts. Protests over the financing of the Act by older persons and some organizations reinforced the impression that older Americans want new benefits without any cost to themselves. Increased federal deficits in the late 1980s and early 1990s have also made it difficult to institute new initiatives for the older population.

LONG-TERM SERVICES

Whatever the changes in public perception of the aged, it is evident that services for this population must be long-term in nature rather than oriented to short-term crises. In a senior center, long-term services means the planning of programs for members who will attend the center for many years. The same is true of adult daycare centers oriented to very frail older individuals. Long-term educational programs must be offered in a framework that emphasizes continued intellectual growth rather than discrete one-time short courses.

The most pressing, and the most costly, initiatives in the next few decades will be for long-term care intended to assist the severely impaired older person. Nursing homes, home care, and adult daycare are the most widely discussed elements in these efforts. Private long-term care insurance that pays for home care services and nursing homes is an important innovation, but its current high cost and restricted benefit structure limit its usefulness. The development of an adequate method of financing various forms of nursing home care that does not destroy the life savings of individuals will require a major commitment of public or public/private funds.

At least four major issues will need to be resolved in the upcoming discussion of a revised long-term care system (OMB Watch, 1990).

- Whether financing will be financed through payroll taxes, general taxes, or some new mechanism
- Whether benefits will begin immediately or after the individual has begun to use the long-term care program for some defined period
- Whether the government would bear all of the costs of the program or whether some portion would have to be paid by the private individual
- Whether the coverage would include Medicare beneficiaries, only the elderly, or other groups such as chronically ill children.

INNOVATION AND THE AGING NETWORK

The role of the public aging network in long-term care and in the provision of programs and services to older people is more in question now than it has ever been since the passage of the Older Americans Act in 1965. As Hudson and Kingson (1991) reaffirm, there can be no question that the intent of the Older Americans Act was to serve all older persons, regardless of their situation. Over time, as the economic situation of the older population has improved, it has seemed more important to stress the needs of economically needy, socially needy, and impaired older persons.

The tension between targeting for these needy older populations, while at the same time providing quality programs and services for all older people, has created problems. One result is increased complexity in the Older Americans Act. The Act now has increased specificity about targeting and accountability and a variety of new initiatives such as the new Title VII (originally proposed by the National Association of State Units on Aging). For many readers, the 1992 OAA amendments will appear a sprawling, confusing document that attempts to deal with all possible circumstances affecting the elderly through a series of programs and services that seem to have no central focus.

To some extent, the growth of provisions in the OAA is a positive reflection of the growth of the field of aging and groups concerned about specific issues. It is questionable, however, whether one major piece of legislation based on the administrative structure of State Units on Aging and Area Agencies on Aging can effectively embody all of these concerns.

There are arguments that AAAs should become coordinators of all community programs and services. In the American social welfare structure, coordination is a difficult task because of the myriad of administrative arrangements that exist to provide services at state and local levels. Many of the most crucial programs and services for the aged are not under control of the Administration on Aging. These include transportation, housing, education, and health care. Because the American social welfare structure is organized along these functional lines (e.g. transportation), an agency concerned with a specific population group (e.g. the aged) has difficulty pulling together the resources and overcoming the "turf" issues that will enable it to mount effective methods. In the 1960s the federal Office of Economic Opportunity, organized to coordinate programs for the poor, encountered the same obstacles. Even if it were possible to implement, coordination of programs and services for older people by the AAA would not necessarily reduce costs for long-term care, delay nursing home placement, or lead to positive changes in functioning among older people (Fortinsky, 1991).

The expansion of the field of aging has also brought many new groups into the service provision arena. Hospitals, concerned about reduced numbers of inpatients, are promoting outpatient and in-home services. Private firms have begun to develop products specifically geared to older people, and the housing industry has grown very interested in the potential retirement and life care community markets. Voluntary agencies now provide services similar to those offered through public agencies. Employers are beginning to offer elder care programs for employees. Private case managers have developed a network around the country to serve families who can afford these services; private adult daycare programs have also begun to appear in some locales. The public sector, which involves State Units on Aging and Area Agencies on Aging, is now only one element in an enlarged service delivery complex concerned about older people (Quirk, 1991).

The failure of federal funding to grow has made it difficult for AoA to maintain its past programs at an adequate level. Area Agencies on Aging increasingly chafe at federal guidelines about their programs since, for many, less than half of their current budget stems from federal funds (Fortinsky, 1991). The 1992 amendments, whatever their good intentions, will fail to have an impact unless major infusions of monies become available during upcoming federal budgets. There is no expectation that these larger sums of money will become available and county and local governments have struggled in recent years to find new sources of revenue.

One possible source of revenue is cost-sharing. Whether sharing the costs of the programs with consumers is the appropriate mechanism for financing efforts of AAAs and State Units on Aging is a major point for debate in the 1990s. A second method of increasing income is for public agencies to offer services to corporations. Many Area Agencies on Aging are currently involved in the development of elder care services in the workplace. These services include education, caregiver consultation, and case management. In Massachusetts, one AAA offers elder care for the Stride Rite Corporation, the General Accounting Office, and General Equipment Corporation.

The model for these initiatives is Public-Private Partnerships (PPP) in which AAAs cooperate with profit-making organizations to provide services to older persons (Boich & Hyde, 1990). While these PPPs may allow AAAs to expand their programs and services, they also raise questions that need to be confronted. Among these questions are whether the involvement of AAAs in these new partnerships will·not siphon off their interest in other non-income generating activities. There is also the possibility that in their endeavor to develop these income producing partnerships, the AAAs will lose sight of the low-income and minority elderly who cannot afford these new services or who are located in less accessible communities. The 1992 OAA amendments require all AAAs to disclose the PPPs in which they are engaged and to demonstrate that rather than diluting the quality of the services they provide, these partnerships will enhance the quality of the services. The AAA must also provide assurances that the partnership does not result in employees of the private organization receiving preferential treatment.

Cost-sharing and Private-Public Partnerships do not resolve the issue of future directions for the public aging network and, in particular, the role of the Older Americans Act. Alternatives to the approach currently embodied in the latest amendments of the Older Americans Act are possible. This approach would narrow the Act's focus to a few priority services that are targeted at frail and impaired older persons and low-income elderly. While this approach would clarify the intent of the Act, it would certainly negate its universal emphasis and, over time, perhaps result in means-testing for eligibility.

A change in direction for the aging network cannot be made without extensive discussion and evaluation of the effectiveness of programs operated through the aging network. Unfortunately, evaluation of these programs is weak, partly due to a lack of standards. Rather than the effects of a program on any number of criteria, reports by AAAs, the State, and the AoA stress numbers of participants, numbers of meals served, or numbers of older workers placed in jobs. Kutza (1991) views these "failures to be self-critical" (p. 67) as weakening the aging network. The reluctance to be self-critical, however, also reflects the maturity of the aging network and the self-protective desire of agencies to ensure their continued funding and existence. Full-scaled valid evaluations of aging network programs now confront an aging network less concerned about innovation than survival, particularly in a period of economic uncertainty.

The dilemma of increased demands, but limited resources, may force an intensive reexamination of the effectiveness of programs, the simplification of access to important programs and services, and the development of programs designed to deal with some of the most difficult remaining problems such as long-term care.

These goals cannot be accomplished in a framework which views pro-

grams and services for the aged as separate from those for other populations. Social welfare advocates must unite in a framework that sees the
needs of children, the aged, minority populations, and other groups as
interrelated rather than competitive. A failure to bridge seeming differences in needs will mean continued competition for social welfare dollars, a competition that will eventually defeat the best intents of all advocacy groups.

REFERENCES

Binstock, R. (1972). Responsibility for the care of the geriatric patient: Legal,
    psychological and ethical issues. *Journal of Geriatric Psychiatry, 5*, 146–
    159.
Boich, L., & Hyde, J. (1990). Public policy and public-private partnerships. *Mi-
    nority aging exchange, 3*(1), 1–3.
Butler, R. (1975). *Why survive?* New York: Harper and Row.
Fortinsky, R. (1991). Coordinated, comprehensive community care and the
    Older Americans Act. *Generations, 15*(3), 39–42.
Gelfand, D., Olsen, J., & Block, M. (1978). Two generations of elderly in the
    changing American family: Implications for aging services. *The Family Co-
    ordinator, 27*, 395–404.
Hudson, R., & Kingson, E. (1991). Inclusive and fair: The case for universality
    in social programs. *Generations, 15*(3), 51–56.
Kingson, E., Hirshorn, B., & Cornman, J. C. (1986). *Ties that bind*. Washing-
    ton, DC: Seven Locks Press.
Kutza, E. (1991). The Older Americans Act of 2000: What should it be? *Genera-
    tions, 15*(3), 65–68.
OMB Watch. (1990). *Long-term care policy: Where are we going?* Univ. of Mas-
    sachusetts, Boston: Gerontology Institute.
Quirk, D. (1991). The aging network: An agenda for the nineties and beyond.
    Generations, 15(3), 23–26.
U.S. Senate, Special Committee on Aging, American Association of Retired Per-
    sons, Federal Council on the Aging, & U.S. Administration on Aging.
    (1991). *Aging America: Trends and projections, 1991 edition*. Washington,
    DC: Authors.

Appendix A

National Nonprofit Resources Groups in Aging

Administration on Aging (AoA), Office of Human Development, U.S. Department of Health and Human Services, Washington, D.C. 20402; (202) 245-0213.

Coordinates programs, services, and research to help older Americans. Administers and authorizes funds for major programs. Operates National Clearinghouse on Aging, which collects, stores, and disseminates information about the elderly. Responds to all inquiries from the general public. State agencies and local Area Agencies on Aging offer consultation, grant application assistance, program information, and help to individuals.

AoA is the major starting point for all program information. As advocate for the elderly, AoA is committed to coordinated action of all federal agencies with programs and services involving older people and to the development of comprehensive information and referral programs. If you cannot locate your area agency in the phone directory, contact the mayor or local executive's office.

Publications: *Aging*, monthly magazine updating national, state, and local resources, legislation, and agency news.

Other: *AoA Fact Sheets*, technical assistance documents, and other materials to meet the needs of the aged, general public, planners, and gerontologists. Publication list available.

Special Committee on Aging. U.S. Senate, G-255 Dirksen Senate Office Building, Washington, D.C. 20510; (202) 224-5364 or 224-1467.

Studies and conducts hearings on all issues related to problems and opportunities for older people; sponsors appropriate legislation. Publishes findings and *Memorandum*, an occasional news sheet updating Congressional action on bills affecting the elderly and announcing future hearings. All public inquiries answered; written requests preferred.

Select Committee on Aging, U.S. Congress, 712 HOB Annex 1, Washington, D.C. 20515; (202) 225-9375.

Studies problems of older Americans, ways to encourage utilization of their skills and knowledge, policies for coordinating government and private programs. Holds hearings and publishes findings. Investigative body with no legislative jurisdiction; information resource for legislators and public. Phone or written inquiries answered; published reports available to public.

ACTION, 806 Connecticut Avenue, N.W., Washington, D.C. 20525; (800) 424-8580.

Federal volunteer agency administering Peace Corps, VISTA, and Older American Volunteer Programs: SCORE, which draws on the skills of retired business people; Foster Grandparents, volunteers who work with children on a one-to-one basis; Retired Senior Volunteers Program (RSVP), retirees who volunteer service to helping organizations; and Senior Companions, older people who serve older people with special needs.

Grants made available by 10 federal regional and 47 state offices to private nonprofit or public community organizations on cost-sharing basis. For information on site sponsorship or volunteer participation, call toll-free number, local office on aging, or local RSVP program office.

Food & Nutrition Service (FNS), U.S. Department of Agriculture, Washington, D.C. 20036; (202) 447-8371.

Coordinates federal food stamp programs. Information available here or more directly from food stamp offices in most major cities. Six regional FNS offices: San Francisco, Dallas, Chicago, Atlanta, Princeton, Waltham; may provide consultation or speakers in areas of nutrition or food management. Surplus food for use by nonprofit, tax-exempt, residential institutions may be available from FNS; contact regional offices.

Editor's note: While food distribution for congregate dining programs may be coordinated by this office, the Nutrition Program for the Elderly is directed by AoA, and inquiries should be addressed to AoA or its area agencies. Meals delivered to homebound elderly as part of this program may be paid for with food stamps; contact food stamp offices for information.

Publications: *Cooking for Two*, large-print recipe book; U.S. Government Printing Office, PA–1043, $1.25.

American Society on Aging, 833 Market St., Suite 512, San Francisco, CA. 94103; (415) 882–2910. The ASA provides a national forum for the discussion of major programmatic and policy issues in aging for practitioners and academics. Society based projects (e.g., Aging in the Neighborhood), conferences and publications are supported by a national membership.

Publications: *Aging Today, Generations* (quarterly journal).

Asociacion Nacional Por Personas Mayores (National Association for Spanish Speaking Elderly), 3875 Wilshire Boulevard, Suite 1401, Los Angeles, California 90010; (213) 487–1922.

The Asociacion Nacional serves all segments of the Hispanic older population. Administers a five-state employment program for low-income persons 55 and over, a national needs assessment of the Hispanic elderly, and technical assistance to local regional and national organizations serving Hispanic elderly. National and local conferences on Hispanic elderly.

Publications: Newsletters and legislative bulletin for members.

National Caucus on the Black Aged, 1424 K Street, N.W., Suite 500, Washington, D.C., 20005; (202) 637–8400.

Advocates attention and programs for the black aged. Recommends public policies responsive to the needs of the older black American.

Conducts research, curriculum development in the area of black aging, training of black professionals in gerontology, training of black elderly to assume leadership roles in services to black aged, and aids in participation of minority social organizations and businesses in service delivery to the elderly. Also conducts employment program for rural black elderly and operates elderly housing. National and local conferences on black aged.

Publications: Newsletters, job bank publications; reports on health, research, curriculum, and theoretical and policy perspectives on black aged.

National Council on the Aging (NCOA), 409 Third St., S.W., Second Floor, Washington, D.C. 20024; (202) 479-1200.

Professional organization providing training, consultation, and technical assistance, under contract, to public and private agencies working with older people. Maintains Center for Public Policy, which monitors legislation, research department, and extensive library containing books, journals, pamphlets, and local project reports. Library is open to public. Special projects include the National Voluntary Organizations (NVOILA) and Generations United.

National Institute of Industrial Gerontology provides analysis and information in the areas of age, employment policies, job design, and retirement. National Institute of Senior Centers (NISC) guides local center personnel in operations, community coordination, and upgrading services.

Publications: Free membership periodicals include: *Perspectives on Aging*, bimonthly magazine of general interest; *Current Literature on Aging*, quarterly summary of recent publications with brief annotations; *Senior Center Report*, NISC's monthly newsletter containing news of successful center programs, new resources; NVOILA *Newsletter*, irregular newsletter of voluntary groups concerned with the provision of alternatives to institutional care.

Other: NCOA actively publishes in areas of interest to those working with or planning services for the elderly. Current publications list available.

National Indian Council on Aging, P.O. Box 2088, Albuquerque, New Mexico 87103; (506) 242-9305.

The overall purpose of the council is to bring about improved comprehensive services to the Indian and Alaskan Native elderly. Membership consists of 40 Indian and Alaskan Native individuals, of whom 12 constitute the board of directors. The council encourages legislative action, communication, and cooperation with service provider agencies, dissemination of information to the Indian communities, and supportive resources; and, when necessary, it intercedes with appropriate agencies to provide access to resources.

Publications: *National Indian Council on Aging NEWS*, $2.00

Other: Reports: *Tribal Nursing Homes* and *State Regulations*; and *American Indian Elderly: A National Profile* (1981).

American Association of Retired Persons/National Retired Teachers Association (AARP/NRTA), 601 E St., N.W., Washington, D.C., 20049; (202) 434-2277.

National organization of older Americans with 2,000 local chapters. Services include legislative representation at the federal and state levels; mail-order pharmacy service for prescription medicine and other health needs; a well-developed preretirement education training program, Action for Independent Maturity (AIM); continuing education at the Institute of Lifetime Learning and its extensions; the Church Relations Office, which explores ways to expand services to older congregants; a travel service and insurance plan. Programs designed for chapter involvement: Health Education, Driver Improvement, Crime Prevention, Consumer Information, Senior Community Service Aides Project, and Widowhood Project.

Publications: *Modern Maturity*, bimonthly magazine of general interest and information for retired people; *News Bulletin*, practical monthly magazine; Better Retirement Series, individual booklets written for the older person: *Consumer, Food, Health, Hobby, Home, Job, Legal, Moving, Pet, Safety, Anti-Crime*, and *Psychology Guide*, single copies free.

Other: Booklets geared to retirement preparation and the older person to parallel the various program activities; *Dynamic Maturity*, AIM magazine for the preretirement year.

National Council of Senior Citizens (NCSC), 925 15th Street, N.W., Washington, D.C. 20005; (202) 347-8800.

Information service to strengthen grassroots-oriented social and legislative action program. Prepares Congressional testimony on critical issues such as Medicare, age discrimination, improved housing, health care, and pension reform. Membership open to individuals of all ages and to senior clubs and groups. Nonprofit services include a mail-order drug program, health insurance, and travel service.

Publications: *Senior Citizens News*, monthly legislative newspaper for members.

The National Center for Citizen Involvement, 1111 N. 19th St., Arlington, VA 22209; (703) 276-0542.

Advocate for voluntary action. Prime source of information on successful programs involving volunteers; files on over 5,000 projects are updated regularly. Strengthens voluntary action movement through leadership education in training volunteers and volunteer administrators; consultations and materials in the areas of public relations, fund development, community resources assessment, information systems development. Community impact through 31 state offices and local Voluntary Action Centers.

Publications: *Voluntary Action News*, bimonthly magazine for volunteers or organizations—includes program profiles, legislative updates, and book reviews—$4.00; *Voluntary Action Leadership*, quarterly forum for volunteers leaders and administrators, free.

Gray Panthers, 311 South Juniper Street, Philadelphia, Pennsylvania 19104; (215) 505-6555.

Eschews special interest focus; advocates change that will benefit people of all ages. Nationally, monitors issues of social justice and joins coalition groups speaking out on issues of health care, consumer fraud, nursing home reform, public transportation. Some 32 units in 18 states engage in community social action and legislative lobbying. Speakers bureau. Assists local groups to organize.

Publications: *Network: Age and Youth in Action, Health Watch, Media Watch Guide.*

Gerontological Society, 1275 K Street, N.W., Washington, D.C. 20005; (202) 842-1275.

Promotes scientific study of aging and application of research findings. Four areas of education stressed at annual meeting: biology; clinical medicine; behavioral and social sciences; social planning, research, and practice.

Publications: *Journals of Gerontology*, bimonthly journal of original scientific research (emphasis on data analysis, methodology); *Gerontologist*, bimonthly journal of applied research (interpretive).

National Hispanic Council on Aging, 2713 Ontario Rd., N.W., Washington, D.C. 20009; (202) 745-2521. The NHCoA is a membership-based organization that promotes the well being of the Hispanic elderly through demonstration projects, research, policy analysis, training, development of educational and informational resources. The NHCoA provides an opportunity to the Hispanic elderly to use the resources of an organized effort to promote and facilitate the process of self help and mutual help to find resolution to their many problems.

Publications: Newsletters: *Noticias, Noticias en Espanol* and *Alliance.*

National Association of Area Agencies on Aging, 1112 16th St., N.W., Suite 100, Washington, D.C. 20036; (202) 296-8130.

National Association of State Units on Aging, 2033 K St., N.W., Suite 304, Washington, D.C. 20006; (202) 785-0707.

Appendix B

**THE OLDER AMERICANS ACT OF 1965,
AS AMENDED**

Updated to Reflect Provisions of PL-102-375
"The Older Americans Act Amendments of 1992"

Older Americans Act of 1965, As Amended

Incorporates Amendments Made by Older Americans Act Amendments of 1992, PL 102-375—September 30, 1992

OLDER AMERICANS ACT OF 1965, AS AMENDED
(42 U.S. CODE, § 3001, ET SEQ)

Language which was added in 1992 is in italics. The text of the Act that was not amended is set in normal type.

OLDER AMERICANS ACT OF 1965
(Public Law 89–73)

AN ACT TO provide assistance in the development of new or improved programs to help older persons through grants to the States for community planning and services and for training, through research, development, or training project grants, and to establish within the Department of Health, Education and Welfare an operating agency to be designated as the "Administration on Aging".

Be it enacted by the Senate and House of Representatives of the United States of America in Congress assembled, That this Act may be cited as the "Older Americans Act of 1965".

TITLE I—DECLARATION OF OBJECTIVES; DEFINITIONS

Declaration of Objectives for Older Americans

Sec. 101. The Congress hereby finds and declares that, in keeping with the traditional American concept of the inherent dignity of the individual in our democratic society, the older people of our Nation are entitled to, and it is the joint and several duty and responsibility of the governments of the United States, the several States and their political subdivisions, and of Indian tribes to assist our older people to secure equal opportunity to the full and free enjoyment of the following objectives:

263

(1) An adequate income in retirement in accordance with the American standard of living.

(2) The best possible physical and mental health which science can make available and without regard to economic status.

(3) Obtaining and maintaining suitable housing, independently selected, designed and located with reference to special needs and functional limitations and available at costs which older citizens can afford.

(4) Full restorative services for those who require institutional care, and a comprehensive array of community-based, long-term care services adequate to appropriately sustain older people in their communities and in their homes, *including support to family members and other persons providing voluntary care to older individuals needing long-term care services.*

(5) Opportunity for employment with no discriminatory personnel practices because of age.

(6) Retirement in health, honor, dignity—after years of contribution to the economy.

(7) Participating in and contributing to meaningful activity within the widest range of civic, cultural, education and training and recreational opportunities.

(8) Efficient community services, including access to low-cost transportation, which provide a choice in supported living arrangements and social assistance in a coordinated manner and which are readily available when needed, with emphasis on maintaining a continuum of care for the vulnerable elderly.

(9) Immediate benefit from proven research knowledge which can sustain and improve health and happiness.

(10) Freedom, independence, and the free exercise of individual initiative in planning and managing their own lives, full participation in the planning and operation of community-based services and programs provided for their benefit, and protection against abuse, neglect, and exploitation.

Definitions

Sec. 102.* For the purposes of this Act—

(1) The term "Secretary" means the Secretary of Health and Human Services, except that for purposes of Title V such term means the Secretary of Labor.

(2) *The term "Commissioner" means, unless the context otherwise requires, the Commissioner of the Administration.*

(3) The term "State" means any of the several States, the District of Columbia, the Virgin Islands, the Commonwealth of Puerto Rico, Guam, Ameri-

*NOTE: Section 102 has confusing subsection references (8, 8,8, 9, 9). See sections 136, 146, and 182(b) of P.L. 100-175.

can Samoa, the Commonwealth of the Northern Mariana Islands, and the Trust Territory of the Pacific Islands.

(4) The term "nonprofit" as applied to any agency, institution, or organization means an agency, institution, or organization which is, or is owned and operated by, one or more corporations or associations no part of the net earnings of which inures, or may lawfully inure, to the benefit of any private shareholder or individual.

(5) The term "Indian" means a person who is a member of an Indian tribe.

(6) Except for the purposes of title VI of this Act, the term "Indian tribe" means any tribe, band, nation, or other organized group or community of Indians (including any Alaska Native village or regional or village corporation as defined in or established pursuant to the Alaska Native Claims Settlement Act (Public Law 92–203; 85 Stat. 688), which (A) is recognized as eligible for the special programs and services provided by the United States to Indians because of their status as Indians; or (B) is located on, or in proximity to, a Federal or State reservation or rancheria.

(7) Except for the purposes of title VI of this Act, the term "tribal organization" means the recognized governing body of any Indian tribe, or any legally established organization of Indians which is controlled, sanctioned, or chartered by such governing body. In any case in which a contract is let or grant made to an organization to perform services benefiting more than one Indian tribe, the approval of each such Indian tribe shall be a prerequisite to the letting or making of such contract or grant.

(8) The term 'disability' means (except when such term is used in the phrase 'severe disability', 'developmental disabilities', 'physical or mental disability', 'physical and mental disabilities', or 'physical disabilities') a disability attributable to mental or physical impairment, or a combination of mental and physical impairments, that results in substantial functional limitations in 1 or more of the following areas of major life activity:

(A) self-care, (B) receptive and expressive language, (C) learning, (D) mobility, (E) self-direction, (F) capacity for independent living, (G) economic self-sufficiency, (H) cognitive functioning, and (I) emotional adjustment.

(9) The term 'Trust Territory of the Pacific Islands' includes the Federated States of Micronesia, the Republic of the Marshall Islands, and the Republic of Palau.

(10) The term 'assistive technology' means technology, engineering methodologies, or scientific principles appropriate to meet the needs of, and address the barriers confronted by, older individuals with functional limitations.

(11) The term 'severe disability' means a severe, chronic disability attributable to mental or physical impairment, or a combination of mental and physical impairments, that—

(A) is likely to continue indefinitely; and

(B) results in substantial functional limitation in 3 or more of the major life activities specified in subparagraphs (A) through (G) of paragraph (8).

(12) The term 'information and referral' includes information relating to assistive technology.

(13) The term 'abuse' means the willful—

(A) infliction of injury, unreasonable confinement, intimidation, or cruel punishment with resulting physical harm, pain, or mental anguish; or

(B) deprivation by a person, including a caregiver, of goods or services that are necessary to avoid physical harm, mental anguish, or mental illness.

(14) The term 'Administration' means the Administration on Aging.

(15) The term 'adult child with a disability' means a child who—

(A) is 18 years of age or older;

(B) is financially dependent on an older individual who is a parent of the child; and

(C) has a disability.

(16) The term 'aging network' means the network of—

(A) State agencies, area agencies on aging, title VI grantees, and the Administration; and

(B) organizations that—

(i)(I) are providers of direct services to older individuals; or

(II) are institutions of higher education; and

(ii) receive funding under this Act.

(17) The term 'area agency on aging' means an area agency on aging designated under section 305(a)(2)(A) or a State agency performing the functions of an area agency on aging under section 305(b)(5).

(18) The term 'art therapy' means the use of art and artistic processes specifically selected and administered by an art therapist, to accomplish the restoration, maintenance, or improvement of the mental, emotional, or social functioning of an older individual.

(19) The term 'board and care facility' means an institution regulated by a State pursuant to section 1616(e) of the Social Security Act (42 U.S.C. 1382e(e)).

(20) The term 'caregiver' means an individual who has the responsibility for the care of an older individual, either voluntarily, by contract, by receipt of payment for care, or as a result of the operation of law.

(21) The term 'caretaker' means a family member or other individual who provides (on behalf of such individual or of a public or private agency, organization, or institution) uncompensated care to an older individual who needs supportive services.

(22) The term 'case management service'—

(A) means a service provided to an older individual, at the direction of the older individual or a family member of the individual—

(i) by an individual who is trained or experienced in the case management skills that are required to deliver the services and coordination described in subparagraph (B); and

(ii) to assess the needs, and to arrange, coordinate, and monitor an optimum package of services to meet the needs, of the older individual; and

(B) includes services and coordination such as—

(i) comprehensive assessment of the older individual (including the physical, psychological, and social needs of the individual);

(ii) development and implementation of a service plan with the older individual to mobilize the formal and informal resources and services identi-

fied in the assessment to meet the needs of the older individual, including coordination of the resources and services—

(I) with any other plans that exist for various formal services, such as hospital discharge plans; and

(II) with the information and assistance services provided under this Act;

(iii) coordination and monitoring of formal and informal service delivery, including coordination and monitoring to ensure that services specified in the plan are being provided;

(iv) periodic reassessment and revision of the status of the older individual with—

(I) the older individual; or

(II) if necessary, a primary caregiver or family member of the older individual; and

(v) in accordance with the wishes of the older individual, advocacy on behalf of the older individual for needed services or resources.

(23) The term 'dance-movement therapy' means the use of psychotherapeutic movement as a process facilitated by a dance-movement therapist, to further the emotional, cognitive, or physical health of an older individual.

(24) The term 'elder abuse' means abuse of an older individual.

(25) The term 'elder abuse, neglect and exploitation' means abuse, neglect, and exploitation, of an older individual.

(26) The term 'exploitation' means the illegal or improper act or process of an individual, including a caregiver, using the resources of an older individual for monetary or personal benefit, profit, or gain.

(27) The term 'focal point' means a facility established to encourage the maximum collocation and coordination of services for older individuals.

(28) The term 'frail' means, with respect to an older individual in a State, that the older individual is determined to be functionally impaired because the individual—

(A)(i) is unable to perform at least two activities of daily living without substantial human assistance, including verbal reminding, physical cuing, or supervision; or

(ii) at the option of the State, is unable to perform at least three such activities without such assistance; or

(B) due to a cognitive or other mental impairment, requires substantial supervision because the individual behaves in a manner that poses a serious health or safety hazard to the individual or to another individual.

(29) The term 'greatest economic need' means the need resulting from an income level at or below the poverty line.

(30) The term 'greatest social need' means the need caused by noneconomic factors, which include

(A) physical and mental disabilities;

(B) language barriers; and

(C) cultural, social, or geographical isolation, including isolation caused by racial or ethnic status, that—

(i) restricts the ability of an individual to perform normal daily tasks; or

(ii) threatens the capacity of the individual to live independently.

(31) The term 'information and assistance service' means a service for older individuals that—

(A) provides the individuals with current information on opportunities and services available to the individuals within their communities, including information relating to assistive technology;

(B) assesses the problems and capacities of the individuals;

(C) links the individuals to the opportunities and services that are available;

(D) to the maximum extent practicable, ensures that the individuals receive the services needed by the individuals, and are aware of the opportunities available to the individuals, by establishing adequate followup procedures; and

(E) serves the entire community of older individuals, particularly—

(i) older individuals with greatest social need; and

(ii) older individuals with greatest economic need.

(32) The term 'institution of higher education' has the meaning given the term in section 1201(a) of the Higher Education Act of 1965 (20 U.S.C. 1141(a)).

(33) The term 'legal assistance'—

(A) means legal advice and representation provided by an attorney to older individuals with economic or social needs; and

(B) includes—

(i) to the extent feasible, counseling or other appropriate assistance by a paralegal or law student under the direct supervision of an attorney; and

(ii) counseling or representation by a nonlawyer where permitted by law.

(34) The term 'long-term care facility' means—

(A) any skilled nursing facility, as defined in section 1819(a) of the Social Security Act (42 U.S.C. 1395i-3(a);

(B) any nursing facility, as defined in section 1919(a) of the Social Security Act (42 U.S.C. 1396r(a));

(C) for purposes of sections 307(a)(12) and 712, a board and care facility; and

(D) any other adult care home similar to a facility or institution described in subparagraphs (A) through (C).

(35) The term 'multipurpose senior center' means a community facility for the organization and provision of a broad spectrum of services, which shall include provision of health (including mental health), social, nutritional, and educational services and the provision of facilities for recreational activities for older individuals.

(36) The term 'music therapy' means the use of musical or rhythmic interventions specifically selected by a music therapist to accomplish the restoration, maintenance, or improvement of social or emotional functioning, mental processing, or physical health of an older individual.

(37) The term 'neglect' means—

(A) The failure to provide for oneself the goods or services that are necessary to avoid physical harm, mental anguish, or mental illness; or

(B) the failure of a caregiver to provide the goods or services.

(38) The term 'older individual' means an individual who is 60 years of age or older.

(39) The term 'physical harm' means bodily injury, impairment, or disease.

(40) The term 'planning and service area' means an area designated by a State agency under section 305(a)(1)(E), including a single planning and service area described in section 305(b)(5)(A).

(41) The term 'poverty line' means the official poverty line (as defined by the Office of Management and Budget, and adjusted by the Secretary in accordance with section 673(2) of the Community Services Block Grant Act (42 U.S.C. 9902(2)).

(42) The term 'representative payee' means a person who is appointed by a governmental entity to receive, on behalf of an older individual who is unable to manage funds by reason of a physical or mental incapacity, any funds owed to such individual by such entity.

TITLE II—*ADMINISTRATION*

Establishment of Administration on Aging

Sec. 201. (a) *There is established in the Office of the Secretary an Administration on Aging which shall be headed by a Commissioner on Aging (hereinafter in this Act referred to as the "Commissioner").* Except for title V, the Administration shall be the agency for carrying out this Act. There shall be a direct reporting relationship between the Commissioner and the Secretary. In the performance of the functions of the Commissioner, the Commissioner shall be directly responsible to the Secretary. The Secretary shall not approve or require any delegation of the functions of the Commissioner *(including the functions of the Commissioner carried out through regional offices)* to any other officer not directly responsible to the Commissioner.

(b) The Commissioner shall be appointed by the President by and with the advice and consent of the Senate.

(c)(1) *There is established in the Administration, an Office for American Indian, Alaskan Native, and Native Hawaiian Programs.*

(2) The Office shall be headed by an Associate Commissioner on American Indian, Alaskan Native, and Native Hawaiian Aging appointed by the Commissioner.

(3) The Associate Commissioner on American Indian, Alaskan Native, and Native Hawaiian Aging shall—

(A)(i) evaluate the adequacy of outreach under title III and title VI for older Native Americans and recommend to the Commissioner necessary action to improve service delivery, outreach, coordination between title III and title VI services, and particular problems faced by older Indians and Hawaiian Natives; and

(ii) include a description of the results of such evaluation and recommendations in the annual report required by section 207(a) to be submitted by the Commissioner;

(B) serve as the effective and visible advocate in behalf of older Native Americans within the Department of Health and Human Services and with other departments and agencies of the Federal Government regarding all Federal policies affecting older Native Americans; *with particular attention to services provided to Native Americans by the Indian Health Service;*

(C) coordinate activities between other Federal departments and agencies to assure a continuum of improved services through memoranda of agreements or through other appropriate means of coordination;

(D) administer and evaluate the grants provided under this Act to Indian tribes, public agencies and nonprofit private organizations serving Hawaiian Natives;

(E) recommend to the Commissioner policies and priorities with respect to the development and operation of programs and activities conducted under the Act relating to older Native Americans;

(F) collect and disseminate information related to problems experienced by older Native Americans *including information (compiled with assistance from public or nonprofit private entities, including institutions of higher education, with experience in assessing the characteristics and health status of older individuals who are Native Americans) on elder abuse, in-home care, health problems, and other problems unique to Native Americans;*

(G) develop research plans, and conduct and arrange for research, in the field of American Native aging with a special emphasis on the gathering of statistics on the status of older Native Americans;

(H) develop and provide technical assistance and training programs to grantees under title VI,

(I) promote coordination—

(i) between the administration of title III and the administration of title VI; and

(ii) between programs established under title III by the Commissioner and programs established under title VI by the Commissioner; including sharing among grantees information on programs funded, and on training and technical assistance provided, under such titles; and

(J) serve as the effective and visible advocate on behalf of older individuals who are Indians, Alaskan Natives, and Native Hawaiians, in the States to promote the enhanced delivery of services and implementation of programs, under this Act and other Federal Acts, for the benefit of such individuals;

(d)(1) There is established in the Administration the Office of Long-Term Care Ombudsman Programs (in this subsection referred to as the 'Office').

(2)(A) The Office shall be headed by an Associate commissioner for Ombudsman Programs (in this subsection referred to as the 'Associate Commissioner') who shall be appointed by the Commissioner from among individuals who have expertise and background in the fields of long-term care advocacy and management. The Associate Commissioner shall report directly to the Commissioner.

(B) No individual shall be appointed Associate Commissioner if—
(i) the individual has been employed within the previous 2 years by—
(I) a long-term care facility;
(II) a corporation that then owned or operated a long-term care facility; or
(III) an association of long-term care facilities;
(ii) the individual—
(I) has an ownership or investment interest (represented by equity, debt, or other financial relationship) in a long-term care facility or long-term care service; or
(II) receives, or has the right to receive, directly or indirectly remuneration (in cash or in kind) under a compensation arrangement with an owner or operator of a long-term care facility; or
(iii) the individual, or any member of the immediate family of the individual, is subject to a conflict of interest.
(3) The Associate Commissioner shall—
(A) serve as an effective and visible advocate on behalf of older individuals who reside in long-term care facilities, within the Department of Health and Human Services and with other departments, agencies, and instrumentalities of the Federal Government regarding all Federal policies affecting such individuals;
(B) review and make recommendations to the commissioner regarding—
(i) the approval of the provisions in State plans submitted under section 30(a) that relate to State Long-Term Care Ombudsman programs; and
(ii) the adequacy of State budgets and policies relating to the programs;
(C) after consultation with State Long-Term Care Ombudsmen and the State agencies, make recommendations to the Commissioner regarding—
(i) policies designed to assist State Long-Term Care Ombudsmen; and
(ii) methods to periodically monitor and evaluate the operation of State Long-Term Care Ombudsman programs, to ensure that the programs satisfy the requirements of section 307(a)(12) and section 712, including provision of service to residents of board and care facilities and of similar adult care facilities;
(D) keep the Commissioner and the Secretary fully and currently informed about—
(i) problems relating to State Long-Term Care Ombudsman programs; and
(ii) the necessity for, and the progress toward, solving the problems;
(E) review, and make recommendations to the Secretary and the Commissioner regarding, existing and proposed Federal legislation, regulations and policies regarding the operation of State Long-Term Care Ombudsman programs;
(F) make recommendations to the Commissioner and the Secretary regarding the policies of the Administration, and coordinate the activities of the Administration with the activities of other Federal entities, State and local entities, and nongovernmental entities, relating to State Long-Term Care Ombudsman programs;

(G) supervise the activities carried out under the authority of the Administration that relate to State Long-Term Care Ombudsman programs;

(H) administer the National Ombudsman Resource Center established under section 202(a)(21) and make recommendations to the Commissioner regarding the operation of the National Ombudsman Resource Center;

(I) advocate, monitor, and coordinate Federal and State activities of Long-Term Care Ombudsmen under this Act;

(J) submit to the Speaker of the House of Representatives and the President pro tempore of the Senate an annual report on the effectiveness of services provided under section 307(a)(12) and section 712;

(K) have authority to investigate the operation or violation of any Federal law administered by the Department of Health and Human Services that may adversely affect the health, safety, welfare, or rights of older individuals; and

(L) not later than 180 days after the date of the enactment of the Older Americans Act Amendments of 1992, establish standards applicable to the training required by section 712(h)(4).

Functions of Commissioner

Sec. 202. (a) It shall be the duty and function of the Administration to—

(1) serve as the effective and visible advocate for the elderly within the Department of Health and Human Services and with other departments, agencies, and instrumentalities of the Federal Government by maintaining active review and commenting responsibilities over all Federal policies affecting the elderly;

(2) collect and disseminate information related to problems of the aged and aging;

(3) directly assist the Secretary in all matter pertaining to problems of the aged and aging;

(4) administer the grants provided by this Act;

(5) develop plans, conduct and arrange for research in the field of aging, and assist in the establishment and implementation of programs designed to meet the needs of older individuals for supportive services, including nutrition, hospitalization, education and training services (including preretirement training, and continuing education), low-cost transportation and housing, and health (including mental health) services;

(6) provide technical assistance and consultation to States and political subdivisions thereof with respect to programs for the aged and aging;

(7) prepare, publish, and disseminate educational materials dealing with the welfare of older individuals;

(8) gather statistics (including statistics regarding the results of outreach activities and application assistance provided under section 306(a)(6)(P) in the field of aging which other Federal agencies are not collecting, and take whatever action is necessary to achieve coordination of activities carried out or assisted by all departments, agencies, and instrumentalities of the Federal Government with respect to the collection, preparation and dissemination of information relevant to older individuals;

(9) stimulate more effective use of existing resources and available services for the aged and aging, including existing legislative protections with particular emphasis on the application of the Age Discrimination in Employment Act of 1967;

(10) Develop basic policies and set priorities with respect to the development and operation of programs and activities conducted under authority of this Act;

(11) *coordinate Federal programs and activities related to such purposes;*

(12) coordinate, and assist in, the planning and development by public (including Federal, State, and local agencies) and private organizations or programs for older individuals with a view to the establishment of a nationwide network of comprehensive, coordinated services and opportunities for such individuals;

(13) convene conferences of such authorities and officials of public (including Federal, State, and local agencies) and nonprofit private organizations concerned with the development and operation of programs for older individuals as the Commissioner deems necessary or proper for the development and implementation of policies related to the purposes of this act;

(14) develop and operate programs providing services and opportunities as authorized by this Act which are not otherwise provided by existing programs for older individuals;

(15) carry on a continuing evaluation of the programs and activities related to the purposes of this Act, with particular attention to the impact of medicare and medicaid, the Age Discrimination in Employment Act of 1967, and the programs of the National Housing Act relating to housing for the elderly and the setting of standards for the licensing of nursing homes, intermediate care homes, and other facilities providing care for older people;

(16) provide information and assistance to private organizations for the establishment and operation by them of programs and activities related to the purposes of this Act;

(17) develop, in coordination with other agencies, a national plan for meeting the needs of trained personnel in the field of aging, and for training persons for carrying out programs related to the purposes of this Act, and conduct and provide for the conducting of such training;

(18) consult with national organizations representing minority individuals to develop and disseminate training packages and to provide technical assistance efforts designed to assist State and area agencies *and service providers in providing services to older individuals with the greatest economic need or individuals with greatest social need, with particular attention to and specific objectives for providing services to low-income minority individuals;*

(19) collect for each fiscal year, for fiscal years beginning after September 30, 1988, directly or by contract, statistical data regarding programs and activities carried out with funds provided under this Act, including—

(A) with respect to each type of service *or activity* provided with such funds—

(i) the aggregate amount of such funds expended to provide such service *or activity;*

(ii) the number of individuals who received such service *or activity;* and

(iii) the number of units of such service *or activity* provided;

(B) the number of senior centers which received such funds; and

(C) the extent to which each area agency on aging designated under section 305(a) satisfied the requirements of paragraphs (2) and (5)(A) of section 306(a)

(20) obtain from—

(A) the Department of Agriculture information explaining the requirements for eligibility to receive benefits under the Food Stamp Act of 1977; and

(B) the Social Security Administration information explaining the requirements for eligibility to receive supplemental security income benefits under title XVI of the Social Security Act (or assistance under a State plan program under title XVI of that Act);

(21)(A) establish and operate the National Ombudsman Resource Center (in this paragraph referred to as the 'Center'), under the administration of the Associate Commissioner for Ombudsman Programs, that will—

(i) by grant or contract—

(I) conduct research;

(II) provide training, technical assistance, and information to State Long-Term Care Ombudsmen;

(III) analyze laws, regulations, programs, and practices; and

(IV) provide assistance in recruiting and retaining volunteers for State Long-Term Care Ombudsman programs by establishing a national program for recruitment efforts that utilizes the organizations that have established a successful record in recruiting and retaining volunteers for ombudsman or other programs; relating to Federal, State, and local long-term care ombudsman policies; and

(ii) assist State Long-Term Care Ombudsmen in the implementation of State Long-Term Care Ombudsman programs; and

(B) make available to the Center not less than the amount of resources made available to the Long-Term Care Ombudsman National Resource Center for fiscal year 1990;

(22) issue regulations, and conduct strict monitoring of State compliance with the requirements in effect, under this Act to prohibit conflicts of interest and to maintain the integrity and public purpose of services provided and service providers, under this Act in all contractual and commercial relationships, and include in such regulations a requirement that as a condition of being designated as an area agency on aging such agency shall—

(A) disclose to the Commissioner and the State agency involved—

(i) the identity of each nongovernmental entity with which such agency has a contract or commercial relationship relating to providing any service to older individuals; and

(ii) the nature of such contract or such relationship;

(B) demonstrate that a loss or diminuition in the quantity or quality of the services provided, or to be provided, under this Act by such

agency has not resulted and will not result from such contract or such relationship;

(C) demonstrate that the quantity or quality of the services to be provided under this Act by such agency will be enhanced as a result of such contract or such relationship; and

(D) on the request of the Commissioner or the State, for the purpose of monitoring compliance with this Act (including conducting an audit), disclose all sources and expenditures of funds received or expended to provide services to older individuals;

(23) encourage, and provide technical assistance to, States and area agencies on aging to carry out outreach to inform older individuals with greatest economic need who may be eligible to receive, but are not receiving, supplemental security income benefits under title XVI of the Social Security Act (42 U.S.C. 1381 et seq.) (or assistance under a State plan program under such title), medical assistance under title XIX of such Act (42 U.S.C. 1396 et seq.), and benefits under the Food Stamp Act of 1977 (7 U.S.C. 2011 et seq.), of the requirements for eligibility to receive such benefits and such assistance;

(24) establish information and assistance services as priority services for older individuals;

(25) develop guidelines for area agencies on aging to follow in choosing and evaluating providers of legal assistance;

(26) develop guidelines and a model job description for choosing and evaluating legal assistance developers referred to in sections 307(a)(18) and 731(b)(2);

(27)(A) conduct a study to determine ways in which Federal funds might be more effectively targeted to low-income minority older individuals, and older individuals residing in rural areas, to better meet the needs of States with a disproportionate number of older individuals with greatest economic need and older individuals with greatest social need;

(B) conduct a study to determine ways in which Federal funds might be more effectively targeted to better meet the needs of States with disproportionate numbers of older individuals, including methods of allotting funds under title III, using the most recent estimates of the population of older individuals; and

(C) not later than January 1, 1994, submit a report containing the findings resulting from the studies described in subparagraphs (A) and (B) to the Speaker of the House of Representatives and the President pro tempore of the Senate;

(28) provide technical assistance, training, and other means of assistance to State agencies, area agencies on aging, and service providers regarding State and local data collection and analysis;

(29) design and implement, for purposes of compliance with paragraph (19), uniform data collection procedures for use by State agencies, including—

(A) uniform definitions and nomenclature;

(B) standardized data collection procedures;

(C) a participant identification and description system;

*(D) procedures for collecting information on gaps in services needed
by older individuals, as identified by service providers in assisting clients through the provision of the supportive services; and*

*(E) procedures for the assessment of unmet needs for services under
this Act; and*

*(30) require that all Federal grants and contracts made under this title
and title IV be made in accordance with a competitive bidding process
established by the Commissioner by regulation;*

and distribute such information, in written form, to State agencies, for redistribution to area agencies on aging, to carry out outreach activities and application assistance under section 307(a)(31).

(b) In order to strengthen the involvement of the Administration in the development of policy alternatives in long-term care and to insure that the development of community alternatives is given priority attention, the Commissioner shall—

(1) develop planning linkages with health systems agencies designated under section 1515 of the Public Health Service Act (42 U.S.C. 300 1-4), with utilization and quality control peer review organizations under title XI of the Social Security Act, with the Alcohol, Drug Abuse, and Mental Health Administration and the Administration on Developmental Disabilities;

(2) participate in all departmental and interdepartmental activities which concern issues of institutional and non-institutional long-term health care services development;

(3) review and comment on all departmental regulations and policies regarding community health and social service development for the elderly; and

*(4) participate in all departmental and interdepartmental activities
to provide a leadership role for the Administration, State agencies, and
area agencies on aging in the development and implementation of a
national community-based long-term care program for older
individuals.*

(c)(1) In executing the duties and functions of the Administration under this Act and carrying out the programs and activities provided for by this Act, the Commissioner, in consultation with the Director of the ACTION Agency, shall take all possible steps to encourage and permit voluntary groups active in supportive services, including youth organizations active at the high school or college levels, to participate and be involved individually or through representative groups in such programs and activities to the maximum extent feasible, through the performance of advisory and consultative functions, and in other appropriate ways;

*(2)(A) In executing the duties and functions of the Administration under
this Act and in carrying out the programs and activities provided for by this
Act, the Commissioner shall act to encourage and assist the establishment
and use of—*

*(i) area volunteer service coordinators, as described in section 306(a)(12),
by area agencies on aging; and*

*(ii) State volunteer service coordinators, as described in section
307(a)(31), by State agencies.*

(B) The Commissioner shall provide technical assistance to the area and State volunteer services coordinators;

(d)(1) The Commissioner shall establish and operate the National Center on Elder Abuse (in this subsection referred to as the 'Center').

(2) In operating the Center, the Commissioner shall—

(A) annually compile, publish, and disseminate a summary of recently conducted research on elder abuse, neglect, and exploitation;

(B) develop and maintain an information clearinghouse on all programs (including private programs) showing promise of success, for the prevention, identification, and treatment of elder abuse, neglect, and exploitation;

(C) compile, publish, and disseminate training materials for personnel who are engaged or intend to engage in the prevention, identification, and treatment of elder abuse, neglect, and exploitation;

(D) provide technical assistance to State agencies and to other public and nonprofit private agencies and organizations to assist the agencies and organizations in planning, improving, developing, and carrying out programs and activities relating to the special problems of elder abuse, neglect, and exploitation; and

(E) conduct research and demonstration projects regarding the causes, prevention, identification, and treatment of elder abuse, neglect, and exploitation.

(3)(A) The Commissioner shall carry out paragraph (2) through grants or contracts.

(B) The Commissioner shall issue criteria applicable to the recipients of funds under this subsection. To be eligible to receive a grant or enter into a contract under subparagraph (A), an entity shall submit an application to the Commissioner at such time, in such manner, and containing such information as the Commissioner may require.

(C) The Commissioner shall—

(i) establish research priorities for making grants or contract to carry out paragraph (2)(E); and

(ii) not later than 60 days before the date on which the Commissioner establishes such priorities, publish in the Federal Register for public comment a statement of such proposed priorities.

(4) The Commissioner shall make available to the Center such resources as are necessary for the Center to carry out effectively the functions of the Center under this Act and not less than the amount of resources made available to the Resource Center on Elder Abuse for fiscal year 1990.

(e)(1)(A) The Commissioner shall make grants or enter into contracts with eligible entities to establish the National Aging Information Center (in this subsection referred to as the 'Center') to—

(i) provide information about education and training projects established under part A, and research and demonstration projects, and other activities, established under part B, of title IV to persons requesting such information;

(ii) annually compile, analyze, publish, and disseminate—

(I) statistical data collected under subsection (a)(19);

(II) census data on aging demographics; and

(III) data from other Federal agencies on the health, social, and eco-

nomic status of older individuals and on the services provided to older individuals;

(iii) biennially compile, analyze, publish, and disseminate statistical data collected on the functions, staffing patterns, and funding sources of State agencies and area agencies on aging;

(iv) analyze the information collected under section 201(c)(3)(F) by the Associate Commissioner on American Indian, Alaskan Native, and Native Hawaiian Aging, and the information provided by the Resource Centers on Native American Elders under section 429E;

(v) provide technical assistance, training, and other means of assistance to State agencies, area agencies on aging, and service providers, regarding State and local data collection and analysis; and

(vi) be a national resource on statistical data regarding aging;

(B) To be eligible to receive a grant or enter into a contract under subparagraph (A), an entity shall submit an application to the Commissioner at such time, in such manner, and containing such information as the Commissioner may require.

(C) Entities eligible to receive a grant or enter into a contract under subparagraph (A) shall be organizations with a demonstrated record of experience in education and information dissemination.

(2)A) The commissioner shall establish procedures specifying the length of time that the Center shall provide the information described in paragraph (1) with respect to a particular project or activity. The procedures shall require the Center to maintain the information beyond the term of the grant awarded, or contract entered into, to carry out the project or activity.

(B) The Commissioner shall establish the procedures described in subparagraph (A) after consultation with—

(i) practitioners in the field of aging;

(ii) older individuals;

(iii) representatives of institutions of higher education;

(iv) national aging organizations;

(v) State agencies;

(vi) area agencies on aging;

(vii) legal assistance providers;

(viii) service providers; and

(ix) other persons with an interest in the field of aging.

(g) OBLIGATION OF FUNDS.—Not later than March 1, 1993, the Commissioner shall obligate, from the funds appropriated under the Older Americans Act of 1965 (42 U.S.C. 3001 et seq.) for fiscal year 1993—

(1) to carry out section 202(a)(21) of such Act (as added by subsection (b)(2) of this section), not less than the amount made available from appropriations for fiscal year 1990 under such Act for making grants and entering into contracts to establish and operate the National Long-Term Care Ombudsman Resource Center; and

(2) to carry out section 202(d)(4) of such Act (as added by subsection (e) of this section), not less than the amount made available from appropriations for fiscal year 1990 under such Act for making grants and entering into contracts to establish and operate the National Aging Resource Center on Elder Abuse.

(h) DEADLINE FOR DEVELOPMENT OF PROCEDURES.—Not later than 1 year after the date of the enactment of this Act, the data collection procedures required by section 202(a)(29) of the Older Americans Act of 1965 shall be developed by the Commissioner on Aging, jointly with the Assistant Secretary of Planning and Evaluation of the Department of Health and Human Services, after—

(1) requesting advisory information under such Act from State agencies, local governments, area agencies on aging, recipients of grants under title VI of such Act, and local providers of services under such Act; and

(2) considering the data collection systems carried out by State agencies in the States then identified as exemplary by the General Accounting Office.

Not later than 1 year after developing such data collection procedures, the Commissioner on Aging shall test such procedures, submit to the Speaker of the House of Representatives and the President pro tempore of the Senate a report summarizing the results of such test, and implement such procedures (as modified, if appropriate, to reflect such results).

Federal Agency Consultation

Sec. 203. (a)(1) The Commissioner, in carrying out the objectives and provisions of this Act, shall coordinate, advise, consult with, and cooperate with the head of each department, agency, or instrumentality of the Federal Government proposing or administering programs or services substantially related to the objectives of this Act, with respect to such programs or services. In particular, the Commissioner shall coordinate, advise, consult, and cooperate with the Secretary of Labor in carrying out title V and with the ACTION Agency in carrying out this Act.

(2) The head of each department, agency, or instrumentality of the Federal Government proposing to establish programs and services substantially related to the objectives of this Act shall consult with the Commissioner prior to the establishment of such programs and services. To achieve appropriate coordination, the head of each department, agency, or instrumentality of the Federal Government administering any program substantially related to the objectives of this Act, particularly administering any program referred to in subsection (b), shall consult and cooperate with the Commissioner in carrying out such program. In particular, the Secretary of Labor shall consult and cooperate with the Commissioner in carrying out the Job Training Partnership Act (29 U.S.C. 1501 et seq.).

(3) The head of each Federal department, agency, or instrumentality of the Federal Government administering programs and services substantially related to the objectives of this Act shall collaborate with the Commissioner in carrying out this Act, and shall develop a written analysis, for review and comment by the Commissioner, of the impact of such programs and services on—

(A) older individuals (with particular attention to low-income minority older individuals) and eligible individuals (as defined in section 507); and

(B) the functions and responsibilities of State agencies and area agencies on aging.

(b) For the purposes of subsection (a), programs related to the purposes of this Act shall include—

(1) the Job Training Partnership Act,

(2) title II of the Domestic Volunteer Service Act of 1973,

(3) titles XVI, XVIII, XIX, and XX of the Social Security Act,

(4) sections 231 and 232 of the National Housing Act,

(5) the United States Housing Act of 1937,

(6) section 202 of the Housing Act of 1959,

(7) title I of the Housing and Community Development Act of 1974,

(8) title I of the Higher Education Act of 1965, and the Adult Education Act,

(9) section 3, 9, and 16 of the Urban Mass Transportation Act of 1964,

(10) the Public Health Service Act, including block grants under title XIX of such Act,

(11) the Low-Income Home Energy Assistance Act of 1981,

(12) part A of the Energy Conservation in Existing Buildings Act of 1976, relating to weatherization assistance for low income persons,

(13) the Community Services Block Grant Act,

(14) demographic statistics and analysis programs conducted by the Bureau of the Census under title 13, United States Code,

(15) parts II and III of title 38, United States Code,

(16) the Rehabilitation Act of 1973,

(17) the Developmental Disabilities and Bill of Rights Act, *and*

(18) The Edward Byrne Memorial State and Local Law Enforcement Assistance Programs, established under part E of title I of the Omnibus Crime Control and Safe Streets Act of 1968 (42 U.S.C. 3750–3766b).

Sec. 203A. Consultation with state agencies, area agencies on aging and Native American grant recipients.

The Commissioner shall consult and coordinate with State agencies, area agencies on aging,and recipients of grants under title VI in the development of Federal goals, regulations, program instructions, and policies under this Act.

Federal Council on the Aging

Sec. 204. (a)(1) There is established a Federal Council on the Aging to be composed of 15 members. *Except as provided in subsection (b)(1)(A), members shall serve for terms of 3 years, ending on March 31 regardless of the actual date of appointment; and* without regard to the provisions of title 5, United States Code. Members shall be appointed by each appointing authority so as to be representative of rural and urban older individuals, national organizations with an interest in aging, business, labor, minorities, Indian tribes and the general public. At least three of the members appointed *from among individuals who have expertise and experience in the field of aging* by each appointing authority shall be older individuals. No full-time officer or employee of the Federal Government may be appointed as a member of the Council.

(2) Members appointed to the Federal Council on the Aging established by this section prior to the date of enactment of the Older Americans Act Amendments of *1992* who are serving on such date, shall continue to serve on the Federal council established by paragraph (1) of this subsection until members are appointed in accordance with subsection (b)(1).

(A)(i) The initial members of the Federal Council on the Aging shall be appointed on April 1, 1993, as follows:

(I) 5 members, who shall be referred to as class 1 members, shall be appointed for a term of 1 year;

(II) 5 members, who shall be referred to as class 2 members, shall be appointed for a term of 2 years; and

(III) 5 members, who shall be referred to as class 3 members, shall be appointed for a term of 3 years.

(ii) Members appointed in 1994 and each third year thereafter shall be referred to as class 1 members. Members appointed in 1995 and each third year thereafter shall be referred to as class 2 members. Members appointed in 1996 and each third year thereafter shall be referred to as class 3 members.

(B)(i) Members of each class shall be appointed *from among individuals who have expertise and experience in the field of aging* in the manner prescribed by this subparagraph.

(ii) Of the members of class 1, two shall be appointed by the President, two by the President pro tempore of the Senate upon the recommendation of the Majority Leader and the Minority Leader, and one by the Speaker of the House of Representatives upon the recommendation of the Majority Leader and the Minority Leader.

(iii) Of the Members of class 2, two shall be appointed by the President, one by the President pro tempore of the Senate upon the recommendation of the Majority Leader and the Minority Leader, and two by the Speaker of the House of Representatives upon the recommendation of the Majority Leader and the Minority Leader.

(iv) Of the Members of class 3, one shall be appointed by the President, two by the President pro tempore of the Senate upon the recommendation of the Majority Leader and Minority Leader, and two by the Speaker of the House of Representatives upon the recommendation of the Majority Leader and the Minority Leader.

(2) Any member appointed to fill a vacancy occurring prior to the expiration of the term for which such member's predecessor was appointed shall be appointed only for the remainder of such term. Members shall be eligible for reappointment and may serve after the expiration of their terms until their successors have taken office.

(3) Any vacancy in the Council shall not affect its powers, but shall be filled in the same manner by which the original appointment was made.

(4) Members of the Council shall, while serving on business of the Council be entitled to receive compensation at a rate not to exceed the daily rate specified for grade GS–18 in section 5332 of title 5, United States Code,

including travel-time, and while so serving away from their homes or regular places of business, they may be allowed travel expenses, including per diem in lieu of subsistence, in the same manner as the expenses authorized by section 5703(b) of title 5, United States Code, for persons in the Government service employed intermittently.

(c) The President shall designate the Chairperson from among the members appointed to the Council. The Council shall meet at the call of the Chairperson at least quarterly.

(d) The Council shall—

(1) advise and assist the President on matters relating to the special needs of Older Americans;

(2) *directly advise the Commissioner on matters affecting the special needs of older individuals for services and assistance under this Act;*

(3) review and evaluate, on a continuing basis, Federal policies regarding the aging and programs and other activities affecting the aging conducted or assisted by all Federal departments and agencies for the purposes of appraising their value and their impact on the lives of older Americans *and of identifying duplication and gaps among the types of services provided under such programs and activities;*

(4) serve as a spokesman on behalf of older Americans by making recommendations to the President, to the Secretary, to the Commissioner, and to the Congress with respect to Federal policies regarding the aging and federally conducted or assisted programs and other activities relating to or affecting them;

(5) inform the public about the problems and needs of the aging by collecting and disseminating information, conducting or commissioning studies and publishing the results thereof, and by issuing publications and reports; and

(6) provide public forums for discussing and publicizing the problems and needs of the aging and obtaining information relating thereto by conducting public hearings, and by conducting or sponsoring conferences, workshops, and other such meetings.

(e) The Council shall have staff personnel, appointed by the Chairperson, to assist it in carrying out its activities. The head of each Federal department and agency shall make available to the Council such information and other assistance as it may require to carry out its activities.

(f) Beginning with the year 1974 the Council shall make *interim reports* and an annual report of its findings and recommendations to the President not later than March 31 of each year. The President shall transmit each such report to the Congress together with his comments and recommendations.

(g) There are authorized to be appropriated to carry out this section $300,000 for the fiscal year *1992 and such sums as may necessary for fiscal years 1993, 1994 and 1995.*

Administration of the Act

Sec. 205. *(a)(1)* In carrying out the purposes of this Act, the Commissioner is authorized to:

(A) provide consultative services and technical assistance to public or nonprofit private agencies and organizations;

(B) provide short-term training and technical instructions;

(C) conduct research and demonstrations;

(D) collect, prepare, publish, and disseminate special educational or informational materials, including reports of the projects for which funds are provided under this Act; and

(E) provide staff and other technical assistance to the Federal Council on the Aging.

(b) In administering the functions of the Administration under this Act, the Commissioner may utilize the services and facilities of any agency of the Federal Government and of any other public or nonprofit agency or organization, in accordance with agreements between the Commissioner and the head thereof, and is authorized to pay therefor, in advance or by way of reimbursement, as may be provided in the agreement.

(c) Not later than 120 days after the date of the enactment of the Older Americans Act Amendments of 1987, the Secretary shall issue and publish in the Federal Register proposed regulations for the administration of this Act. After allowing a reasonable period for public comment on such proposed rules and not later than 90 days after such publication, the Secretary shall issue, in final form, regulations for the administration of this Act.

(d) Not later than September 1 of each fiscal year, the Commissioner shall make available to the public, for the purpose of facilitating informed public comment, a statement of proposed specific goals to be achieved by implementing this Act in the first fiscal year beginning after the date on which such statement is made available.

(e) For the purpose of carrying out this section, there are authorized to be appropriated such sums as may be necessary.

(2)(A) *The Commissioner shall designate an officer or employee who shall serve on a full-time basis and who shall be responsible for the administration of the nutrition services described in subparts 1, 2, and 3 of part C of title III and shall have duties that include—*

(i) designing, implementing, and evaluating nutrition programs;

(ii) developing guidelines for nutrition providers concerning safety, sanitary handling of food, equipment, preparation, and food storage;

(iii) disseminating information to nutrition service providers about nutrition advancements and developments;

(iv) promoting coordination between nutrition service providers and community-based organizations serving older individuals;

(v) developing guidelines on cost containment;

(vi) defining a long range role for the nutrition services in community-based care systems;

(vii) developing model menus and other appropriate materials for serving special needs populations and meeting cultural meal preferences; and

(viii) providing technical assistance to the regional offices of the Administration with respect to each duty described in clauses (i) through (vii).

(B) The regional offices of the Administration shall be responsible for disseminating, and providing technical assistance regarding the guidelines and information described in clauses (ii), (iii), and (v) of subparagraph (A) to

State agencies, area agencies on aging, and persons that provide nutrition services under part C of title III.

(C) The officer or employee designated under subparagraph (A) shall—

(i) have expertise in nutrition and dietary services and planning; and

(ii)(I) be a registered dietitian;

(II) be a credentialed nutrition professional; or

(III) have education and training that is substantially equivalent to the education and training for a registered dietitian or a credentialed nutrition professional.

Evaluation

Sec. 206. (a) The Secretary shall measure and evaluate the impact of all programs authorized by this Act, their effectiveness in achievement stated goals in general, and in relation to their cost, their impact on related programs, *their effectiveness in targeting for services under this Act unserved older individuals with greatest economic need (including low-income minority individuals) and unserved older individuals with greatest social need (including low-income minority individuals)* and their structure and mechanisms for delivery of services, including, where appropriate, comparisons with appropriate control groups composed of persons who have not participated in such programs. Evaluations shall be conducted by persons not immediately involved in the administration of the program or project evaluated.

(b) The Secretary may not make grants or contracts under title IV of this[1] Act until the Secretary develops and publishes general standards to be used by the Secretary in evaluating the programs and projects assisted under such title. Results of evaluations conducted pursuant to such standards shall be included in the reports required by section 207.

(c) In carrying out evaluations under this section, the Secretary shall, whenever possible, arrange to obtain the opinions of program and project participants about the strengths and weaknesses of the programs and projects, and conduct, where appropriate, evaluations which compare the effectiveness of related programs in achieving common objectives. In carrying out such evaluations, the Secretary shall consult with organizations concerned with older individuals, including those representing minority individuals and older individuals with disabilities.

(d) The Secretary shall annually publish summaries and analyses of the results of evaluative research and evaluation of program and project impact and effectiveness, including, as appropriate, health and nutrition education demonstration projects conducted under section 307(f) the full contents of which shall be transmitted to Congress, be disseminated to Federal, State, and local agencies and private organizations with an interest in aging, and be accessible to the public.

[1]This amendment effective on December 8, 1984, per Sec. 803(b)(1), P.L.98-459.

(e) The Secretary shall take the necessary action to assure that all studies, evaluations, proposals, and data produced or developed with Federal funds shall become the property of the United States.

(f) Such information as the Secretary may deem necessary for purposes of the evaluations conducted under this section shall be made available to him, upon request, by the departments and agencies of the executive branch.

(g)(1) Not later than June 30, 1994, the Commissioner, in consultation with the Assistant Secretary for Planning and Evaluation of the Department of Health and Human Services, shall complete an evaluation of nutrition services provided under this Act, to evaluate for fiscal years 1992 and 1993—

(A) their effectiveness in serving special populations of older individuals;

(B) the quality of nutrition provided by such services;

(C) average meal costs (including the cost of food, related administrative costs, and the cost of supportive services relating to nutrition services), taking into account regional differences and size of projects;

(D) the characteristics of participants;

(E) the applicability of health, safety, and dietary standards;

(F) the appraisal of such services by recipients;

(G) the efficiency of delivery and administration of such services;

(H) the amount, sources, and ultimate uses of funds transferred under section 308(b)(5) to provide such services;

(I) the amount, sources, and uses of other funds expended to provide such services, including the extent to which funds received under this Act are used to generate additional funds to provide such services;

(J) the degree of nutritional expertise used to plan and manage coordination with other State and local services;

(K) nonfood cost factors incidental to providing nutrition services under this Act;

(L) the extent to which commodities provided by the Secretary of Agriculture under section 311(a) are used to provide such services;

(M) and for the 8-year period ending September 30, 1992, the characteristics, and changes in the characteristics, of such nutrition services;

(N) differences between older individuals who receive nutrition services under section 331 and older individuals who receive nutrition services under section 336, with specific reference to age, income, health status, receipt of food stamp benefits, and limitations on activities of daily living;

(O) the impact of the increase in nutrition services provided under section 336, the factors that caused such increase, and the effect of such increase on nutrition services authorized under section 336;

(P) how, and the extent to which, nutrition services provided under this Act generally, and under section 331 specifically, are integrated with long-term care programs;

(Q) the impact of nutrition services provided under this Act on older individuals, including the impact on their dietary intake and opportunities for socialization;

(R) the adequacy of the daily recommended dietary allowances described in section 339; and

(S) the impact of transferring funds under section 308(b)(5) and how funds transferred under such section are expended to provide nutrition services.

(2)(A)(i) The Commissioner shall establish an advisory council to develop recommendations for guidelines on efficiency and quality in furnishing nutrition services described in subparts 1, 2, and 3 of part C of title III.

(ii) The council shall be composed of members appointed by the Commissioner from among individuals nominated by the Secretary of Agriculture, the American Dietetic Association, the Dietary Managers Association, the National Association of Nutrition and Aging Service Programs, the National Association of Meal Programs, the National Association of State Units on Aging, the National Association of Area Agencies on Aging, and other appropriate organizations.

(B) Not later than June 30, 1993, the Commissioner, in consultation with the Secretary of Agriculture and taking into consideration the recommendations of the council, shall publish interim guidelines of the kind described in subparagraph (A)(i);

(3) Not later than September 30, 1994, the Secretary shall—

(A) submit to the President, the Speaker of the House of Representatives, and the President pro tempore of the Senate recommendations and final guidelines to improve nutrition services provided under this Act; and

(B) require the Commissioner to implement such recommendations administratively, to the extent feasible;

(h) The Secretary may use such sums as may be necessary, but not to exceed $3,000,000 (of which not to exceed $1,500,000 shall be available from funds appropriated to carry out title III and not to exceed $1,500,000 shall be available from funds appropriated to carry out title IV), to conduct directly evaluations under this section. No part of such sums may be reprogrammed, transferred, or used for any other purpose. Funds expended under this subsection shall be justified and accounted for by the Secretary.

Reports

Sec. 207. (a) Not later than one hundred and twenty days after the close of each fiscal year, the Commissioner shall prepare and submit to the President and to Congress a full and complete report on the activities carried out under this Act. Such annual reports shall include statistical data reflecting services and activities provided individuals during the preceding fiscal year. Such annual reports shall include—

(1) statistical data reflecting services and activities provided to individuals during the preceding fiscal year;

(2) statistical data collected under section 202(a)(19);

(3) an analysis of the information received under section 306(b)(2)(D) by the Commissioner;

(4) statistical data and an analysis of information regarding the effectiveness of the State agency and area agencies on aging in targeting services to older individuals with the greatest economic or social

needs, with particular attention to low-income minority individuals, low-income individuals, and frail individuals (including individuals with any physical or mental functional impairment) *and*

(5) a description of the implementation of the plan required by Section 202(a)(17)

(b)(1) Not later than *March 1* of each year, the Commissioner shall compile a report—

(A) summarizing and analyzing the data collected under section 307(a)(12)(C) for the then most recently concluded fiscal year;

(B) identifying significant problems and issues revealed by such data (with special emphasis on problems relating to quality of care and residents' rights);

(C) discussing current issues concerning the long-term care ombudsman programs of the States; and

(D) making recommendations regarding legislation and administrative actions to resolve such problems.

(2) The Commissioner shall submit the report required by paragraph (1) to—

(A) the Select Committee on Aging of the House of Representatives;

(B) the Special Committee on Aging of the Senate;

(C) the Committee on Education and Labor of the House of Representatives; and

(D) the Committee on Labor and Human Resources of the Senate.

(3) The Commissioner shall provide the report required by paragraph (1), and make the State reports required by section 307(a)(12)(H)(i) available, to—

(A) the Administrator of the Health Care Finance Administration;

(B) the Office of the Inspector General of the Department of Health and Human Services;

(C) the Office of Civil Rights of the Department of Health and Human Services;

(D) the Administrator of the Veterans' Administration; and

(E) the public agencies and private organizations designated under section 307(a)(12)(A).

(c) The Commissioner shall, as part of the annual report submitted under subsection (a), prepare and submit a report on the evaluations required to be submitted under section 307(a)(31)(D), together with such recommendations as the Commissioner deems appropriate. In carrying out this subsection, the Commissioner shall consider—

(1) the number of older individuals reached through outreach activities supported under section 306(a)(6)(P);

(2) the dollar amount of the assistance and benefits received by older individuals as a result of such activities;

(3) the cost of such activities in terms of the number of individuals reached and the dollar amount described in paragraph (2);

(4) the effect of such activities on supportive services and nutrition services furnished under title III of this Act *and*

(5) the effectiveness of State and local efforts to target older individuals with greatest economic need (including low-income minority

individuals) and older individuals with greatest social need (including low-income minority individuals) to receive services under this Act.

Joint Funding of Projects

Sec. 208. Pursuant to regulations prescribed by the President and to the extent consistent with the other provisions of this Act, where funds are provided for a single project by more than one Federal agency to any agency or organization assisted under this Act, the Federal agency principally involved may be designated to act for all in administering the funds provided. In such cases, a single non-Federal share requirement may be established according to the proportion of funds advanced by each Federal agency, and any such agency may waive any technical grant or contract requirement (as defined by such regulations) which is inconsistent with the similar requirements of the administering agency or which the administering agency does not impose.

Advance Funding

Sec. 209. (a) For the purpose of affording adequate notice of funding available under this Act, appropriations under this Act are authorized to be included in the appropriation Act for the fiscal year preceding the fiscal year for which they are available for obligation.

(b) In order to effect a transition to the advance funding method of timing appropriation action, subsection (a) shall apply notwithstanding that its initial application will result in the enactment in the same year (whether in the same appropriation Act or otherwise) of two separate appropriations, one for the then current fiscal year and one for the succeeding fiscal year.

Application of Other Laws

Sec. 210. (a) The provision and requirements of the Act of December 5, 1974 (Public Law 93–510; 88 Stat. 1604) shall not apply to the administration of the provisions of this Act or to the administration of any program or activity under this Act.

(b) no part of the costs of any project under any title of this Act may be treated as income or benefits to any eligible individual (other than any wage or salary to such individual) for the purpose of any other program or provision of Federal or State law.

Sec. 211. Study of Effectiveness of State Long-Term Care Ombudsman Programs. Not later than January 1, 1994, the Commissioner on Aging shall, in consultation with State agencies, State Long-term Care Ombudsmen, the National Ombudsman Resource Center established under section 202(a)(2l) of the Older Americans Act of 1965 (as added by section 202(b)(2) of this Act), and professional ombudsmen associations, directly, or by grant or contract, conduct a study, and submit a report to the committees specified in section 207(b)(2) of such Act, analyzing separately with respect to each State—

(1) the availability of services, and the unmet need for services, under the State Long-Term Care Ombudsman programs in effect under sections 307(a)(12) and 712 of the Older Americans Act of 1965 (42 U.S.C. 3001 et seq.) to residents of long-term care facilities (as defined in section 102 of such Act);

(2) the effectiveness of the programs in providing the services to the residents, including residents of board and care facilities (as defined in section 102 of such Act) and of similar adult care facilities;

(3) the adequacy of Federal and other resources available to carry out the programs on a statewide basis in each State;

(4) compliance and barriers to such compliance of the States in carrying out the programs;

(5) any actual and potential conflicts of interest in the administration and operation of the programs; and

(6) the need for and feasibility of providing ombudsman services to older individuals (as defined in section 102 of such Act) who are not in long-term care facilities and who use long-term care services and other health care services, by analyzing and assessing current State agency practices in programs in which the State Long-Term Care Ombudsmen provide services to older individuals in settings in addition to long-term care facilities, taking into account variations in—

(A) settings where services are provided;

(B) the types of clients served;

(C) the types of complaints and problems handled;

(D) State regulation of long-term care provided in settings other than long-term care facilities; and

(E) possible conflicts of interest between the State Long-Term Care Ombudsman programs under such Act and area agencies on aging (as defined in section 102 of such Act) who provide to older individuals long-term care services both in such settings and in long-term care facilities.

Sec. 212. Study on Board and Care Facility Quality. (a) ARRANGEMENT FOR STUDY COMMITTEE.—The Secretary of Health and Human Services shall enter into an arrangement, in accordance with subsection (d), to establish a study committee described in subsection (c) to conduct a study through the Institute of Medicine of the National Academy of Sciences on the quality of board and care facilities for older individuals (as defined in section 102 of the Older Americans Act of 1965 (42 U.S.C. 3001 et seq.)) and the disabled.

(b) SCOPE OF STUDY.—The study shall include—

(1) an examination of existing quality, health, and safety requirements for board and care facilities and the enforcement of such requirements for their adequacy and effectiveness, with special attention to their effectiveness in promoting good personal care;

(2) an examination of, and recommendations with respect to, the appropriate role of Federal, State, and local governments in assuring the health and safety of residents of board and care facilities; and

(3) specific recommendations to the Congress and the Secretary, by not later than 20 months after the date of the enactment of this Act, concerning the establishment of minimum national standards for the quality, health, and safety of residents of such facilities and the enforcement of such standards.

(c) COMPOSITION OF STUDY COMMITTEE.—The study committee shall be composed of members as appointed from among the following:
(1) NATIONAL ACADEMY OF SCIENCES.—The members of the National Academy of Sciences with experience in long-term care. The members so appointed shall include—
(A) physicians;
(B) experts on the administration of drugs to older individuals, and disabled individuals receiving long-term care services; and
(C) experts on the enforcement of life-safety codes in long-term care facilities.
(2) RESIDENTS.—Residents of board and care facilities (including privately owned board and care facilities), and representatives of such residents or of organizations that advocate on behalf of such residents. Members so appointed shall include—
(A) residents of a nonprofit board and care facility; or
(B) individuals who represent—
(i) residents of nonprofit board and care facilities; or
(ii) organizations that advocate on behalf of residents of nonprofit board and care facilities.
(3) OPERATORS.—Operators of board and care facilities (including privately owned board and care facilities), and individuals who represent such operators or organizations that represent the interests of such operators. Member so appointed shall include—
(A) operators of a nonprofit board and care facility; or
(B) individuals who represent—
(i) operators of nonprofit board and care facilities; or
(ii) organizations that represent the interests of operators of nonprofit board and care facilities.
(4) OFFICERS.—
(A) STATE OFFICERS.—Elected and appointed State officers who have responsibility relating to the health and safety of residents of board and care facilities.
(B) REPRESENTATIVES.—Representatives of such officers or of organizations representing such officers.
(C) OTHER INDIVIDUALS.—Other individuals with relevant expertise.
(d) USE OF INSTITUTE OF MEDICINE.—The Secretary shall request the National Academy of Sciences, through the Institute of Medicine, to establish, appoint, and provide administrative support for the study committee under an arrangement under which the actual expenses incurred by the Academy in carrying out such functions will be paid by the Secretary. If the National Academy of Sciences is willing to do so, the Secretary shall enter into such arrangement with the Academy.
(e) INVOLVEMENT OF OTHERS.—
(1) GOVERNMENT OFFICIALS.—The study committee shall conduct its work in a manner that provides for the consultation with Members of Congress or their representatives, officials of the Department of Health and Human Services, and officials of State and local governments who are not members of the study committee.
(2) EXPERTS.—The study committee may consult with any individual or

organization with expertise relating to the issues involved in the activities of the study committee.

(f) REPORT.—Not later than 20 months after an arrangement is entered into under subsection (d), the study committee shall submit, to the Secretary, the Speaker of the House of Representatives, and the President pro tempore of the Senate, a report containing the results of the study referred to in subsection (a) and the recommendations made under subsection (b).

(g) BOARD AND CARE FACILITY DEFINED.—In this section the term "board and care facility" means a facility describe in section 1616(e) of the Social Security Act (42 U.S.C. 1372e(e)).

(h) AUTHORIZATION.—There are authorized to be appropriated to carry out this section $1,500,000 for fiscal year 1992 and such sums as may be necessary for subsequent fiscal years.

Sec. 213. Study on Home Care Quality. (a) ESTABLISHMENT STUDY OF COMMITTEE.—The Secretary of Health and Human Services shall enter into an arrangement, in accordance with subsection (d), to establish a study committee described in subsection (c) to conduct a study through the Institute of Medicine of the National Academy of Sciences on the quality of home care services for older individuals and disabled individuals.

(b) SCOPE OF STUDY.—The study shall include—

(1) an examination of existing quality, health and safety requirements for home care services and the enforcement of such requirements for their adequacy, effectiveness, and appropriateness;

(2) an examination of, and recommendations with respect to, the appropriate role of Federal, State, and local governments in ensuring the health and safety of patients and clients of home care services; and

(3) specific recommendations to the Congress and the Secretary, not later than 20 months after the date of the enactment of this Act, concerning the establishment of minimum national standards for the quality, health, and safety of patients and clients of such services and the enforcement of such standards.

(c) COMPOSITION OF STUDY COMMITTEE.—The study committee shall be composed of members appointed from among—

(1) individuals with experience in long-term care, including nonmedical home care services;

(2) patients and clients of home care services (including privately provided home care services and services funded under the Older Americans Act of 1965) or individuals who represent such patients and clients or organizations that advocate on behalf of such patients and clients;

(3) providers of home care services (including privately provided home care services and services funded under the Older Americans Act of 1965) or individuals who represent such providers or organizations that advocate on behalf of such providers;

(4) elected and appointed State officers who have responsibility relating to the health and safety of patients and clients of home care services, or representatives of such officers or of organizations representing such officers; and

(5) other individuals with relevant expertise.

(d) USE OF INSTITUTE OF MEDICINE.—The Secretary shall request the National Academy of Sciences, through the Institute of Medicine, to establish, appoint, and provide administrative support for the study committee under an arrangement under which the actual expenses incurred by the Academy in carrying out such functions will be paid by the Secretary. If the National Academy of Sciences is willing to do so, the Secretary shall enter into such arrangement with the Academy.

(e) INVOLVEMENT OF OTHERS.—

(1) MEMBERS AND OFFICIALS.—The committee shall conduct its work in a manner that provides for consultation with Members of Congress or their representatives, officials of the Department of Health and Human Services, and officials of State and local governments who are not members of the committee.

(2) INDIVIDUAL OR ORGANIZATION WITH EXPERTISE.—The committee may consult with any individual or organization with expertise relating to the issues involved in the activities of the committee.

(f) REPORT.—Not later than 20 months after an arrangement is entered into under subsection (d), the committee shall submit, to the Secretary, the Speaker of the House of Representatives, and the President pro tempore of the Senate, a report containing the results of the study referred to in subsection (a).

(g) AUTHORIZATION.—There are authorized to be appropriated to carry out this section $1,000,000 for fiscal year 1992 and such sums as may be necessary for subsequent fiscal years.

Sec. 214. Nutrition Education. The Commissioner and the Secretary of Agriculture may provide technical assistance and appropriate material to agencies carrying out nutrition education programs in accordance with section 307(a)(13)(J).

Sec. 215. Authorization of Appropriations. (a) ADMINISTRATION.—For purposes of carrying out this Act, there are authorized to be appropriated for the Administration such sums as may be necessary for fiscal years 1992, 1993, 1994, and 1995.

(b) SALARIES AND EXPENSE.—There are authorized to be appropriated for salaries and expenses of the Administration on Aging—

(1) $17,000,000 for fiscal year 1992, $20,000,000 for fiscal year 1993, $24,000,000 for fiscal year 1994, and $29,000,000 for fiscal year 1995; and

(2) such additional sums as may be necessary for each such fiscal year to enable the Commissioner to provide for not fewer than 300 full-time employees (or the equivalent thereof) in the Administration on Aging.

TITLE III—GRANTS FOR STATE AND COMMUNITY PROGRAMS ON AGING

Part A—General Provisions

Purpose; Administration

Sec. 301. (a)1 It is the purpose of his title to encourage and assist State agencies and area agencies on aging to concentrate resources in order to de-

velop greater capacity and foster the development and implementation of comprehensive and coordinated systems to serve older individuals by entering into new cooperative arrangements in each State with the persons described in paragraph (2) for the planning, and for the provision of, supportive services, and multipurpose senior centers, in order to—

(A) secure and maintain maximum independence and dignity in a home environment for older individuals capable of self care with appropriate supportive services;

(B) remove individual and social barriers to economic and personal independence for older individuals; and

(C) provide a continuum of care for the vulnerable *older individuals; and*

(D) secure the opportunity for older individuals to receive managed in-home and community-based long-term care services.

(2) The persons referred to in paragraph (1) include—

(A) State agencies and area agencies on aging;

(B) other State agencies, including agencies that administer home and community care programs;

(C) Indian tribes, tribal organizations, and Native Hawaiian organizations;

(D) the providers, including voluntary organizations or other private sector organizations, of supportive services, nutrition services, and multipurpose senior centers; and

(E) organizations representing or employing older individuals or their families.

(b)(1) In order to effectively carry out the purpose of this title, *the Commissioner shall administer programs under this title through the Administration.*

(2) In carrying out the provisions of this title, the Commissioner may request the technical assistance and cooperation of the Department of Education, the Department of Labor, the Department of Housing and Urban Development, the Department of Transportation, the Office of Community Services, the Veteran's Administration, the Alcohol, Drug Abuse, and Mental Health Administration, and such other agencies and departments of the Federal Government as may be appropriate.

(c) The Commissioner shall provide technical assistance and training (by contract, grant, or otherwise) to State long-term care ombudsman programs established under Section 307(a)(12), and to individuals designated under such section to be representatives of a long-term care ombudsman, in order to enable such ombudsmen and such representatives to carry out the ombudsman program effectively.

Definitions

Sec. 302. For the purpose of this title—

(1) the term "comprehensive and coordinated system" means a system for providing all necessary supportive services, including nutrition services, in a manner designed to—

(A) facilitate accessibility to, and utilization of, all supportive services and nutrition services provided within the geographic area served by such system by any public or private agency or organization;

(B) develop and make the most efficient use of supportive services and nutrition services in meeting the needs of older individuals;

(C) use available resources efficiently and with a minimum of duplication; and

(D) encourage and assist public and private entities that have unrealized potential for meeting the service needs of older individuals to assist the older individuals on a voluntary basis.

(2) The term "unit of general purpose local government" means—

(A) a political subdivision of the State whose authority is general and not limited to only one function or combination of related functions; or

(B) an Indian tribal organization.

(3) The term "education and training service" means a supportive service designed to assist older individuals to better cope with their economic, health, and personal needs through services such as consumer education, continuing education, health education, preretirement education, financial planning, and other education and training services which will advance the objectives of this Act.

(4) The term "multipurpose senior center" means a community facility for the organization and provision of a broad spectrum of services, which shall include, but not be limited to, provision of health (including mental health), social, nutritional, and educational services and the provision of facilities for recreational activities for older individuals.

Authorization of Appropriations; Uses of Funds

Sec. 303. Supportive Services and Senior Centers.—(a)(1) There are authorized to be appropriated *$461,376,000 for fiscal year 1992 and such sums as may be necessary for fiscal years 1993, 1994, and 1995.*

(2) Funds appropriated under paragraph (1) shall be available to carry out section 712.

(b)(1) Congregate Nutrition Services.—There are authorized to be appropriated $505,000,000 for fiscal year 1992 and such sums as may be necessary for fiscal years 1993, 1994, and 1995, for the purpose of making grants under subpart 1 of Part C of this title.

(2) Home-Delivered Nutrition Services.—There are authorized to be appropriate $120,000,000 for fiscal year 1992 and such sums as may be necessary for fiscal years 1993, 1994, and 1995.

(3) School-Based Meals.—There are authorized to be appropriated $15,000,000 for fiscal years 1993, 1994, and 1995 to carry out subpart 3 or part C of this title (relating to school-based meals for volunteer older individuals and multigenerational programs).

(c) Grants made under parts B and subparts 1 and 2 of Part C of this title may be used for paying part of the cost of—

(1) the administration of area plans by area agencies on aging designated under section 305(a) (2) (A), including the preparation of area plans on aging consistent with section 306 and the evaluation of activities carried out under such plans; and

(2) the development of comprehensive and coordinated systems for supportive services, congregate and home delivered nutrition services under subparts 1 and 2 of part C, the development and operation of multipurpose senior centers, and the delivery of legal assistance.

(d) In-Home Services.—There are authorized to be appropriated $45,388,000 for fiscal year 1992 and such sums as may be necessary for fiscal years 1993, 1994, and 1995.

(e) Special Needs.—There are authorized to be appropriated such sums as may be necessary for fiscal years 1993, 1994, and 1995.

(f) Disease Prevention and Health Promotion.—There are authorized to be appropriated $25,000,000 for fiscal years 1992 and such sums as may be necessary for fiscal years 1993, 1994 and 1995.

(g) Supportive Activities for Caregivers.—There are authorized to be appropriated $15,000,000 for fiscal years 1992 and such sums as may be necessary for fiscal years 1993, 1994, and 1995, to carry out part G (relating to supportive activities for caretakers).

Allotment; Federal Share

Sec. 304. (a)(1) Subject to paragraphs (2) and (3) from the sums appropriated under section 303 for each fiscal year, each State shall be allotted an amount which bears the same ratio to such sums as the population aged 60 or older in such State bears to the population aged 60 or older in all States, except that (A) no State shall be allotted less than one-half of 1 percent of the sum appropriated for the fiscal year for which the determination is made; (B) Guam, the Virgin Islands, and the Trust Territory of the Pacific Islands, shall each be allotted not less than one-fourth of 1 percent of the sum appropriated for the fiscal year for which the determination is made; and (C) American Samoa and the Commonwealth of the Northern Mariana Islands shall each be allotted not less than one-sixteenth of 1 percent of the sum appropriated for the fiscal year for which the determination is made. For the purposes of paragraph (3) and the exception contained in clause (A) only, the term "State" does not include Guam, American Samoa, the Virgin Islands, the Trust Territory of the Pacific Islands, and the Commonwealth of the Northern Mariana Islands.

(2) No State shall be allotted less than the total amount allotted to the State under paragraph (1) of this subsection and section 308 for fiscal year 1987.

(3) No State shall be allotted, from the amount appropriated *under section 303(g)*, less than $50,000 for any fiscal year;

(4) The number of individuals aged 60 or older in any State and in all States shall be determined by the Commissioner on the basis of the most recent *data available from the Bureau of the Census, and other reliable demographic data satisfactory to the Commissioner.*

(b) Whenever the Commissioner determines that any amount allotted to a State under part B or C for a fiscal year under this section will not be used by such State for carrying out the purposes for which the allotment was made, the Commissioner shall make such allotment available for carrying out such purpose to one or more other States to the extent the Commissioner determines that such other States will be able to use such additional amount for carrying out such purpose. Any amount made available to a State from an appropriation for a fiscal year in accordance with the preceding sentence shall, for purposes of this title, be regarded as part of such State's allotment (as determined under subsection (a) for such year, but shall remain available until the end of the succeeding fiscal year.

(c) If the Commissioner finds that any State has failed to qualify under the State plan requirements of section 307 *or the commissioner does not approve the funding formula required under Section 305(a)(2)(C)* the Commissioner shall withhold the allotment of funds to such State referred to in subsection (a). The Commissioner shall disburse the funds so withheld directly to any public or private nonprofit institution or organization, agency, or political subdivision of such State submitting an approved plan under section 307, which includes an agreement that any such payment shall be matched in the proportion determined under subsection (d)(1)(D) for such State, by funds or in-kind resources from non-Federal sources.

(d)(1) From any State's allotment, after the application of section 308(b), under this section for any fiscal year—

(A) such amount as the State agency determines, but not more than 10 percent thereof, shall be available for paying such percentage as the agency determines but not more than 75 percent, of the cost of administration of area plans;

(B) such amount (excluding any amount attributable to funds appropriated under section 303(a)(3) as the State agency determines to be adequate for conducting an effective ombudsman program under section 307(a)(12) shall be available for conducting such program;

(C) *Not less than $150,000 and not more than 4 percent of the amount allotted to the State for carrying out part B, shall be available for conducting outreach demonstration projects under section 706; and*

(D) the remainder of such allotment shall be available to such State only for paying such percentage as the State agency determines but not more than 85 percent of the cost of supportive services, senior centers, and nutrition services under this title provided in the State as a part of a comprehensive and coordinated system in planning and services areas for which there is an area plan approved by the State agency.

(2) The non-Federal share shall be in cash or in kind. In determining the amount of the non-Federal share, the Commissioner may attribute fair market value to services and facilities contributed from non-Federal sources.

(e) *Grants made from allotments received under this title may be used for paying for the costs of providing for an area volunteer services coordinator (as described in section 306(a)(12)) or a State volunteer services coordinator (as described in section 307(a)(31)).*

Organization

Sec. 305. (a) In order for a State to be eligible to participate in programs of grants to States from allotments under this title—

(1) the State shall, in accordance with regulations of the Commissioner, designate a State agency as the sole State agency to—

(A) develop a State plan to be submitted to the Commissioner for approval under section 307;

(B) administer the State plan within such State;

(C) be primarily responsible *for planning, policy development, administration, coordination, priority setting, and evaluation of all State activities related to the objectives of this Act;*

(D) serve as an effective and visible advocate for the elderly by reviewing and commenting upon all State plans, budgets, and policies which affect the elderly and providing technical assistance to any agency, organization, association, or individual representing the needs of the elderly; and

(E) divide the State into district planning and service areas (or in the case of a State specified in subsection (b)(5)(A), designate the entire State as a single planning and service area), in accordance with guidelines issued by the Commissioner, after considering the geographical distribution of individuals aged 60 and older in the State, the incidence of the need for supportive services, nutrition services, multipurpose senior centers, and legal assistance, the distribution of older individuals who have greatest economic need (with particular attention to low-income minority individuals) residing in such areas, the distribution of older individuals who have the greatest social need (with particular attention to low-income minority individuals) residing in such areas, the distribution of older Indians residing in such areas, the distribution of resources available to provide such services or centers, the boundaries of existing areas within the State which were drawn for the planning or administration of supportive services programs, the location of units of general purpose local government within the State, and any other relevant factors; and

(2) the State agency shall—

(A) except as provided in subsection (b)(5), designate for each such area after consideration of the views offered by the unit or units of general purpose local government in such area, a public or private nonprofit agency or organization as the area agency on aging for such area;

(B) provide assurances, satisfactory to the Commissioner, that the State agency will take into account, in connection with matters of general policy arising in the development and administration of the State plan for any fiscal year, the views of recipients of supportive services or nutrition services, or individuals using multipurpose senior centers provided under such plan;

(C) in consultation with area agencies, in accordance with guidelines issued by the Commissioner, and using the best available data, develop and publish for review and comment a formula for distribution within the State of funds received under this title that takes into account—

(i) the geographical distribution of older individuals in the State; and

(ii) the distribution among planning and service areas of older individuals with greatest economic need and older individuals with greatest social need, with particular attention to low-income minority older individuals;

(D) submit its formula developed under subclause (C) to the Commissioner for approval;

(E) provide assurances that preference will be given to providing services to older individuals with the greatest economic or social needs, with particular attention to low-income minority individuals, and include proposed methods of carrying out the preference in the State plan;

(F) provide assurances that the State agency will require use of outreach efforts described in section 307(a)(24); and

(G)(i) set specific objectives, in consultation with area agencies on aging, for each planning and service area for providing services funded under this title to low-income minority older individuals;

(ii) provide an assurance that the State agency will undertake specific program development, advocacy, and outreach efforts focused on the needs of low-income minority older individuals; and

(iii) provide a description of the efforts described in clause (ii) that will be undertaken by the State agency.

(b)(1) In carrying out the requirement of clause (1) of subsection (a), the State may designate as a planning and service area any unit of general purpose local government which has a population of 100,000 or more. In any case in which a unit of general purpose local government makes application to the State agency under the preceding sentence to be designated as a planning and service area, the State agency shall, upon request, provide an opportunity for a hearing to such unit of general purpose local government. A State may designate as a planning and service area under clause (1) of subsection (a) any region within the State recognized for purposes of area-wide planning which includes one or more such units of general purpose local government when the State determines that the designation of such a regional planning and service area is necessary for, and will enhance, the effective administration of the programs authorized by this title. The State may include in any planning and service area designated under clause (1) of subsection (a) such additional areas adjacent to the unit of general purpose local government or regions so designated as the State determines to be necessary for, and will enhance the effective administration of the programs authorized by this title.

(2) The State is encouraged in carrying out the requirement of clause (1) of subsection (a) to include the area covered by the appropriate economic development district involved in any planning and service area designated under such clause, and to include all portions of an Indian reservation within a single planning and service area, if feasible.

(3) The chief executive officer of each State in which a planning and service area crosses State boundaries, or in which an interstate Indian reservation is located, may apply to the Commissioner to request redesignation

as an interstate planning and service area comprising the entire metropolitan area or Indian reservation. If the Commissioner approves such an application, the Commissioner shall adjust the State allotments of the areas within the planning and service area in which the interstate planning and service area is established to reflect the number of older individuals within the area who will be served by an interstate planning and service area not within the State.

(4) Whenever a unit of general purposes local government, a region, a metropolitan area or an Indian reservation is denied designation under the provisions of clause (1) of subsection (a), such unit of general purpose local government, region, metropolitan area, or Indian reservation may appeal the decision of the State agency to the Commissioner. The Commissioner shall afford such unit, region, metropolitan area, or Indian reservation an opportunity for a hearing. In carrying out the provisions of this paragraph, the Commissioner may approve the decision of the State agency, disapprove the decision of the State agency or require the State agency to designate the unit, region, area, or Indian reservation appealing the decision as a planning and service area, or take such other action as the Commissioner deems appropriate.

(5)(A) A State which on or before October 1, 1980, had designated, with the approval of the Commissioner, a single planning and service area covering all of the older individuals in the State, in which the State agency was administering the area plan, may after that date designate one or more additional planning and service areas within the State to be administered by public or private nonprofit agencies or organizations as area agencies on aging, after considering the factors specified in subsection (a)(1)(E). The State agency shall continue to perform the functions of an area agency *on aging* for any area of the State not included in a planning and service area for which an area agency *on aging* has been designated.

(B) Whenever a State agency designates a new area agency on aging after the date of enactment of the Older Americans Act Amendments of 1984, the State agency shall give the right of first refusal to a unit of general purpose local government if (i) such unit can meet the requirements of subsection (c), and (ii) the boundaries of such a unit and the boundaries of the area are reasonably contiguous.

(c) An area agency on aging designated under subsection (a) shall be—
    (1) an established office of aging which is operating within a planning and service area designated under subsection (a);
    (2) any office or agency of a unit of general purpose local government, which is designated to function only for the purpose of serving as an area agency *on aging* by the chief elected official of such unit;
    (3) any office or agency designated by the appropriate chief elected officials of any combination of units of general purpose local government to act only on behalf of such combination for such purpose;
    (4) any public or nonprofit private agency in a planning and service area, or any separate organizational unit within such agency, which is under the supervision or direction for this purpose of the designated State agency and which can and will engage only in the

planning or provision of a broad range of supportive services, or nutrition services within such planning and service area; or

(5) in the case of a State specified in subsection (b)(5), the State agency;

and shall provide assurance, determined adequate by the State agency, that the area agency *on aging* will have the ability to develop an area plan and to carry out, directly or through contractual or other arrangements, a program in accordance with the plan within the planning and service area. In designating an area agency on aging within the planning and service area or within any unit of general purpose local government designated as a planning and service area the State shall give preference to an established office on aging, unless the State agency finds that no such office within the planning and service area will have the capacity to carry out the area plan.

(d) The publication for review and comment required by clause (2)(C) of subsection (a) shall include—

(A) a descriptive statement of the formula's assumptions and goals, and the application of the definitions of greatest economic or social need,

(B) a numerical statement of the actual funding formula to be used,

(C) a listing of the population, economic, and social data to be used for each planning and service area in the State, and

(D) a demonstration of the allocation of funds, pursuant to the funding formula, to each planning and service area in the State.

(C)(i) A State agency shall establish and follow appropriate procedures to provide due process to affected parties, if the State agency initiates an action or proceeding to—

(I) revoke the designation of the area agency on aging under subsection (a);

(II) designate an additional planning and service area in a State;

(III) divide the State into different planning and services areas; or

(IV) otherwise affect the boundaries of the planning and service areas in the State.

(ii) The procedures described in clause (i) shall include procedures for—

(I) providing notice of an action or proceeding described in clause (i);

(II) documenting the need for the action or proceeding;

(III) conducting a public hearing for the action or proceeding;

(IV) involving area agencies on aging, service providers, and older individuals in the action or proceeding; and

(V) allowing an appeal of the decision of the State agency in the action or proceeding to the Commissioner.

(iii) An adversely affected party involved in an action or proceeding described in clause (i) may bring an appeal described in clause (ii)(V) on the basis of—

(I) the facts and merits of the matter that is the subject of the action or proceeding; or

(II) procedural grounds.

(iv) In deciding an appeal described in clause (ii)(V), the Commissioner may affirm or set aside the decision of the State agency. If the Commissioner

sets aside the decision, and the State agency has taken an action described in subclauses (I) through (III) of clause (i), the State agency shall nullify the action.

Area Plans

Sec. 306. (a) Each area agency on aging designated under section 305(a)(2)(A) shall, in order to be approved by the State agency, prepare and develop an area plan for a planning and service area for a two-, three-, or four-year period determined by the State agency, with such annual adjustments as may be necessary. Each such plan shall be based upon a uniform format for area plans within the State prepared in accordance with section 307(a)(1). Each such plan shall—

(1) provide, through a comprehensive and coordinated system, for supportive services, nutrition services, and, where appropriate, for the establishment, maintenance, or construction of multipurpose senior centers, within the planning and service area covered by the plan, including determining the extent of need for supportive services, nutrition services, and multipurpose senior centers in such area (taking into consideration, among other things, the number of older individuals with low incomes residing in such area, the number of older individuals who have greatest economic need (with particular attention to low-income minority individuals) residing in such area, the number of older individuals who have greatest social need (with particular attention to low-income minority individuals) residing in such area, and the number of older Indians residing in such area, and the efforts of voluntary organizations in the community), evaluating the effectiveness of the use of resources in meeting such need, and entering into agreements with providers of supportive services, nutrition services, or multipurpose senior centers in such area, for the provision of such services or centers to meet such need;

(2) provide assurances that an adequate proportion, as required under section 307(a)(22), of the amount allotted for part B to the planning and service area will be expended for the delivery of each of the following categories of services—

(A) services associated with access to services (transportation, outreach, *information and assistance, and case management services);*

(B) in-home services (homemaker and home health aide, visiting and telephone reassurance, and chore maintenance, and supportive services for families of elderly victims of Alzheimer's disease and related disorders with neurological and organic brain dysfunction); and

(C) legal assistance; and specify annually in such plan, as submitted or amended, in detail the amount of funds expended for each such category during the fiscal year most recently concluded;

(3)(A) designate, where feasible, a focal point for comprehensive service delivery in each community giving special consideration to designating multipurpose senior centers including multipurpose senior centers operated by organizations referred to in paragraph (6)(E)(ii) as such focal point; and

(B) specify in grants, contracts, and agreements implementing the plan, the identity of each focal point so designated.

(4) provide for the establishment and maintenance of information and assistance services in sufficient numbers to assure that all older individuals within the planning and service area covered by the plan will have reasonably convenient access to such services with particular emphasis on linking services available to isolated older individuals and older individuals with Alzheimer's disease or related disorders with neurological and organic brain dysfunction (and the caretakers of individuals with such disease or disorders);

(5)(A)(i) to provide assurances that the area agency on aging will set specific objectives for providing services to older individuals with the greatest economic or social needs, include specific objectives for providing services to low-income minority individuals, and include proposed methods of carrying out preferences in the area plan;

(ii) provide assurances that the area agency on aging will include in each agreement made with a provider of any service under this title, a requirement that such provider will—

(I) specify how the provider intends to satisfy the service needs of low-income minority individuals in the area served by the provider;

(II) to the maximum extent feasible, provide services to low-income minority individuals in accordance with their need for such services; and

(III) meet specific objectives established by the area agency on aging, for providing services to low-income minority individuals within the planning and service area; and

(iii) with respect to the fiscal year preceding the fiscal year for which such plan is prepared—

(I) identify the number of low-income minority older individuals in the planning and service area;

(II) describe the methods used to satisfy the service needs of such minority older individuals; and

(III) provide information on the extent to which the area agency on aging met the objectives discussed in clause (i);

(6) provide that the area agency on aging will;

(A) conduct periodic evaluations of, and public hearing on, activities carried out under the area plan and an annual evaluation of the effectiveness of outreach conducted under paragraph (5)(B);

(B) furnish appropriate technical assistance, and timely information in a timely manner, to providers of supportive services, nutrition services, or multipurpose senior centers in the planning and service area covered by the area plan;

(C) take into account in connection with matters of general policy arising in the development and administration of the area plan, the view of recipients of services under such plan;

(D) serve as the advocate and focal point for the elderly within the community *(in cooperation with agencies, organizations, and individuals participating in activities under the plan)* by monitoring, evaluating, and commenting upon all policies, programs, hearings, levies, and community actions which will affect the elderly;

(E)*(i)* where possible, enter into arrangements with organizations providing day care services for children or adults, and respite for families, so as to provide opportunities for older individuals to aid or assist on a voluntary basis in the delivery of such services to children, adults, and families; *and*

(ii) if possible regarding the provision of services under this title, enter into arrangements and coordinate with organizations that have a proven record of providing services to older individuals, that—

(I) were officially designated as community action agencies or community action programs under section 210 of the Economic Opportunity Act of 1964 (42 U.S.C. 2790) for fiscal year 1981, and did not lose the designation as a result of failure to comply with such Act; or

(II) came into existence during fiscal year 1982 as direct successors in interest to such community action agencies or community action programs; and that meet the requirements under section 675(c)(3) of the Community Services Block Grant Act (42 U.S.C. 9904(c)(3));

(F) establish an advisory council consisting of older individuals (including minority individuals) who are participants or who are eligible to participate in programs assisted under this Act, representatives of older individuals, local elected officials, providers of veterans' health care (if appropriate), and the general public, to advise continuously the area agency *on aging* on all matters relating to the development of the area plan, the administration of the plan and operations conducted under the plan;

(G) develop and publish methods by which priority of services is determined, particularly with respect to the delivery of services under clause (2);

(H) *establish effective and efficient procedures for coordination of;*

(i) entities conducting programs that receive assistance under this Act within the planning and service area served by the agency; and

(ii) entities conducting other Federal programs for older individuals at the local level, with particular emphasis on entities conducting programs described in section 203(b), within the area;

(I) conduct efforts to facilitate the coordination of community-based, long-term care services designed to retain individuals in their homes, thereby deferring unnecessary, costly institutionalization, and designed to *include the development of case management services as a component of the long-term care services;*

(J) identify the public and private nonprofit entities involved in the prevention, identification, and treatment of the abuse, neglect, and exploitation of older individuals, and based on such identification, determine the extent to which the need for appropriate services for such individuals is unmet;

(K) facilitate the involvement of long-term care providers in the coordination of community-based long-term care services and work to ensure community awareness of and involvement in addressing the needs of residents of long-term care facilities;

(L) coordinate the categories of services specified in paragraph (2) for which the area agency on aging is required to expend funds under Part B, with activities of community-based organizations established for the benefit of victims of Alzheimer's disease and the families of such victims;

(M) coordinate any mental health services provided with funds expended by the area agency on aging for part B with the mental health services provided by community health centers and by other public agencies and nonprofit private organizations;

(N) if there is a significant population of older Indians in the planning and service area of the area agency *on aging,* the area agency *on aging* shall conduct outreach activities to identify older Indians in such area and shall inform such older Indians of the availability of assistance under this Act;

(O)(i) compile available information on institutions of higher education in the planning and service area regarding—

(I) the courses of study offered to older individuals by such institutions;

(II) the policies of such institutions with respect to the enrollment of older individuals with little or no payment of tuition, on a space available basis, or on another special basis; and include in such compilation such related supplementary information as may be necessary; and

(ii) based on the results of such compilation, make a summary of such information available to older individuals at multipurpose senior centers, congregate nutrition sites, and other appropriate places; and

(P) establish a grievance procedure for older individuals who are dissatisfied with or denied services under this title;

(Q) enter into voluntary arrangements with nonprofit entities (including public and private housing authorities and organizations) that provide housing (such as housing under section 202 of the Housing Act of 1959 (12 U.S.C. 1701Q) to older individuals, to provide—

(i) leadership and coordination in the development, provision, and expansion of adequate housing, supportive services, referrals, and living arrangements for older individuals; and

(ii) advance notification and nonfinancial assistance to older individuals who are subject to eviction from such housing;

(R) list the telephone number of the agency in each telephone directory that is published, by the provider of local telephone service, for residents in any geographical area that lies in whole or in part in the service and planning area served by the agency—

(i) under the name 'Area Agency on Aging';

(ii) in the unclassified section of the directory; and

(iii) to the extent possible, in the classified section of the direc-

tory, under a subject heading designated by the Commissioner by regulation; and

(S) identify the needs of older individuals and describe methods the area agency on aging will use to coordinate planning and delivery of transportation services (including the purchase of vehicles) to assist older individuals, including those with special needs, in the area;

(7) provide assurances that any amount received under part D will be expended in accordance with such part;

(8) provide assurances that any amount received under part E will be expended in accordance with such part;

(9) provide assurances that any amount received under part F will be expended in accordance with such part;

(10) provide assurances that any amount received under part G will be expended in accordance with such part;

(11) provide assurances that the area agency on aging, in carrying out the State Long-Term Care Ombudsman program under section 307(a)(12), will expend not less than the total amount of funds appropriated under this Act and expended by the agency in fiscal year 1991 in carrying out such a program under this title.

(12) in the discretion of the area agency on aging, provide for an area volunteer services coordinator, who shall—

(A) encourage, and enlist the services of, local volunteer groups to provide assistance and services appropriate to the unique needs of older individuals within the planning and service area;

(B) encourage, organize, and promote the use of older individuals as volunteers to local communities within the area; and

(C) promote the recognition of the contribution made by volunteers to programs administered under the area plan;

(13)(A) describe all activities of the area agency on aging, whether funded by public or private funds; and

(B) provide an assurance that the activities conform with—

(i) the responsibilities of the area agency on aging, as set forth in this subsection; and

(ii) the laws, regulations, and policies of the State served by the area agency on aging;

(14) provide assurances that the area agency on aging will—

(A) maintain the integrity and public purpose of services provided, and service providers, under this title in all contractual and commercial relationships;

(B) disclose to the Commissioner and the State agency—

(i) the identity of each nongovernmental entity with which such agency has a contract or commercial relationship relating to providing any service to older individuals; and

(ii) the nature of such contract or such relationships;

(C) demonstrate that a loss or diminution in the quantity or quality of the services provided, or to be provided, under this title by such agency has not resulted and will not result from such contract or such relationship;

(D) demonstrate that the quantity or quality of the services to be

provided under this title by such agency will be enhanced as a result of such contract or such relationship; and

(E) on the request of the Commissioner or the State, for the purpose of monitoring compliance with this Act (including conducting an audit), disclose all sources and expenditures of funds such agency receives or expends to provide services to older individuals;

(15) provide assurances that funds received under this title will not be used to pay any part of a cost (including an administrative cost) incurred by the area agency on aging to carry out a contract or commercial relationship that is not carried out to implement this title;

(16) provide assurances that preference in receiving services under this title will not be given by the area agency on aging to particular older individuals as a result of a contract or commercial relationship that is not carried out to implement this title;

(17) provide assurances that projects in the planning and service area will reasonably accommodate participants as described in section 307(a)(13)(G);

(18) provide assurances that the area agency on aging will, to the maximum extent practicable, coordinate the services it provides under this title with services provided under title VI;

(19)(A) provide an assurance that the area agency on aging will pursue activities to increase access by older individuals who are Native Americans to all aging programs and benefits provided by the agency, including programs and benefits under this title, if applicable; and

(B) specify the ways in which the area agency on aging intends to implement the activities; and

(20) provide that case management services provided under this title through the area agency on aging will—

(A) not duplicate case management services provided through other Federal and State programs;

(B) be coordinated with services described in subparagraph (A); and

(C) be provided by—

(i) a public agency; or

(ii) a nonprofit private agency that—

(I) does not provide, and does not have a direct or indirect ownership or controlling interest in, or a direct or indirect affiliation or relationship with, an entity that provides, services other than case management services under this title; or

(II) is located in a rural area and obtains a waiver of the requirement described in subclause (I).

(b)(1) Each State, in approving area agency plans under this section, shall waive the requirement described in clause (2) of subsection (a) for any category of services described in such clause if the area agency on aging demonstrates to the State agency that services being furnished for such category in the area are sufficient to meet the need for such services in such area.

(2)(A) Before an area agency on aging requests a waiver under paragraph (1) of this subsection, the area agency on aging shall conduct a timely public hearing in accordance with the provisions of this paragraph. The area agency on aging requesting a waiver shall notify all interested parties in the area of the public hearing and furnish the interested parties with an opportunity to testify.

(B) the area agency on aging shall prepare a record of the public hearing conducted pursuant to subparagraph (A) and shall furnish the record of the public hearing with the request for a waiver made to the State under paragraph (1).

(C) Whenever the State agency proposes to grant a waiver to an area agency *on aging* under this subsection, the State agency shall publish the intention to grant such a waiver together with the justification for the waiver at least 30 days prior to the effective date of the decision to grant the waiver. An individual or service provider from the area with respect to which the proposed waiver applies is entitled to request a hearing before the State agency on the request to grant such waiver. If within the 30-day period described in the first sentence of this subparagraph, an individual or service provider requests a hearing under this subparagraph, the State agency shall afford such individual or provider an opportunity for a hearing.

(D) If the State agency waives the requirement described in clause (2) of subsection (a), the State agency shall provide to the Commissioner—

(i) a report regarding such waiver that details the demonstration made by the area agency on aging to obtain such waiver;

(ii) a copy of the record of the public hearing conducted pursuant to subparagraph (a); and

(iii) a copy of the record of any public hearing conducted pursuant to subparagraph (C).

(c)(1) Subject to regulations prescribed by the Commissioner, an area agency on aging designated under section 305(a)(2)(A) or, in areas of a State where no such agency has been designated, the State agency, may enter into agreements with agencies administering programs under the Rehabilitation Act of 1973, and titles XIX and XX of the Social Security Act for the purpose of developing and implementing plans for meeting the common need for transportation services of individuals receiving benefits under such Acts and older individuals participating in programs authorized by this title.

(2) In accordance with an agreement entered into under paragraph (1), funds appropriated under this title may be used to purchase transportation services for older individuals and may be pooled with funds made available for the provision of transportation services under the Rehabilitation Act of 1973, and titles XIX and XX of the Social Security Act.

(d) An area agency on aging may not require any provider of legal assistance under this title to reveal any information that is protected by the attorney-client privilege.

(e)(1) If the head of a State agency finds that an area agency on aging has failed to comply with Federal or State laws, including the area plan requirements of this section, regulations, or policies, the

State may withhold a portion of the funds to the area agency on aging available under this title.

(2)(A) The head of a State agency shall not make a final determination withholding funds under paragraph (1) without first affording the area agency on aging due process in accordance with procedures established by the State agency.

(B) At a minimum, such procedures shall include procedures for—

(i) providing notice of an action to withhold funds;

(ii) providing documentation of the need for such action; and

(iii) at the request of the area agency on aging, conducting a public hearing concerning the action.

(3)(A) If a State agency withholds the funds, the State agency may use the funds withheld to directly administer programs under this title in the planning and service area served by the area agency on aging for a period not to exceed 180 days, except as provided in subparagraph (B).

(B) If the State agency determines that the area agency on aging has not taken corrective action, or if the State agency does not approve the corrective action, during the 180-day period described in subparagraph (A), the State agency may extend the period for more than 90 days.

State Plans

SEC. 307. (a) Except as provided *in the succeeding sentence and* section 309(a), each State, in order to be eligible for grants from its allotment under this title for any fiscal year, shall submit to the Commissioner a State plan for a two-, three-, or four-year period determined by the State agency, which such annual revisions as are necessary, which meets such criteria as the Commissioner may by regulation prescribe. *If the Commissioner determines, in the discretion of the Commissioner, that a State failed in 2 successive years to comply with the requirements under this title, then the State shall submit to the Commissioner a State plan for a 1-year period that meets such criteria, for subsequent years until the Commissioner determines that the State is in compliance with such requirements. Each such plan shall comply with all of the following requirements:*

(1) The plan shall contain assurances that the State plan will be based upon areas plans developed by area agencies on aging within the State designated under section 305(a)(2)(A) and that the State will prepare and distribute a uniform format for use by area agencies *on aging* in developing area plans under section 306.

(2) The plan shall provide that each area agency on aging designated under section 305(a)(2)(A) will develop and submit to the State agency for approval an area plan which complies with the provisions of section 306.

(3)(A) The plan shall provide that the State agency will evaluate the need for supportive services (including legal assistance *and transportation services*), nutrition services, and multipurpose senior centers within the

State and determine the extent to which existing public or private programs meet such need. *To conduct the evaluation, the State agency shall use the procedures implemented under section 202(a)(29).*

(B) The plan shall provide assurances that the State agency will spend in each fiscal year, for services to older individuals residing in rural areas in the State assisted under this title, an amount equal to not less than 105 percent of the amount expended for such services (including amounts expended under title V and title VII) in fiscal year 1978.

(4) The plan shall provide for the use of such methods of administration (including methods relating to the establishment and maintenance of personnel standards on a merit basis, except that the Commissioner shall exercise no authority with respect to the selection, tenure of office, or compensation of any individual employed in accordance with such methods) as are necessary for the proper and efficient administration of the plan, and where necessary, provide for the reorganization and reassignment of functions to assure such efficient administration.

(5) The plan shall provide that the State agency will afford an opportunity for a hearing upon request to any area agency on aging submitting a plan under this title, to any provider of a service under such a plan, or to any applicant to provide a service under such a plan. *The State Agency shall establish and publish procedures for requesting and conducting such a hearing.*

(6) The plan shall provide that the State agency will make such reports, in such form, and containing such information, as the Commissioner may require, and comply with such requirements as the Commissioner may impose to insure the correctness of such reports.

(7)(A) The plan shall provide satisfactory assurance that such fiscal control and fund accounting procedures will be adopted as may be necessary to assure proper disbursement of, and accounting for, Federal funds paid under this title to the State, including any such funds paid to the recipients of a grant or contract.

(B) The plan shall provide assurances that—

(i) no individual (appointed or otherwise) involved in the designation of the State agency or an area agency on aging, or in the designation of the head of any subdivision of the State agency or of an area agency on aging, is subject to a conflict of interest prohibited under this Act;

(ii) no officer, employee, or other representative of the State agency or an area agency on aging is subject to a conflict of interest prohibited under this Act; and

(iii) mechanisms are in place to identify and remove conflicts of interest prohibited under this Act.

(C) The plan shall provide assurances that the State agency and each area agency on aging will—

(i) maintain the integrity and public purpose of services provided, and service providers, under the State plan in all contractual and commercial relationships;

(ii) disclose to the Commissioner—

(I) the identity of each nongovernmental entity with which the State

agency or area agency on aging has a contract or commercial relationship relating to providing any service to older individuals; and

(II) the nature of such contract or such relationship;

(iii) demonstrate that a loss or diminution in the quantity or quality of the services provided, or to be provided, under this Act by such agency has not resulted and will not result from such contract or such relationship;

(iv) demonstrate that the quantity or quality of the services to be provided under the State plan will be enhanced as a result of such contract or such relationship; and

(v) on the request of the Commissioner, for the purpose of monitoring compliance with this Act (including conducting an audit), disclose all sources and expenditures of funds the State agency and area agency on aging receive or expend to provide services to older individuals.

(8) The plan shall provide that the State agency will conduct periodic evaluations of, and public hearings on, activities and projects carried out under the State plan, including an evaluation of the effectiveness of the State agency in reaching older individuals with the greatest economic or social needs, with particular attention to low-income minority individuals. In conducting such evaluations and public hearings, the State agency shall solicit the views and experiences of entities that are knowledgeable about the needs and concerns of low-income minority older individuals.

(9) The plan shall provide for establishing and maintaining information and assistance services in sufficient numbers to assure that all older individuals in the State who are not furnished adequate information and referral services under section 306(a)(4) will have reasonably convenient access to such services.

(10) The plan shall provide that no supportive services, nutrition services or in-home services (as defined in section 342, will be directly provided by the State agency or an area agency on aging, except where, in the judgment of the State agency, provision of such services by the State agency or an area agency on aging is necessary to assure an adequate supply of such services, or where such services are directly related to such services, or where such services are directly related to such State or area agency on aging's administrative functions, or where such services of comparable quality can be provided more economically by such State or area agency on aging.

(11) The plan shall provide that subject to the requirements of merit employment systems of State and local governments—

(A) preference shall be given to older individuals; and

(B) special consideration shall be given to individuals with formal training in the field of aging (including an educational specialty or emphasis in aging and a training degree or certificate in aging) or equivalent professional experience in the field of aging for any staff positions (full time or part time) in State and area agencies for which such individuals qualify.

(12) The plan shall provide assurances that the State agency will carry out, through the Office of the State Long-Term Care Ombudsman, a State Long-term Care Ombudsman program in accordance with section 712 and this title.

(A) the State agency will establish and operate, either directly or by contract or other arrangement with any public agency or other appropriate private nonprofit organization, other than an agency or organization which is responsible for licensing or certifying long-term care services in the State or which is an association (or an affiliate of such an association) of long-term care facilities (including any other residential facility for older individuals), an Office of the State Long-Term Care Ombudsman (in this paragraph referred to as the 'Office') and shall carry out through the Office a long-term care ombudsman program which provides an individual who will on a full-time basis—

(i) investigate and resolve complaints made by or on behalf of older individuals who are residents of long-term care facilities relating to action, inaction, or decisions of providers, or their representatives, of long-term care services, of public agencies, or of social service agencies, which may adversely affect the health, safety, welfare, or rights of such residents;

(ii) provide for training staff and volunteers and promote the development of citizen organizations to participate in the ombudsman program; and

(iii) carry out such other activities as the Commissioner deems appropriate.

(B) The State agency will establish procedures for appropriate access by the ombudsman to long-term care facilities and patients' records, including procedures to protect the confidentiality of such records and ensure that the identity of any complainant or resident will not be disclosed without the written consent of such complainant or resident, or upon court order.

(C) The State agency will establish a statewide uniform reporting system to collect and analyze data relating to complaints and conditions in long-term care facilities for the purpose of identifying and resolving significant problems, with provision for submission of such data to the agency of the State responsible for licensing or certifying long-term care facilities in the State and to the Commissioner on a regular basis.

(D) The State agency will establish procedures to assure that any files maintained by the ombudsman program shall be disclosed only at the discretion of the ombudsman having authority over the disposition of such files, except that the identity of any complainant or resident of a long-term care facility shall not be disclosed by such ombudsman unless—

(i) such complainant or resident, or the individual's legal representative, consents in writing to such disclosure; or

(ii) such disclosure is required by court order.

(E) In planning and operating the ombudsman program, the State agency will consider the views of area agencies on aging, older individuals, and provider agencies.

(F) The State agency will—

(i) ensure that no individuals (whether by appointment or otherwise) or the designation of the head of any subdivision of the Office is subject to a conflict of interest;

(ii) ensure that no officer, employee or other representative of the Office is subject to a conflict of interest; and
(iii ensure that mechanisms are in place to identify and remedy any such or other similar conflicts.
(G) The State agency will—
(i) ensure that adequate legal counsel is available to the Office for advice and consultation and that legal representation is provided to any representative of the Office against whom suit or other legal action is brought in connection with the performance of such representative's official duties; and
(ii) ensure that the Office has the ability to pursue administrative, legal, and other appropriate remedies on behalf of residents of long-term care facilities.
(H) The State agency will require the Office to—
(i) prepare an annual report containing data and findings regarding the types of problems experienced and complaints received by or on behalf of individuals residing in long-term care facilities, and to provide policy, regulatory, and legislative recommendations to solve such problems, resolve such complaints, and improve the quality of care and life in long-term care facilities;
(ii) analyze and monitor the development and implementation of Federal, State, and local laws, regulations, and policies with respect to long-term care facilities and services in that State, and recommend any changes in such laws, regulations, and policies deemed by the Office to be appropriate;
(iii) provide information to public agencies, legislators, and others, as deemed necessary by the Office, regarding the problems and concerns, including recommendations related to such problems and concerns, of older individuals residing in long-term care facilities;
(iv) provide for the training of the Office staff, including volunteers and other representatives of the Office in—
(I) Federal, State, and local laws, regulations, and policies with respect to long-term care facilities in the State;
(II) investigative techniques; and
(III) such other matters as the State deems appropriate;
(v) coordinate ombudsman services with the protection and advocacy systems for individuals with developmental disabilities and mental illness established under part A of the Developmental Disabilities Assistance and Bill of Rights Act (42 U.S.C. 6001 et seq.) and under the Protection and Advocacy for Mentally Ill individuals Act of 1986 (Public Law 99-319); and
(vi) include any area of local ombudsman entity designated by the State Long Term Care Ombudsman as a subdivision of the Office. Any representative of an entity designated in accordance with the preceding sentence (whether an employee or an unpaid volunteer) shall be treated as a representative of the Office for purposes of this paragraph.
(I) The State will ensure that no representative of the Office will

be liable under State law for the good faith performance of official duties.

(J) The State will—

(i) ensure that willful interference with representatives of the Office in the performance of their official duties (as defined by the Commissioner) shall be unlawful;

(ii) prohibit retaliation and reprisals by a long-term care facility or other entity with respect to any resident or employee for having filed a complaint with, or providing information to, the Office; and

(iii) provide for appropriate sanctions with respect to such interference, retaliation, and reprisals; and

(iv) ensure that representatives of the Office shall have—

(I) access to long-term care facilities and their residents; and

(II) with the permission of a resident or resident's legal guardian, have access to review the resident's medical and social records or, if a resident is unable to consent to such review and has no legal guardian, appropriate access to the resident's medical and social records.

(K) The State agency will prohibit any officer, employee, or other representative of the Office to investigate any complaint filed with the Office unless the individual has received such training as may be required under subparagraph (G)(iv) and has been approved by the long-term care ombudsman as qualified to investigate such complaints.

(13) The plan shall provide with respect to nutrition services that—

(A) each project providing nutrition services will be available to individuals aged 60 or older and to their spouses, and may be made available to handicapped or disabled individuals who have not attained 60 years of age but who reside in housing facilities occupied primarily by the elderly at which congregate nutrition services are provided;

(B) primary consideration shall be given to the provision of meals in a congregate setting, except that each area agency *on aging* (i) may award funds made available under this title *other than under section 303(b)(3)* to organizations for the provision of home delivered meals to older individuals in accordance with the provisions of subpart 2 of part C, based upon a determination of need made by the recipient of a grant or contract entered into under this title, without requiring that such organizations also provide meals to older individuals in a congregate setting; and (ii) shall, in awarding such funds, select such organizations in a manner which complies with the provisions of subclause (H);

(C)(i) each project will permit recipients of grants or contracts to solicit voluntary contributions for meals furnished in accordance with guidelines established by the Commissioner, taking into consideration the income ranges of eligible individuals in local communities and other sources of income of the recipients of a grant or contract; and (ii) such voluntary contributions will be used to increase the number of meals served by the project involved, to facilitate access to such meals, and to provide other supportive services directly related to nutrition services;

(D) in the case of meals served in a congregate setting, a site for such services and for comprehensive supportive services is furnished in as close proximity to the majority of eligible individuals' residences as feasible, with particular attention upon a multipurpose senior center, a school, a church, or other appropriate community facility, preferably within walking distance where possible, and where appropriate, transportation to such site is furnished.

(E) each project will establish outreach activities which assure that the maximum number of eligible individuals may have an opportunity to participate.

(F) each project *will establish and administer the nutrition project with the advice of dietitians (or individuals with comparable expertise)*, persons competent in the field of service in which the nutrition project is being provided, who are knowledgeable with regard to the needs of older individuals;

(G) each project will provide special menus, where feasible and appropriate to meet the particular dietary needs arising from the health requirements, religious requirements, or ethnic backgrounds of eligible individuals.

(H) each area agency *on aging* will give consideration where feasible, in the furnishing of home delivered meals to the use of organizations which (i) have demonstrated an ability to provide home delivered meals efficiently and reasonably; and (ii) furnish assurances to the area agency *on aging* that such an organization will maintain efforts to solicit voluntary support and that funds made available under this title to the organization will not be used to supplant funds from non-Federal sources;

(I) each area agency *on aging* shall establish procedures that will allow nutrition project administrators the option to offer a meal, on the same basis as meals are provided to elderly participants, to individuals providing volunteer services during the meal hours, and to individuals with disabilities who reside at home with and accompany older individuals who are eligible under this Act;

(J) each nutrition project shall provide nutrition education on at least a semiannual basis to participants in programs described in part C;

(K) each project shall comply with applicable provisions of State or local laws regarding the safe and sanitary handling of food, equipment, and supplies used in the storage, preparation, service, and delivery of meals to an older individual;

(L) the State agency will monitor, coordinate, and assist in the planning of nutritional services, with the advice of a dietitian or an individual with comparable expertise; and

(M) the State agency will—

(i) develop nonfinancial criteria for eligibility to receive nutrition services under section 336; and

(ii) periodically evaluate recipients of such services to determine whether they continue to meet such criteria.

(14) The plan shall provide, with respect to the acquisition (in fee simple or by lease for 10 years or more), alteration, or renovation of existing facilities (or the construction of new facilities in any area in which there are no suitable structures available, as determined by the State agency, after full consideration of the recommendations made by area agencies on aging to be a focal point for the delivery of services assisted under this title) to serve as multipurpose senior centers, that—

(A) the plan contains or is supported by reasonable assurances that (i) for not less than 10 years after acquisition, or not less than 20 years after the completion of construction, the facility will be used for the purpose for which it is to be acquired or constructed, unless for unusual circumstances the Commissioner waives the requirement of this division; (ii) sufficient funds will be available to meet the non-Federal share of the cost of acquisition or construction of the facility; (iii) sufficient funds will be available when acquisition or construction is completed, for effective use of the facility for the purpose for which it is being acquired or constructed; and (iv) the facility will not be used and is not intended to be used for sectarian instruction or as a place for religious worship;

(B) the plan contains or is supported by reasonable assurance that, in the case of purchase or construction, there are no existing facilities in the community suitable for leasing as a multipurpose senior center;

(C) the plans and specifications for the facility are in accordance with regulations relating to minimum standards of construction, promulgated with particular emphasis on securing compliance with the requirements of the Act of August 12, 1968, commonly known as the Architectural Barriers Act of 1968;

(D) the plan contains or is supported by adequate assurance that any laborer or mechanic employed by any contractor or subcontractor in the performance of work on the facility will be paid wages at rates not less than those prevailing for similar work in the locality as determined by the Secretary of Labor in accordance with the Act of March 3, 1931 (40 U.S.C. 276a—276A-5, commonly known as the Davis-Bacon Act), and the Secretary of Labor shall have, with respect to the labor standards specified in this clause, the authority and functions set forth in reorganization plan numbered 14 of 1950 (15 FR 3176; 64 Stat. 1267), and section 2 of the Act of June 13, 1934 (40 U.S.C. 276c); and

(E) the plan contains assurances that the State agency will consult with the Secretary of Housing and Urban Development with respect to the technical adequacy of any proposed alteration or renovation.

(15) The plan shall provide that with respect to legal assistance—

(A) the plan contains assurances that area agencies on aging will (i) enter into contracts with providers of legal assistance which can demonstrate the experience or capacity to deliver legal assistance; (ii) include in any such contract provisions to assure that any recipient of funds under division (i) will be subject to specific restrictions and regulations promulgated under the Legal Services Corporation Act (other than restrictions and regulations governing eligibility for legal assistance under such Act and governing membership of local governing boards) as determined appropriate by the Commissioner; and (iii) attempt to involve the private bar in legal assistance activities authorized under this title, including groups within the private bar furnishing services to older individuals on a pro bono and reduced fee basis:

(B) the plan contains assurances that no legal assistance will be furnished unless the grantee—administers a program designed to provide legal assistance to older individuals with social or economic need and has agreed, if the grantee is not a Legal Services Corporation project grantee, to coordinate its services with existing Legal Services Corporation projects in the planning and service area in order to concentrate the use of funds provided under this title on individuals with the greatest such need and the area agency *on aging* makes a finding after assessment, pursuant to standards for service promulgated by the Commissioner, that any grantee selected is the entity best able to provide the particular services;

(C) The State agency will provide for the coordination of the furnishing of legal assistance to older individuals within the State, and provide advice and technical assistance in the provision of legal assistance to older individuals within the State and support the furnishing of training and technical assistance for legal assistance for older individuals;

(D) the plan contains assurances, to the extent practicable, that legal assistance furnished under the plan will be in addition to any legal assistance for older individuals being furnished with funds from sources other than this Act and that reasonable efforts will be made to maintain existing levels of legal assistance for older individuals; and

(E) the plan contains assurances that area agencies on aging will give priority to legal assistance related to income, health care, long-term care, nutrition, housing, utilities, protective services, defense of guardianship, abuse, neglect and age discrimination.

(16) The plan shall, whenever the State desires to, provide for a fiscal year for services for the prevention of abuse of older individuals—

(A) the plan contains assurances that any area agency on aging carrying out such services will conduct a program consistent with relevant State law and coordinated with existing State adult protective service activities for—

(i) public education to identify and prevent abuse of older individuals;

(ii) receipt of reports of abuse of older individuals;

(iii) active participation of older individuals participating in programs under this Act through outreach, conferences, and referral of such individuals to other social service agencies or sources of assistance where appropriate and consented to by the parties to be referred; and

(iv) referral of complaints to law enforcement or public protective service agencies where appropriate;

(B) the State will not permit involuntary or coerced participation in the program of services described in this clause by alleged victims, abusers, or their households; and

(C) all information gathered in the course of receiving reports and making referrals shall remain confidential unless all parties to the complaint consent in writing to the release of such information, except that such information may be released to a law enforcement or public protective service agency.

(17) The plan shall provide assurances that each State will provide inservice training opportunities for personnel of agencies and programs funded under this Act.

(18) The plan shall provide assurances that each State will assign personnel *(one of whom shall be known as a legal assistance developer)* to provide State leadership in developing legal assistance programs for older individuals throughout the State.

(19) The plan shall provide, with respect to education and training services, assurances that area agencies on aging may enter into grants and contracts with providers of education and training services which can demonstrate the experience or capacity to provide such services (except that such contract authority shall be effective for any fiscal year only to such extent, or in such amounts, as are provided in the appropriations Act).

(20) The plan shall provide assurances that, if a substantial number of the older individuals residing in any planning and service area in the State are of limited English-speaking ability, then the State will require the area agency on aging for each such planning and service area—

(A) to utilize, in the delivery of outreach services under sections 306(a)(2)(A) and 306(a)(6)(P), the services of workers who are fluent in the language spoken by a predominant number of such older individuals who are of limited English-speaking ability; and

(B) to designate an individual employed by the area agency on aging, or available to such area agency on aging on a full-time basis, whose responsibilities will include—

(i) taking such action as may be appropriate to assure that counseling assistance is made available to such older individuals who are of limited English-speaking ability in order to assist such older individuals in participating in programs and receiving assistance under this Act; and

(ii) providing guidance to individuals engaged in the delivery of supportive services under the area plan involved to enable such individuals to be aware of cultural sensitivities and to take into account effectively linguistic and cultural differences.

(21) The plan shall provide assurances that the State agency, in carrying out the State Long-Term Care Ombudsman program under section 307(a)(12), will expend not less than the total amount expended by the agency in fiscal year 1991 in carrying out such a program under this title.

(22) The plan shall specify a minimum percentage of the funds received by each area agency *on aging* for part B that will be expended, in the absence of the waiver granted under section 306(b)(1), by such area agency to provide each of the categories of services specified in section 306(a)(2).

(23) The plan shall, with respect to the fiscal year preceding the fiscal year for which such plan is prepared—

(A) identify the number of low-income minority older individuals in the State; and

(B) describe the methods used to satisfy the service needs of such minority older individuals.

(24) the plan shall provide assurances that the State agency will require outreach efforts that will—

(A) identify older individuals eligible for assistance under this Act with special emphasis on

(i) *older individuals residing in rural areas;*

(ii) *older individuals with greatest economic need (with particular attention to low-income minority individuals);*

(iii) *older individuals with greatest social need (with particular attention to low-income minority individuals);*

(iv) *older individuals with severe disabilities;*

(v) *older individuals with limited English-speaking ability; and*

(vi) *older individuals with Alzheimer's disease or related disorders with neurological and organic brain dysfunction (and the caretakers of such individuals); and*

(B) *inform the older individuals referred to in clauses (i) through (vi) of subparagraph (A), and the caretakers of such individuals, of the availability of such assistance.*

(25) The plan shall provide, with respect to the needs of older individuals with severe disabilities, assurances that the State will coordinate planning, identification, assessment of needs, and service for older individuals with disabilities with particular attention to individuals with severe disabilities with the State agencies with primary responsibility for individuals with disabilities, including severe disabilities, and develop collaborative programs, where appropriate, to meet the needs of older individuals with disabilities.

(26) The plan shall provide assurances that area agencies on aging will conduct efforts to facilitate the coordination of community-based, long-term care services, pursuant to section 306(a)(6)(I), for older individuals who—

(A) reside at home and are at risk of institutionalization because of limitations on their ability to function independently;

(B) are patients in hospitals and are at risk of prolonged institutionalization; or

(C) are patients in long-term care facilities, but who can return to their homes if community-based services are provided to them.

(27) The plan shall provide assurances of consultation and coordination in planning and provision of in-home services under section 341 with State and local agencies and private nonprofit organizations which administer and provide services relating to health, social services, rehabilitation, and mental health services.

(28) The plan shall provide assurances that if the State receives funds appropriated under section 303(e), the State agency and area agencies on aging will expend such funds to carry out part E.

(29) The plan shall, with respect to the fiscal year preceding the fiscal

year for which such plan is prepared, describe the methods used to satisfy the service needs of older individuals who reside in rural areas.

(30) The plan shall *include the assurances and description required by section 705(a).*

(31)(A) If 50 percent or more of the area plans in the State provide for an area volunteer services coordinator, as described in section 306(a)(12), the State plan shall provide for a State volunteer services coordinator, who shall—

> *(i) encourage area agencies on aging to provide for area volunteer services coordinators;*
>
> *(ii) coordinate the volunteer services offered between the various area agencies on aging;*
>
> *(iii) encourage, organize, and promote the use of older individuals as volunteers to the State;*
>
> *(iv) provide technical assistance, which may include training, to area volunteer services coordinators; and*
>
> *(v) promote the recognition of the contribution made by volunteers to the programs administered under the State plan.*
>
> *(B) If fewer than 50 percent of the area plans in the State provide for an area volunteer services coordinator, the State plan may provide for the State volunteer services coordinator described in subparagraph (A).*

(32) The plan shall provide assurances that special efforts will be made to provide technical assistance to minority providers of services.

(33) The plan—

> *(A) shall include the statement and the demonstration required by paragraphs (2) and (4) of section 305(d); and*
>
> *(B) may not be approved unless the Commissioner approves such statement and such demonstration.*

(34) The plan shall provide an assurance that the State agency will coordinate programs under this title and title VI, if applicable.

(35) The plan shall—

> *(A) provide an assurance that the State agency will pursue activities to increase access by older individuals who are Native Americans to all aging programs and benefits provided by the agency, including programs and benefits under this title, if applicable; and*
>
> *(B) specify the ways in which the State agency intends to implement the activities.*

(36) If case management services are offered to provide access to supportive services, the plan shall provide that the State agency shall ensure compliance with the requirements specified in section 306(a)(20).

(37) The plan shall identify for each fiscal year, the actual and projected additional costs of providing services under this title, including the cost of providing access to such services, to older individuals residing in rural areas in the State (in accordance with a standard definition of rural areas specified by the Commissioner).

(38) The plan shall provide assurances that funds received under this title will not be used to pay any part of a cost (including an administrative

*cost) incurred by the State or an area agency on aging to carry out a contract
or commercial relationship that is not carried out to implement this title.*

*(39) The plan shall provide assurances that preference in receiving ser-
vices under this title will not be given by the area agency on aging to particular older individuals as a result of a contract or commercial relationship
that is not carried out to implement this title.*

*(40) The plan shall provide assurances that if the State receives funds
appropriated under section 303(g) the State agency and area agencies on aging will expend such funds to carry out part G.*

*(41) The plan shall provide assurances that demonstrable efforts will be
made—*

> *(A) to coordinate services provided under this Act with other State
> services that benefit older individuals; and*
>
> *(B) to provide multigenerational activities, such as opportunities
> for older individuals to serve as mentors or advisers in child care,
> youth day care, educational assistance, at-risk youth intervention, juve-
> nile delinquency treatment, and family support programs.*

*(42) The plan shall provide assurances that the State will coordinate
public services within the State to assist older individuals to obtain transportation services associated with access to services provided under this title, to
services under title VI, to comprehensive counseling services, and to legal
assistance.*

*(43) The plan shall provide that the State agency shall issue guidelines
applicable to grievance procedures required by section 306(a)(6)(P).*

*(44) The plan shall include assurances that the State has in effect a
mechanism to provide for quality in the provision of in-home services under
this title.*

(b)(1) The Commissioner shall approve any State plan which the Commissioner finds fulfills the requirements of subsection (a) *except the Commissioner may not approve such plan unless the Commissioner determines
that the formula submitted under section 305(a)(2)(D) complies with the
guidelines in effect under section 305(a)(2)(C).*

(2) The Commissioner, in approving any State plan under this section,
may waive the requirement described in clause (3)(B) of subsection (a) if the
State agency demonstrates to the Commissioner that the service needs of
older individuals residing in rural areas in the State are being met, or that
the number of older individuals residing in such rural areas is not sufficient
to require the State agency to comply with the requirement described in
clause (3)(B) of subsection (a).

(c)*(1)* The Commissioner shall not make a final determination disap-
proving any State plan, or any modification thereof, or make a final determination that a State is ineligible under section 305, without first affording the
State reasonable notice and opportunity for a hearing.

*(2) Not later than 30 days after such final determination, a State dissatis-
fied with such final determination may appeal such final determination to
the Secretary for review. If the State timely appeals such final determination
in accordance with subsection (e)(1), the Secretary shall dismiss the appeal
filed under this paragraph.*

(3) If the State is dissatisfied with the decision of the Secretary after re-

view under paragraph (2), the State may appeal such decision not later than 30 days after such decision and in the manner described in subsection (e). For purposes of appellate review under the preceding sentence, a reference in subsection (e) to the Commissioner shall be deemed to be a reference to the Secretary.

(d) Whenever the Commissioner, after reasonable notice and opportunity for a hearing to the State agency, finds that—

(1) the State is eligible under section 305,

(2) The State plan has been so changed that it no longer complies substantially with the provisions of subsection (a), or

(3) in the administration of the plan there is a failure to comply substantially with any such provision of subsection (a), the Commissioner shall notify such State agency that no further payments from its allotments under section 304 and section 308 will be made to the State (or, in the Commissioner's discretion, that further payments to the State will be limited to projects under or portions of the State plan not affected by such failure), until the Commissioner is satisfied that there will no longer be any failure to comply. Until the Commissioner is so satisfied, no further payments shall be made to such State from its allotments under section 304 and 308 (or payments shall be limited to projects under or portions of the State plan not affected by such failure). The Commissioner shall, in accordance with regulations the Commissioner shall prescribe, disburse the funds so withheld directly to any public or nonprofit private organization or agency or political subdivision of such State submitting an approved plan in accordance with the provisions of this section. Any such payment shall be matched in the proportions specified in section 304.

(e)(1) A State which is dissatisfied with a final action of the Commissioner under subsection (b), (c), or (d) may appeal to the United States court of appeals for the circuit in which the State is located, by filing a petition with such court within 30 days after such final action. A copy of the petition shall be forthwith transmitted by the clerk of the court to the Commissioner, or any officer designated by the Commissioner for such purpose. The Commissioner thereupon shall file in the court the record of the proceedings on which the Commissioner's action is based, as provided in section 2112 of title 28, United States Code.

(2) Upon the filing of such petition, the court shall have jurisdiction to affirm the action of the Commissioner or to set it aside, in whole or in part, temporarily or permanently, but until the filing of the record, the Commissioner may modify or set aside the Commissioner's order. The findings of the Commissioner as to the facts, if supported by substantial evidence, shall be conclusive, but the court, for good cause shown, may remand the case to the Commissioner to take further evidence, and the Commissioner shall, within 30 days, file in the court the record of those further proceedings. Such new or modified findings of fact shall likewise be conclusive if supported by substantial evidence. The judgment of the court affirming or setting aside, in whole or in part, any action of the Commissioner shall be fi-

nal, subject to review by the Supreme Court of the United States upon certiorari or certification as provided in section 1254 of title 28, United States Code.

(3) The commencement of proceedings under this subsection shall not, unless so specially ordered by the court, operate as a stay of the Commissioner's action.

(f)(1) Neither a State, nor a State agency, may require any provider of legal assistance under this title to reveal any information that is protected by the attorney-client privilege.

(2) Information disclosed under section 306(a)(14)(B)(i) or subsection (a)(7)(C)(ii)(I) may be disclosed to the public by the State agency or the State only if such information could be disclosed under section 552 of title 5, United States Code, by an agency of the United States.

Planning, Coordination, Evaluation, and Administration of State Plans

Sec. 308. (a)(1) Amounts available to States under subsection (b)(1) may be used to make grants to States for paying such percentages as each State agency determines, but not more than 75 percent, of the cost of the administration of its State plan, including the preparation of the State plan, the evaluation of activities carried out under such plan, the collection of data and the carrying out of analyses related to the need for supportive services, nutrition services, and multipurposes senior centers within the State, and dissemination of information so obtained, the provision of short-term training to personnel of public or nonprofit private agencies and organizations engaged in the operation of programs authorized by this Act, and the carrying out of demonstration projects of statewide significance relating to the initiation, expansion, or improvement of services assisted under this title.

(2) Any sums available to a State under subsection (b)(1) for part of the cost of the administration of its State plan which the State determines is not needed for such purpose may be used by the State to supplement the amount available under section 304(d)(1)(A) to cover part of the cost of the administration of area plans.

(3) Any State which has *been* designated a single planning and service area under section 305(a)(1)(E) covering all, or substantially all, of the older individuals in such State, as determined by the Commissioner, may elect to pay part of the costs of the administration of State and area plans either out of sums received under this section or out of sums made available for the administration of area plans under section 304(d)(1)(A), but shall not pay such costs out of sums received or allotted under both such sections.

(A)(b)(1) if for any fiscal year the aggregate amount appropriated under section 303 does not exceed $800,000,000, then—

(A) except as provided in clause (B), the greater of 5 percent of the allotment to a State under section 304(a)(1) or $300,000; and

(B) in the case of Guam, American Samoa, the Virgin Islands, the Trust Territory of the Pacific Islands, and the Commonwealth of the

Northern Mariana Islands, the greater of 5 percent of such allotment of $75,000;

shall be available to such State to carry out the purposes of this section.

(2) if for any fiscal year the aggregate amount appropriated under section 303 exceeds $800,000,000, then—

(A) except as provided in clause (ii), the greater of 5 percent of the allotment to a State under section 304(a)(1) or $500,000; and

(B) in the case of Guam, American Samoa, the Virgin Islands, the Trust Territory of the Pacific Islands, and the Commonwealth of the Northern Mariana Islands, the greater of 5 percent of such allotment or $100,000;

shall be available to such State to carry out the purposes of this section.

(3)(A) If the aggregate amount appropriated under section 303 for a fiscal year does not exceed $800,000,000, then any State which desires to receive amounts, in addition to amounts allotted to such State under paragraph (1), to be used in the administration of its State plan in accordance with subsection (a) may transmit an application to the Commissioner in accordance with this paragraph. Any such application shall be transmitted in such form, and according to such procedures, as the Commissioner may require, except that such application may not be made as part of, or as an amendment to, the State plan.

(B) The Commissioner may approve any application transmitted by a State under paragraph (A) if the Commissioner determines, based upon a particularized showing of need, that—

(i) the State will be unable to fully and effectively administer its State plan and to carry out programs and projects authorized by this title unless such additional amounts are made available by the Commissioner;

(ii) the State is making full and effective use of its allotment under paragraph (1) and of the personnel of the State agency and area agencies designated under section 305(a)(2)(A) in the administration of its State plan in accordance with subsection (a); and

(iii) the State agency and area agencies *on aging of such State are carrying out,* on a full-time basis, programs and activities which are in furtherance of the purposes of this Act.

(C) The Commissioner may approve that portion of the amount requested by a State in its application under subparagraph (A) which the Commissioner determines has been justified in such application.

(D) Amounts which any State may receive in any fiscal year under this paragraph may not exceed three-fourths of 1 percent of the sum of the amounts allotted under section 304(a) to such State to carry out the State plan for such fiscal year.

(E) No application by a State under subparagraph (A) shall be approved unless it contains assurances that no amounts received by the State under this paragraph will be used to hire any individual to fill a job opening created by the action of the State in laying off or terminating the employment of any employee not supported under this Act in anticipation of filling the vacancy so created by hiring an employee to be supported through use of amounts received under this paragraph.

(4)(A) Notwithstanding any other provision of this title, *and except as provided in subparagraph (B)*, with respect to funds *received by a State and attributable to funds appropriated under paragraph (1) or (2) of section 303(b)*, the State may elect in its plan under section 307(a)(13) regarding part C of this title, to transfer *not more than 30 percent of the funds so received* between subpart 1 and subpart 2 of part C for use as the State considers appropriate to meet the needs of the area served. The Commissioner shall approve any such transfer unless the Commissioner determines that such transfer is not consistent with the purposes of this Act.

(B) If a State demonstrates, to the satisfaction of the Commissioner, that funds received by the State and attributable to funds appropriated under paragraph (1) or (2) of section 303(b), including funds transferred under subparagraph (A) without regard to this subparagraph, for fiscal year 1993, 1994, 1995, or 1996 are insufficient to satisfy the need for services under subpart 1 or subpart 2 of part C, then the Commissioner may grant a waiver that permits the State to transfer under subparagraph (A) to satisfy such need—

(i) an additional 18 percent of the funds so received for fiscal year 1993;

(ii) an additional 15 percent of the funds so received for each of the fiscal years 1994 and 1995; and

(iii) an additional 10 percent of the funds so received for fiscal year 1996.

(5)(A) Notwithstanding any other provision of this title and except as provided in subparagraph (B), of the funds received by a State attributable to funds appropriated under subsection (a)(1), and paragraphs (1) and (2) of subsection (b), of section 303, the State may elect to transfer not more than 30 percent for fiscal year 1993, not more than 25 percent for fiscal year 1994, not more than 25 percent for fiscal year 1995, and not more than 20 percent for fiscal year 1996, between programs under part B and part C, for use as the State considers appropriate. The State shall notify the Commissioner of any such election.

(B)(i) If a State demonstrates, to the satisfaction of the Commissioner, that funds received by the State and attributable to funds appropriated under part B or part C (including funds transferred under subparagraph (A) without regard to this subparagraph) for fiscal year 1994 or 1995 are insufficient to satisfy the need for services under such part, then the Commissioner may grant a waiver that permits the State to transfer under subparagraph (A) to satisfy such need an additional 5 percent of the funds so received for such fiscal year.

(ii) If a State demonstrates, to the satisfaction of the commissioner, that funds received by the State and attributable to funds appropriated under part B or part C (including funds transferred under subparagraph (A) without regard to this subparagraph) for fiscal year 1996 are insufficient to satisfy the need for services under such part, then the Commissioner may grant a waiver that permits the State to transfer under subparagraph (A) to satisfy such need an additional 8 percent of the funds so received for such fiscal year.

(C) At a minimum, the application described in subparagraph (A) shall include a description of the amount to be transferred, the purposes of the

transfer, the need for the transfer, and the impact of the transfer on the provision of services from which the funding will be transferred. The Commissioner shall approve or deny the application in writing.

(6) A State agency may not delegate to an area agency on aging or any other entity the authority to make a transfer under paragraph (4)(A) or (5)(A).

(7) The Commissioner shall annually collect, and include in the report required by section 207(a), data regarding the transfers described in paragraphs (4)(A) and (5)(A), including—

    (A) the amount of funds involved in the transfers, analyzed by State;

    (B) the rationales for the transfers;

    (C) in the case of transfers described in paragraphs (4)(A) and (5)(A), the effect on the transfers of the provision of services, including the effect on the number of meals served, under—

        (i) subpart 1 of part C; and

        (ii) subpart 2 of part C; and

    (D) in the case of transfers described in paragraph (5)(A)—

        (i) in the case of transfers to part B, information on the supportive services, or services provided through senior centers, for which the transfers were used; and

        (ii) the effect of the transfers on the provision of services provided under—

        (I) part B; and

        (II) part C, including the effect on the number of meals served.

Payments

Sec. 309. (a) Payments of grants or contracts under this title may be made (after necessary adjustments resulting from previously made overpayments or underpayments) in advance or by way of reimbursement, and in such installments, as the Commissioner may determine. From a State's allotment for a fiscal year which is available under section 308 the Commissioner may pay to a State which does not have a State plan approved under section 307 such amounts as the Commissioner deems appropriate for the purpose of assisting such State in developing a State plan.

(b)(1) For each fiscal year, not less than 25 percent of the non-Federal share of the total expenditures under the State plan which is required by section 304(d) shall be met from funds from State or local public sources.

(2) Funds required to meet the non-Federal share required by section 304(d)(1)(D), in amounts exceeding the non-Federal share required prior to fiscal year 1981, shall be met from State sources.

(c) A State's allotment under section 304 for a fiscal year shall be reduced by the percentage (if any) by which its expenditures for such year from State sources under its State plan approved under section 307 are less than its average annual expenditures from such sources for the period of 3 fiscal years preceding such year.

Disaster Relief Reimbursements

Sec. 310. (a)(1) The Commissioner may provide reimbursements to any State, upon application for such reimbursement, for funds such State makes available to area agencies on aging in such State for the delivery of supportive services (and related supplies) during any major disaster declared by the President in accordance with the Disaster Relief Act of 1974.

(2) Total payments to all States under paragraph (1) in any fiscal year shall not exceed 2 percent of the total amount appropriate and available to carry out title IV.

(3) If the Commissioner decides, in the 5-day period beginning on the date such disaster is declared by the President, to provide an amount of reimbursement under paragraph (1) to a State, then the Commissioner shall provide not less than 75 percent of such amount to such State not less than 5 days after the date of such decision.

(b)(1) At the beginning of each fiscal year the Commissioner shall set aside, for payment to States under subsection (a), an amount equal to 2 percent of the total amount appropriated and available to carry out title IV.

(2) Amounts set aside under paragraph (1) which are not obligated by the end of the third quarter of any fiscal year shall be made available for carrying out the purposes of section 422.

(c) Nothing in this section shall be construed to prohibit expenditures by States for disaster relief for older individuals in excess of amounts reimbursable under this section, by using funds made available to them under other sections of this Act or under other provisions of Federal or State law, or from private sources.

Availability of Surplus Commodities

Sec. 311. (a)(1) Agricultural commodities and products purchased by the Secretary of Agriculture under section 32 of the Act of August 24, 1935 (7 U.S.C. 612c), shall be donated to a recipient of a grant or contract to be used for providing nutrition services in accordance with the provisions of this title.

(2) The Commodities Credit Corporation shall dispose of food commodities under section 416 of the Agricultural Act of 1949 (7 U.S.C. 1431) by donating them to a recipient of a grant or contract to be used for providing nutrition services in accordance with the provisions of this title.

(3) Dairy products purchased by the Secretary of Agriculture under section 709 of the Food and Agriculture Act of 1965 (7 U.S.C. 1446a–1) shall be used to meet the requirements of programs providing nutrition services in accordance with the provisions of this title.

(4)(A) Subject to the authorization of appropriations specified in subsection (c), in donating commodities under this subsection, the Secretary of Agriculture *shall maintain*

(i) for fiscal year 1992, a level of assistance equal to the greater of—

(I) a per meal rate equal to the amount appropriated under subsection (c) for fiscal year 1992, divided by the number of meals served in the preceding fiscal year; or

(II) 61 cents per meal; and

(ii) for fiscal year 1993 and each subsequent fiscal year, an annually programmed level of assistance equal to the greater of—

(I) a per meal rate equal to the amount appropriated under subsection (c) for the fiscal year, divided by the number of meals served in the preceding fiscal year; or

(II) 61 cents per meal, adjusted in accordance with changes in the series for food away from home, of the Consumer Price Index for All Urban Consumers, published by the Bureau of Labor Statistics of the Department of Labor, based on the 12-month period ending on July 1 of the preceding year.

(B) Among the commodities delivered under this subsection, the Secretary shall give special emphasis to high protein foods, meat, and meat alternates. The Secretary of Agriculture, in consultation with the Commissioner, is authorized to prescribe the terms and conditions respecting the donating of commodities under this subsection.

(b)(1) Notwithstanding any other provision of law, a State may, for purposes of the programs authorized by this Act, elect to receive cash payments in lieu of donated foods for all or any portion of its project. In any case in which a State makes such an election, the Secretary of Agriculture shall make cash payments to such State in an amount equivalent in value to the donated foods which the State otherwise would have received if such State had retained its commodity distribution.

(2) When such payments are made, the State agency shall promptly and equitably disburse any cash it receives in lieu of commodities to recipients of grants or contracts. Such disbursements shall only be used by such recipients of grants or contracts to purchase United States agricultural commodities and other foods for their nutrition projects.

(3) Nothing in this subsection shall be construed to authorize the Secretary of Agriculture to require any State to elect to receive cash payments under this subsection.

(c)(1)(A) There are authorized to be appropriated *$250,000,000 for fiscal year 1992, $310,000,000 for fiscal year 1993, $380,000,000 for fiscal year 1994, and $460,000,000 for fiscal year 1995,* to carry out the provisions of this section (other than subsection (a)(1)).

(B) Effective on the first day of the first month beginning after the date of enactment of the Older Americans Act Amendments of 1984, no State may receive reimbursement under the provisions of this section unless the State submits final reimbursement claims for meals within 90 days after the last day of the quarter for which the reimbursement is claimed.

(2)(A) Except as provided in subparagraph (B), in any fiscal

year in which compliance with subsection (a)(4) of this section costs more than the amounts authorized under paragraph (1) of this subsection for that fiscal year the Secretary of Agriculture shall reduce the cents per meal level determined pursuant to subsection (a)(4) for that fiscal year as necessary to meet the authorization of appropriations for that fiscal year.

(B) In each fiscal year, the final reimbursement claims shall be adjusted to use the full amount appropriated under this subsection for the fiscal year.

Multipurpose Senior Centers: Recapture of Payments

Sec. 312. If, within 10 years after acquisition, or within 20 years after the completion of construction, of any facility for which funds have been paid under this title—

(1) the owner of the facility ceases to be a public or nonprofit private agency or organization; or

(2) the facility ceases to be used for the purposes for which it was acquired (unless the Commissioner determines, in accordance with regulations, that there is good cause for releasing the applicant or other owner from the obligation to do so);

the United States shall be entitled to recover from the applicant or other owner of the facility an amount which bears to the then value of the facility (or so much thereof as constituted an approved project or projects) the same ratio as the amount of such Federal funds bore to the cost of the facility financed with the aid of such funds. Such value shall be determined by agreement of the parties or by action brought in the United States district court for the district in which such facility is situated.

Audit

Sec. 313. (a) The Commissioner and The Comptroller General of the United States or any of their duly authorized representatives shall have access for the purpose of audit and examination to any books, documents, papers, and records that are pertinent to a grant or contract received under this title.

(b) State agencies and area agencies on aging shall not request information or data from providers which is not pertinent to services furnished pursuant to this Act or a payment made for such services.

(a) PROMOTION.—

The Commissioner shall require entities that provide in-home services under this title to promote the rights of each older individual who receives such services. Such rights include the following:

(1) The right—

(A) to be fully informed in advance about each in-home service provided by such entity under this title and about any change in such service that may affect the well-being of such individual; and

(B) to participate in planning and changing an in-home service pro-

vided under this title by such entity unless such individual is judicially adjudged incompetent.

(2) The right to voice a grievance with respect to such service that is or fails to be so provided, without discrimination or reprisal as a result of voicing such grievance.

(3) The right to confidentiality of records relating to such individual.

(4) The right to have the property of such individual treated with respect.

(5) The right to be fully informed (orally and in writing), in advance of receiving an in-home service under this title, of such individual's rights and obligations under this title.

Part B—Supportive Services and Senior Centers

Program Authorized

Sec. 321. (a) The Commissioner shall carry out a program for making grants to States under State plans approved under section 307 for any of the following supportive services:

(1) health (including mental health) education and training, welfare, informational, recreational, homemaker, counseling, or referral services;

(2) transportation services to facilitate access to supportive services or nutrition services, or both:

(3) services designed to encourage and assist older individuals to use the facilities and services *(including information and assistance services)* available to them *including language translation services to assist older individuals with limited-English speaking ability to obtain services under this title.*

(4) services designed (A) to assist older individuals to obtain adequate housing, including residential repair and renovation projects designed to enable older individuals to maintain their homes in conformity with minimum housing standards; (b) to adapt homes to meet the needs of older individuals who have physical disabilities; (C) to prevent unlawful entry into residences of elderly individuals, through the installation of security devices and through structural modifications or alterations of such residences *or (D) to receive applications from older individuals for housing under section 202 of the Housing Act of 1959 (12 U.S.C. 1701Q);*

(5) services designed to assist older individuals in avoiding institutionalization and to assist individuals in long-term care institutions who are able to return to their communities, including client assess-

ment through case management and integration and coordination of community services such as pre-institution evaluation and screening and home health services, homemaker services, shopping services, escort services, reader services, and letter writing services, through resource development and management to assist such individuals to live independently in a home environment;

(6) services designed to provide *to older individuals* legal assistance and other counseling service and assistance, including

(A) tax counseling and assistance, financial counseling, and counseling regarding appropriate health and life insurance coverage;

(B) representation—

(i) of individuals who are wards (or are allegedly incapacitated); and

(ii) in guardianship proceedings of older individuals who seek to become guardians, if other adequate representation is unavailable in the proceedings; and

(C) provision, to older individuals who provide uncompensated care to their adult children with disabilities, of counseling to assist such older individuals with permanency planning for such children;

(7) services designed to enable older individuals to attain and maintain physical and mental well-being through programs of regular physical activity, exercise, *music therapy, art therapy, and dance-movement therapy;*

(8) services designed to provide health screening to detect or prevent illnesses, or both, that occur most frequently in older individuals;

(9) services designed to provide *for older individuals, preretirement counseling and assistance in planning for and assessing future post-retirement needs with regard to public and private insurance, public benefits, lifestyle changes, relocation, legal matters, leisure time, and other appropriate matters;*

(10) services of an ombudsman at the State level to receive, investigate, and act on complaints by older individuals who are residents of long-term care facilities and to advocate for the well-being of such individuals;

(11) services which are designed to meet the unique needs of older individuals who are disabled, *and of older individuals who provide uncompensated care to their adult children with disabilities;*

(12) services to encourage the employment of older workers including job *and second career* counseling and, where appropriate, job development, referral, and placement;

(13) crime prevention services and victim assistance programs for older individuals;

(14) a program, to be known as "Senior Opportunities and Services", designed to identify and meet the needs of older, poor individuals 60 years of age or older in one or more of the following areas: (A) development and provision of new volunteer services; (B) effective referral to existing health, employment, housing, legal, consumer, transportation, and other services; (C) stimulation and creation of additional services and programs to remedy gaps and deficiencies in

presently existing services and programs; and (D) such other services as the Commissioner may determine are necessary or especially appropriate to meet the needs of the older poor and to assure them greater self-sufficiency;

(15) services for the prevention of abuse of older individuals in accordance with clause (16) of section 307(a);

(16) in service training and State leadership for legal assistance activities;

(17) health and nutrition education services, *including information concerning prevention, diagnosis, treatment, and rehabilitation of age-related diseases and chronic disabling conditions;*

(18) services designed to enable mentally impaired older individuals to attain and maintain emotional well-being and independent living through a coordinated system of support services;

(19) services designed to support family members and other persons providing voluntary care to older individuals that need long-term care services;

(20) services designed to provide information and training for individuals who are or may become guardians or representative payees of older individuals, including information on the powers and duties of guardians and representative payees and on alternatives to guardianships;

(21) services to encourage and facilitate regular interaction between school-age children and older individuals, including visits in long-term care facilities, multipurpose senior centers, and other settings;

(22) or any other services;

if such services meet standards prescribed by the Commissioner and are necessary for the general welfare of older individuals.

For purposes of paragraph (5), the term 'client assessment through case management' includes providing information relating to assistive technology.

(b)(1) The Commissioner shall carry out a program for making grants to States under State plans approved under section 307 for the acquisition, alteration, or renovation of existing facilities, including mobile units, and where appropriate, construction of facilities to serve as multipurpose senior centers.

(2) Funds made available to a State under this part may be used for the purpose of assisting in the operation of multipurpose senior centers and meeting all or part of the costs of compensating professional and technical personnel required for the operation of multipurpose senior centers.

Part C—Nutrition Service

Subpart 1—Congregate Nutrition Services

Program Authorized

Sec. 331. The Commissioner shall carry out a program for making grants to States under State plans approved under section 307 for the establishment and operation of nutrition projects—

(1) which, 5 or more days a week *(except in a rural area where such frequency is not feasible (as defined by the Commissioner by regulation) and a lesser frequency is approved by the State agency)* provide at least one hot or other appropriate meal per day and any additional meals which the recipient of a grant or contract under this subpart may elect to provide;

(2) which shall be provided in congregate settings; and

(3) which may include nutrition educational services and other appropriate nutrition services for older individuals.

Subpart 2—Home Delivered Nutrition Services

Program Authorized

Sec. 336. The Commissioner shall carry out a program for making grants to States under State plans approved under section 307 for the establishment and operation of nutrition projects for older individuals which, 5 or more days a week *(except in a rural area where such frequency is not feasible (as defined by the Commissioner by regulation) and a lesser frequency is approved by the State agency) provide at least one home delivered hot, cold, frozen, dried, canned, or supplemental foods (with a satisfactory storage life) meal per day and any additional meals which the recipient of a grant or contract under this subpart may elect to provide.*

Criteria

Sec. 337. The Commissioner, in consultation with organizations of and for the aged, blind, and disabled, and with representatives from the American Dietetic Association, *the Dietary Manager's Association,* the National Association of Area Agencies on Aging, the National Association of Meals Programs, Incorporated, and any other appropriate group, shall develop minimum criteria of efficiency and quality for the furnishing of home delivered meal services for projects described in section 336. The criteria required by this section shall take into account the ability of established home delivered meals programs to continue such services without major alteration in the furnishing of such services.

Subpart 3—School-Based Meals for Volunteer Older Individuals and Multigenerational Programs

Sec. 338. ESTABLISHMENT.

(a) IN GENERAL.—The Commissioner shall establish and carry out, under State plans approved under section 307, a program for making grants to States to pay for the Federal share of establishing and operating projects in public elementary and secondary schools (including elementary and sec-

ondary schools for Indian children operated with Federal assistance, or operated by the Department of the Interior, and referred to in section 1005(d)(2) of the Elementary and Secondary Education Act of 1965 (20 U.S.C. 2711(d)(2)) that—

> (1) provide hot meals, each of which ensures a minimum of one-third of the daily recommended dietary allowances as established by the Food and Nutrition Board of the National Research Council of the National Academy of Sciences,· to volunteer older individuals—
> (A) while such schools are in session;
> (B) during the summer; and
> (C) unless waived by the State involved, on the weekdays in the school year when such schools are not in session;
> (2) provide multigenerational activities in which volunteer older individuals and students interact;
> (3) provide social and recreational activities for volunteer older individuals;
> (4) develop skill banks that maintain and make available to school officials information on the skills and preferred activities of volunteer older individuals, for purposes of providing opportunities for such individuals to serve as tutors, teacher aides, living historians, special speakers, playground supervisors, lunchroom assistants, and in other roles; and
> (5) provide opportunities for volunteer older individuals to participate in school activities (such as classes, dramatic programs, and assemblies) and use school facilities.

(b) FEDERAL SHARE.—The Federal share of the cost of establishing and operating nutrition and multigenerational activities projects under this subpart shall be 85 percent.

SEC. 338A. APPLICATION AND SELECTION OF PROVIDERS.

(a) CONTENTS OF APPLICATION.—To be eligible to carry out a project under the program established under this subpart, an entity shall submit an application to a State agency. Such application shall include—

> (1) a plan describing the project proposed by the applicant and comments on such plan from the appropriate area agency on aging and the appropriate local educational agency (as defined in section 1471 of the Elementary and Secondary Education Act of 1965 (20 U.S.C. 2891));
> (2) an assurance that the entity shall pay not more than 85 percent of the cost of carrying out such project from funds awarded under this subpart;
> (3) an assurance that the entity shall pay not less than 15 percent of such cost, in cash or in kind, from non-Federal sources;
> (4) information demonstrating the need for such project, including a description of—
> (A) the nutrition services and other services currently provided under this part in the geographic area to be served by such project; and

(B) the manner in which the project will be coordinated with such services; and

(5) such other information and assurances as the Commissioner may require by regulation.

(b) SELECTION AMONG APPLICANTS.—In selecting grant recipients from among entities that submit applications under subsection (a) for a fiscal year, the State agency shall—

(1) give first priority to entities that carried out a project under this subpart in the preceding fiscal year;

(2) give second priority to entities that carried out a nutrition project under subpart 1 of title VI in the preceding fiscal year; and

(3) give third priority to entities whose applications include a plan that involves a school with greatest need (as measured by the dropout rate, the level of substance abuse, and the number of children who have limited-English proficiency or who participate in projects under section 1015 of the Elementary and Secondary Education Act of 1965 (20 U.S.C. 2025)).

SEC. 338B. REPORTS.

(a) REPORTS BY STATES.—Not later than 60 days after the end of a fiscal year for which a State receives a grant under this subpart, such State shall submit to the Commissioner a report evaluating the projects carried out under this subpart by such State in such fiscal year. Such report shall include for each project—

(1) a description of—

(A) persons served;

(B) multigenerational activities carried out; and

(C) additional needs of volunteer older individuals and students; and

(2) recommendations for any appropriate modifications to satisfy the needs described in paragraph (1)(C).

(b) REPORTS BY COMMISSIONER.—Not later than 120 days after the end of a fiscal year for which funds are appropriated to carry out this subpart, the Commissioner shall submit to the Speaker of the House of Representatives and the President pro tempore of the Senate a report summarizing, with respect to each State, the reports submitted under subsection (a) for such fiscal year.

Subpart 4—General Provisions

SEC. 339. COMPLIANCE WITH DIETARY GUIDELINES.

A State that establishes and operates a nutrition project under this part shall ensure that the meals provided through the project—

(1) comply with the Dietary Guidelines for Americans, published by the Secretary and the Secretary of Agriculture; and

(2) provide to each participating older individual—

(A) a minimum of 33 1/3 percent of the daily recommended dietary allowances as established by the Food and Nutrition Board of the National Research Council of the National Academy of Sciences, if the project provides 1 meal per day;
(B) a minimum of 66 2/3 percent of the allowances if the project provides 2 meals per day; and
(C) 100 percent of the allowances if the project provides 3 meals per day.

SEC. 339A. PAYMENT REQUIREMENT.

Payments made by a State agency or an area agency on aging for nutrition services (including meals) provided under part A, B, or C may not be reduced to reflect any increase in the level of assistance provided under section 311.

Part D—In-Home Services for Frail Older Individuals

Definition of In-Home Services

Program Authorized

Sec. 341. (a) The Commissioner shall carry out a program for making grants to States under State plans approved under section 307 to provide in-home services to frail older individuals, including in-home supportive services for older individuals who are victims of Alzheimer's disease and related disorders with neurological and organic brain dysfunction, and to the families of such victims.

(b) In carrying out the provisions of this part, each area agency *on aging* shall coordinate with other community agencies and voluntary organizations providing counseling and training *for family caretakers* and support service personnel in management of care, functional and needs assessment services, assistance with locating, arranging for, and coordinating services, case management, and counseling prior to admission to nursing home to prevent premature institutionalization.

Definitions

Sec. 342. For purposes of this part, the term 'in-home services' includes
(1) homemaker and home health aides;
(2) visiting and telephone reassurance;
(3) chore maintenance;
(4) in-home respite care for families, including adult day care as a respite service for families;
(5) minor modification of homes that is necessary to facilitate the abil-

ity of older individuals to remain at home and that is not available under other programs, except that not more than $150 per client may be
expended under this part for such modification;

(6) personal care services; and

(7) other in-home services as defined—

(A) by the State agency in the State plan submitted in accordance with
section 307; and

(B) by the area agency on aging in the area plan submitted in accordance with section 306.

State Criteria

Sec. 343. The State agency shall develop eligibility criteria for providing
in-home services to frail older individuals which shall take into account—

(1) age;

(2) greatest economic need;

(3) noneconomic factors contributing to the frail condition; and

(4) noneconomic and nonhealth factors contributing to the need for
such services.

Maintenance of Effort

Sec. 344. Funds made available under this part shall be in addition to,
and may not be used to supplant, any funds that are or would otherwise be
expended under any Federal, State, or local law by a State or unit of general
purpose local government (including area agencies on aging which have in
their planning and services areas existing services which primarily serve
older individuals who are victims of Alzheimer's disease and related disorders with neurological and organic brain dysfunction, and the families of
such victims).

Part E—Additional Assistance for Special Needs of Older Individuals

Program Authorized

Sec. 351. The Commissioner shall carry out a program for making grants
to States under State plans approved under section 307 to provide services,
consistent with the purpose of this title, designed to satisfy special needs of
older individuals. Such services include—

(1) transportation associated with services provided under this title;

(2) outreach regarding such services;

(3) targeting such services to older individuals with greatest economic
need or greatest social need;

(4) services under the ombudsman program established under section
307(a)(12); and

(5) any other service under this title—

(A) for which the State demonstrates to satisfaction of the Commissioner that there is unmet need; and

(B) which is appropriate to improve the quality of life of older individuals, particularly those with greatest economic need and those with greatest social need.

Part F—*DISEASE PREVENTION AND HEALTH PROMOTION SERVICES*

Program Authorized

Sec 361. (a) The Commissioner shall carry out a program for making grants to States under State plans approved under section 307 *to provide disease prevention and health promotion services and information at multipurpose senior centers, at congregate meal sites, through home delivered meals programs, or at other appropriate sites. In carrying out such program, the Commissioner shall consult with the Directors of the Centers for Disease Control and the National Institute on Aging.*

(b) The Commissioner shall, to the extent possible, assure that services provided by other community organizations and agencies are used to carry out the provisions of this part.

Distribution to Area Agencies *on Aging*

Sec 362. The State agency shall give priority, in carrying out this part, to areas of the State—

(1) which are medically underserviced; and

(2) in which there are a large number of older individuals who have the greatest economic need for such services.

Definitions

Sec 363. As used in this part, the term 'disease prevention and health promotion services' means—

(1) health risk assessments;

(2) routine health screening, which may include hypertension, glaucoma, cholesterol, cancer, vision, hearing, diabetes, and nutrition screening;

(3) nutritional counseling and educational services for individuals and their primary caregivers;

(4) health promotion programs, including programs relating to chronic disabling conditions (including osteoporosis and cardiovascular disease) prevention and reduction of effects, alcohol and substance abuse reduction, smoking cessation, weight loss and control, and stress management;

(5) programs regarding physical fitness, group exercise, and music, art, and dance-movement therapy, including programs for multigenerational participation that are provided by—

(A) an institution of higher education;

(B) a local educational agency, as defined in section 1471 of the Elementary and Secondary Education Act of 1965 (20 U.S.C. 2891); or

(C) a community-based organization;

(6) home injury control services, including screening of high-risk home environments and provision of educational programs on injury prevention (including fall and fracture prevention) in the home environment;

(7) screening for the prevention of depression, coordination of community mental health services, provision of educational activities, and referral to psychiatric and psychological services;

(8) educational programs on the availability, benefits, and appropriate use of preventive health services covered under title XVIII of the Social Security Act (42 U.S.C. 1395 et seq.);

(9) medication management screening and education to prevent incorrect medication and adverse drug reactions;

(10) information concerning diagnosis, prevention, treatment, and rehabilitation of age-related diseases and chronic disabling conditions, including osteoporosis, cardiovascular diseases, and Alzheimer's disease and related disorders with neurological and organic brain dysfunction; and

(11) gerontological counseling; and

(12) counseling regarding social services and followup health services based on any of the services described in paragraphs (1) through (11).

The term shall not include services for which payment may be made under title XVIII of the Social Security Act (42 U.S.C. 1395 et seq.).

Part G—Supportive Activities for Caretakers Who Provide In-Home Services to Frail Older Individuals

SEC. 381. PROGRAM AUTHORIZED.

The Commissioner shall carry out a program for making grants to States under State plans approved under section 307 to carry out a program to provide supportive activities for caretakers who provide in-home services to frail older individuals (including older individuals who are victims of Alzheimer's disease ore related disorders with neurological and organic brain dysfunction). Such supportive activities may include—

(1) providing training and counseling for such caretakers;

(2) technical assistance to such caretakers to assist them to form or to participate in support groups;

(3) providing information—

(A) to frail older individuals and their families regarding how to obtain in-home services and respite services; and

(B) to caretakers who provide such services, regarding—

(i) how to provide such services; and

(ii) sources of nonfinancial support available to them as a result of their providing such services; and

(4) maintaining lists of individuals who provide respite services for the families of frail older individuals.

SEC. 382. DEFINITIONS.

For purposes of this part, the term 'in-home services' has the meaning given such term in section 342.
SEC. 383. MAINTENANCE OF EFFORT.
Section 344 shall apply with respect to funds made available under this part, in the same manner as such section applies to funds made available under part D.

TITLE IV—TRAINING, RESEARCH, AND DISCRETIONARY PROJECTS AND PROGRAMS

Statement of Purpose

Sec. 401. It is the purpose of this title to expand the Nation's knowledge and understanding of aging and the aging process, to design and test innovative ideas in programs and services for older individuals *and publicly disseminate the results of the tests, to replicate such programs and services under this Act* and to help meet the needs for trained personnel in the field of aging through—

(1) placing a priority on the education and training of personnel to work with and on behalf of older individuals, with special emphasis on minority individuals, low-income individuals, frail individuals, and individuals with disabilities;

(2) research and development of effective practice in the field of aging;

(3) demonstration projects directly related to the field of aging; and

(4) dissemination of information on aging and the aging process acquired through such programs to public and private organizations or programs for older individuals.

Administration

Sec. 402. (a) In order to carry out the provisions of this title effectively, the Commissioner shall administer this title through the Administration.

(b) In carrying out the provisions of this title, the Commissioner may request the technical assistance and cooperation of the Department of Education, the National Institutes of Health, the Veteran's Administration, Alcohol, Drug Abuse, and Mental Health Administration, and such other agencies and departments of the Federal Government as may be appropriate.

(c) The Commissioner shall ensure that grants and contracts under this title are equitably awarded to agencies, organizations, and institutions representing minorities.

(d) The Commissioner shall, in developing priorities, consistent with the requirements of this title, for awarding grants and entering into contracts under this title, consult annually with State agencies, area agencies on aging, recipients of grants under title VI, institutions of higher education, organizations representing beneficiaries of services under this Act, and other organizations, and individuals, with expertise in aging issues.

(e) The Commissioner shall ensure that grants and contracts awarded under this title—
(1) are evaluated for their benefit to older individuals, and to programs under this Act; and
(2) comply with the requirements under this Act.

Part A—Education and Training

Purpose

Sec. 410. The purpose of this part is to improve the quality of service and to help meet critical shortages of adequately trained personnel for programs in the field of aging by—

(1) identifying both short- and long-range manpower needs in the field of aging;

(2) providing a broad range of educational and training opportunities to meet those needs;

(3) attracting a greater number of qualified personnel *with particular emphasis on attracting minority individuals* into the field of aging;

(4) helping to upgrade personnel training programs to make them more responsive to the need in the field of aging; and

(5) establishing and supporting multidisciplinary centers of gerontology (including centers of gerontology to improve, enhance, and expand minority personnel and training programs) and providing special emphasis that will improve, enhance, and expand existing training programs.

Grants and Contracts

Sec. 411. (a) The Commissioner shall make grants and enter into contracts to achieve the purpose of this part. The purposes for which such grants and contracts shall be made include the following:

(1) To provide comprehensive and coordinated nondegree education, training programs, and curricula at institutions of higher education and at other research, training, or educational organizations, for practitioners in the fields of nutrition, health (including mental health) care, supportive *gerontology services*, housing, and long-term care, including the expansion and enhancement of existing inservice education and training programs.

(2) To provide inservice training opportunities to the personnel of State offices, area agencies *on aging*, senior centers, and nutrition *and counseling* programs to strengthen their capacity to remain responsive to the needs of older individuals *with special emphasis on using culturally sensitive practices.*

(3) To provide courses on aging and the dissemination of information about aging to the public through institutions of higher education and other public and nonprofit private organizations and agencies.

(4) To provide in-service training opportunities and courses of instruc-

tion on aging to Indian tribes through public and nonprofit Indian aging organizations.

(b) To achieve the purpose of this title, the Administration shall conduct both—

(1) long-term educational activities to prepare personnel for careers in the field of aging; and

(2) short-term inservice training and continuing education activities *for State agency and area agency on aging* personnel, and other personnel, in the field of aging or preparing to enter the field of aging.

(c) In making grants and contracts under this part, the Commissioner shall give special consideration to the recruitment and training of personnel, volunteers, and those individuals preparing for employment in that part of the field of aging which relates to providing services to individuals with disabilities and to individuals with Alzheimer's disease and related disorders with neurological and organic brain dysfunction and providing family respite services with respect to such individuals.

(d) In making grants or contracts under this part, the Commissioner shall ensure that all projects and activities related to personnel training shall include specific data on the number of individuals to be trained and the number of older individuals to be served through such training activities by public and nonprofit agencies, State and area agencies on aging, institutions of higher education, and other organizations.

(e) From amounts appropriated under 431(b), the Commissioner shall make grants and enter into contracts under this part to establish and carry out a program under which service providers (including family physicians, clergy, and other professionals) will receive training—

(1) comprised of—

(A) intensive training regarding normal aging, recognition of problems of older individuals, and communication with providers of mental health services; and

(B) advanced clinical training regarding means of assessing and treating the problems of older individuals;

(2) provided by—

(A) faculty and graduate students in programs of human development and family studies at an institution of higher education;

(B) mental health professionals; and

(C) nationally recognized consultants with expertise regarding the mental health problems of individuals residing in rural areas; and

(3) held in public hospitals throughout each State in which the program is carried out.

(5) To provide annually a national meeting to train directors of programs under title VI.

Multidisciplinary Centers of Gerontology

Sec. 412. (a) The Commissioner may make grants to public and private nonprofit agencies, organizations, and institutions for the purpose of establishing or supporting multidisciplinary centers of gerontology, and gerontology centers of special emphasis (including emphasis on nutrition, employment, health (including mental health), disabilities (including severe

disabilities), income maintenance *counseling services,* supportive services, and minority populations). Such centers shall conduct research and policy analysis and function as a technical resource for the Commissioner, policymakers, service providers, and the Congress. Multidisciplinary centers of gerontology shall—
    (1) recruit and train personnel;
    (2) conduct basic and applied research directed toward the development of information related to aging;
    (3) stimulate the incorporation of information on aging into the teaching of biological, behavioral, and social sciences at colleges and universities;
    (4) help to develop training programs in the field of aging at schools of public health, education, *social work, and psychology* and other appropriate schools within colleges and universities;
    (5) serve as a repository of information and knowledge on aging;
    (6) provide consultation and information to public and voluntary organizations, including State *agencies and area agencies on aging* which serve the needs of older individuals in planning and developing services provided under other provisions of this Act; and
    (7) if appropriate, provide information relating to assistive technology.
    (b) Centers supported under this section shall provide data to the Commissioner on the projects and activities for which fund are provided under this title. Such data shall include the number of personnel trained, the number of older individuals served, the number of schools assisted, and other information that will facilitate achieving the purposes of this Act.

Part B—Research, Demonstrations, and Other Activities

Purpose

Sec. 420. The purpose of this part is to improve the quality and efficiency of programs serving older individuals through research and development projects, and demonstration projects, designed to—
    (1) develop and synthesize knowledge about aging from multidisciplinary perspectives;
    (2) establish an information base of data and practical experience;
    (3) examine effective models of planning and practice that will improve or enhance services provided under other provisions of this Act;
    (4) evaluate the efficacy, quality, efficiency, and accessibility of programs and services for older individuals; and
    (5) develop, implement, and evaluate innovative planning and practice strategies to address the needs, concerns, and capabilities of older individuals.

Research and Development Projects

Sec. 421. (a) The Commissioner may make grants to any public or nonprofit private agency, organization, or institution, and may enter into contracts with any agency, organization, institution, or individual to support research and development related to the purposes of this Act, evaluation of the results of such research and development activities, and collection and dissemination of information concerning research findings, demonstration results, and other materials developed in connection with activities assisted under this title, and conducting of conferences and other meetings for purposes of exchange of information and other activities related to the purposes of this title. Appropriate provisions for the dissemination of resulting information shall be a requirement for all grants made under this section.

(b) Each research and development activity proposal for which funds are requested under subsection (a) shall include a concise policy or practical application statement.

(c)(1) The Commissioner shall select, to the extent practicable, for assistance under subsection (a) research activities which will, not later than three years after the date of the enactment of the Older Americans Act Amendments of 1984, collectively—

(A) contribute to the establishment and maintenance of a demographic data base which contains information on the population of older individuals generally and older individuals categorized by age, sex, race, geographical location, and such other factors as the Commissioner deems useful for the purpose of formulating public policy;

(B) identify the future needs of older individuals;

(C) identify the kinds of comprehensiveness of programs required to satisfy such needs; and

(D) identify the kinds and number of personnel required to carry out such programs.

(2) The Commissioner shall select, to the extent practicable, for assistance under subsection (a) demonstration projects which test research results and implement innovative ways of satisfying the needs of, and delivering services to, older individuals.

Demonstration Projects

Sec. 422. (a)(1) The Commissioner may, after consultation with the State agency in the State involved, make grants to any public agency or nonprofit private organization or enter into contracts with any agency or organization within such State for paying part or all of the cost of developing or operating nationwide, statewide, regional, metropolitan area, county, city, or community model projects which will demonstrate methods to improve or expand supportive services or nutrition services or otherwise promote the well-being of older individuals. The Commissioner shall give special consideration to the funding of rural area agencies on aging to conduct model projects devoted to the special needs of the rural elderly. Such projects shall include alternative health care delivery systems, advocacy and out-reach programs, and transportation services.

(2) The Commissioner may, after consultation with the State agency in the State involved, make grants to or enter into contracts with public or private institutions of higher education having graduate programs with capability in public health, the medical sciences, psychology, pharmacology, nurs-

ing, social work, health education, nutrition, or gerontology, for the purpose of designing and developing prototype health education and promotion programs for the use of State and area agencies on aging in implementing *disease prevention and health promotion programs (including coordinated multidisciplinary research projects on the aging process).*

(b) In making grants and contracts under (a)(1), the Commissioner shall give special consideration to projects designed to—

(1) meet the supportive services needs of elderly victims of Alzheimer's disease and related disorders with neurological and organic brain dysfunction and their families, including—

(A) home health care for such victims;

(B) adult day health care for such victims; and

(C) homemaker aids, transportation, and in-home respite care for the families, particularly spouses, of such victims;

(2) the special health care needs of the elderly, including—

(A) the location of older individuals who are in need of mental health services or who have severe disabilities;

(B) the provision of, or arrangements for the provision of, medical differential diagnoses of older individuals to distinguish between their need for mental health services and other medical care;

(C) the specification of the mental health needs of older individuals, and the mental health and support services required to meet such needs;

(D) the provision of—

(i) the mental health and support services specified in subclause (C) in the communities; or

(ii) such services for older individuals in nursing homes and intermediate care facilities, and training of the employees of such homes and facilities in the provision of such services; and

(E) the identification and provision of services to older individuals with severe disabilities; and

(3) assist in meeting the special housing needs of older individuals by—

(A) providing financial assistance to such individuals, who own their own homes, necessary to enable them (i) to make the repairs or renovations to their homes, which are necessary for them to meet minimum standards, and (ii) to install security devices, and to make structural modifications or alterations, designed to prevent unlawful entry; and

(B) studying and demonstrating methods of adapting existing housing, or construction of new housing, to meet the needs of older individuals suffering from physical disabilities;

(4) provide education and training to older individuals designed to enable them to lead more productive lives by broadening the education, occupational, cultural, or social awareness of such older individuals;

(5) provide preretirement education information and relevant services (including the training of personnel to carry out such programs and the conduct of research with respect to the development and operation of such programs) to individuals planning retirement;

(6) meet the special need of, and improve the delivery of services to,

older individuals who are not receiving adequate services under other provisions of this Act, with emphasis on the needs of low-income, minority, Indian, and limited English-speaking individuals and the rural elderly;

(7) develop or improve methods of coordinating all available supportive services for the homebound elderly, blind, and disabled by establishing demonstration projects in ten States, in accordance with subsection (c);

(8) improve transportation systems for the rural elderly;

(9) provide expanded, innovative volunteer opportunities to older individuals which are designed to fulfill unmet community needs, while at the same time avoiding duplication of existing volunteer programs, which may include *projects furnishing multigenerational services by older individuals addressing the needs of children, such as—*

(A) tutorial services in elementary and special schools;

(B) after school programs for latchkey children; and

(C) voluntary services for child care and youth day care programs;

(10) meet the service needs of older individuals who provide uncompensated care to their adult children with disabilities, for supportive services relating to such care, including—

(A) respite services; and

(B) legal advice, information, and referral services to assist such older individuals with permanency planning for such children;

(11) advance the understanding of the efficacy and benefits of providing music therapy, art therapy, or dance-movement therapy to older individuals through—

(A) projects that—

(i) study and demonstrate the provision of music therapy, art therapy, or dance-movement therapy to older individuals who are institutionalized or at risk of being institutionalized; and

(ii) provide music therapy, art therapy, or dance-movement therapy—

(I) in nursing homes, hospitals, rehabilitation centers, hospices, or senior centers;

(II) through disease prevention and health promotion services programs established under part F of title III;

(III) through in-home service programs established under part D of title III;

(IV) through multigenerational activities described in section 307(a)(41)(B) of subpart 3 of part C of title III;

(V) through supportive services described in section 321(a)(21); or

(VI) through disease prevention and health promotion services described in section 363(5); and

(B) education, training, and information dissemination projects, including—

(i) projects for the provision of gerontological training to music therapists, and education and training of individuals in the aging network regarding the efficacy and benefits of music therapy for older individuals; and

(ii) projects for disseminating to the aging network and to music therapists background materials on music therapy, best practice manuals, and other information on providing music therapy to older individuals; and

(12)(A) establish, in accordance with subparagraph (B), nationwide,

statewide, regional, metropolitan area, county, city, or community model volunteer service credit projects to demonstrate methods to improve or expand supportive services or nutrition services, or otherwise promote the wellbeing of older individuals;

(B) for purposes of paying part or all of the cost of developing or operating the projects, in the fiscal year, make not fewer than three and not more than five grants to, or contracts with, public agencies or nonprofit private organizations in such State; and

(C) ensure that the projects will be operated in consultation with the ACTION Agency and will permit older individuals who are volunteers to earn, for services furnished, credits that may be redeemed later for similar volunteer services.

(d)(1) Whenever appropriate, grants made and contracts entered into under this section shall be developed in consultation with an appropriate gerontology center.

(2)(A) Grants made and contracts entered into under this section shall include provisions for the appropriate dissemination of project results.

(B) An agency or organization that receives a grant or enters into a contract to carry out a project described in subparagraph (A) or (B)(i) of subsection (b)(11) shall submit to the Commissioner a report containing—

(i) the results, and findings based on the results, of such project; and

(ii) the recommendations of the agency or organization, if the agency or organization provided music therapy, regarding means by which music therapy could be made available, in an efficient and effective manner, to older individuals who would benefit from the therapy.

Special Projects in Comprehensive Long-Term Care

Sec. 423 (a) DEFINITIONS.—As used in this section:

(1) PROJECT.—The term 'Project' means a Project to Improve the Delivery of Long-Term Care Services.

(2) RESOURCE CENTER.—The term 'Resource Center' means a Resource Center for Long-Term Care.

(b) RESOURCE CENTERS.—

(1) GRANTS AND CONTRACTS.—The Commissioner shall award grants to, or enter into contracts with, eligible entities to support the establishment or operation of not fewer than four and not more than seven Resource Centers in accordance with paragraph 2).

(2) REQUIREMENTS.—

(A) FUNCTIONS.—Each Resource Center that receives funds under this subsection shall, with respect to subjects within an area of specialty of the Resource Center—

(i) perform research;

(ii) provide for the dissemination of results of the research; and

(iii) provide technical assistance and training to State agencies and area agencies on aging.

(B) AREA OF SPECIALTY.—For purposes of subparagraph (A) the term 'area of specialty' means—

(i) Alzheimer's disease and related dementias, and other cognitive impairments;

(ii) client assessment and case management;

(iii) data collection and analysis;

(iv) home modification and supportive services to enable older individuals to remain in their homes;

(v) consolidation and coordination of services;

(vi) linkages between acute care, rehabilitative services, and long-term care, facilities and providers;

(vii) decisionmaking and bioethics;

(viii) supply, training, and quality of long-term care personnel, including those who provide rehabilitative services;

(ix) rural issues, including barrier to access to services;

(x) chronic mental illness;

(xi) populations with greatest social need and populations with greatest economic need, with particular attention to low-income minorities; and

(xii) an area of importance as determined by the Commissioner.

(c) PROJECTS.—The Commissioner shall award grants to, or enter into contracts with, eligible entities to support the entities in establishing and carrying out not fewer than 10 Projects.

(d) USE OF FUNDS.—

(1) IN GENERAL.—Except as provided in paragraph *(2)*, an eligible entity may use funds received under a grant or contract—

(A) described in subsection *(b)(1)* to pay for part or all of the cost (including startup cost) of establishing and operating a new Resource Center, or of operating a Resource Center in existence on the day before the date of the enactment of the Older Americans Act Amendments of 1992; or

(B) described in subsection *(c)* to pay for part or all of the cost (including startup cost) of establishing and carrying out a Project.

(2) REIMBURSABLE DIRECT SERVICES.—None of the funds may be used to pay for direct services that are eligible for reimbursement under title XVIII, XIX, or XX of the Social Security Act *(42 U.S.C. 1395 et seq., 1396 et seq., or 1397 et seq.)*.

(e) PREFERENCE.—In awarding grants, and entering into contracts, under this section, the Commissioner shall give preference to entities that demonstrate that—

(l) adequate State standards have been developed to ensure the quality of services provided under the grant or contract; and

(2) the entity has made a commitment to carry out programs under the grant or contract with each State agency responsible for the administration of title XIX or XX of the Social Security Act.

(f) APPLICATION.—

(1) IN GENERAL.—To be eligible to receive funds under a grant or contract described in subsection *(b)(1)* or *(c)*, an entity shall submit an application to the Commissioner at such time, in such manner, and containing such information as the Commissioner may require.

(2) PROJECT APPLICATION.—An entity seeking a grant or contract under subsection *(c)* shall submit an application to the Commissioner containing, at a minimum—

(A) information identifying and describing gaps, weaknesses, or other problems in the delivery of long-term care services in the State or geographic area to be served by the entity, including—
(i) duplication of functions in the delivery of such services, including duplication at the State and local level;
(ii) fragmentation of systems, especially in coordinating services to populations of older individuals and other populations;
(iii) barriers to access for populations with greatest social need and populations with greatest economic need, including minorities and residents of rural areas;
(iv) lack of financing for such services;
(v) lack of availability of adequately trained personnel to provide such services; and
(vi) lack of a range of chronic care services (including rehabilitative strategies) that promote restoration, maintenance, or improvement of function in older individuals;
(B) a plan to address the gaps, weaknesses, and problems described in clauses (i) through (v); and
(C) information describing the extent to which the entity will coordinate with area agencies on aging and service providers in carrying out the proposed Project.
(g) ELIGIBLE ENTITIES.—
(1) RESOURCE CENTERS.—Entities eligible to receive grants, or enter into contracts, under subsection (b)(1) shall be—
(A) institutions of higher education; and
(B) other public agencies and nonprofit private organizations.
(2) PROJECTS.—Entities eligible to receive grants, or enter into contracts, under subsection (c) include—
(A) State agencies; and
(B) in consultation with State agencies—
(i) area agencies on aging;
(ii) institutions of higher education; and
(iii) other public agencies and nonprofit private organizations.
(h) REPORT.—The Commissioner shall include in the annual report to the Congress required by section 207, a report on the grants awarded, and contracts entered into, under this section including—
(l) an analysis of the relative effectiveness, and recommendations for any changes, of the projects of Resource Centers funded under subsection (b)(1) in the fiscal year for which the Commissioner is preparing the annual report; and
(2) an evaluation of the needs identified, the agencies utilized, and the effectiveness of the approaches used by projects funded under subsection (c).
(i) AVAILABILITY OF FUNDS.—The Commissioner shall make available for carrying out subsection (b) for each fiscal year not less than the amount made available in fiscal year 1991 for making grants and entering into contracts to establish and operate Resource Centers under section 423 as in effect on the day before the date of the enactment of the Older Americans Act Amendments of 1992.

(b) OBLIGATION.—Not later than 60 days after the date of enactment of this Act, the Commissioner shall obligate, from the funds appropriated under section 431(a)(1) of the Older Americans Act of 1965 (42 U.S.C. 3037(a)(1)) for fiscal year 1992—
   (1) not less than the amount described in section 423(i) of such Act (42 U.S.C. 3035b(i)) for carrying out section 423 (b)(1) of such Act; and
   (2) such sums as may be necessary for carrying out section 423(c) of such Act.

Special Demonstration and Support Projects for Legal Assistance for Older Individuals

Sec. 424. (a) The Commissioner shall make grants and enter into contracts, in order to—
   (1) provide a national legal assistance support system (operated by one or more grantees or contractors) of activities to State and area agencies on aging for providing, developing, or supporting legal assistance for older individuals, including—
      (A) case consultations;
      (B) training;
      (C) provision of substantive legal advice and assistance; and
      (D) assistance in the design, implementation, and administration of legal assistance delivery systems to local providers of legal assistance for older individuals; and
   (2) support demonstration projects to expand or improve the delivery of assistance to older individuals with social or economic needs.
   (b) Any grants or contracts made under subsection (a)(2) shall contain assurances that the requirements of section 307(a)(15) are met.
   (c) To carry out subsection (a)(1), the Commissioner shall make grants to or enter into contracts with national nonprofit legal assistance organizations experienced in providing support, on a nationwide basis, to local legal assistance providers.

National Impact Activities

Sec. 425. (a)(1) The Commissioner may carry out directly or through grants or contracts—
   (A) innovation and development projects and activities of national significance which show promise of having substantial impact on the expansion or improvement of supportive services, nutrition services, or multipurpose senior centers, or otherwise promoting the well-being of older individuals; and
   (B) dissemination of information activities related to such programs.
   (2) The Commissioner shall carry out, directly or through grants or contracts, special training programs and technical assistance designed to improve services to minorities.
   (b) An amount not to exceed 15 percent of any sums appropriated under section 431 may be used for carrying out this section.

Utility and Home Heating Cost Demonstration Project

Sec. 426. *The Secretary may, after consultation with the appropriate State agency,* make grants to pay for part or all of the costs of developing model projects which show promise of relieving older individuals of the excessive burdens of high utility service and home heating costs. Any such project shall give special consideration to projects under which a business concern is engaged in providing home heating oil for utility services to low-income older individuals at a cost which is substantially lower than providing home heating oil or utility services to other individuals.

Ombudsman and Advocacy Demonstration Projects

Sec. 427. (a) The Commissioner is authorized to make grants to not less than three nor more than ten States to demonstrate and evaluate cooperative projects between the State long-term care ombudsman program, *legal assistance agencies,* and the State protection and advocacy systems for developmental disabilities and mental illness, established under part A of the Developmental Disabilities Assistance and Bill of Rights Act (42 U.S.C. 6001 et seq.) and under the protection and Advocacy for Mentally Ill Individuals Act of 1986 (Public Law 99–319).

(b) The Commissioner on Aging shall prepare and submit to the Congress a report of the study and evaluation required by subsection (a). Such report shall contain such recommendations as the Commissioner on Aging deems appropriate.

Consumer Protection Demonstration Projects for Services Provided in the Home

Sec. 428. (a)(1) The Commissioner is authorized to make grants to not fewer than 6 nor more than 10 States to demonstrate and evaluate the effectiveness of consumer protection projects for services provided to older individuals in the home that are furnished or assisted with public funds.

(2) Grants made under this section shall be used to test different approaches to protecting older individuals with regard to services in the home. Such projects may provide consumer protection through State and local ombudsmen, legal assistance agencies, and other community service agencies.

(b) No grant may be made under this section unless an application is made to the Commissioner at such time, in such manner, and containing such information as the Commissioner may reasonably require. Each such application shall—

(1) describe activities for which assistance is sought;

(2) provide for an evaluation of the activities for which assistance is sought; and

(3) provide assurance that the applicant will prepare and submit a report to the Commissioner on the activities conducted with assistance under this section and the evaluation of such activities.

(c) In approving applications under this section, the Commissioner shall assure equitable geographic distribution of assistance.

(d) The Commissioner shall, as part of the annual report submitted under section 207, prepare and submit a report on the evaluation submitted under this section, together with such recommendations as the Commissioner deems appropriate. In carrying out this section, the Commissioner shall include in the report—

(1) a description of the demonstration projects assisted under this section;

(2) an evaluation of the effectiveness of each such project; and

(3) recommendations of the Commissioner with respect to the desirability and feasibility of carrying out on a nation-wide basis a consumer protection program for services in the home.

(e) Consumer protection projects carried out under this section—

(1) may include, but are not limited to, consumer education, the use of consumer hotlines, receipt and resolution of consumer complaints, and advocacy; and

(2) may not address medical services.

SEC. 429. DEMONSTRATION PROJECTS FOR MULTIGENERATIONAL ACTIVITIES.

(a) GRANTS AND CONTRACTS.—The Commissioner may award grants and enter into contracts with eligible organizations to establish demonstration projects that provide older individuals with multigenerational activities.

(b) USE OF FUNDS.—An eligible organization shall use funds made available under a grant awarded, or a contract entered into, under subsection (a)—

(1) to carry out a demonstration project that provides multigenerational activities, including any professional training appropriate to such activities for older individuals; and

(2) to evaluate the project in accordance with subsection (f).

(c) AWARDS.—In awarding grants and entering into contracts under subsection (a), the Commissioner shall give preference to—

(1) eligible organizations with a demonstrated record of carrying out multigenerational activities; and

(2) eligible organizations proposing projects that will serve older individuals with greatest economic need (with particular attention to low-income minority individuals).

(d) APPLICATION.—To be eligible to receive a grant or enter into a contract under subsection (a), an organization shall submit an application to the Commissioner at such time, in such manner, and accompanied by such information as the Commissioner may reasonably require.

(e) ELIGIBLE ORGANIZATIONS.—Organizations eligible to receive a grant or enter into a contract under subsection (a) shall be organizations that employ, or provide opportunities for, older individuals in multigenerational activities.

(f) LOCAL EVALUATION AND REPORT.—

(1) EVALUATION.—Each organization receiving a grant or a contract under subsection (a) to carry out a demonstration project shall evaluate the activities assisted under the project to determine the effectiveness of multigenerational activities, the impact of such activities on child care and youth day care programs, and the impact on older individuals involved in such project.

(2) REPORT.—The organization shall submit a report to the Commissioner containing the evaluation not later than 6 months after the expiration of the period for which the grant or contract is in effect.

(g) REPORT TO CONGRESS.—Not later than 6 months after the Commissioner receives the reports described in subsection (f)(2), the Commissioner shall prepare and submit to the Speaker of the House of Representatives and the President pro tempore of the Senate a report that assesses the evaluations and includes, at a minimum—

(1) the names or descriptive titles of the demonstration projects funded under subsection (a);

(2) a description of the nature and operation of the projects;

(3) the name and address of the individual or governmental entity that conducted the projects;

(4) a description of the methods and success of the projects in recruiting older individuals as employees and volunteers to participate in the project;

(5) a description of the success of the projects retaining older individuals involved in the projects as employees and as volunteers; and

(6) the rate of turnover of older individual employees and volunteers in the projects.

(h) DEFINITION.—As used in this section, the term 'multigenerational activity' includes an opportunity to serve as a mentor or adviser in a child care program, a youth day care program, an educational assistance program, an at-risk youth intervention program, a juvenile delinquency treatment program, or a family support program.

SEC. 429A. SUPPORTIVE SERVICES IN FEDERALLY ASSISTED HOUSING DEMONSTRATION PROGRAM.

(a) GRANTS.—The Commissioner shall award grants to eligible agencies to establish demonstration programs to provide services described in subsection (b) to older individuals who are residents in federally assisted housing (referred to in this section as 'residents').

(b) USE OF GRANTS.—An eligible agency shall use a grant awarded under subsection (a) to conduct outreach and to provide to residents services including—

(1) meal services;

(2) transportation;

(3) personal care, dressing, bathing, and toileting;

(4) housekeeping and chore assistance;

(5) nonmedical counseling;

(6) case management;

(7) other services to prevent premature and unnecessary institutional-ization; and

(8) other services provided under this Act.

(c) AWARD OF GRANTS.—The Commissioner shall award grants under subsection (a) to agencies in a variety of geographic settings, including urban and rural settings.

(d) APPLICATION.—To be eligible to receive a grant under subsection (a), an agency shall submit an application to the Commissioner at such time, in such manner, and containing such information as the Commissioner may require, including, at a minimum—

(1) information demonstrating a lack of, and need for, services described in subsection (b) in federally assisted housing projects in the geographic area proposed to be served by the applicant;

(2) a comprehensive plan to coordinate with housing facility management to provide services to frail older individuals who are in danger of premature or unnecessary institutionalization;

(3) information demonstrating initiative on the part of the agency to address the supportive service needs of residents;

(4) information demonstrating financial, in-kind, or other support available to the applicant from State or local governments, or from private resources;

(5) an assurance that the agency will participate in the development of the comprehensive housing affordability strategy under section 105 of the Cranston-Gonzalez National Affordable Housing Act (42 U.S.C. 12705) and seek funding for supportive services under the Department of Housing and Urban Development or the Farmers Home Administration;

(6) an assurance that the agency will target services to low-income minority older individuals and conduct outreach;

(7) an assurance that the agency will comply with the guidelines described in subsection (f); and

(8) a plan to evaluate the eligibility of older individuals for services under the federally assisted housing demonstration program, which plan shall include a professional assessment committee to identify such individuals.

(e) ELIGIBLE AGENCIES.—Agencies eligible to receive grants under this section shall be State agencies and area agencies on aging.

(f) GUIDELINES.—The Commissioner shall issue guidelines for use by agencies that receive grants under this section—

(1) regarding the level of frailty that older individuals shall meet to be eligible for services under a demonstration program established under this section; and

(2) for accepting voluntary contributions from residents who receive services under such a program.

(g) EVALUATIONS AND REPORTS.—

(1) AGENCIES.—Each agency that receives a grant under subsection (a) to establish a demonstration program shall, not later than 3 months after the end of the period for which the grant is awarded—

(A) evaluate the effectiveness of the program; and

(B) submit a report containing the evaluation to the Commissioner.

(2) COMMISSIONER.—The Commissioner shall, not later than 6 months af-

ter the end of the period for which the Commissioner awards grants under
subsection (a)—

(A) evaluate the effectiveness of each demonstration program that receives a grant under subsection (a); and

(B) submit a report containing the evaluation to the Speaker of the
House of Representatives and the President pro tempore of the Senate.

SEC. 429B. NEIGHBORHOOD SENIOR CARE PROGRAM.

(a) DEFINITIONS.—As used in this section;

(1) HEALTH AND SOCIAL SERVICES.—The term 'health and social services' includes skilled nursing care, personal care, social work services, homemaker
services, health and nutrition education, health screening, home health aid
services, and specialized therapies.

(2) VOLUNTEER SERVICES.—The term 'volunteer services' includes peer
counseling, chore services, help with mail and taxes, transportation, socialization, health and social services, and other similar services.

(b) SERVICE GRANTS.—

(1) IN GENERAL.—The Commissioner may award grants to eligible entities
to establish neighborhood senior care programs, in order to encourage professionals to provide volunteer services to local residents who are older individuals and who might otherwise have to be admitted to nursing homes and
to hospitals.

(2) PREFERENCE.—In awarding grants under this section, the Commissioner shall give preference to applicants experienced in operating community programs and programs meeting the independent living needs of older
individuals

(3) ADVISORY BOARD.—The Commissioner shall establish an advisory
board to provide guidance to grant recipients regarding the neighborhood
senior care programs. Not fewer than two-thirds of the members of the advisory board shall be residents in communities served by the grant recipients.

(4) APPLICATION.—To be eligible to receive a grant under this section, an
entity shall submit an application to the Commissioner at such time, in such
manner, and containing such information as the Commissioner may reasonably require. Each application shall—

(A) describe the activities in the program for which assistance is
sought;

(B) describe the neighborhood in which volunteer services are to be
provided under the program, and a plan for integration of volunteer services
within the neighborhood;

(C)(i) provide assurances that nurses, social workers, and community
volunteers providing volunteer services and an outreach coordinator involved with the project live in the neighborhood; or

(ii)(I) reasons that it is not possible to provide such assurances; and

(II) assurances that nurses, social workers, community volunteers and
the outreach coordinator will be assigned repeatedly to the particular neighborhood; and

(D) provide for an evaluation of the activities for which assistance is sought.

(c) TECHNICAL RESOURCE CENTER.—The Commissioner shall, to the extent appropriations are available, enter into a contract with an applicant described in subsection (b)(2) to establish a technical resource center that will—

(1) assist the Commissioner in developing criteria for, and in awarding grants to communities to establish, neighborhood senior care organizations that will implement neighborhood senior care programs under subsection (b);

(2) assist communities interested in establishing such a neighborhood senior care program;

(3) coordinate the neighborhood senior care programs;

(4) provide ongoing analysis of and collection of data on the neighborhood senior care programs and provide such data to the Commissioner;

(5) serve as a liaison to State agencies interested in establishing neighborhood senior care programs; and

(6) take any further actions as required by regulation by the Commissioner.

SEC. 429C. INFORMATION AND ASSISTANCE SYSTEMS DEVELOPMENT PROJECTS.

(a) GRANTS.—The Commissioner may—

(1) make grants to State agencies, and, in consultation with State agencies, to area agencies on aging to support the improvement of information and assistance services, and systems of services, operated at the State and local levels; and

(2) make grants to organizations to provide training and technical assistance to State agencies, area agencies on aging, and providers of supportive services—

(A) to support a national telephone access service to inform older individuals, families, and caregivers about State and local information and assistance services funded under this Act; and

(B) to support the improvement of information and assistance services, and systems of services, operated at the State and local levels.

(b) APPLICATION.—To be eligible to receive a grant under subsection (a) an agency or organization shall submit an application to the Commissioner at such time, in such manner, and containing such information as the Commissioner may specify.

(c) GUIDELINES.—The Commissioner shall establish guidelines for the operation of the national telephone access service described in subsection (a)(2)(A).

(d) EVALUATION AND REPORT.—

(1) EVALUATION.—The Commissioner shall conduct an evaluation of the effectiveness of the national telephone service described in subsection (a)(2)(A) in providing information and assistance services to older individuals,

families, and caregivers about State and local information and assistance services.

(2) REPORT.—Not later than January 1, 1995, the Commissioner shall submit the evaluation described in paragraph (1) to the Speaker of the House of Representatives and the President pro tempore of the Senate.

SEC. 429D. SENIOR TRANSPORTATION DEMONSTRATION PROGRAM GRANTS.

(a) ESTABLISHMENT.—The Commissioner shall establish and carry out senior transportation demonstration programs. In carrying out the programs, the Commissioner shall award grants to not fewer than five eligible entities for the purpose of improving the mobility of older individuals and transportation services for older individuals (referred to in this section as 'senior transportation services').

(b) USE OF FUNDS.—Grants made under subsection (a) may be used to—

(1) develop innovative approaches for improving access by older individuals to supportive services under part B of title III, nutrition services under part C of title III, health care, and other important services;

(2) develop comprehensive and integrated senior transportation services; and

(3) leverage additional resources for senior transportation services by—

(A) coordinating various transportation services; and

(B) coordinating various funding sources for transportation services, including—

(i) sources of assistance under—

(I) sections 9, 16(b)(2), and 18 of the Urban Mass Transportation Act of 1964 (49 U.S.C. app.); and

(II) titles XIX and XX of the Social Security Act (42 U.S.C. 1396 et seq. and 1397 et seq.); and

(ii) State and local sources.

(c) AWARD OF GRANTS.—

(1) PREFERENCE.—In awarding grants under subsection (a), the Commissioner shall give preference to entities that—

(A) demonstrate special needs for enhancing senior transportation services and resources for the services within the geographic area served by the entities;

(B) establish plans to ensure that senior transportation services are coordinated with general public transportation services and other specialized transportation services;

(C) demonstrate the ability to utilize the broadest range of available transportation and community resources to provide senior transportation services;

(D) demonstrate the capacity and willingness to coordinate senior transportation services with services provided under title III and with general public transportation services and other specialized transportation services; and

(E) establish plans for senior transportation demonstration programs de-

signed to serve the special needs of low-income, rural, frail, and other at-risk, transit-dependent older individuals.

(2) RURAL ENTITIES.—The Commissioner shall award not less than 50 percent of the grants authorized under this section to entities located in, or primarily serving, rural areas.

(d) APPLICATION.—An entity that seeks a grant under this section shall submit an application to the Commissioner at such time, in such manner, and containing such information as the Commissioner may require, including at a minimum—

(1) information describing senior transportation services for which the entity seeks assistance;

(2) a comprehensive strategy for developing a coordinated transportation system or leveraging additional funding resources, to provide senior transportation services;

(3) information describing the extent to which the applicant intends to coordinate the services of the applicant with the services of other transportation providers;

(4) a plan for evaluating the effectiveness of the proposed senior transportation demonstration program and preparing a report containing the evaluation to be submitted to the Commissioner; and

(5) such other information as may be required by the Commissioner.

(e) ELIGIBLE ENTITIES.—Entities eligible to receive grants under this section shall be—

(1) State agencies;

(2) area agencies on aging; and

(3) other public agencies and nonprofit organizations.

(f) REPORT.—

(1) PREPARATION.—The Commissioner shall prepare, either directly or through grants or contracts, annual reports on the senior transportation demonstration programs established under this section. The reports shall contain an assessment of the effectiveness of each demonstration project and recommendations regarding legislative, administrative, and other initiatives needed to improve the access to and effectiveness of transportation services for older individuals.

(2) SUBMISSION.—The Commissioner shall submit the report described in paragraph (1) to the Speaker of the House of Representatives and the President pro tempore of the Senate.

SEC. 429E. RESOURCE CENTERS ON NATIVE AMERICAN ELDERS.

(a) ESTABLISHMENT.—The Commissioner shall make grants or enter into contracts with not fewer than two and not more than four eligible entities to establish and operate Resource Centers on Native American Elders (referred to in this section as 'Resource Centers'). The Commissioner shall make such grants or enter into such contracts for periods of not less than 3 years.

(b) FUNCTIONS.—

(1) IN GENERAL.—Each Resource Center that receives funds under this section shall—

(A) gather information;

(B) perform research;

(C) provide for the dissemination of results of the research; and

(D) provide technical assistance and training to entities that provide services to Native Americans who are older individuals.

(2) AREAS OF CONCERN.—In conducting the functions described in paragraph (1), a Resource Center shall focus on priority areas of concern for the Resource Centers regarding Native Americans who are older individuals, which areas shall be—

(A) health problems;

(B) long-term care, including in-home care;

(C) elder abuse; and

(D) other problems and issues that the Commissioner determines are of particular importance to Native Americans who are older individuals.

(c) PREFERENCE.—In awarding grants and entering into contracts under subsection (a), the Commissioner shall give preference to institutions of higher education that have conducted research on, and assessment of, the characteristics and needs of Native Americans who are older individuals.

(d) CONSULTATION.—In determining the type of information to be sought from, and activities to be performed by, Resource Centers, the Commissioner shall consult with the Associate Commissioner on American Indian, Alaskan Native, and Native Hawaiian Aging and with national organizations with special expertise in serving Native Americans who are older individuals.

(e) ELIGIBLE ENTITIES.—Entities eligible to receive a grant or enter into a contract under subsection (a) shall be institutions of higher education with experience conducting research and assessment on the needs of older individuals.

(f) REPORT TO CONGRESS.—The Commissioner, with assistance from each Resource Center, shall prepare and submit to the Speaker of the House of Representatives and the President pro tempore of the Senate an annual report on the status and needs including the priority areas of concern of Native Americans who are older individuals.

SEC. 429F. DEMONSTRATION PROGRAMS FOR OLDER INDIVIDUALS WITH DEVELOPMENTAL DISABILITIES.

(a) DEFINITION.—As used in this section:

(1) DEVELOPMENTAL DISABILITY.—The term 'developmental disability' has the meaning given the term in section 102(5) of the Developmental Disabilities Assistance and Bill of Rights Act (42 U.S.C. 6001(5)).

(2) IN-HOME SERVICE.—The term 'in-home service' has the meaning given the term section 342.

(b) ESTABLISHMENT.—The Commissioner shall make grants to State agencies to provide services in accordance with subsection (c).

(c) USE OF FUNDS.—A State agency may use a grant awarded under subsection (b) to provide services for older individuals with developmental disabilities, and for older individuals with caretaker responsibilities for developmentally disabled children, including—

(1) child care and youth day care programs;

(2) programs to integrate the individuals into existing programs for older individuals;

(3) respite care;

(4) transportation to multipurpose senior centers and other facilities and services;

(5) supervision;

(6) renovation of multipurpose senior centers;

(7) provision of materials to facilitate activities for older individuals with developmental disabilities, and for older individuals with caretaker responsibilities for developmentally disabled children;

(8) training of State agency, area agency on aging, volunteer, and multipurpose senior center staff, and other service providers, who work with such individuals; and

(9) in-home services.

(d) APPLICATION.—To be eligible to receive a grant under this section, a State agency shall submit an application to the Commissioner at such time, in such manner, and containing such information as the Commissioner may require.

SEC. 429G. HOUSING DEMONSTRATION PROGRAMS.

(a) HOUSING OMBUDSMAN DEMONSTRATION PROGRAMS.—

(1) GRANTS.—The Commissioner shall award grants to eligible agencies to establish housing ombudsman programs.

(2) USE OF GRANTS.—An eligible agency shall use a grant awarded under paragraph (1) to—

(A) provide the services described in subparagraph (B) through—

(i) professional and volunteer staff to older individuals who are—

(I) participating in federally assisted and other publicly assisted housing programs; or

(II) seeking Federal, State, and local housing programs; and

(ii)(I) the State Long-Term Care Ombudsman program under section 307(a)(12) or section 712;

(II) a legal services or assistance organization or through an organization that provides both legal and other social services;

(III) a public or not-for-profit social services agency; or

(IV) an agency or organization concerned with housing issues but not responsible for publicly assisted housing.

(B) establish a housing ombudsman program that provides information, advice, and advocacy services including—

(i) direct assistance, or referral to services, to resolve complaints or problems;

(ii) provision of information regarding available housing programs, eligibility, requirements, and application processes;

(iii) counseling or assistance with financial, social, familial, or other related matters that may affect or be influenced by housing problems;

(iv) advocacy related to promoting—

(I) the rights of the older individuals who are residents in publicly assisted housing programs; and

(II) the quality and suitability of housing in the programs; and

(v) assistance with problems related to housing regarding—

(I) threats of eviction or eviction notices;

(II) older buildings;

(III) functional impairments as the impairments relate to housing;

(IV) unlawful discrimination;

(V) regulations of the Department of Housing and Urban Development and the Farmers Home Administration;

(VI) disability issues;

(VII) intimidation, harassment, or arbitrary management rules;

(VIII) grievance procedures;

(IX) certification and recertification related to programs of the Department of Housing and Urban Development and the Farmers Home Administration; and

(X) issues related to transfer from one project or program to another; and

(3) AWARD OF GRANTS.—The Commissioner shall award grants under paragraph *(1)* to agencies in rural, urban, and other settings.

(4) APPLICATION.—To be eligible to receive a grant under paragraph *(1)*, an agency shall submit an application to the Commissioner at such time, in such manner, and containing such information as the Commissioner may require, including, at a minimum—

(A) an assurance that the agency will conduct training of professional and volunteer staff who will provide services through the housing ombudsman demonstration program;

(B) in the case of an application submitted by an area agency on aging, an endorsement of the program by the State agency serving the State in which the program will be established, and an assurance by the State agency that the agency will work with the area agency in carrying out the program; and

(C) a plan to involve in the demonstration program the Secretary of the Department of Housing and Urban Development, the Administrator of the Farmers Home Administration, any individual or entity described in paragraph *(2)(A)* through which the agency intends to provide the services, and other agencies involved in publicly assisted housing programs.

(5) ELIGIBLE AGENCIES.—Agencies eligible to receive grants under this section shall include—

(A) State agencies;

(B) area agencies on aging; and

(C) other nonprofit entities, including providers of services under the State Long-Term Care Ombudsman program and the elder rights and legal assistance development program described in chapters 2 and 4, respectively, of subtitle A of title VII.

(b) Foreclosure and Eviction Assistance and Relief Services Demonstration Programs.—

(1) Grants.—The Commissioner shall make grants to States to carry out demonstration programs to develop methods or implement laws—

(A) to prevent or delay the foreclosure on housing owned and occupied by older individuals or the eviction of older individuals from housing the individuals rent;

(B) to obtain alternative housing as a result of such foreclosure or eviction; and

(C) to assist older individuals to understand the rights and obligations of the individuals under laws relating to housing ownership and occupancy.

(2) Notification Process.—A State that receives a grant under paragraph *(1)* shall establish methods, including a notification process—

(A) to assist older individuals who are incapable of, or have difficulty in, understanding the circumstances and consequences of foreclosure on or eviction from housing the individuals occupy; and

(B) to coordinate the program for which such grant is received with the activities of tenant organizations, tenant-landlord mediation organizations, public housing entities, and area agencies on aging, to provide more effectively assistance or referral to services to relocate or prevent eviction of older individuals from housing the individuals occupy.

(c) Evaluations and Reports.—

(1) Agencies.—Each agency or State that receives a grant under subsection *(a)* or *(b)* to establish a demonstration program shall, not later than 3 months after the end of the period for which the grant is awarded—

(A) evaluate the effectiveness of the program; and

(B) submit a report containing the evaluation to the Commissioner.

(2) Commissioner.—The Commissioner shall, not later than 6 months after the end of the period for which the Commissioner awards a grant under subsection *(a)* or *(b)*—

(A) evaluate the effectiveness of each demonstration program that receives the grant; and

(B) submit a report containing the evaluation to the Speaker of House of Representatives and the President pro tempore of the Senate.

SEC. 429H. PRIVATE RESOURCE ENHANCEMENT PROJECTS.

(a) Grants.—

(1) In General.—The Commissioner may make grants to, and enter into contracts with, State agencies and area agencies on aging, to carry out demonstration projects that generate non-Federal resources (including cash and in-kind contributions), in order to increase resources available to provide additional services under title III.

(2) Maintenance of Resources.—Resources generated with a grant made, or contract entered into, under subsection *(a)* shall be in addition to, and may not be used to supplant, any resource that is or would otherwise be

available under any Federal, State, or local law to a State, State agency, area agency on aging, or unit of general purpose local government (as defined in section 302(2) to provide such services.

(3) Use of Resources.—Resources generated with a grant made, or a contract entered into, under subsection (a) shall be used to provide supportive services in accordance with title III. The requirements under this Act that apply to funds received under title III by States to carry out title III shall apply with respect to such resources.

(b) Award of Grants and Contracts.—

(1) Regional Distribution.—The Commissioner shall ensure that States and area agencies on aging in all standard Federal regions of the United States, established by the Office of Management and Budget, receive grants and contracts under subsection (a) on an equitable basis.

(2) Distribution Based on Need.—Within such regions, the Commissioner shall give preference to applicants that provide services under title III in geographical areas that contain a large number of older individuals with greatest economic need or older individuals with greatest social need.

(c) Monitoring.—The Commissioner shall monitor how—

(1) grants are expended, and contracts are carried out, under subsection (a); and

(2) resources generated under such grants and contracts are expended, to ensure compliance with this section.

SEC. 429I. CAREER PREPARATION FOR THE FIELD OF AGING.

(a) Grants.—The Commissioner shall make grants to institutions of higher education, historically black colleges or universities, Hispanic Centers of Excellence in Applied Gerontology, and other educational institutions that serve the needs of minority students, to provide education and training to prepare students for careers in the field of aging.

(b) Definitions.—For purposes of subsection (a);

(1) Hispanic Center of Excellence in Applied Gerontology.—The term 'Hispanic Center of Excellence in Applied Gerontology' means an institution of higher education with a program in applied gerontology that—

(A) has a significant number of Hispanic individuals enrolled in the program, including individuals accepted for enrollment in the program;

(B) has been effective in assisting Hispanic students of the program to complete the program and receive the degree involved;

(C) has been effective in recruiting Hispanic individuals to attend the program, including providing scholarships and other financial assistance to such individuals and encouraging Hispanic students of secondary educational institutions to attend the program; and

(D) has made significant recruitment efforts to increase the number and placement of Hispanic individuals serving in faculty or administrative positions in the program.

(2) Historically Black College or University.—The term 'historically black college or university' has the meaning given the term 'part B institution' in section 322(2) of the Higher Education Act of 1965 (20 U.S.C. 1061(2)).

SEC. 429J. PENSION RIGHTS DEMONSTRATION PROJECTS.—

. (a) DEFINITIONS.—As used in this section:

(1) PENSION RIGHTS INFORMATION PROGRAM.—The term 'pension rights information program' means a program described in subsection (c).

(2) PENSION AND OTHER RETIREMENT BENEFITS.—The term 'pension and other retirement benefits' means private, civil service, and other public pensions and retirement benefits, including benefits provided under—

(A) the Social Security program under title II of the Social Security Act (42 U.S.C. 401 et seq.);

(B) the railroad retirement program under the Railroad Retirement Act of 1974 (45 U.S.C. 231 et seq.);

(C) the government retirement benefits programs under the Civil Service Retirement System set forth in chapter 83 of title 5, United States Code, the Federal Employees Retirement System set forth in chapter 84 of title 5, United States Code, or other Federal retirement systems; or

(D) the Employee Retirement Income Security Act (29 U.S.C. 1001 et seq.).

(b) ESTABLISHMENT.—The Commissioner shall establish and carry out pension rights demonstration projects.

(c) PENSION RIGHTS INFORMATION PROGRAMS.—

(1) USE OF FUNDS.—In carrying out the projects specified in subsection (b), the Commissioner shall, to the extent appropriations are available, award grants to six eligible entities to establish programs to provide outreach, information, counseling, referral, and assistance regarding pension and other retirement benefits, and rights related to such benefits.

(2) AWARD OF GRANTS.—

(A) TYPE OF ENTITY.—The Commissioner shall award under this subsection—

(i) four grants to State agencies or area agencies on aging; and

(ii) two grants to nonprofit organizations with a proven record of providing—

(I) services related to retirement of older individuals; or

(II) specific pension rights counseling.

(B) PANEL.—In awarding grants under this subsection, the Commissioner shall use a citizen advisory panel that shall include representatives of business, labor, national senior advocates, and national pension rights advocates.

(C) CRITERIA.—In awarding grants under this subsection, the Commissioner in consultation wiht the panel, shall use as criteria—

(i) evidence of commitment of an agency or organization to carry out a proposed pension rights information program;

(ii) the ability of the agency or organization to perform effective outreach to affected populations, particularly populations identified as in need of special outreach; and

(iii) reliable information that the population to be served by the agency or organization has a demonstrable need for the services proposed to be provided under the program.

(3) APPLICATION.—

(A) IN GENERAL.—To be eligible to receive a grant under this subsection, an entity shall submit an application to the Commissioner at such time, in such manner, and containing such information as the Commissioner may require, including, at a minimum—
(i) a plan for the establishment of a pension rights information program to serve a specific geographic area; and
(ii) an assurance that staff members (including volunteer staff members) have no conflict of interest in providing the services described in the plan.
(B) PLAN.—The plan described in paragraph (1) shall provide for a program that—
(i) establishes a State or area pension rights information center;
(ii) provides counseling (including direct counseling and assistance to individuals needing information) and information that may assist individuals in establishing rights to, obtaining, and filing claims or complaints related to, pension and other retirement benefits;
(iii) provides information on sources of pension and other retirement benefits, including the benefits under programs described in subsection (a)(1);
(iv) makes referrals to legal services and other advocacy programs;
(v) establishes a system of referral to State, local, and Federal departments or agencies related to pension and other retirement benefits;
(vi) provides a sufficient number of staff positions (including volunteer positions) to ensure information, counseling, referral, and assistance regarding pension and other retirement benefits;
(vii) provides training programs for staff members, including volunteer staff members of the programs described in subsection (a)(1);
(viii) makes recommendations to the Administration, the Department of Labor and other local, State, and Federal agencies concerning issues for older individuals related to pension and other retirement benefits; and
(ix) establishes an outreach program to provide information, counseling, referral, and assistance regarding pension and other retirement benefits, with particular emphasis on outreach to women, minorities, and low-income retirees.
(d) TRAINING PROGRAM.—
(1) USE OF FUNDS.—In carrying out the projects described in subsection (b), the Commissioner shall, to the extent appropriations are available, award a grant to an eligible entity to establish a training program to provide—
(A) information to the staffs of entities operating pension rights information programs; and
(B) assistance to the entities and assist such entities in the design of program evaluation tools
(2) ELIGIBLE ENTITY.—Entities eligible to receive grants under this subsection include nonprofit private organizations with records of providing national information, referral, and advocacy in matters related to pension and other retirement benefits.
(3) APPLICATION.—To be eligible to receive a grant under this subsection, an entity shall submit an application to the Commissioner at such time, in such manner, and containing such information as the Commissioner may require.

(e) DURATION.—The Commissioner may award grants under subsection (c) or (d) for periods not to exceed 18 months.

(f) REPORT TO CONGRESS.—

(1) PREPARATION.—The Commissioner shall prepare a report that—

(A) summarizes the distribution of funds authorized for grants under this section and the expenditure of such funds;

(B) summarizes the scope and content of training and assistance provided under a program carried out under this section and the degree to which the training and assistance can be replicated;

(C) outlines the problems that individuals participating in programs funded under this section encountered concerning rights related to pension and other retirement benefits; and

(D) makes recommendations regarding the manner in which services provided in programs funded under this section can be incorporated into the ongoing programs of State agencies, area agencies on aging, multipurpose senior centers, and other similar entities.

(2) SUBMISSION.—Not later than 30 months after the date of the enactment of this section, the Commissioner shall submit the report described in paragraph (1) to the Committee on Education and Labor of the House of Representatives and the Committee on Labor and Human Resources of the Senate.

(g) ADMINISTRATIVE EXPENSES.—Of the funds appropriated under section 431(a)(1) to carry out this section for a fiscal year, not more than $100,000 may be used by the Administration for administrative expenses in carrying out this section.

Part C—General Provisions

Authorization of Appropriations

Sec. 431. (a)(1) There are authorized to be appropriated to carry out the provisions of this title (other than the provision specified in subsection (b)) $72,000,000 for fiscal year 1992, and such sums as may be necessary for fiscal years 1993, 1994, and 1995.

(2) Not less than 1 percent of the amount appropriated under paragraph (1) for each fiscal year shall be made available to carry out section 202(d).

(b) There are authorized to be appropriated to carry out section 411(e), $450,000 for each of fiscal years 1992, 1993, 1994, and 1995.

(c) No funds may be appropriated under this title—

(1) may be transferred to any office or other authority of the Federal Government which is not directly responsible to the Commissioner;

(2) may be used for any program or activity which is not specifically authorized by this title; or

(3) may be combined with funds appropriated under any other Act if the purpose of combining funds is to make a single discretionary grant or a single discretionary payment, unless such funds appropriated under this ti-

tle are separately identified in such grant or payment and are used for the purposes of this title.

3. Paragraph (3) inapplicable to any grant or payment made before Oct. 9, 1984, per Sec. 803(b)(3), P. L. 98–459.

Payments of Grants

Sec. 432. (a) To the extent the Commissioner deems it appropriate, the Commissioner shall require the recipient of any grant or contract under this title to contribute money, facilities, or services for carrying out the project for which such grant or contract was made.

(b) Payments under this title pursuant to a grant or contract may be made (after necessary adjustment, in the case of grants, on account of previously made overpayments or underpayments) in advance or by way of reimbursement, and in such installments and on such conditions, as the Commissioner may determine.

(c) The Commissioner shall make no grant or contract under this title in any State which has established or designated a State agency for purposes of title III unless the Commissioner

(1) consults with the State agency prior to issuing the grant or contract; and

(2) informs the State agency of the purposes of the grant or contract when the grant or contract is issued.

Responsibilities of Commissioner

Sec. 433. (a) The Commissioner shall be responsible for the administration, implementation, and making of grants and contracts under this title and shall not delegate authority under this title to any other individual, agency, or organization.

(b)(1) Not later than January 1 following each fiscal year, the Commissioner shall submit, to the Speaker of the House of Representatives and the President pro tempore of the Senate, a report for such fiscal year that describes each project and each program—

(A) for which funds were provided under this title; and

(B) that was completed in the fiscal year for which such report is prepared.

(2) Such report shall contain—

(A) the name or descriptive title of each project or program;

(B) the name and address of the individual or governmental entity that conducted such project or program;

(C) a specification of the period throughout which such project or program was conducted;

(D) the identity of each source of funds expended to carry out such project or program and the amount of funds provided by each such source;

(E) an abstract describing the nature and operation of such project or program; and

(F) a bibliography identifying all published information relating to such project or program; and

(c)(1) The Commissioner shall establish by regulation and implement a process to evaluate the results of projects and programs carried out under this title.

(2) The Commissioner shall—

(A) make available to the public each evaluation carried out under paragraph (1); and

(B) use such evaluation to improve services delivered, or the operation of projects and programs carried out, under this Act.

TITLE V—COMMUNITY SERVICE EMPLOYMENT FOR OLDER AMERICANS

Sec. 501. This title may be cited as the "Older American Community Service Employment Act".

Older American Community Service Employment Program

Sec. 502. (a) In order to foster and promote useful part-time opportunities in community service activities for unemployed low-income persons who are fifty-five years old or older *and who have poor employment prospects* the Secretary of Labor (hereinafter in this title referred to as the "Secretary") is authorized to establish an older American community service employment program.

(b)(1) In order to carry out the provisions of this title, the Secretary is authorized to enter into agreements with public or private nonprofit agencies or organizations, including national organizations, agencies of a State government or a political subdivision of a State (having elected or duly appointed governing officials), or a combination of such political subdivisions, or tribal organizations in order to further the purposes and goals of the program. Such agreements may include provisions for the payment of costs, as provided in subsection (c), of projects developed by such organizations and agencies in cooperation with the Secretary toward the cost of any project established or administered by any such organization or agency unless the Secretary determines that such project—

(A) will provide employment only for eligible individuals, except for necessary technical, administrative, and supervisory personnel, but such personnel shall, to the fullest extent possible, be recruited from among eligible individuals;

(B) will provide employment for eligible individuals in the community in which such individuals reside, or in nearby communities;

(C) will employ eligible individuals in services related to publicly owned and operated facilities projects, or projects sponsored by organizations, other than political parties, exempt from taxation under the provisions of section 501(c)(3) of the Internal Review Code of 1954, except projects involving the construction, operation, or maintenance of any facility used or to be used as a place for sectarian religious instruction or worship;

(D) will contribute to the general welfare of the community;

(E) will provide employment for eligible individuals;

(F)(i) will result in an increase in employment opportunities over those opportunities which would otherwise be available; (ii) will not result in the displacement of currently employed workers (including partial displacement, such as a reduction in the hours of non-overtime work or wages or employment benefits); and (iii) will not impair existing contracts or results in the substitution of Federal funds for other funds in connection with work that would otherwise be performed;

(G) will not employ or continue to employ any eligible individual to perform work the same or substantially the same as that performed by any other person who is on layoff;

(H) will utilize methods of recruitment and selection (including listing of job vacancies with the employment agency operated by any State or political subdivision thereof) which will assure that the maximum number of eligible individuals will have an opportunity to participate in the project;

(I) will include such training as may be necessary to make the most effective use of the skills and talents of those individuals who are participating, and will provide for the payment of the reasonable subsistence allowance;

(J) will assure that safe and healthy conditions of work will be provided, and will assure that persons employed in community service jobs assisted under this title shall be paid wages which shall not be lower than whichever is the highest of (i) the minimum wage which would be applicable to the employee under the Fair Labor Standards Act of 1938, if section 6(a)(1) of such Act applied to the participant and if the participant were not exempt under section 13 thereof, (ii) the State or local minimum wage for the most nearly comparable covered employment, or (iii) the prevailing rates of pay for persons employed in similar public occupations by the same employer;

(K) will be established or administered with the advice of persons competent in the field of service in which employment is being provided, and of persons who are knowledgeable with regard to the needs of older persons;

(L) will authorize pay for necessary transportation costs of eligible individuals which may be incurred in employment in any project funded under this title, in accordance with regulations promulgated by the Secretary;

(M) will assure, that to the extent feasible, such project will serve the needs of minority, limited English-speaking, and Indian eligible individuals who have greatest economic need, at least in proportion to their numbers in the State and take into consideration their rates of poverty and unemployment;

(N)(i) will prepare an assessment of—

(I) the participants' skills and talents;

(II) their need for supportive services; and

(III) their physical capabilities; except to the extent such project has, for the particular participant involved, an assessment of such skills and talents, such need, or such capabilities prepared recently pursuant to another em-

ployment or training program (such as a program under the Job Training Partnership Act (29 U.S.C. 1501 et seq.) or the Carl D. Perkins Vocational and Applied Technology Education Act (20 U.S.C. 2301 et seq.));

(ii) will provide to eligible individuals training and employment counseling based on strategies that identify appropriate employment objectives and the need for supportive services, developed as a result of the assessment provided for in clause (i); and

(iii) will provide counseling to participants on their progress in meeting such objectives and satisfying their need for supportive services;

(O) will authorize funds to be used, to the extent feasible, to include individuals participating in such project under any State unemployment insurance plan; and

(P) will post in such project work place a notice, and will make available to each person associated with such project a written explanation, clarifying the law with respect to allowable and unallowable political activities under chapter 15 of title 5, United States Code applicable to the project and to each category of individuals associated with such project and containing the address and telephone number of the Inspector General of the Department of Labor, to whom questions regarding the application of such chapter may be addressed.

(2) The Secretary is authorized to establish, issue, and amend such regulations as may be necessary to effectively carry out the provisions of this title.

(3) The Secretary shall develop alternatives for innovative work modes and provide technical assistance in creating job opportunities through work sharing and other experimental methods to prime sponsors, labor organizations, groups representing business and industry and workers as well as to individual employers, where appropriate.

(4) The Secretary may enter into an agreement with the Administrator of the Environmental Protection Agency to establish a Senior Environmental Employment Corps.

(c)(1) The Secretary is authorized to pay not to exceed 90 per cent of the cost of any project which is the subject of an agreement entered into under subsection (b), except that the Secretary is authorized to pay all of the costs of any such project which is (A) an emergency or disaster project, or (B) a project located in an economically depressed area, as determined by the Secretary in consultation with the Secretary of Commerce and the Director of the Office of Community Services of the Department of Health and Human Services.

(2) The non-Federal share shall be in cash or in kind. In determining the amount of the non-Federal share, the Secretary is authorized to attribute fair market value to services and facilities contributed from non-Federal sources.

(3) Of the amount for any project to be paid by the Secretary under this subsection, not more than 13.5 percent for fiscal year 1987 and each fiscal year thereafter shall be available for paying the costs of administration for such project, except that—

(A) whenever the Secretary determines that it is necessary to carry out the project assisted under this title, based on information submitted by the public or private nonprofit agency or organization with which the Secretary has an agreement under subsection (b), the Secretary may increase the amount available for paying the cost of administration to an amount not more than 15 percent of the cost of such project; and

(B) whenever the public or private nonprofit agency or organization with which the Secretary has an agreement under subsection (b) demonstrates to the Secretary that—

(i) major administrative cost increases are being incurred in necessary program components, including liability insurance, payments for workers' compensation, costs associated with achieving unsubsidized placement goals, and other operation requirements imposed by the Secretary;

(ii) the number of employment positions in the project will decline if the amount available for paying the cost of administration is not increased; or

(iii) the size of the project is so small that the amount of administrative expenses incurred to carry out the project necessarily exceed 13.5 percent of the amount for such project; the Secretary shall increase the amount available for the fiscal year for paying the cost of administration to an amount not more than 15 percent of the cost of such project.

(d)(1) Whenever a national organization or other program sponsor conducts a project *within a planning and service area in a State such organization or program sponsor shall conduct such project in consultation with the area agency on aging of the planning and service area and shall submit to the State agency and the area agency on aging* a description of such project to be conducted in the State, including the location of the project, 30 days prior to undertaking the project, for review and comment according to guidelines the Secretary shall issue to assure efficient and effective coordination of programs under this title.

(2) The Secretary shall review on his own initiative or at the request of any public or private nonprofit agency or organization, or an agency of the State government, the distribution of programs under this title within the State including the distribution between urban and rural areas within the State. For each proposed reallocation of programs within a State, the Secretary shall give notice and opportunity for a hearing on the record by all interested individuals and make a written determination of his findings and decision.

(e)(1) The Secretary, in addition to any other authority contained in this title, shall conduct experimental projects designed to assure second career training and the placement of eligible individuals in employment opportunities with private business concerns. The Secretary shall enter into such agreements with States, public agencies, nonprofit private organizations and private business concerns as may be necessary to conduct the experimental projects authorized by this subsection. The Secretary, from amounts reserved under section 506*(a)(2)(A)* in any fiscal year, may pay all of the costs of any agreements entered into under the provisions of this subsection. The Secretary shall, to the extent feasible, assure equitable geographic distribution of projects authorized by this subsection.

(2) *The Secretary shall issue and amend from time to time* criteria de-

signed to assure that agreements entered into under paragraph (1) of this subsection—

(A) will involve different kinds of work modes, such as flextime, job sharing, and other arrangements relating to reduced physical exertion;

(B) will emphasize projects involving second careers and job placement and give consideration to placement in growth industries and in jobs reflecting new technological skills and;

(C) require the coordination of projects carried out under such agreements, with the programs carried out under section 124 of the Job Training Partnership Act (29 U.S.C. 1534).

(3)(A) The Secretary shall carry out an evaluation of the second career training job placement projects authorized by this subsection.

(B) The evaluation shall include but not be limited to the projects described in paragraph (2).

(C) The Secretary shall prepare and submit, not later than one year after the enactment of the Older Americans Act Amendments of 1981, to the Congress an interim report describing the agreements entered into under paragraph (1) and the design for the evaluation required by this paragraph. The Secretary shall prepare and submit to the President and the Congress a final report on the evaluation required by this paragraph not later than February 1, 1984, together with his findings and such recommendations, including recommendations for additional legislation, as the Secretary deems appropriate.

(D) The Secretary shall make the final report submitted under subparagraph (C) available to interested private business concerns.

(4) For the purpose of this subsection, "eligible individual" means any individual who is 55 years of age or older and who has an income equal to or less than the intermediate level retired couples budget as determined annually by the Bureau of Labor Statistics.

Administration

Sec. 503. (a)*(1)* In order to effectively carry out the provisions of this title, the Secretary shall, through the Commissioner of the Administration consult with the State agency and the appropriate area agencies on aging established under section 305(a)(2) with regard to—

(A) the localities in which community service projects of the type authorized by this title are most needed;

(B) consideration of the employment situations and the type of skills possessed by available local individuals who are eligible to participate; and

(C) potential projects and the number and percentage of eligible individuals in the local population.

(2) The Secretary of Labor and the Commissioner shall coordinate the programs under this title and the programs under titles III, IV, and VI to increase job opportunities available to older individuals.

(b)(1) *The Secretary shall* coordinate the program assisted under this title with programs authorized under the Job Training Partnership Act, the Community Services Block Grant Act, and the Vocational Educational Act of 1984. *The Secretary shall coordinate the administration of titles III, IV, and VI by the Commissioner, to increase the likelihood that eligible individuals for whom employment opportunities under this title are available and who need services under such titles receive such services.* Appropriations under this Act may not be used to carry out any program under the Job Training Partnership Act, the Community Services Block Grant Act, or the Vocational Education Act of 1984.

(2) The Secretary shall distribute to grantees under this title, for distribution to program enrolles, and at no cost to grantees or enrolles, informational materials developed and supplied by the Equal Employment Opportunity Commission and other appropriate Federal agencies which the Secretary determines are designed to help enrolles identify age discrimination and understand their rights under the Age Discrimination in Employment Act of 1967.

(c) In carrying out the provisions of this title, the Secretary is authorized to use, with their consent, the services, equipment, personnel, and facilities of Federal and other agencies with or without reimbursement, and on a similar basis to cooperate with other public and private agencies and instrumentalities in the use of services, equipment, and facilities.

(d) Payments under this title may be made in advance or by way of reimbursement and in such installments as the Secretary may determine.

(e) The Secretary shall not delegate any function of the Secretary under this title to any other department or agency of the Federal Government.

(f) In carrying out the provisions of this title, the Secretary may fund and expand projects concerning the Senior Environmental Employment Corps and energy conservation from sums appropriated under section 508 for such fiscal year. *The preceding sentence shall not be construed to prohibit carrying out projects under this title jointly with programs, projects, or activities under any Act specified in such sentence.*

Participants Not Federal Employees

Sec. 504. (a) Eligible individuals who are employed in any project funded this title shall not be considered to be Federal employees as a result of such employment and shall not be subject to the provisions of part III of title 5, United States Code.

(b) No contract shall be entered into under this title with a contractor who is, or whose employees are, under State law, exempted from operation of the State workmen's compensation law, generally applicable to employees, unless the contractor shall undertake to provide either through insurance by a recognized carrier, or by self-insurance, as authorized by State law, that the persons employed under the contract shall enjoy workmen's compensation coverage equal to that provided by law for covered employment.

Interagency Cooperation

Sec. 505. (a) The Secretary shall consult with and obtain the written views of *the Commission* prior to the establishment of rules or the establishment of general policy in the administration of this title.

(b) The Secretary shall consult and cooperate with the Director of the

Office of Community Services, the Secretary of Health and Human Services, and the heads of other Federal agencies carrying out related programs, in order to achieve optimal coordination with such other programs. In carrying out the provisions of this section, the Secretary shall promote programs or projects of a similar nature. Each Federal agency shall cooperate with the Secretary in disseminating information relating to the availability of assistance under this title and in promoting the identification and interests of individuals eligible for employment in projects assisted under this title.

(c) In administering projects under this title concerning the Senior Environmental Employment Corps and energy conservation, the Secretary shall consult with the Administrator of the Environmental Protection Agency and the Secretary of Energy and shall enter into an agreement with the Administrator and the Secretary of Energy to coordinate programs conducted by them with such projects.

(d)(1) The Secretary shall promote and coordinate carrying out projects under this title jointly with programs, projects, or activities under other Acts that provide training and employment opportunities to eligible individuals.

(2) The Secretary shall consult with the Secretary of Education to promote and coordinate carrying out projects under this title jointly with employment and training programs in which eligible individuals may participate that are carried out under the Carl D. Perkins Vocational and Applied Technology Education Act (20 U.S.C. 2301 et seq.).

Equitable Distribution of Assistance

Sec. 506. (a)(1)(A) Subject to subparagraph (B) and paragraph (2), from sums appropriated under this title for each fiscal year, the Secretary shall first reserve such sums as may be necessary for national grants or contracts with public agencies and public or nonprofit private organizations to maintain the level of activities carried on under such grants or contracts at least at the level of such activities supported under this title and under any other provision of Federal law relating to community service employment programs for older Americans in fiscal year 1978.

(B)(i)(I) For each fiscal year in which the sums appropriated under this title exceed the amount appropriated under this title for fiscal year 1978, the Secretary shall reserve not more than 45 percent of such excess, except as provided in subclause (II), to carry out clauses (ii), (iii), and (v).

(II) The Secretary shall reserve a sum sufficient to carry out clauses (iii) and (v).

(III) The Secretary in awarding grants and contracts under this paragraph from the sum reserved under this paragraph shall, to the extent feasible, assure an equitable distribution of activities under such grants and contracts designed to achieve the allotment among the States described in paragraph (3) of this subsection.

(ii) The Secretary shall reserve such sums as may be necessary for national grants or contracts with public or nonprofit national Indian aging organizations with the ability to provide employment services to older Indians and with national public or nonprofit Pacific Island and Asian American ag-

ing organizations with the ability to provide employment services to older Pacific Island and Asian Americans.

(iii) If the amount appropriated under this title for a fiscal year exceeds 102 percent oft he amount appropriated under this title for fiscal year 1991, for each fiscal year described in clause (iv), the Secretary shall reserve for recipients of national grants and contracts under this paragraph such portion of the excess amount as the Secretary determines to be appropriate and is—

(I) at least 25 percent of the excess amount; or

(II) the portion required to increase the amount made available under this paragraph to each of the recipients so that the amount equals 1.3 percent of the amount appropriated under this title for fiscal year 1991.

(iv) From the portion reserved under clause (iii), the Secretary shall increase the amount made available under this paragraph to each of the recipients—

(I) for each fiscal year before the fiscal year described in subclause (II), so that such amount equals, or more closely approaches, such 1.3 percent; and

(II) for the first fiscal year for which the portion is sufficient to make available under this paragraph to each of the recipients the amount equal to such 1.3 percent, so that such amount is not less than such 1.3 percent.

(v) For each fiscal year after the fiscal year described in clause (iv)(II), the Secretary shall make available under this paragraph to each of the recipients an amount not less than such 1.3 percent.

(C) Preference in awarding grants and contracts under this paragraph shall be given to national organizations, and agencies, of proven ability in providing employment services to eligible individuals under this program and similar programs. The Secretary, in awarding grants and contracts under this section, shall, to the extent feasible, assure an equitable distribution of activities under such grants and contracts, in the aggregate, among the States, taking into account the needs of underserved States, subject to subparagraph (B)(i)(III).

(2)(A) From sums appropriated under this title for each fiscal year after September 30, 1978, the Secretary shall reserve an amount which is at least 1 percent and not more than 3 percent of the amount appropriated in excess of the amount appropriated for fiscal year 1978 for the purpose of entering into agreements under section 502(e), relating to improved transition to private employment.

(B) After the Secretary makes the reservations required by paragraph (1)(B) and subparagraph (A), the remainder of such excess shall be allotted to the appropriate public agency of each State pursuant to paragraph (3).

(3) The Secretary shall allot to the State agency on aging on each State the remainder of the sums appropriated for any fiscal year under section 508 so that each State will receive an amount which bears the same ratio to such remainder as the product of the number of persons aged fifty-five or over in the State and the allotment percentage of such State bears to the sum of the corresponding product for all States, except that (A) no State shall be allotted less than one-half of 1 percent of the remainder of the sums appropriated for the fiscal year for which the determination is made, or $100,000, whichever is greater, and (B) Guam, American Samoa, the Com-

monwealth of the Northern Mariana Islands, the Virgin Islands, and the Trust Territory of the Pacific Islands shall each be allotted an amount which is not less than one-fourth of 1 per centum of the remainder of the sums appropriated for the fiscal year for which the determination is made, or $50,000, whichever is greater. For the purpose of the exception contained in this paragraph the term "State" does not include Guam, American Samoa, the Commonwealth of the Northern Mariana Islands, the Virgin Islands, and the Trust Territory of the Pacific Islands.

(4) For the purpose of this subsection—

(A) the allotment percentage of each State shall be 100 percent less that percentage which bears the same ratio to 50 percentum as the per capita income of such State bears to the per capita income of the United States, except that (i) the allotment percentage shall in no case be more than 75 per centum or less than 33 1/3 per centum, and (ii) the allotment percentage for the District of Columbia, the Commonwealth of Puerto Rico, Guam, the Virgin Islands, American Samoa, the Commonwealth of the Northern Mariana Islands, and the Trust Territory of the Pacific Islands shall be 75 percent;

(B) the number of persons aged fifty-five or over in any State and in all States, and the per capita income in any State and in all States, shall be determined by the Secretary on the basis of the most satisfactory data available to *the Secretary*, and

(C) for the purpose of determining the allotment percentage, the term "United States" means the fifty States and the District of Columbia.

(b) The amount allotted for projects within any State under subsection (a) for any fiscal year which the Secretary determines will not be required for such year shall be reallotted, from time to time and on such dates during such year as the Secretary may fix, to projects within other States in proportion to the original allotments to projects within such States under subsection (a) for such year, but with such proportionate amount for any of such other States being reduced to the extent it exceeds the sum the Secretary estimates that projects within such State need and will be able to use for such year; and the total of such reductions shall be similarly reallotted among the States whose proportionate amounts were not so reduced. Any amount reallotted to a State under this subsection during a year shall be deemed part of its allotment under subsection (a) for such year.

(c) The amount apportioned for projects within each State under subsection (a) shall be apportioned among areas within each such State in an equitable manner, taking into consideration (1) the proportion which eligible individuals in each such area bears to the total number of such individuals, respectively, in that State, (2) the relative distribution of such individuals residing in rural and urban areas within the State, *and (3) the relative distribution of (A) such individuals who are individuals with greatest economic need, (B) such individuals who are minority individuals, and (C) such individuals who are individuals with greatest social need.*

(d) The Secretary shall require the State agency for each State receiving funds under this title to report at the beginning of each fiscal year on such State's compliance with subsection (c). Such report shall include the names and geographic location of all projects assisted under this title and carried out in the State and the amount allotted to each such project.

Definitions

Sec. 507. As used in this title—

(1) the term "eligible individual" means an individual who is fifty-five years old or older, who has a low income (including any such individual whose income is not more than 125 percent of the *poverty line*, except that, pursuant to regulations prescribed by the Secretary, any such individual who is sixty years old or older shall have priority for the work opportunities provided for under this title;

(2) the term "community service" means social, health, welfare, and educational services (particularly literacy tutoring), legal and other counseling services and assistance, including tax counseling and assistance and financial counseling, and library, recreational, and other similar services; conservation, maintenance, or restoration of natural resources; community betterment or beautification; antipollution and environmental quality efforts, weatherization activities; economic development; and such other services essential and necessary to the community as the Secretary, by regulation, may prescribe:

(3) the term "program" means the older American community service employment program established under this title

(4) the term 'Pacific Island and Asian Americans' means Americans having origins in any of the original peoples of the Far East, Southeast Asia, the Indian Subcontinent, or the Pacific Islands.

Authorization of Appropriations

Sec. 508. (a) There is authorized to be appropriated to carry out this title—

(1) $470,671,000 for fiscal year 1992, ad such sums as may be necessary for years 1993, 1994, and 1995; and

(2) such additional sums as may be necessary for each such fiscal year to enable the Secretary, through programs under this title, to provide for at least 70,000 part-time employment positions for eligible individuals. For purposes of paragraph (2), "part-time employment position" means an employment position within a workweek of at least 20 hours.

(b) Amounts appropriated under this section for any fiscal year shall be used during the annual period which begins on July 1 of the calendar year immediately following the beginning of such fiscal year and which ends on June 30 of the following calendar year. The Secretary may extend the period during which such amounts may be obligated or expended in the case of a particular organization or agency receiving funds under this title if the Secretary determines that such extension is necessary to ensure the effective use of such funds by such organization or agency. Any such extension shall be for a period of not more than 60 days after the end of such annual period.

Employment Assistance and Federal Housing and Food Stamp Programs

Sec. 509. Funds received by eligible individuals from projects carried out under the program established in this title shall not be considered to be income of such individuals for purposes of determining the eligibility of such individuals, or of any other persons, to participate in any housing program for which Federal funds may be available or for any income determination under the Food Stamp Act of 1977.

The 1987 Amendments Deleted the Text of Title VI in its entirely and substituted the following:

SEC. 510. DUAL ELIGIBILITY.

In the case of projects under this title carried out jointly with programs carried out under the Job Training Partnership Act, eligible individuals shall be deemed to satisfy the requirements of section 203 of such Act (29 U.S.C. 1603) that are applicable to adults.

SEC. 511. TREATMENT OF ASSISTANCE.

Assistance furnished under this title shall not be construed to be financial assistance described in section 245(A)(h)(1)(A) of the Immigration and Nationality Act (8 U.S.C. 1255a(h)(1)(A)).

TITLE VI—GRANTS FOR NATIVE AMERICANS

Statement of Purpose

Sec. 601. It is the purpose of this title to promote the delivery of supportive services, including nutrition services to American Indians, Alaskan Natives, and Native Hawaiians that are comparable to services provided under title III.

Sense of Congress

Sec. 602. It is the sense of the Congress that older Indians, older Alaskan Natives, and older Native Hawaiians are a vital resource entitled to all benefits and services available and that such services and benefits should be provided in a manner that preserves and restores their respective dignity, self-respect, and cultural identities.

Part A—Indian Program

Findings

Sec. 611. (a) The Congress finds that the older Indians of the United States—

(1) are a rapidly increasing population;

(2) suffer from high unemployment;

(3) live in poverty at a rate estimated to be as high as 61 percent;

(4) have a life expectancy between 3 and 4 years less than the general population;

(5) lack sufficient nursing homes, other long-term care facilities, and other health care facilities;

(6) lack sufficient Indian area agencies on aging;

(7) frequently live in substandard and over-crowded housing;

(8) receive less than adequate health care;

(9) are served under this title at a rate of less than 19 percent of the total national Indian elderly population living on Indian reservations; and

(10) are served under title III at a rate of less than 1 percent of the total participants under that title.

Eligibility

Sec. 612. (a) A tribal organization of an Indian tribe is eligible for assistance under this part only if—

(1) the tribal organization represents at least 50 individuals who are 60 years of age or older; and

(2) the tribal organization demonstrates the ability to deliver supportive services, including nutritional services.

(b) For the purposes of this part, the terms 'Indian tribe' and 'tribal organization' have the same meaning as in section 4 of the Indian Self-Determination and Education Assistance Act (25 U.S.C. 450b).

Grants Authorized

Sec. 613. The Commissioner may make grants to eligible tribal organizations to pay all of the costs for delivery of supportive services and nutrition services for older Indians.

Applications

Sec. 614. (a) No grant may be made under this part unless the eligible tribal organization submits an application to the Commissioner which meets such criteria as the Commissioner may by regulation prescribe. Each such application shall—

(1) provide that the eligible tribal organization will evaluate the need for supportive and nutrition services among older Indians to be represented by the tribal organization;

(2) provide for the use of such methods of administration as are necessary for the proper and efficient administration of the program to be assisted;

(3) provide that the tribal organization will make such reports in such form and containing such information, as the Commissioner may reasonably require, and comply with such requirements as the Commissioner may impose to assure the correctness of such reports;

(4) provide for periodic evaluation of activities and projects carried out under the application;

(5) establish objectives consistent with the purposes of this part toward which activities under the application will be directed, identify obstacles to the attainment of such objectives, and indicate the manner in which the tribal organization proposes to overcome such obstacles;

(6) provide for establishing and maintaining information and assistance services to assure that older Indians to be served by the assistance made available under this part will have reasonably convenient access to such services;

(7) provide a preference for Indians aged 60 and older for full or part-time staff positions wherever feasible;

(8) provide assurances that either directly or by way of grant or contract with appropriate entities nutrition services will be delivered to older Indians represented by the tribal organization substantially in compliance with the provisions of part C of title III, except that in any case in which the need for nutritional services for older Indians represented by the tribal organization is already met from other sources, the tribal organization may use the funds otherwise required to be expended under this clause for supportive services;

(9) contain assurances that the provisions of sections 307(a)(14)(A) (i) and (iii), 307(a)(14)(B), and 307(a)(14)(C) will be complied with whenever the application contains provisions for the acquisition, alteration, or renovation of facilities to serve as multipurpose senior centers;

(10) provide that any legal or ombudsman services made available to older Indians represented by the tribal organization will be substantially in compliance with the provisions of title III relating to the furnishing of similar services;

(11) provide satisfactory assurance that fiscal control and fund accounting procedures will be adopted as may be necessary to assure proper disbursement of, and accounting for, Federal funds paid under this part to the tribal organization, including any funds paid by the tribal organization to a recipient of a grant or contract, and;

(b) For the purpose of any application submitted under this part, the tribal organization may develop its own population statistics, with certification from the Bureau of Indian Affairs, in order to establish eligibility.

(c) The Commission(sic) shall approve any application which complies with the provisions of subsection (a).

(d) Whenever the Commissioner determines not to approve an application submitted under subsection (a) the Commission(sic) shall—

(1) state objections in writing to the tribal organization within 60 days after such decision;

(2) provide to the extent practicable technical assistance to the tribal organization to overcome such stated objections; and

(3) provide the tribal organization with a hearing, under such rules and regulations as the Commissioner may prescribe.

(e) Whenever the Commissioner approves an application of a tribal organization under this part, funds shall be awarded for not less than 12 months.

(12) contain assurances that the tribal organization will coordinate services provided under this part with services provided under title III in the same geographical area.

SEC. 614A. DISTRIBUTION OF FUNDS AMONG TRIBAL ORGANIZATIONS.

(a) MAINTENANCE OF 1991 AMOUNTS.—Subject to the availability of appropriations to carry out this part, the amount of the grant (if any) made under this part to a tribal organization for fiscal year 1992 and for each subsequent fiscal year shall be not less than the amount of the grant made under this part to the tribal organization for fiscal year 1991.

(B) USE OF ADDITIONAL AMOUNTS APPROPRIATED.—If the funds appropriated to carry out this part in a fiscal year subsequent to fiscal year 1991 exceed the funds appropriated to carry out this part in fiscal year 1991, then the amount of the grant (if any) made under this part to a tribal organization for the subsequent fiscal year shall be—

(1) increased by such amount as the Commissioner considers to be appropriate, in addition to the amount of any increase required by subsection (a), so that the grant equals or more closely approaches the amount of the grant made under this part to the tribal organization for fiscal year 1980; or

(2) an amount the Commissioner considers to be sufficient if the tribal organization did not receive a grant under this part for either fiscal year 1980 or fiscal year 1991.

Surplus Educational Facilities

Sec. 615. (a) Notwithstanding any other provision of law, the Secretary of the Interior through the Bureau of Indian Affairs shall make available surplus Indian educational facilities to tribal organizations, and nonprofit organizations with tribal approval, for use as multipurpose senior centers. Such centers may be altered so as to provide extended care facilities, community center facilities, nutrition services, child care services, and other supportive services.

(b) Each eligible tribal organization desiring to take advantage of such surplus facilities shall submit an application to the Secretary of the Interior at such time and in such manner, and containing or accompanied by such information, as the Secretary of the Interior determines to be necessary to carry out the provisions of this section.

Part B—Native Hawaiian Program

Findings

Sec. 621. The Congress finds the older Native Hawaiians—

(1) have a life expectancy 10 years less than any other ethnic group in the State of Hawaii;

(2) rank lowest on 9 of 11 standard health indices for all ethnic groups in Hawaii;

(3) are often unaware of social services and do not know how to go about seeking such assistance; and

(4) live in poverty at a rate of 34 percent.

Eligibility

Sec. 622. A public or private nonprofit organization having the capacity to provide services under this part for Hawaiian Natives is eligible for assistance under this part only if—

(1) the organization will serve at least 50 individuals who have attained 60 years of age or older; and

(2 the organization demonstrates the ability to deliver supportive services, including nutrition services.

Grants Authorized

Sec. 623. The Commissioner may make grants to public and nonprofit private organizations to pay all the costs for the delivery of supportive services and nutrition services to older Native Hawaiians.

Application

Sec. 624. (a) No grant may be made under this part unless the public or nonprofit private organization submits an application to the Commissioner which meets such criteria as the Commissioner may by regulation prescribe. Each such application shall—

(1 provide that the organization will evaluate the need for supportive and nutrition services among older Native Hawaiians to be represented by the organization;

(2) provide for the use of such methods of administration as are necessary for the proper and efficient administration of the program to be assisted;

(3) provide assurance that the organization will coordinate its activities with the State agency on aging *and with the activities carried out under title III in the same geographical area;*

(4) provide that the organization will make such reports in such form and containing such information as the Commissioner may reasonably require, and comply with such requirements as the Commissioner may impose to ensure the correctness of such reports;

(5) provide for periodic evaluation of activities and projects carried out under the application;

(6) establish objectives, consistent with the purpose of this title, toward which activities described in the application will be directed, identify obstacles to the attainment of such objectives, and indicate the manner in which the organization proposes to overcome such obstacles;

(7) provide for establishing and maintaining information *and assistance* services to assure that older Native Hawaiians to be served by the assistance made available under this part will have reasonably convenient access to such services;

(8) provide a preference for Native Hawaiians age 60 and older for full or part-time staff positions wherever feasible;

(9) provide that any legal or ombudsman services made available to older Native Hawaiians represented by the nonprofit private organization will be substantially in compliance with the provisions of title III relating to the furnishing and similar service; and

(10) provide satisfactory assurances that the fiscal control and fund accounting procedures will be adopted as may be necessary to assure proper disbursement of, and accounting for, Federal funds paid under this part to the nonprofit private organization, including any funds paid by the organization to a recipient of a grant or contract.

(b) The Commissioner shall approve any application which complies with the provisions of subsection (a).

(c) Whenever the Commissioner determines not to approve an application submitted under subsection (a) the Commissioner shall—

(1) state objections in writing to the nonprofit private organizations within 60 days after such decision;

(2) provide to the extent practicable technical assistance to the nonprofit private organization to overcome such stated objections; and

(3) provide the organization with a hearing under such rules and regulations as the Commissioner may prescribe.

(d) Whenever the Commissioner approves an application of a nonprofit private or public organization under this part funds shall be awarded for not less than 12 months.

SEC. 624A. DISTRIBUTION OF FUNDS AMONG ORGANIZATIONS.

Subject to the availability of appropriations to carry out this part, the amount of the grant (if any) made under this part to an organization for fiscal year 1992 and for each subsequent fiscal year shall be not less than the amount of the grant made under this part to the organization for fiscal year 1991.

Definition

Sec. 625. For the purposes of this part, the term 'Hawaiian Native' means any individual any of whose ancestors were natives of the area which consists of the Hawaiian Islands prior to 1778.

Part C—General Provisions

Administration

Sec. 631. In establishing regulations for the purpose of part A the Commissioner shall consult with the Secretary of the Interior.

Payments

Sec. 632. Payments may be made under this title (after necessary adjustments, in the case of grants, on account of previously made overpayments

or underpayments) in advance or by way of reimbursement in such installments and on such conditions, as the Commissioner may determine.

Authorization of Appropriations

Sec. 633 (a) *There are authorized to be appropriated $30,000,000 for fiscal
year 1992 and such sums as may be necessary for fiscal years 1993, 1994, and
1995, to carry out this title (other than section 615).*

*(b) Of the amount appropriated under subsection (a) for each fiscal
year—*

(1) 90 percent shall be available to carry out part A; and

(2) 10 percent shall be available to carry out part B.

TITLE VII—ALLOTMENTS FOR VULNERABLE ELDER RIGHTS PROTECTION ACTIVITIES

Subtitle A—State Provisions

CHAPTER 1—GENERAL STATE PROVISIONS

SEC. 701. ESTABLISHMENT.

*The Commissioner, acting through the Administration, shall establish
and carry out a program for making allotments to States to pay for the cost
of carrying out vulnerable elder rights protection activities.*

SEC. 703. AUTHORIZATION OF APPROPRIATIONS.

*(a) OMBUDSMAN PROGRAM.—There are authorized to be appropriated to
carry out chapter 2, $40,000,000 for fiscal year 1992 and such sums as may be
necessary for fiscal years 1993, 1994, and 1995.*

*(b) PREVENTION OF ELDER ABUSE, NEGLECT, AND EXPLOITATION.—There are au-
thorized to be appropriated to carry out chapter 3, $15,000,000 for fiscal year
1992 and such sums as may be necessary for fiscal years 1993, 1994, and
1995.*

*(c) STATE ELDER RIGHTS AND LEGAL ASSISTANCE DEVELOPMENT PROGRAM.—There
are authorized to be appropriated to carry out chapter 4, $10,000,000 for fis-
cal year 1992 and such sums as may be necessary for fiscal years 1993, 1994,
and 1995.*

*(d) OUTREACH, COUNSELING, AND ASSISTANCE PROGRAM.—There are autho-
rized to be appropriated to carry out chapter 5, $15,000,000 for fiscal year
1992 and such sums as may be necessary for fiscal years 1993, 1994, and
1995.*

SEC. 703. ALLOTMENT.

(a) IN GENERAL.—

(1) POPULATION.—In carrying out the program described in section 701, the Commissioner shall initially allot to each State, from the funds appropriated under section 702 for each fiscal year, an amount that bears the same ratio to the funds as the population of older individuals in the State bears to the population of older individuals in all States.

(2) MINIMUM ALLOTMENTS.—

(A) IN GENERAL.—After making the initial allotments described in paragraph (1), the Commissioner shall adjust the allotments on a pro rata basis in accordance with subparagraphs (B) and (C).

(B) GENERAL MINIMUM ALLOTMENTS.—

(i) MINIMUM ALLOTMENT FOR STATES.—No State shall be allotted less than one-half of 1 percent of the funds appropriated under section 702 for the fiscal year for which the determination is made.

(ii) MINIMUM ALLOTMENT FOR TERRITORIES.—Guam, the United States Virgin Islands, and the Trust Territory of the Pacific Islands, shall each be allotted not less than one-fourth of 1 percent of the funds appropriated under section 702 for the fiscal year for which the determination is made. American Samoa and the Commonwealth of the Northern Mariana Islands shall each be allotted not less than one-sixteenth of 1 percent of the sum appropriated under section 702 for the fiscal year for which the determination is made.

(C) MINIMUM ALLOTMENTS FOR OMBUDSMAN AND ELDER ABUSE PROGRAMS.—

(1) OMBUDSMAN PROGRAM.—No State shall be allotted for a fiscal year, from the funds appropriated under section 702(a), less than the amount allotted to the State under section 304 in fiscal year 1991 to carry out the State Long-Term Care Ombudsman program under title III.

(ii) ELDER ABUSE PROGRAMS.—No State shall be allotted for a fiscal year, from the funds appropriated under section 702(b), less than the amount allotted to the State under section 304 in fiscal year 1991 to carry out programs with respect to the prevention of elder abuse, neglect, and exploitations under title III.

(D) DEFINITION.—For the purposes of this paragraph, the term 'State' does not include Guam, American Samoa, the United States Virgin Islands, the Trust Territory of the Pacific Islands, and the Commonwealth of the Northern Mariana Islands.

(b) REALLOTMENT.—

(1) IN GENERAL.—If the Commissioner determines that any amount allotted to a State for a fiscal year under this section will not be used by the State for carrying out the purpose for which the allotment was made, the Commissioner shall make the amount available to a State that the Commissioner determines will be able to use the amount for carrying out the purpose.

(2) AVAILABILITY.—Any amount made available to a State from an appropriation for a fiscal year in accordance with paragraph (1) shall, for purposes of this subtitle, be regarded as part of the allotment of the State (as determined under subsection (a)) for the year, but shall remain available until the end of the succeeding fiscal year.

(c) WITHHOLDING.—If the Commissioner finds that any State has failed to carry out this title in accordance with the assurances made and description provided under section 705, the Commissioner shall withhold the allotment of funds to the State. The Commissioner shall disburse the funds withheld directly to any public or nonprofit private institution or organization, agency, or political subdivision of the State submitting an approved plan containing the assurances and description.

SEC. 704. ORGANIZATION.

In order for a State to be eligible to receive allotments under this subtitle—

(1) the State shall demonstrate eligibility under section 305;

(2) the State agency designated by the State shall demonstrate compliance with the applicable requirements of section 305; and

(3) each area agency on aging designated by the State agency and participating in such a program shall demonstrate compliance with the applicable requirements of section 305.

SEC. 705. ADDITIONAL STATE PLAN REQUIREMENTS.

(a) ELIGIBILITY.—In order to be eligible to receive an allotment under this subtitle, a State shall include in the State plan submitted under section 307—

(1) an assurance that the State, in carrying out any chapter of this subtitle for which the State receives funding under this subtitle, will establish programs in accordance with the requirements of the chapter and this chapter;

(2) an assurance that the State will hold public hearings, and use other means, to obtain the view of older individuals, area agencies on aging, recipients of grants under title VI, and other interested persons and entities regarding programs carried out under this subtitle;

(3) an assurance that the State, in consultation with area agencies on aging, will identify and prioritize statewide activities aimed at ensuring that older individuals have access to, and assistance in securing and maintaining, benefits and rights;

(4) an assurance that the State will use funds made available under this subtitle for a chapter in addition to, and will not supplant, any funds that are expended under any Federal or State law in existence on the day before the date of the enactment of this subtitle, to carry out the vulnerable elder rights protection activities described in the chapter;

(5) an assurance that the State will place no restrictions, other than the requirements referred to in clauses (i) through (iv) of section 712(a)(5)(C), on the eligibility of entities for designation as local Ombudsman entities under section 712(a)(5);

(6) an assurance that, with respect to programs for the prevention of elder abuse, neglect, and exploitation under chapter 3—

(A) in carrying out such programs the State agency will conduct a program of services consistent with relevant State law and coordinated with existing State adult protective services activities for—

(i) public education to identify and prevent elder abuse;

(ii) receipt of reports of elder abuse;

(iii) active participation of older individuals participating in programs under this Act through outreach, conferences, and referral of such individuals to other social service agencies or sources of assistance if appropriate and if the individuals to be referred consent; and

(iv) referral of complaints to law enforcement or public protective service agencies if appropriate;

(B) the State will not permit involuntary or coerced participation in the program of services described in subparagraph (A) by alleged victims, abusers, or their households; and

(C) all information gathered in the course of receiving reports and making referrals shall remain confidential except—

(i) if all parties to such complaint consent in writing to the release of such information;

(ii) if the release of such information is to a law enforcement agency, public protective service agency, licensing or certification agency, ombudsman program, or protection or advocacy system; or

(iii) upon court order;

(7) an assurance that the State agency—

(A) from funds appropriated under section 702(d) for chapter 5, will make funds available to eligible area agencies on aging to carry out chapter 5 and, in distributing such funds among eligible area agencies, will give priority to area agencies on aging based on—

(i) the number of older individuals with greatest economic need, and older individuals with greatest social need, residing in their respective planning and service areas; and

(ii) the inadequacy in such areas of outreach activities and application assistance of the type specified in chapter 5;

(B) will require, as a condition of eligibility to receive funds to carry out chapter 5, an area agency on aging to submit an application that—

(i) describes the activities for which such funds are sought;

(ii) provides for an evaluation of such activities by the area agency on aging; and

(iii) includes assurances that the area agency on aging will prepare and submit to the State agency a report of the activities conducted with funds provided under this paragraph and the evaluation of such activities;

(C) will distribute to area agencies on aging—

(i) the eligibility information received under section 202(a)(20) from the Administration; and

(ii) information, in written form, explaining the requirements for eligibility to receive medical assistance under title XIX of the Social Security Act (42 U.S.C. 1396 et seq.); and

(D) will submit to the Commissioner a report on the evaluations required to be submitted under subparagraph (B); and

(8) a description of the manner in which the State agency will carry out

this title in accordance with the assurances described in paragraphs (1) through (7).

(b) PRIVILEGE.—Neither a State, nor a State agency, may require any provider of legal assistance under this subtitle to reveal any information that is protected by the attorney-client privilege.

SEC. 706. DEMONSTRATION PROJECTS.

(a) ESTABLISHMENT.—From amounts made available under section 304(d)(1)(C) after September 30, 1992, each State may provide for the establishment of at least one demonstration project, to be conducted by one or more area agencies on aging within the State, for outreach to older individuals with greatest economic need with respect to—

(1) benefits available under title XVI of the Social Security Act (42 U.S.C. 1381 et seq.) (or assistance under a State program established in accordance with such title);

(2) medical assistance available under title XIX of such Act (42 U.S.C. 1396 et seq.); and

(3) benefits available under the Food Stamp Act of 1977 (7 U.S.C. 2011 et seq.).

(b) BENEFITS.—Each outreach project carried out under subsection (a) shall—

(1) provide to older individuals with greatest economic need information and assistance regarding their eligibility to receive the benefits and assistance described in paragraphs (1) through (3) of subsection (a);

(2) be carried out in a planning and service area that has a high proportion of older individuals with greatest economic need, relative to the aggregate number of older individuals in such area; and

(3) be coordinated with State and local entities that administer benefits under such titles.

SEC. 708. OMBUDSMAN PROGRAMS.

Title VII of the Older Americans Act of 1965 (as added by section 701 of this Act) is amended by adding at the end the following:

CHAPTER 2—OMBUDSMAN PROGRAMS

SEC. 711. DEFINITIONS.

As used in this chapter:

(1) OFFICE.—The term 'Office' means the office established in section 712(a)(1)(A).

(2) OMBUDSMAN.—The term 'Ombudsman' means the individual described in section 712(a)(2).

(3) LOCAL OMBUDSMAN ENTITY.—The term 'local Ombudsman entity' means an entity designated under section 712(a)(5)(A) to carry out the duties described in section 712(a)(5)(B) with respect to a planning and service area or other substate area.

(4) PROGRAM.—The term 'program' means the State Long-Term Care Ombudsman program established in section 712(a)(1)(B).

(5) REPRESENTATIVE.—The term 'representative' includes an employee or volunteer who represents an entity designated under section 712(a)(5)(A) and who is individually designated by the Ombudsman.

(6) RESIDENT.—The term 'resident' means an older individual who resides in a long-term care facility.

SEC. 712. STATE LONG-TERM CARE OMBUDSMAN PROGRAM.

(a) ESTABLISHMENT.—

(1) IN GENERAL.—In order to be eligible to receive an allotment under section 703 from funds appropriated under section 702(a), a State agency shall, in accordance with this section—

(A) establish and operate an Office of the State Long-Term Care Ombudsman; and

(B) carry out through the Office a State Long-Term Care Ombudsman program.

(2) OMBUDSMAN.—The Office shall be headed by an individual, to be known as the State Long-Term Care Ombudsman, who shall be selected from among individuals with expertise and experience in the fields of long-term care and advocacy.

(3) FUNCTIONS.—The Ombudsman shall serve on a full-time basis, and shall, personally or through representatives of the Office—

(A) identify, investigate, and resolve complaints that—

(i) are made by, or on behalf of, residents; and

(ii) relate to action inaction, or decisions, that may adversely affect the health, safety, welfare, or rights of the residents (including the welfare and rights of the residents with respect to the appointment and activities of guardians and representative payees), of—

(I) providers, or representatives of providers, of long-term care services;

(II) public agencies; or

(III) health and social service agencies;

(B) provide services to assist the residents in protecting the health, safety, welfare, and rights of the residents;

(C) inform the residents about means of obtaining services provided by providers or agencies described in subparagraph (A)(ii) or services described in subparagraph (B);

(D) ensure that the residents have regular and timely access to the services provided through the Office and that the residents and complainants;

(E) represent the interests of the residents before governmental agencies and seek administrative, legal, and other remedies to protect the health, safety, welfare, and rights of the residents;

(F) provide administrative and technical assistance to entities designated under paragraph (5) to assist the entities in participating in the program;

(G)(i) analyze, comment on, and monitor the development and implementation of Federal, State, and local laws, regulations, and other governmental policies and actions, that pertain to the health, safety, welfare, and rights of the residents, with respect to the adequacy of long-term care facilities and services in the State;

(H) recommend any changes in such laws, regulations, policies, and actions as the Office determines to be appropriate; and

(iii) facilitate public comment on the laws, regulations, policies, and actions;

(H)(i) provide for training representatives of the Office;

(ii) promote the development of citizen organizations, to participate in the program; and

(III) provide technical support for the development of resident and family councils to protect the well-being and rights of residents; and

(l) carry out such other activities as the Commissioner determines to be appropriate.

(4) CONTRACTS AND ARRANGEMENTS.—

(A) IN GENERAL.—Except as provided in subparagraph (B), the State agency may establish and operate the Office, and carry out the program, directly, or by contract or other arrangement with any public agency or nonprofit private organization.

(B) LICENSING AND CERTIFICATION ORGANIZATIONS; ASSOCIATIONS.—The State agency may not enter into the contract or other arrangement described in subparagraph (A) with—

(i) an agency or organization that is responsible for licensing or certifying long-term care services in the State; or

(ii) an association (or an affiliate of such an association) of long-term care facilities, or of any other residential facilities for older individuals.

(5) DESIGNATION OF LOCAL OMBUDSMAN ENTITIES AND REPRESENTATIVES.—

(A) DESIGNATION.—In carrying out the duties of the Office, the Ombudsman may designate an entity as a local Ombudsman entity, and may designate an employee or volunteer to represent the entity.

(B) DUTIES.—An individual so designated shall, in accordance with the policies and procedures established by the Office and the State agency—

(i) provide services to protect the health, safety, welfare and rights of residents;

(ii) ensure that residents in the service area of the entity have regular, timely access to representatives of the program and timely responses to complaints and requests for assistance;

(iii) identify, investigate, and resolve complaints made by or on behalf of residents that relate to action, inaction, or decisions, that may adversely affect the health, safety, welfare, or rights of the residents;

(iv) represent the interests of residents before government agencies and

seek administrative, legal, and other remedies to protect the health, safety, welfare, and rights of the residents;

(v)(I) review, and if necessary, comment on any existing and proposed laws, regulations, and other government policies and actions, that pertain to the rights and well-being of residents; and

(II) facilitate the ability of the public to comment on the laws, regulations, policies, and actions;

(vi) support the development of resident and family councils; and

(vii) carry out other activities that the Ombudsman determines to be appropriate.

(C) ELIGIBILITY FOR DESIGNATION.—Entities eligible to be designated as local Ombudsman entities, and individuals eligible to be designated as representatives of such entities, shall—

(i) have demonstrated capability to carry out the responsibilities of the Office;

(ii) be free of conflicts of interest;

(iii) in the case of the entities, be public or nonprofit private entities; and

(iv) meet such additional requirements as the Ombudsman may specify.

(D) POLICIES AND PROCEDURES.—

(i) IN GENERAL.—The State agency shall establish, in accordance with the Office, policies and procedures for monitoring local Ombudsman entities designated to carry out the duties of the Office.

(ii) POLICIES.—In a case in which the entities are grantees, or the representatives are employees, of area agencies on aging, the State agency shall develop the policies in consultation with the area agencies on aging. The policies shall provide for participation and comment by the agencies and for resolution of concerns with respect to case activity.

(iii) CONFIDENTIALITY AND DISCLOSURE.—The State agency shall develop the policies and procedures in accordance with all provisions of this subtitle regarding confidentiality and conflict of interest.

(b) PROCEDURES FOR ACCESS.—

(1) IN GENERAL.—The State shall ensure that representatives of the Office shall have—

(A) access to long-term care facilities and residents;

(B)(i) appropriate access to review the medical and social records of a resident, if—

(I) the representative has the permission of the resident, or the legal representative of the resident; or

(II) the resident is unable to consent to the review and has no legal representative; or

(ii) access to the records as is necessary to investigate a complaint if—

(I) a legal guardian of the resident refuses to give the permission;

(II) a representative of the Office has reasonable cause to believe that the guardian is not acting in the best interests of the resident; and

(III) the representative obtains the approval of the Ombudsman;

(C) access to the administrative record, policies, and documents, to which the residents have, or the general public has access, of long-term care facilities; and

(D) access to and, on request, copies of all licensing and certification records maintained by the State with respect to long-term care facilities.

(2) PROCEDURES.—The State agency shall establish procedures to ensure the access described in paragraph (1).

(c) REPORTING SYSTEM.—The State agency shall establish a statewide uniform reporting system to—

(1) collect and analyze data relating to complaints and conditions in long-term care facilities and to residents for the purpose of identifying and resolving significant problems; and

(2) submit the data, on a regular basis, to—

(A) the agency of the State responsible for licensing or certifying long-term care facilities in the State;

(B) other State and Federal entities that the Ombudsman determines to be appropriate;

(C) the Commissioner; and

(D) the National Ombudsman Resource Center established in section 202(a)(21).

(d) DISCLOSURE.—

(1) IN GENERAL.—The State agency shall establish procedures for the disclosure by the Ombudsman or local Ombudsman entities of files maintained by the program, including records described in subsection (b)(1) or (c).

(2) IDENTITY OF COMPLAINANT OR RESIDENT.—The procedures described in paragraph (1) shall—

(A) provide that, subject to subparagraph (B), the files and records described in paragraph (1) may be disclosed only at the discretion of the Ombudsman (or the person designated by the Ombudsman to disclose the files and records); and

(B) prohibit the disclosure of the identity of any complainant or resident with respect to whom the Office maintains such files or records unless—

(i) the complainant or resident, or the legal representative of the complainant or resident, consents to the disclosure and the consent is given in writing;

(ii)(I) the complainant or resident gives consent orally; and

(II) the consent is documented contemporaneously in a writing made by a representative of the Office in accordance with such requirements as the State agency shall establish; or

(iii) the disclosure is required by court order.

(e) CONSULTATION.—In planning and operating the program, the State agency shall consider the views of area agencies on aging, older individuals and providers of long-term care.

(f) CONFLICT OF INTEREST.—The State agency shall—

(1) ensure that no individual, or member of the immediate family of an individual, involved in the designation of the Ombudsman (whether by appointment or otherwise) or the designation of an entity designated under subsection (a)(5), is subject to a conflict of interest;

(2) ensure that no officer or employee of the Office, representative of a local Ombudsman entity, or member of the immediate family of the officer, employee, or representative, is subject to a conflict of interest;

(3) ensure that the Ombudsman—

(A) does not have a direct involvement in the licensing or certification of a long-term care facility or of a provider of a long-term care service;

(B) does not have an ownership or investment interest (represented by equity, debt, or other financial relationship) in a long-term care facility or a long-term care service;

(C) is not employed by, or participating in the management of, a long-term care facility; and

(D) does not receive, or have the right to receive, directly or indirectly, remuneration (in cash or in kind) under a compensation arrangement with an owner or operator of a long-term care facility; and

(4) establish, and specify in writing, mechanisms to identify and remove conflicts of interest referred to in paragraphs *(1)* and *(2)*, and to identify and eliminate the relationships described in subparagraphs *(A)* through *(D)* of paragraph *(3)*, including such mechanisms as—

(A) the methods by which the State agency will examine individuals, and immediate family members, to identify the conflicts; and

(B the actions that the State agency will require the individuals and such family members to take to remove such conflicts.

(g) LEGAL COUNSEL.—*The State agency shall ensure that—*

(1)(A) adequate legal counsel is available, and is able, without conflict of interest, to—

(i) provide advice and consultation needed to protect the health, safety, welfare, and rights of residents; and

(ii) assist the Ombudsman and representatives of the Office in the performance of the official duties of the Ombudsman and representatives; and

(B) legal representation is provided to any representative of the Office against whom suit or other legal action is brought or threatened to be brought in connection with the performance of the official duties of the Ombudsman or such a representative; and

(2) the Office pursues administrative, legal, and other appropriate remedies on behalf of residents.

(h) ADMINISTRATION.—*The State agency shall require the Office to—*

(1) prepare an annual report—

(A) describing the activities carried out by the Office in the year for which the report is prepared;

(B) containing and analyzing the data collected under subsection *(c)*;

(C) evaluating the problems experienced by, and the complaints made by or on behalf of, residents;

(D) containing recommendations for—

(i) improving quality of the care and life of the residents; and

(ii) protecting the health, safety, welfare, and rights of the residents;

(E)(i) analyzing the success of the program including success in providing services to residents of board and care facilities and other similar adult care facilities; and

(ii) identifying barriers that prevent the optimal operation of the program; and

(F) providing policy, regulatory, and legislative recommendations to solve identified problems, to resolve the complaints, to improve the quality of care and life of residents, to protect the health, safety, welfare, and rights of residents, and to remove the barriers;

(2) analyze, comment on, and monitor the development and implementation of Federal, State, and local laws, regulations, and other government policies and actions that pertain to long-term care facilities and services, and to the health, safety, welfare, and rights of residents, in the State, and recommend any changes in such laws, regulations, and policies as the Office determines to be appropriate;

(3)(A) provide such information as the Office determines to be necessary to public and private agencies, legislators, and other persons, regarding—

(i) the problems and concerns of older individuals residing in long-term care facilities; and

(ii) recommendations related to the problems and concerns; and

(B) make available to the public, and submit to the Commissioner, the chief executive officer of the State, the State legislature, the State agency responsible for licensing or certifying long-term care facilities, and other appropriate governmental entities, each report prepared under paragraph (1);

(4)(A) not later than 1 year after the date of the enactment of this title, establish procedures for the training of the representatives of the Office, including unpaid volunteers, based on model standards established by the Associate Commissioner for Ombudsman Programs, in consultation with representatives of citizen groups, long-term care providers, and the Office, that—

(i) specify a minimum number of hours of initial training;

(ii) specify the content of the training, including training relating to—

(I) Federal, State, and local laws, regulations, and policies, with respect to long-term care facilities in the State;

(II) investigative techniques; and

(III) such other matters as the State determines to be appropriate; and

(iii) specify an annual number of hours of in-service training for all designated representatives; and

(B) require implementation of the procedures not later than 21 months after the date of the enactment of this title;

(5) prohibit any representative of the Office (other than the Ombudsman) from carrying out any activity described in subparagraphs (A) through (G) of subsection (a)(3) unless the representative—

(A) has received the training required under paragraph (4); and

(B) has been approved by the Ombudsman as qualified to carry out the activity on behalf of the Office;

(6) coordinate ombudsman services with the protection and advocacy systems for individuals with developmental disabilities and mental illnesses established under—

(A) part A of the Developmental Disabilities Assistance and Bill of Rights Act (42 U.S.C. 6001 et seq.); and

(B) the Protection and Advocacy for Mentally Ill Individuals Act of 1986 *(42 U.S.C. 10801 et seq.);*

(7) coordinate, to the greatest extent possible, ombudsman services with legal assistance provided under section 306(a)(2)(C), through adoption of memoranda of understanding and other means; and

(8) permit any local Ombudsman entity to carry out the responsibilities described in paragraph (1), (2), (3), (6), or (7).

(i) LIABILITY.—The State shall ensure that no representative of the Office will be liable under State law for the good faith performance of official duties.

(j) NONINTERFERENCE.—The State shall—

(1) ensure that willful interference with representatives of the Office in the performance of the official duties of the representatives (as defined by the Commissioner) shall be unlawful;

(2) prohibit retaliation and reprisals by a long-term care facility or other entity with respect to any resident, employee, or other person for filing a complaint with, providing information to, or otherwise cooperating with any representative of, the Office; and

(3) provide for appropriate sanctions with respect to the interference, re-taliation, and reprisals.

SEC. 713. REGULATIONS.

The Commissioner shall issue and periodically update regulations re-specting—

(1) conflicts of interest by persons described in paragraphs (1) and (2) of section 712(f); and

(2) the relationships described in subparagraphs (A) through (D) of section 712(f)(3).

SEC. 703. PROGRAMS FOR PREVENTION OF ELDER ABUSE, NEGLECT, AND EXPLOITATION.

(a) PURPOSE.—The purpose of this section is to assist States in the de-sign, development, and coordination of comprehensive services of the State and local levels to prevent, treat, and remedy elder abuse, neglect, and exploitation.

(b) PROGRAMS.—Title VII of the Older Americans Act of 1965 (as added by section 701, and amended by section 702) is amended by adding at the end the following:

CHAPTER 3—PROGRAMS FOR PREVENTION OF ELDER ABUSE, NEGLECT, AND EXPLOITATION

SEC. 721. PREVENTION OF ELDER ABUSE, NEGLECT, AND EXPLOITATION.

(a) ESTABLISHMENT.—In order to be eligible to receive an allotment under section 703 from funds appropriated under section 702(b), a State agency

shall, in accordance with this section, and in consultation with area agencies on aging, develop and enhance programs for the prevention of elder abuse, neglect, and exploitation.

(b) USE OF ALLOTMENTS.—The State agency shall use an allotment made under subsection (a) to carry out, through the programs described in subsection (a), activities to develop, strengthen, and carry out programs for the prevention and treatment of elder abuse, neglect, and exploitation, including—

(1) providing for public education and outreach to identify and prevent elder abuse, neglect, and exploitation;

(2) ensuring the coordination of services provided by area agencies on aging with services instituted under the State adult protection service program;

(3) promoting the development of information and data systems, including elder abuse reporting systems, to quantify the extent of elder abuse, neglect, and exploitation in the State;

(4) conducting analyses of State information concerning elder abuse, neglect, and exploitation and identifying unmet service, enforcement, or intervention needs;

(5) conducting training for individuals, professionals, and paraprofessionals, in relevant fields on the identification, prevention, and treatment of elder abuse, neglect, and exploitation, with particular focus on prevention and enhancement of self-determination and autonomy;

(6) providing technical assistance to programs that provide or have the potential to provide services for victims of elder abuse, neglect, and exploitation and for family members of the victims;

(7) conducting special and on-going training, for individuals involved in serving victims of elder abuse, neglect, and exploitation, on the topics of self-determination, individual rights, State and Federal requirements concerning confidentiality, and other topics determined by a State agency to be appropriate; and

(8) promoting the development of an elder abuse, neglect, and exploitation system—

(A) that includes a State elder abuse, neglect, and exploitation law that includes provisions for immunity, for persons reporting instances of elder abuse, neglect, and exploitation, from prosecution arising out of such reporting, under any State or local law;

(B) under which a State agency—

(i) on receipt of a report of known or suspected instances of elder abuse, neglect, or exploitation, shall promptly initiate an investigation to substantiate the accuracy of the report; and

(ii) on a finding of elder abuse, neglect, or exploitation, shall take steps, including appropriate referral, to protect the health and welfare of the abused, neglected, or exploited older individual;

(C) that includes, throughout the State, in connection with the enforcement of elder abuse, neglect, and exploitation laws and with the reporting of suspected instances of elder abuse, neglect, and exploitation—

(i) such administrative procedures;

(ii) such personnel trained in the special problems of elder abuse, neglect, and exploitation prevention and treatment;

(iii) such training procedures;

(iv) such institutional and other facilities (public and private); and

(v) such related multidisciplinary programs and services,

as may be necessary or appropriate to ensure that the State will deal effectively with elder abuse, neglect, and exploitation cases in the State;

(D) that preserves the confidentiality of records in order to protect the rights of older individuals;

(E) that provides for the cooperation of law enforcement officials, courts of competent jurisdiction, and State agencies providing human services with respect to special problems of elder abuse, neglect, and exploitation;

(F) that enables an older individual to participate in decisions regarding the welfare of the older individual, and makes the least restrictive alternatives available to an older individual who is abused, neglected, or exploited; and

(G) that includes a State clearinghouse for dissemination of information to the general public with respect to—

(i) the problems of elder abuse, neglect, and exploitation;

(ii) the facilities described in subparagraph (C)(iv); and

(iii) prevention and treatment methods available to combat instances of elder abuse, neglect, and exploitation.

(c) APPROACH.—In developing and enhancing programs under subsection (a), the State agency shall use a comprehensive approach, in consultation with area agencies on aging, to identify and assist older individuals who are subject to abuse, neglect, and exploitation, including older individuals who live in State licensed facilities, unlicensed facilities, or domestic or community-based settings.

(d) COORDINATION.—In developing and enhancing programs under subsection (a), the State agency shall coordinate the programs with other State and local programs and services for the protection of vulnerable adults, particularly vulnerable older individuals, including programs and services such as—

(1) area agency on aging programs;

(2) adult protective services programs;

(3) the State Long-term Care Ombudsman program established in chapter 2;

(4) protection and advocacy programs;

(5) facility and long-term care provider licensure and certification programs;

(6) medicaid fraud and abuse services, including services provided by a State medicaid fraud control unit, as defined in section 1903(q) of the Social Security Act (42 U.S.C. 1396b(q));

(7) victim assistance programs; and

(8) consumer protection and law enforcement programs, as well as other State and local programs that identify and assist vulnerable older individuals.

(e) REQUIREMENTS.—In developing and enhancing programs under subsection (a), the State agency shall—

(1) not permit involuntary or coerced participation in such programs by alleged victims, abusers, or members of their households;

(2) require that all information gathered in the course of receiving a report described in subsection (b)(8)(B)(i), and making a referral described in subsection (b)(8)(B)(ii), shall remain confidential except—

(A) if all parties to such complaint or report consent in writing to the release of such information;

(B) if the release of such information is to a law enforcement agency, public protective service agency, licensing or certification agency, ombudsman program, or protection or advocacy system; or

(C) upon court order; and

(3) make all reasonable efforts to resolve any conflicts with other public agencies with respect to confidentiality of the information described in paragraph (2) by entering into memoranda of understanding that narrowly limit disclosure of information, consistent with the requirement described in paragraph (2).

(f) DESIGNATION.—The State agency may designate a State entity to carry out the programs and activities described in this chapter.

SEC. 704. STATE ELDER RIGHTS AND LEGAL ASSISTANCE DEVELOPMENT PROGRAM

Title VII of the Older Americans Act of 1965 (as added by section 701 and amended by the preceding sections) is amended by adding at the end the following:

CHAPTER 4—STATE ELDER RIGHTS AND LEGAL ASSISTANCE DEVELOPMENT PROGRAM

SEC. 731. STATE ELDER RIGHTS AND LEGAL ASSISTANCE DEVELOPMENT.

(a) ESTABLISHMENT.—

(1) IN GENERAL.—In order to be eligible to receive an allotment under section 703 from funds appropriated under section 702(c), a State agency shall, in accordance with this section and in consultation with area agencies on aging, establish a program to provide leadership for improving the quality and quantity of legal and advocacy assistance as a means for ensuring a comprehensive elder rights system.

(2) COORDINATION AND ASSISTANCE.—In carrying out the program established under this chapter the State agency shall coordinate, and provide assistance to, area agencies on aging and other entities in the State that assist older individuals in—

(A) understanding the rights of the older individuals;

(B) exercising choice;

(C) benefiting from services and opportunities authorized by law;

(D) maintaining the rights of the older individuals and, in particular, of the older individuals with reduced capacity; and

(E) solving disputes.

(b) FUNCTIONS.—In carrying out this chapter, the State agency shall—

(1) establish a focal point for elder rights policy review, analysis, and advocacy at the State level, including such issues as guardianship, age discrimination, pension and health benefits, insurance, consumer protection, surrogate decisionmaking, protective services, public benefits, and dispute resolution;

(2) provide an individual who shall be known as a State legal assistance developer, and other personnel, sufficient to ensure—

(A) State leadership in securing and maintaining legal rights of older individuals;

(B) State capacity for coordinating the provision of legal assistance;

(C) State capacity to provide technical assistance, training and other supportive functions to area agencies on aging, legal assistance providers, ombudsmen, and other persons as appropriate; and

(D) State capacity to promote financial management services for older individuals at risk of conservatorship;

(3)(A) develop, in conjunction with area agencies on aging and legal assistance providers, statewide standards for the delivery of legal assistance to older individuals; and

(B) provide technical assistance to area agencies on aging and legal assistance providers to enhance and monitor the quality and quantity of legal assistance to older individuals, including technical assistance in developing plans for targeting services to reach the older individuals with greatest economic need and older individuals with greatest social need, with particular attention to low-income minority individuals;

(4) provide consultation to, and ensure, the coordination of activities with the legal assistance provided under title III, services provided by the Legal Service Corporation, and services provided under chapters 2, 3, and 5, as well as other State or Federal programs administered at the State and local levels that address the legal assistance needs of older individuals;

(5) provide for the education and training of professionals, volunteers, and older individuals concerning elder rights, the requirements and benefits of specific laws, and methods for enhancing the coordination of services;

(6) promote, and provide as appropriate, education and training for individuals who are or might become guardians or representative payees of older individuals, including information on—

(A) the powers and duties of guardians or representative payees; and

(B) alternatives to guardianship;

(7) promote the development of, and provide technical assistance concerning, pro bono legal assistance programs, State and local bar committees on aging, legal hot lines, alternative dispute resolution, programs and curricula, related to the rights and benefits of older individuals, in law schools and other institutions of higher education, and other methods to expand access

by older individuals to legal assistance and advocacy and vulnerable elder rights protection activities;

(8) provide for periodic assessments of the status of elder rights in the State, including analysis—

(A) of the unmet need for assistance in resolving legal problems and benefits-related problems, methods for expanding advocacy services, the status of substitute decisionmaking systems and services (including systems and services regarding guardianship, representative payeeship, and advance directives), access to courts and the justice system, and the implementation of civil rights and age discrimination laws in the State; and

(B) of problems and unmet needs identified in programs established under title III and other programs; and

(9) for the purpose of identifying vulnerable elder rights protection activities provided by the entities under this chapter, and coordinating the activities with programs established under title III and chapters 2, 3, and 5, develop working agreements with—

(A) State entities, including the consumer protection agency, the court system, the attorney general, the State equal employment opportunity commission, and other State agencies; and

(B) Federal entities, including the Social Security Administration, Health Care Financing Administration, and the Department of Veterans' Affairs, and other entities.

SEC. 705. OUTREACH, COUNSELING, AND ASSISTANCE PROGRAMS.

(a) PURPOSE.—The purpose of this section is to provide outreach, counseling, and assistance in order to assist older individuals in obtaining benefits under—

(1) public and private health insurance, long-term care insurance, life insurance, and pension plans; and

(2) public programs under which the individuals are entitled to benefits, including benefits under—

(A) the supplemental security income program established under title XVI of the Social Security Act (42 U.S.C. 1381 et seq.);

(B) the medicare program established under title XVIII of the Social Security Act (42 U.S.C. 1395 et seq.);

(C) the medicaid program established under title XIX of the Social SEcurity Act (42 U.S.C. 1395 et eq.);

(D) the program established under the Food Stamp Act of 1977 (7 U.S.C. 2011 et seq.); and

(E) the program established under the Low-Income Home Energy Assistance Act of 1981 (42 U.S.C. 8621 et seq.).

(b) PROGRAM.—Title VII of the Older Americans Act of 1965 (as added by section 701, and amended by the preceding sections) is amended by adding at the end the following:

CHAPTER 5—OUTREACH, COUNSELING, AND ASSISTANCE PROGRAM

SEC. 741. STATE OUTREACH, COUNSELING, AND ASSISTANCE PROGRAM FOR INSURANCE AND PUBLIC BENEFITS.

(a) DEFINITIONS.—As used in this section:

(1) INSURANCE BENEFIT.—The term 'insurance benefit' means a benefit under—

(A) the medicare program established under title XVIII of the Social Security Act (42 U.S.C. 1395 et seq.);

(B) the medicaid program established under title XIX of the Social Security Act (42 U.S.C. 1396 et seq.);

(C) a public or private insurance program;

(D) a medicare supplemental policy; or

(E) a pension plan.

(2) MEDICARE SUPPLEMENTAL POLICY.—The term 'medicare supplemental policy' has the meaning given the term in section 1882(g)(1) of the Social Security Act (42 U.S.C. 1395ss(g)(1)).

(3) PENSION PLAN.—The term 'pension plan' means an employee pension benefit plan, as defined in section 3(2) of the Employee Retirement Income Security Act of 1974 (29 U.S.C. 1002(2)).

(4) PUBLIC BENEFIT.—The term 'public benefit' means a benefit under—

(A) the Federal Old-Age, Survivors, and Disability Insurance Benefits programs under title II of the Social Security Act (42 U.S.C. 401 et seq.);

(B) the medicare program established under title XVIII of the Social Security Act, including benefits as a qualified medicare beneficiary, as defined in section 1905(p) of the Social Security Act;

(C) the medicaid program established under title XIX of the Social Security Act;

(D) the program established under the Food Stamp Act of 1977 (7 U.S.C. 2011 et seq.);

(E) the program established under the Low-Income Home Energy Assistance Act of 1981 (42 U.S.C. 8621 et seq.);

(F) the supplemental security income program established under title XVI of the Social Security Act (42 U.S.C. 1381 et seq.); or

(G) a program determined to be appropriate by the Commissioner.

(5) STATE INSURANCE ASSISTANCE PROGRAM.—The term 'State insurance assistance program' means the program established under subsection (b)(1).

(6) STATE PUBLIC BENEFIT ASSISTANCE PROGRAM.—The term 'State public benefit assistance program' means the program established under subsection (b)(2).

(b) ESTABLISHMENT.—In order to receive an allotment under section 703 from funds appropriated under section 702(d), a State agency shall, in coordination with area agencies on aging and in accordance with this section, establish—

(1) a program to provide to older individuals outreach, counseling, and assistance related to obtaining insurance benefits; and

(2) a program to provide outreach, counseling, and assistance to older individuals who may be eligible for, but who are not receiving, public benefits.

(c) INSURANCE AND PUBLIC BENEFITS.—The State agency shall—

(1) in carrying out a State insurance assistance program—

(A) provide information and counseling to assist older individuals—

(i) in filing claims and obtaining benefits under title XVIII and title XIX of the Social Security Act;

(ii) in comparing medicare supplemental policies and in filing claims and obtaining benefits under such policies;

(iii) in comparing long-term care insurance policies and in filing claims and obtaining benefits under such policies;

(iv) in comparing other types of health insurance policies not described in clause (iii) and in filing claims and obtaining benefits under such policies;

(v) in comparing life insurance policies and in filing claims and obtaining benefits under such policies;

(vi) in comparing other forms of insurance policies not described in clause (v), in comparing pension plans, and in filing claims and obtaining benefits under such policies and plans as the State agency may determine to be necessary; and

(vii) in comparing current and future health and post-retirement needs related to pension plans, and the relationship of benefits under such plans to insurance benefits and public benefits;

(B) establish a system of referrals to appropriate providers of legal assistance, and to appropriate agencies of the Federal or State government regarding the problems of older individuals related to health insurance benefits, other insurance benefits, and public benefits;

(C) give priority to providing assistance to older individuals with greatest economic need;

(D) ensure that services provided under the program will be coordinated with programs established under chapters 2, 3, and 4, and under title III;

(E) provide for adequate and trained staff (including volunteers) necessary to carry out the program;

(F) ensure that staff (including volunteers) of the agency and of any agency or organization described in subsection (d) will not be subject to a conflict of interest in providing services under the program;

(G) provide for the collection and dissemination of timely and accurate information to staff (including volunteers) related to insurance benefits and public benefits;

(H) provide for the coordination of information on insurance benefits between the staff of departments and agencies of the State government and the staff (including volunteers) of the program; and

(I) make recommendations related to consumer protection that may affect individuals eligible for, or receiving, health or other insurance benefits; and

(2) in carrying out a State public benefits assistance program—

(A) carry out activities to identify older individuals with greatest economic need who may be eligible for, but who are not receiving, public benefits;

(B) conduct outreach activities to inform older individuals of the requirements for eligibility to receive such benefits;

(C) assist older individuals in applying for such benefits;

(D) establish a system of referrals to appropriate providers of legal assistance, or to appropriate agencies of the Federal or State government regarding the problems of older individuals related to public benefits;

(E) comply with the requirements specified in subparagraphs (C) through (F) of paragraph (1) with respect to the State public benefits assistance program;

(F) provide for the collection and dissemination of timely and accurate information to staff (including volunteers) related to public benefits;

(G) provide for the coordination of information on public benefits between the staff of State entities and the staff (including volunteers) of the State public benefits assistance program; and

(H) make recommendations related to consumer protection that may affect individuals eligible for, or receiving, public benefits.

(d) ADMINISTRATION.—The State agency may operate the State insurance assistance program and the State public benefits assistance program directly, in cooperation with other State agencies, or under an agreement with a statewide nonprofit organization, an area agency on aging, or another public or nonprofit agency or organization.

(e) MAINTENANCE OF EFFORT.—Any funds appropriated for the activities under this chapter shall supplement, and shall not supplant, funds that are expended for similar purposes under any Federal, State, or local program providing insurance benefits or public benefits.

(f) COORDINATION.—A State that receives an allotment under section 703 and receives a grant to provide services under section 4360 of the Omnibus Reconciliation Act of 1990 (42 U.S.C. 1395b-4) shall coordinate the services with activities provided by the State agency through the programs described in paragraphs (1) and (2) of subsection (b).

SEC. 706. NATIVE AMERICAN ORGANIZATION PROVISIONS.

Title VII of the Older Americans Act of 1965 (as added by section 702, and amended by the preceding sections) is amended by adding at the end the following:

Subtitle B—Native American Organization Provisions

SEC. 751. NATIVE AMERICAN PROGRAM.

(a) ESTABLISHMENT.—The Commissioner, acting through the Associate Commissioner on American Indian, Alaskan Native, and Native Hawaiian Aging, shall establish and carry out a program for—

(1) assisting eligible entities in prioritizing, on a continuing basis, the needs of the service population of the entities relating to elder rights; and

(2) making grants to eligible entities to carry out vulnerable elder rights protection activities that the entities determine to be priorities.

(b) APPLICATION.—In order to be eligible to receive assistance under this subtitle, an entity shall submit an application to the Commissioner, at such time, in such manner, and containing such information as the Commissioner may require.

(c) ELIGIBLE ENTITY.—An entity eligible to receive assistance under this section shall be—

(1) an Indian tribe; or

(2) a public agency, or a nonprofit organization, serving older individuals who are Native Americans.

(d) AUTHORIZATION OF APPROPRIATIONS.—There are authorized to be appropriated to carry out this section, $5,000,000 for fiscal year 1992, and such sums as may be necessary for fiscal years 1993, 1994, and 1995.

SEC. 707. GENERAL PROVISIONS.

Title VII of the Older Americans Act of 1965 (as added by section 701, and amended by the preceding sections) is amended by adding at the end the following:

Subtitle C—General Provisions

SEC. 761. DEFINITIONS.

As used in this title:

(1) ELDER RIGHT.—The term 'elder right' means a right of an older individual.

(2) VULNERABLE ELDER RIGHTS PROTECTION ACTIVITY.—The term 'vulnerable elder rights protection activity' means an activity funded under chapter 2, 3, 4, or 5 of this title.

SEC. 762. ADMINISTRATION.

A State agency or an entity described in section 751(c) may carry out vulnerable elder rights protection activities either directly or through contracts or agreements with public or nonprofit private agencies or organizations, such as—

(1) other State agencies;

(2) area agencies on aging;

(3) county governments;

(4) institutions of higher education;

(5) Indian tribes; or

(6) nonprofit service providers or volunteer organizations.

SEC. 763. TECHNICAL ASSISTANCE.

(a) OTHER AGENCIES.—*In carrying out the provisions of this title, the Commissioner may request the technical assistance and cooperation of such Federal entities as may be appropriate.*

(b) COMMISSIONER.—*The Commissioner shall provide technical assistance and training (by contract, grant, or otherwise) to persons and entities that administer programs established under this title.*

SEC. 764. AUDITS.

(a) ACCESS.—*The Commissioner, the Comptroller General of the United States, and any duly authorized representative of the Commissioner or the Comptroller shall have access, for the purpose of conducting an audit or examination, to any books, documents, papers, and records that are pertinent to financial assistance received under this title.*

(b) LIMITATION.—*State agencies, area agencies on aging, and entities described in section 751(c) shall not request information or data from providers that is not pertinent to services furnished under this title or to a payment made for the services.*

SEC. 708. TECHNICAL AND CONFORMING AMENDMENTS

(a) OMBUDSMAN PROGRAM.—

(1) SOCIAL SECURITY ACT.—

(A) Section 1819 of the social Security Act (42 U.S.C. 1395i–3) is amended in subsections (c)(2)(B)(iii)(II) and (g)(5)(B) by striking "established under section 307(a)(12) of the Older Americans Act of 1965" and inserting established under title III or VII of the Older Americans Act of 1965 in accordance with section 712 of the Act.

(B) Section 1919 of the Social Security Act (42 U.S.C. 1396r) is amended in subsections (c)(2)(B)(iii)(II) and (g)(5)(B) by striking "established under section 307(a)(12) of the Older Americans Act of 1965" and inserting "established under title III or VII of the Older Americans Act of 1965 in accordance with section 712 of the Act".

(2) OLDER AMERICANS ACT OF 1965.—

(A) Section 207(b) of the Older Americans Act of 1965 (42 U.S.C. 3018(b)) is amended—

(i) in paragraph (1)(A), by striking "section 307(a)(12)(C)" and inserting "titles III and VII in accordance with section 712(c)"; and

(ii) in paragraph (3)—

(I) by striking "by section 307(a)(12)(H)(i)" and inserting "under titles III and VII in accordance with section 712(h)(1)"; and

(II) by striking subparagraph (E) and inserting the following:

(E) each public agency or private organization designated as an Office of the State Long-Term Care Ombudsman under title III or VII in accordance with section 712(a)(4)(A).

(B) Section 301(c) of the Older Americans Act of 1965 (42 U.S.C. 3021(c)) is amended by striking section 307(a)(12), and to individuals designated under such section" and inserting "section 307(a)(12) in accordance with section 712, and to individuals within such programs designated under section 712.

(C) Section 351(4) of the Older Americans Act of 1965 (42 U.S.C. 30301(4)) is amended by striking "section 307(a)(12) and inserting titles III and VII in accordance with section 712."

(b) PROGRAMS FOR PREVENTION OF ABUSE, NEGLECT, AND EXPLOITATION.—Section 321(15) of the Older Americans Act of 1965 (42 U.S.C. 3030d(15)) is amended by striking "clause (16) of section 307(a), and inserting "chapter 3 of subtitle A of title VII and section 307(a)(16)".

(c) OUTREACH PROGRAMS.—

(1) Section 202(a)(20) of the Older Americans Act of 1965 (42 U.S.C. 3012(a)(20)) is amended by striking "under section 307(a)(31).

(2) Section 207(c) of the Older Americans Act of 1965 (42 U.S.C. 3018(c)) is amended—

(A) in the first sentence, by striking on the evaluations required to be submitted under section 307(a)(31)(D) and inserting on the outreach activities supported under this Act; and

(B) in paragraph (1), by striking outreach activities supported under section 306(a)(6)(P) and inserting the activities.

(3) Section 303(a)(1) of the Older Americans Act of 1965 (42 U.S.C. 3023(a)(1) is amended by striking for purposes other than outreach activities and application assistance under section 307(a)(31).

(4) Section 307(a)(20)(A) of the Older Americans Act of 1965 (42 U.S.C. 3027(a)(20)(A) is amended by striking sections 306(a)(2)(A) and 306(a)(6)(P)) and inserting section 306(a)(2)(A).

TITLE VIII—AMENDMENTS TO OTHER LAWS; RELATED MATTERS

Subtitle A—Long-Term Health Care Workers

SEC. 801. DEFINITIONS.

As used in this subtitle:

(1) NURSING HOME NURSE AIDE.—The term nursing home nurse aide means an individual employed at a nursing or convalescent home who assists in the care of patients at such home under the direction of nursing and medical staff.

(2) HOME HEALTH CARE AIDE.—The term home health care aide means an individual who—

(A) is employed by a government, charitable, nonprofit, or proprietary agency; and

(b) cares for elderly, convalescent, or handicapped individuals in the home of the individuals by performing routine home assistance (such as housecleaning, cooking, and laundry) and assisting the health care of such individuals under the direction of a physician or nurse.

SEC. 802. INFORMATION REQUIREMENTS.

(a) NATIONAL CENTER FOR HEALTH STATISTICS.—The Director of the National Center for Health Statistics of the Centers for Disease Control shall collect, and prepare a report containing—
(1) demographic information on home health care aides and nursing home nurse aides, including information on the—
(A) age, race, marital status, education, number of children and other dependents, gender, and primary language, of the aides; and
(B) location of facilities at which the aides are employed in—
(i) rural communities; or
(ii) urban or suburban communities; and
(2) information on the role of the aides in providing institution-based and home-based long-term care.
(b) DEPARTMENT OF LABOR.—The Secretary of Labor shall—
(1) collect, and prepare a report containing, information on home health care aides, including—
(A) information on conditions of employment, including—
(i) the length of employment of the aides with the current employer of the aides;
(ii) the number of aides who are—
(I) employed by a for-profit employer;
(II) employed by a nonprofit private employer;
(III) employed by a charitable employer;
(IV) employed by a government employer; or
(V) independent contractors;
(iii) the number of full-time, part-time, and temporary positions for the aides;
(iv) the ratio of the aides to professional staff;
(v) the types of tasks performed by the aides, the level of skill needed to perform the tasks, and whether the tasks are completed in a institution-based or home-based setting; and
(vi) the average number and range of hours worked each week by the aides; and
(B) information on availability of the employment benefits for home health care aides and a description of the benefits, including—
(i) information on health insurance coverage;
(ii) the type of pension plan coverage;
(iii) the amount of vacation leave;
(iv) wage rates; and
(v) the extent of work-related training provided; and
(2) collect, and prepare a report containing, information on nursing home nurse aides, including—

(A) the information described in subparagraphs (A) and (B) or paragraph (1); and

(B) information on—

(i) the type of facility of the employer of the aides, such as a skilled nursing facility, as defined in section 1819(a) of the Social Security Act (42 U.S.C. 1395i–3a)), or an intermediate care facility within the meaning of section 1121(a) of the Social Security Act (42 U.S.C. 1320a(a));

(ii) the number of beds at the facility; and

(iii) the ratio of the aides to residents of the facility.

SEC. 803. REPORTS.

(a) REPORTS TO COMMISSIONER ON AGING.—

(1) TRANSMITTAL.—

(A) NATIONAL CENTER FOR HEALTH STATISTICS REPORT.—Not later than March 1, 1994, the Director of the National Center for Health Statistics of the Centers for Disease Control shall transmit to the Commissioner on Aging the report required by section 802(a).

(B) DEPARTMENT OF LABOR REPORTS.—

(i) HOME HEALTH CARE AIDES.—Not later than March 1, 1993, the Secretary of Labor shall transmit to the Commissioner on Aging a plan for the collection of the information described in section 802(b)(1). Not later than March 1, 1995, the Secretary of Labor shall transmit to the Commissioner on Aging the report required by section 802(b)(1).

(ii) NURSING HOME NURSE AIDES.—Not later than March 1, 1994, the Secretary of Labor shall transmit to the Commissioner on Aging the report required by section 802(b)(2).

(2) PREPARATION.—

(A) NATIONAL CENTER FOR HEALTH STATISTICS REPORT.—The report required by section 802(a) shall be prepared and organized in such a manner as the Director of the National Center for Health Statistics may determine to be appropriate.

(B) DEPARTMENT OF LABOR REPORTS.—The reports required by paragraphs (1) and (2) of section 802(b) shall be prepared and organized in such a manner as the Secretary of Labor may determine to be appropriate.

(3) PRESENTATION OF INFORMATION.—The reports required by section 802 shall not identify by name individuals supplying information for purposes of the reports. The reports shall present information collected in the aggregate.

(b) REPORT TO CONGRESS.—The Commissioner on Aging shall review the reports required by section 802 and shall submit to the appropriate committees of Congress a report containing—

(1) the reports required by section 802;

(2) the comments of the Commissioner on the reports; and

(3) additional information, regarding the roles of nursing home nurse aides and home health care aides in providing long-term care, obtained through the State Long-Term Care Ombudsman program established under sections 307(a)(12) and 712 of the Older Americans Act of 1965.

SEC. 804. OCCUPATIONAL CODE.

The Secretary of Labor shall include an occupational code covering nursing home nurse aides and an occupational code covering home health care aides in each wage survey of relevant industries conducted by the Department of Labor that begins after the date of enactment of this Act.

Subtitle B—National School Lunch Act

SEC. 811. MEALS PROVIDED THROUGH ADULT DAY CARE CENTERS.

(a) IN GENERAL.—Section 17(o)(2)(A)(i) of the National School Lunch Act (42 U.S.C. 1766(o)(2)(A)(i) is amended by inserting, or a group living arrangement, after homes.

(b) EFFECTIVE DATE.—The amendment made by subsection (a) shall take effect as if the amendment had been included in the Older Americans Act Amendments of 1987.

Subtitle C—Native American Programs

SEC. 831. SHORT TITLE.

This subtitle may be cited as the Native American Programs Act Amendments of 1992.

SEC. 822 AMENDMENTS.

The Native American Programs Act of 1974 (42 U.S.C. 2991 et seq.) is amended—

(1) in section 803 (42 U.S.C. 2991b)—

(A) by striking Secretary each place the term appears and inserting Commissioner; and

(B) in the first sentence of subsection (a)—

(i) by striking Indian organizations and inserting Indian and Alaska Native organizations; and

(ii) by striking nonreservation area and inserting area that is not an Indian reservation or Alaska Native village;

(2) in section 803 A (42 U.S.C. 2991b-1)—

(A) in subsection (a)(1)—

(i) by striking one agency and all that follows through of Native Hawaiians and inserting the Office of Hawaiian Affairs of the State of Hawaii (referred to in this section as the Office);

(ii) by striking 5-year; and

(iii) in subparagraph (A) by striking such agency or Native Hawaiian organization and inserting the Office;

(B) by striking agency or organization to which a grant is awarded under subsection (a)(1) of this section each place the term appears and inserting Office;

(C by striking agency or organization each place the term appears and inserting Office;

(D) by striking Secretary each place the term appears and inserting Commissioner;

(E) in subsection (a)(2) by inserting before the period at the end the following: and a requirement that the grantee contribute to the revolving loan fund an amount of non-Federal funds equal to the amount of such grant;

(F) by striking subsection (b)(6);

(G) in subsection (f)(1) by striking fiscal years 1988, 1989, and 1990 the aggregate amount of $3,000,000 for all such fiscal years and inserting each of the fiscal years 1992, 1993, and 1994, $1,000,000;

(H) by striking subsection (f)(3); and

(I) by striking subsection (g) and inserting the following:

(g)(1) The Commissioner, in consultation with the Office, shall submit a report to the President pro tempore of the Senate and the Speaker of the House of Representatives not later than January 1 following each fiscal year, regarding the administration of this section in such fiscal year.

(2) Such report shall include the views and recommendations of the Commissioner with respect to the revolving loan fund established under subsection (a)(1) and with respect to loans made from such fund, and shall—

(A) describe the effectiveness of the operation of such fund in improving the economic and social self-sufficiency of Native Hawaiians;

(B) specify the number of loans made in such fiscal year;

(C) specify the number of loans outstanding as of the end of such fiscal year; and

(D) specify the number of borrowers who fail in such fiscal year to repay loans in accordance with the agreements under which such loans are required to be repaid.;

(3) after section 803A (42 U.S.C. 2991b–1) by inserting the following:

ESTABLISHMENT OF ADMINISTRATION FOR NATIVE AMERICANS

SEC. 803B. (a) There is established in the Department of Health and Human Services (referred to in this title as the Department) the Administration for Native Americans (referred to in this title as the Administration), which shall be headed by a Commissioner of the Administration for Native Americans (referred to in this title as the Commissioner). The Administration shall be the agency responsible for carrying out the provisions of this title.

(b) The Commissioner shall be appointed by the President, by and with the advice and consent of the Senate.

(c) The Commissioner shall—

(1) provide for financial assistance, loan funds, technical assistance,

training, research and demonstration projects, and other activities, described in this title;

(2) serve as the effective and visible advocate on behalf of Native Americans within the Department, and with other departments and agencies of the Federal Government regarding all Federal policies affecting Native Americans;

(3) with the assistance of the Intra-Departmental Council on Native American Affairs established by subsection (d)(1), coordinate activities within the Department leading to the development of policies, programs, and budgets, and their administration affecting Native Americans, and provide quarterly reports and recommendations to the Secretary;

(4) collect and disseminate information related to the social and economic conditions of Native Americans, and assist the Secretary in preparing an annual report to the Congress about such conditions;

(5) give preference to individuals who are eligible for assistance under this title, in entering into contracts for technical assistance, training, and evaluation under this title; and

(6) encourage agencies that carry out projects under this title, to give preference to such individuals in hiring and entering into contracts to carry out such projects.

(d)(1) There is established in the Office of the Secretary the Intra-Departmental Council on Native American Affairs. The Commissioner shall be the chairperson of such council and shall advise the Secretary on all matters affecting Native Americans that involve the Department. The Director of the Indian Health Service shall serve as vice chairperson of the Council.

(2) The membership of the Council shall be the heads of principal operating divisions within the Department, as determined by the Secretary, and such persons in the Office of the Secretary as the Secretary may designate.

(3) In addition to the duties described in subsection (c)(3), the Council shall, within 180 days following the date of the enactment of the Native American Programs Act Amendments of 1992, prepare a plan, including legislative recommendations, to allow tribal governments and other organizations described in section 803(a) to consolidate grants administered by the Department and to designate a single office to oversee and audit the grants. Such plan shall be submitted to the committees of the Senate and the House of Representatives having jurisdiction over the Administration for Native Americans.

(e) The Secretary shall assure that adequate staff and administrative support is provided to carry out the purpose of this title. In determining the staffing levels of the Administration, the Secretary shall consider among other factors the unmet needs of the Native American population, the need to provide adequate oversight and technical assistance to grantees, the need to carry out the activities of the Council, the additional reporting requirements established, and the staffing levels previously maintained in support of the Administration;

(4) by striking section 804 (42 U.S.C. 2991c) and inserting the following:

TECHNICAL ASSISTANCE AND TRAINING

SEC. 804. The Commissioner shall provide, directly or through other arrangements—

(1) technical assistance to the public and private agencies in planning, developing, conducting, and administering projects under this title;

(2) short-term in-service training for specialized or other personnel that is needed in connection with projects receiving financial assistance under this title; and

(3) upon denial of a grant application, technical assistance to a potential grantee in revising a grant proposal.;

(5) in section 805 (42 U.S.C. 2991d) by striking Secretary each place the term appears and inserting Commissioner;

(6) in section 806 (42 U.S.C. 2991d-1) by striking Secretary each place the term appears and inserting Commissioner;

(7) in section 807 (42 U.s.C. 2991e) by striking Secretary each place the term appears and inserting Commissioner;

(8) in section 808 (42 U.S.C. 2991f) by striking Secretary each place the term appears and inserting Commissioner;

(9) in section 809 (42 U.S.C. 2991g) by striking Secretary each place the term appears and inserting Commissioner;

(10) in section 810 (42 U.s.C. 2991h)—

(A) by striking "Secretary" and inserting Commissioner;

(b) by designating the text as subsection (a); and

(C) by adding at the end the following;

(b) If an application is rejected on the grounds that the applicant is ineligible or that activities proposed by the applicant are ineligible for funding, the applicant may appeal to the Secretary, not later than 30 days after the date of receipt of notification of such rejection, for a review of the grounds for such rejection. On appeal, if the Secretary finds that an applicant is eligible or that its proposed activities are eligible, such eligibility shall not be effective until the next cycle of grant proposals are considered by the Administration;

(11) in section 811 (42 U.S.C. 2992)—

(A) by striking Secretary each place the term appears and inserting Commissioner;

(B) in subsection (a)—

(i) by inserting (1) after (a), and

(ii) by adding at the end the following:

(2) the projects assisted under this title shall be evaluated in accordance with this section not less frequently than at 3-year intervals.;

(12) after section 811 (42 U.S.C. 2992) by inserting the following:

ANNUAL REPORT

SEC. 811A. The Secretary shall, not later than January 31 of each year, prepare and transmit to the President pro tempore of the Senate and the Speaker of the House of Representatives an annual report on the social and economic conditions of American Indians, Native Hawaiians, other Native American Pacific islanders (including American Samoan Natives), and Alaska Natives, together with such recommendations to Congress as the Secretary considers to be appropriate.;

(13) after section 812 (42 U.S.C. 2992a) by inserting the following:

STAFF

SEC. 812A. In all personnel actions of the Administration, preference shall be given to individuals who are eligible for assistance under this title. Such preference shall be implemented in the same fashion as the preference given to veterans referred to in section 2108(3)(C) of title 5, United States Code. The Commissioner shall take such additional actions as may be necessary to promote recruitment of such individuals for employment in the Administration;

(14) by striking section 813 (42 U.S.C. 2992b) and inserting the following:

ADMINISTRATION

SEC. 813. Nothing in this title shall be construed to prohibit interagency funding agreements made between the Administration and other agencies of the Federal Government for the development and implementation of specific grants or projects.;

(15) in section 816(a) (42 U.S.C. 2992d(a))—

(A) by striking 1988 and all that follows and inserting 1992, 1993, 1994, and 1995,; an

(B) by striking and 803A and inserting a comma and 803A, subsection (e) of this section, and any other provision of this title for which there is an express authorization of appropriations;

(16) in section 816(b) (42 U.S.C. 2992d(b)) by striking and 803A and inserting a comma and 803A, 804, subsection (e) of this section, and any other provision of this title for which there is an express authorization of appropriations;

(17) in section 816(c)(1) (42 U.S.C. 2992d(c)(1))—

(A) by striking (1) Except as provided in paragraph (2), there are and inserting There are; and

(B) by striking 1988, 1989, 1990, and 1991 and inserting 1992, 1993, 1994, and 1995;

(18) by striking section 816(c)(2) (42 U.S.C. 2992d(c)(2));

(19) in section 816(d) by striking 1991;

(20) in section 816 (42 U.S.C. 2992d) by adding at the end the following:

(e)(1) For fiscal years 1992 and 1993, there are authorized to be appropriated such sums as may be necessary for the purpose of—

(A) establishing demonstration projects to conduct research related to Native American studies and Indian policy development; and

(B) continuing the development of a detailed plan, based in part on the results of the projects, for the establishment of a National Center for Native American Studies and Indian Policy Development.

(2) Such a plan shall be delivered to the Congress not later than 30 days after the date of enactment of this subsection.; and

(21) in sections 802, 803(a), 806(a)(2), 808, and 815(2) (42 U.S.C. 2991a, 2991b(a), 2991d–1(a)(2), 2991f, and 2992c(2)) by striking Alaskan Native each place the term appears and inserting Alaska Native.

TITLE II—WHITE HOUSE CONFERENCE ON AGING

(b) FINDINGS.—Section 201(a) of the Older Americans Act Amendments of 1987 (42 U.S.C. 3001 note) is amended—

(1) in paragraph (1)—

(A by striking 51,400,000 in 1986 and inserting 52,923,000 in 1990; and

(B) by striking 101,700,000 and inserting 103,646,000;

(2) in paragraph (2) by striking every 6 and inserting every 8; and

(3) by amending paragraph (3) to read as follows:

(3) the out-of-pocket costs to older individuals for health care increased from 12.3 percent in 1977 to 18.2 percent in 1988.

SEC. 832. CONFERENCE REQUIRED.

Section 202 of the Older Americans Act Amendments of 1987 (72 U.S.C. 3001 note) is amended—

(1) in subsection (a) by striking The President may call a White House Conference on Aging in 1991 and inserting, Not later than December 31, 1994 the President shall convene the White House Conference on Aging;

(2) in subsection (c) by striking paragraphs (1) through (6) and inserting the following:

(1) to increase the public awareness of the interdependence of generations and the essential contributions of older individuals to society for the well-being of all generations;

(2) to identify the problems facing older individuals and the commonalities of the problems with problems of younger generations;

(3) to examine the well-being of older individuals, including the impact the wellness of older individuals has on our aging society:

(4) to develop such specific and comprehensive recommendations for executive and legislative action as may be appropriate for maintaining and improving the well-being of the aging;

(5) to develop recommendations for the coordination of Federal policy with State and local needs and the implementation of such recommendations; and

(6) to review the status and multigenerational value of recommendations adopted at previous White House Conferences on Aging; and

(3) in subsection (d)(2) by adding at the end the following: Delegates shall include individuals who are professionals, individuals who are nonprofessionals, minority individuals, and individuals from low-income families.

SEC. 833. CONFERENCE ADMINISTRATION.

Section 203 of the Older Americans Act Amendments of 1987 (42 U.S.C. 3001 note) is amended—

(1) in subsection (a)—

(A) in paragraph (2), by inserting (including organizations representing older Indians) after appropriate organizations;

(B) in paragraph (3)—

(i) by striking prepare and; and

(ii) by inserting prepared by the Policy Committee, after agenda;

(C) by redesignating paragraphs (1) through (5) as paragraphs (2) through (6), respectively; and

(D) by inserting before paragraph (2), as so redesignated, the following:

(1) provide written notice to all members of the Policy Committee of each meeting, hearing, or working session of the Policy Committee not later than 48 hours before the occurrence of such meeting, hearing, or working session;

(2) in subsection (b)—

(A) in the matter preceding paragraph (1), by striking assure and inserting and as part of the White House Conference on Aging, ensure;

(B) in paragraph (1), by striking will and inserting shall;

(C) by striking paragraphs (2) and (3);

(D) by inserting after paragraph (1) the following:

(2) the agenda prepared under subsection (a)(4) for the Conference is published in the Federal Register not later than 30 days after such agenda is approved by the Policy Committee, and the Secretary may republish such agenda together with the recommendations of the Secretary regarding such agenda,; and

(E) by redesignating paragraphs (4) through (6) as paragraphs (3) through (5), respectively; and

(3) by adding at the end the following:

(c) GIFTS.—The Secretary may accept, on behalf of the United States, gifts (in cash or in kind, including voluntary and uncompensated services), which shall be available to carry out this title. Gifts of cash shall be available in addition to amounts appropriated to carry out this title.

(d) RECORDS.—The Secretary shall maintain records regarding—

(1) the sources, amounts, and uses of gifts accepted under subsection (c); and

(2) the identity of each person receiving assistance to carry out this title, and the amount of such assistance received by each such person.

SEC. 834. POLICY COMMITTEE; RELATED COMMITTEES.

Section 204 of the Older Americans Act Amendments of 1987 (42 U.S.C. 3001 note) is amended—

(1) by amending the heading to read as follows:

SEC. 804. POLICY COMMITTEE; RELATED COMMITTEES;

(2) in subsection (b) by striking (b) OTHER COMMITTEES.—and inserting the following:

(2) OTHER COMMITTEES.—;

(3) in subsection (a)—

(A) by striking (a) ADVISORY COMMITTEE.—The Secretary and inserting (b) ADVISORY AND OTHER COMMITTEES.—

(1) IN GENERAL.—The President; and

(B) by adding at the end the following: The President shall consider for appointment to the advisory committee individuals recommended by the Policy Committee;

(4) by inserting before subsection (b), as so redesignated, the following:

(a) POLICY COMMITTEE.—

(1) ESTABLISHMENT.—There is established a Policy Committee comprised of 25 members to be selected, not later than 90 days after the enactment of the Older Americans Act Amendments of 1992, as follows:

(A) PRESIDENTIAL APPOINTEES.—Thirteen members shall be selected by the President and shall include—

(i) 3 members who are officers or employees of the United States; and

(ii) 10 members with experience in the field of aging, who may include representatives of public aging agencies, institution-based organizations, and minority aging organizations.

(B) HOUSE APPOINTEES.—Four members shall be selected by the Speaker of the House of Representatives, after consultation with the Minority Leader of the House of Representatives, and shall include members of the Committee on Education and Labor of the House of Representatives, the Committee on Ways and Means of the House of Representatives, and the Select Committee on Aging of the House of Representatives. Not more than 3 members selected under this subparagraph may be associated or affiliated with the same political party.

(C) SENATE APPOINTEES.—Four members shall be selected by the Majority Leader of the Senate, after consultation with the Minority Leader of the Senate, and shall include members of the Committee on Labor and Human Resources of the Senate, the Committee on Finance of the Senate, and the Special Committee on Aging of the Senate. Not more than 3 members selected under this subparagraph may be associated or affiliated with the same political party.

(D) JOINT APPOINTEES.—Four members shall be selected jointly by the Speaker of the House of Representatives and the Majority Leader of the Senate, after consultation with the minority leaders of the House and Senate, and shall include representatives with experience in the field of aging, who may include representatives described in subsection (a)(1)(A)(ii). Not more than 2 member selected under this subparagraph may be associated or affiliated with the same political party.

(2) DUTIES OF THE POLICY COMMITTEE.—The Policy Committee shall initially meet at the call of the Secretary, but not later than 30 days after the last

member is selected under subsection (a). Subsequent meetings of the Policy Committee shall be held at the call of the chairperson of the Policy Committee. Through meetings, hearings, and working session, the Policy Committee shall—

(A) make recommendations to the Secretary to facilitate the timely convening of the Conference;

(B) formulate and approve a proposed agenda for the Conference not later than 60 days after the first meeting of the Policy Committee;

(C) make recommendations for participants and delegates of the Conference;

(D) establish the number of delegates to be selected under section 202(d)(2); and

(E) formulate and approve the initial report of the Conference in accordance with section 205.

(3) QUORUM; COMMITTEE VOTING; CHAIRPERSON.—

(A) QUORUM.—Thirteen members shall constitute a quorum for the purpose of conducting the business of the Policy Committee, except that 17 members shall constitute a quorum for purposes of approving the agenda required by paragraph (2)(B) and the report required by paragraph (2)(E).

(B) VOTING.—The Policy Committee shall act by the vote of the majority of the members present.

(C) CHAIRPERSON.—The President shall select a chairperson from among the members of the Policy Committee. The chairperson may vote only to break a tie vote of the other members of the Policy Committee; and

(5) in the first sentence of subsection (c)—

(A) by striking Each such committee and inserting Each committee established under subsection (b); and

(B) by inserting, and individuals who are Native Americans before the period at the end.

SEC. 835. REPORT OF THE CONFERENCE.

Section 205 of the Older Americans Act Amendments of 1987 (42 U.S.C. 3001 note) is amended—

(1) in subsection (a) by striking 60 and inserting 90;

(2) in subsection (b) by striking "Secretary, not later than 180" and inserting Policy Committee, not later than 90;

(3) in subsection (c)—

(A) by striking (c) FINAL REPORT.—The Secretary and inserting the following:

(c) REPORTS.—

(1) INITIAL REPORT.—The Policy Committee;

(B) by striking prepare a final report and inserting prepare and approve an initial report; and

(C) by adding at the end the following:

(2) Not later than 60 days after such initial report is transmitted by the Policy Committee, the Secretary shall publish such initial report in the Federal Register. The Secretary may republish a final report together with such

additional views and recommendations as the Secretary considers to be appropriate; and

(4) in subsection (d)—

(A) in the heading of such subsection by striking SECRETARY *and inserting* POLICY COMMITTEE; *and*

(B) by striking Secretary and inserting "Policy Committee";

SEC. 836. AUTHORIZATION OF APPROPRIATIONS.

Section 207 of the Older Americans Act Amendments of 1987 (42 U.S.C. 3001 note) is amended to read as follows:

SEC. 207. AUTHORIZATION OF APPROPRIATIONS.

(a) AUTHORIZATION.—

(1) IN GENERAL.—*There are authorized to be appropriated such sums as may be necessary for fiscal years 1992 through 1994 to carry out this title.*

(2) CONTRACTS.—*Authority to enter into contracts under this title shall be effective only to the extent, or in such amounts as are, provided in advance in appropriations Acts.*

(b) AVAILABILITY OF FUNDS.—

(1) IN GENERAL.—*Except as provided in paragraph (3), funds appropriated to carry out this title and funds received as gifts under section 203(c) shall remain available for obligation or expenditure until June 30, 1995, or the expiration of the one-year period beginning on the date the Conference adjourns, whichever occurs earlier.*

(2) UNOBLIGATED FUNDS.—*Except as provided in paragraph (3), any such funds neither expended nor obligated before June 30, 1995, or the expiration of the one-year period beginning on the date the Conference adjourns, whichever occurs earlier, shall be available to carry out the Older Americans Act of 1965 (42 U.S.C. 3001 et seq.).*

(3) CONFERENCE NOT CONVENED.—*If the Conference is not convened before June 30, 1994, such funds neither expended nor obligated before such date shall be available to carry out the Older Americans Act of 1965.*

SEC. 837. SAVINGS PROVISION.

All personnel assigned or engaged under section 202(b) or section 203(a)(5) of the Older Americans Act Amendments of 1987 (42 U.s.C. 3001 note) as in effect immediately before the date of the enactment of this Act shall continue to be assigned or engaged under such section after such date notwithstanding the amendments made by this subtitle.

SEC. 838. SENSE OF THE CONGRESS.

It is the sense of the Congress that the White House Conference on Aging should consider the impact of the earnings test in effect under section

203 of the Social Security Act (42 U.S.C. 403) on older individuals who are employed.

SEC. 839. TECHNICAL AMENDMENTS.

(a) DEFINITIONS.—Section 206 of the Older Americans Act Amendments of 1987 (42 U.S.C. 3001 note) is amended—

(1) in paragraph (1), by striking means and all that follows and inserting has the meaning given the term in section 102(17) of the Older Americans Act of 1965 (42 U.S.C. 3002(17).; and

(2) in paragraph (4) by striking authorized in subsection (b).

(b) TABLE OF CONTENTS.—The table of contents of the Older Americans Act Amendments of 1987 (42 U.S.C. note) is amended—

(1) by striking the item relating to title II and inserting the following:

TITLE II—WHITE HOUSE CONFERENCE ON AGING;

and

(2) by striking the item relating to section 204 and inserting the following:

Sec. 204. Policy committee; related committees.

TITLE IX—GENERAL PROVISIONS

SEC. 901. LIMITATION OF AUTHORITY TO ENTER INTO CONTRACTS.

Any authority to enter into contracts under this Act or an amendment made by this Act shall be effective only to the extent or in such amounts as are provided in advance in appropriations Acts.

SEC. 902. REGULATIONS.

Except as otherwise specifically provided, the Secretary of Health and Human Services shall, not later than 120 days after the date of the enactment of this Act, issue proposed regulations to carry out the amendments made by titles I through VII.

SEC. 903. SENSE OF CONGRESS.

(a) IN GENERAL.—It is the sense of the Congress that a recipient of a grant or other Federal financial assistance awarded under this Act or an amendment made by this Act to assist the recipient in purchasing equipment or products should, in expending the assistance, purchase American-made equipment of products, respectively.

(b) NOTICE.—The Secretary of Health and Human Services shall provide procedures to inform such recipients of the sense of the Congress under subsection (a).

SEC. 904. TECHNICAL AMENDMENTS.

(a) The Older Americans Act of 1965 (42 U.S.C. 3001–3057n) is amended—

(1) in section 101(8) by striking the vulnerable elderly and inserting vulnerable older individuals;

(2) in section 102(2) by striking Virgin Islands and inserting United States Virgin Islands;

(3) in section 2019c)(3)—

(A) in subparagraphs (A)(i), (B), (E), and (G) by inserting individuals who are after older the first place it appears in each of such subparagraphs;

(B) in subparagraph (B) by striking older Native Americans the last place it appears and inserting such individuals; and

(C) in subparagraph (E) by striking the Act and inserting this Act;

(4) in section 202—

(A) in subsection (a)—

(i) in paragraph (1) by striking the elderly each place it appears and inserting older individuals;

(ii) in paragraph (15)—

(I) by striking the elderly and inserting older individuals; and

(II) by striking older people and inserting such individuals; and

(iii) in paragraphs (13), (15), (16), and (17) by striking purposes and inserting objectives;

(B) in subsection (b)—

(i) in paragraph (1) by striking with health systems agencies designated under section 1515 of the Public Health Service Act (42 U.S.C. 3001-4); and

(ii) in paragraph (3) by striking the elderly and inserting older individuals;

(5) in section 203(b) by striking purposes the second place it appears and inserting objectives;

(6) in section 204—

(A) in subsection (b)(4) by striking the daily rate specified for grade GS–18 in section 5332 and inserting the daily equivalent of the rate specified for level V of the Executive Schedule under section 5316; and

(B) in paragraphs (1), (3) and (4) of subsection (d), as amended by section 205(c), by striking Americans and inserting individuals;

(7) in section 205(a)(1), as so redesignated by section 206—

(A) by striking purposes and inserting objectives; and

(B) by striking to and inserting to—;

(8) in section 207(a)(4) by striking the greatest economic or social needs and inserting greatest economic need and older individuals with greatest social need;

(9) the last sentence of section 211 is amended by striking purposes and inserting objectives;

(10) in section 304(a)(1)—

(A) by striking aged 60 or older each place it appears, and inserting of older individuals;

(B) by striking Virgin Islands each place it appears and inserting United States Virgin Islands; and

(C) in the last sentence by striking clause and inserting subparagraph;
(11) in section 305—
(A) in subsection (a)—
(i) in paragraph (1)—
(I) in subparagraph (D) by striking the elderly each place it appears and inserting older individuals;
(II) in subparagraph (E) by striking individuals aged 60 and older and inserting older individuals; and
(III) in subparagraph (E) by striking Indians and inserting individuals who are Indians; and
(ii) in paragraph (2)—
(I) in the matter preceding subparagraph (A) by striking clause and inserting paragraph;
(II) in subparagraph (D) by striking subclause and inserting subparagraph; and
(III) in subparagraph (E) by striking the greatest economic or social needs and inserting greatest economic need and older individuals with greatest social need;
(B) in subsection (b)—
(i) in paragraphs (I) and (4) by striking clause (1) of subsection (a) and inserting subsection (a)(1); and
(ii) in paragraph (2) by striking designated under such clause and inserting designated under subsection (a)(1); and
(C) in subsection (d) by striking clause and inserting paragraph;
(12) in section 306—
(A) in subsection (a)—
(i) in paragraph (1) by striking Indians and inserting individuals who are Indians;
(ii) in paragraph (2)(B) by striking elderly and inserting older individuals who are; and
(iii) in paragraph (5)(A)(i) by striking the greatest economic or social needs and inserting greatest economic need and older individuals with greatest social need; and
(iv) in paragraph (6)—
(I) in subparagraph (D) by striking the elderly each place it appears and inserting older individuals;
(II) in subparagraph (GO by striking clause and inserting paragraph;
(III) in subparagraph (N) by striking Indians the first place it appears and inserting individuals who are Indians; and
(IV) in subparagraph (N) by striking elder Indians in such area and shall inform such older Indians and inserting such individuals in such area and shall inform such individuals; and
(B) in subsection (b)—
(i) in paragraph (1)—
(I) by inserting on aging after area agency the first place it appears; and
(II) by striking clause each place it appears and inserting paragraph; and
(ii) in paragraph (2)(D) by striking clause and inserting paragraph;
(13) in section 307—

(A) in subsection (a)—

(i) in paragraph (8) by striking the greatest economic or social needs and inserting greatest economic need and older individuals with greatest social need;

(ii) in paragraph (13)—

(I) in subparagraph (A) by striking individuals aged 60 or older and inserting older individuals;

(II) in subparagraph (A) by striking the elderly and inserting older individuals;

(III) in subparagraph (B) by striking subclause and inserting subparagraph; and

(IV) in subparagraph (I) by striking elderly participants and inserting participating older individuals;

(iii) in paragraph (14)(D) by striking clause and inserting subparagraphs; and

(iv) in paragraph (16)(B) by striking clause and inserting paragraph; and

(B) in subsection (b)(2) by striking clause and inserting paragraph;

(14) in section 308(b)—

(A) in paragraphs (1)(B) and (2)(B) by striking Virgin Islands and inserting United States Virgin Islands; and

(B) in paragraphs (3)(B)(iii) and (4) by striking purposes each place it appears and inserting objectives;

(15) in section 321(a)—

(A) in paragraph (4) by striking elderly and inserting older;

(B) in paragraph (14)—

(i) by striking older, poor individuals 60 years of age or older and inserting low-income older individuals; and

(ii) by striking the older poor and inserting low-income older individuals; and

(C) in paragraph (15) by striking clause and inserting paragraph;

(16) in section 402(b) by striking Alcohol and inserting the Alcohol;

(17) in section 412(b) by striking purposes and inserting objectives;

(18) in section 421(a) by striking purposes and inserting objectives;

(19) in section 422—

(A) in the second sentence of subsection (a)(1) by striking the rural elderly and inserting older individual residing in rural areas;

(B) in subsection (b)—

(i) in paragraph (1) by striking elderly and inserting older individuals who are;

(ii) in paragraph (2) by striking the elderly and inserting older individuals;

(iii) in paragraph (6) by striking the rural elderly and inserting older individuals residing in rural areas; and

(iv) in paragraph (8) by striking the rural elderly and inserting older individuals residing in rural areas;

(20) in section 602 by striking older Indians, older Alaskan Natives, and older Native Hawaiians and inserting older individuals who are Indians, older individuals who are Alaskan Natives, and older individuals who are Native Hawaiians;

(21) in section 611(a)—

(A) in the matter preceding paragraph (1) by inserting individuals who are after older; and

(B) in paragraph (9) by striking Indian elderly population and inserting population of older individuals who are Indians;

(22) in section 613 by inserting individuals who are after older; and

(23) in section 614(a)—

(A) in paragraph (7) by striking Indians aged 60 and older and inserting older individuals who are Indians;

(B) in paragraph (8) by striking clause and inserting paragraph; and

(C) in paragraphs (1), (6), (8), and (10) by inserting individuals who are after older each place it appears.

(b) The Older Americans Community Service Employment Act (42 U.S.C. 3056 et seq.) is amended—

(1) in section 502(b)(1)—

(A) in subparagraph (C) by striking 1954 and inserting 1986; and

(B) in subparagraph (J) by striking persons each place it appears and inserting individuals; and

(2) in paragraphs (3) and (4)(A) of section 506(a) by striking Virgin Islands each place it appears and inserting United States Virgin Islands.

SEC. 905. EFFECTIVE DATES; APPLICATION OF AMENDMENTS.

(a) IN GENERAL.—Except as provided in section 811(b), any other provision of this Act (other than this section), and in subsection (b) of this section, this Act and the amendments made by this Act shall take effect on the date of the enactment of this Act.

(b) APPLICATION OF AMENDMENTS.—

(1) FEDERAL COUNCIL ON AGING.—Incumbent members of the Federal Council on Aging may serve on the Council until their successors are appointed under section 204 of the Older Americans Act of 1965 (42 U.S.C. 3015) as amended by section 205 of this Act.

(2) STATE AND COMMUNITY PROGRAMS ON AGING.—The amendments made by sections 303(a)(2), 303(a)(3), 303(f), 304, 305, 306, 307, 316, 317, and 320 shall not apply with respect to fiscal year 1992.

(3) PROJECT REPORTS.—The amendments made by sections 410, 411, 413, 414, 415, 416, 418, and 419 shall not apply with respect to fiscal year 1992.

(4) COMMUNITY SERVICE EMPLOYMENT.—The amendments made by sections 501, 504, and 506 shall not apply with respect to fiscal year 1992.

(5) INDIAN AND NATIVE HAWAIIAN PROGRAMS.—The amendments made by sections 601 and 603 shall not apply with respect to fiscal year 1992.

(6) VULNERABLE ELDER RIGHTS PROTECTION ACTIVITIES.—The amendments made by title VII shall not apply with respect to fiscal year 1992.

Index